American Gridlock

American Gridlock brings together the country's preeminent experts on the causes, characteristics, and consequences of partisan polarization in U.S. politics and government, with each chapter presenting original scholarship and novel data. This book is the first to combine research on all facets of polarization, among the public (both voters and activists), in our federal institutions (Congress, the presidency, and the Supreme Court), at the state level, and in the media. Each chapter includes a bullet-point summary of its main argument and conclusions, and is written in clear prose that highlights the substantive implications of polarization for representation and policymaking. The authors examine polarization with an array of current and historical data, including public opinion surveys; electoral, legislative, and congressional data; experimental data; and content analyses of media outlets. *American Gridlock*'s theoretical and empirical depth distinguishes it from any other volume on polarization.

James A. Thurber is University Distinguished Professor of Government and Founder and Director of the Center for Congressional and Presidential Studies at American University. In 2010, he won the Walter Beach Pi Sigma American Political Science Association Award for his work combining applied and academic research. He is a fellow of the National Academy of Public Administration and a member of the American Bar Association's Task Force on Lobbying Law Reform. He is the author of multiple books and more than eighty articles and chapters on Congress, congressional-presidential relations, congressional budgeting, congressional reform, interest groups and lobbying, congressional ethics, and campaigns and elections. He co-produced three BBC TV documentaries on the U.S. Congress and elections.

Antoine Yoshinaka is Associate Professor in the Department of Political Science at the State University of New York at Buffalo. He has published numerous articles on elections, parties, and representation in outlets such as *Political Research Quarterly*, *Legislative Studies Quarterly*, *British Journal of Political Science*, and *Electoral Studies*. He has a forthcoming book to be published by Cambridge University Press, titled *Crossing the Aisle: Party Switching by U.S. Legislators in the Postwar Era*.

American Gridlock

The Sources, Character, and Impact of Political Polarization

Edited by

JAMES A. THURBER
American University

ANTOINE YOSHINAKA
State University of New York at Buffalo

CAMBRIDGE
UNIVERSITY PRESS

CAMBRIDGE
UNIVERSITY PRESS

32 Avenue of the Americas, New York NY 10013-2473, USA

Cambridge University Press is part of the University of Cambridge.

It furthers the University's mission by disseminating knowledge in the pursuit of education, learning and research at the highest international levels of excellence.

www.cambridge.org
Information on this title: www.cambridge.org/9781107534698

© Cambridge University Press 2015

First published 2015

A catalogue record for this publication is available from the British Library

ISBN 978-1-107-53469-8 Paperback

For my wife, Claudia
And my family, Mark, Lissette, Kathryn, Greg, Tristan, Bryan, and
Kelsey

– James A. Thurber

To Daniela and Clara

– Antoine Yoshinaka

Contents

Contributors

Alan I. Abramowitz is the Alben W. Barkley Professor of Political Science at Emory University in Atlanta, Georgia. He received his BA from the University of Rochester in 1969 and his PhD from Stanford University in 1976. Dr. Abramowitz has authored or coauthored six books, dozens of contributions to edited volumes, and more than fifty articles in political science journals dealing with political parties, elections, and voting behavior in the United States. He is also one of the nation's leading election forecasters – his Time for Change Model has correctly predicted the popular-vote winner in every presidential election since 1988, including the 2012 election. Dr. Abramowitz's most recent book, *The Polarized Public: Why American Government Is So Dysfunctional*, examines the causes and consequences of growing partisan polarization among political leaders and ordinary Americans.

Samuel J. Abrams is a political scientist with interests in political behavior and culture and methods. He is Professor of Politics and Social Science at Sarah Lawrence College and is a research fellow at the Hoover Institution at Stanford University. His current research interests involve understanding the current "red/blue divide" in the United States and mapping Jewish community's political and electoral behavior. He is also working on a number of projects exploring ideology and partisanship.

Micah Altman is Director of Research and Head Scientist in the Program on Information Science for the MIT Libraries at the Massachusetts Institute of Technology. Dr. Altman is also a nonresident senior fellow at The Brookings Institution. Prior to arriving at MIT, Dr. Altman served at Harvard University for fifteen years as Associate Director of the Harvard-MIT Data Center, Archival Director of the Henry A. Murray Archive, and Senior Research Scientist in the Institute for Quantitative Social Sciences. Dr. Altman conducts work primarily in the fields of social science, information privacy, information science and research methods, and statistical computation, focusing on the intersections of information, technology, privacy, and politics as well as on the dissemination, preservation, reliability, and governance of scientific knowledge. Dr. Altman earned a PhD in social science from the California Institute of Technology and conducted his postdoctoral research at Harvard University. Prior to studying social science, Dr. Altman worked as a software engineer in the Silicon Valley developing software and courses, teaching, and consulting on the subject of high-performance computing.

Kevin Arceneaux is Professor of Political Science, Faculty Affiliate with the Institute for Public Affairs, and Director of the Behavioral Foundations Lab at Temple University. He studies political communication, political psychology, and political behavior, focusing on the interaction between political messages and people's political predispositions. His recent book, *Changing Minds or Changing Channels: Partisan News in an Age of Choice* (2013, coauthored with Martin Johnson), employs novel experimental methods to investigate how human agency shapes the influence of political media. The book was co-winner of the 2014 Goldsmith Book Prize awarded by the Harvard Kennedy School Shorenstein Center on Media, Politics, and Public Policy. He has published articles on the influence of partisan campaigns on voting behavior, the effects of predispositions on attitude formation, the role of human biology in explaining individual variation in predispositions, and experimental methodology. In 2012, Professor Arceneaux received the Emerging Scholar Award from the Elections, Public Opinion, and Voting Behavior Section of the American Political Science Association (APSA). He is an active member of the APSA Experiments in Political Science section, a member of the Experiments in Governance and Politics (EGAP) group, and a Laboratories of Democracies research affiliate. He also serves as an Associate Editor for the *Journal of Experimental Political Science* and, along with Cindy Kam, as a co-editor for the Routledge Series on Experimental Political Science. He has served on the editorial boards of the *American Journal of Political Science* and *Political Communication*. Professor Arceneaux has received research funding from the National Science Foundation, the JEHT Foundation, CIRCLE, and Time-Sharing Experiments for the Social Sciences. His work appears in numerous scholarly journals, including the *American Journal of Political Science, Journal of Politics, British Journal of Political Science, Political Research Quarterly, Quarterly Journal of Political Science, Political Behavior, Political Communication, Political Psychology,* and *Political Analysis*. He received a PhD in political science from Rice University in 2003. Before joining the faculty at Temple University, he completed a postdoctoral fellowship at Yale University.

Brandon L. Bartels is Associate Professor of Political Science at George Washington University. His research and teaching interests center on American politics, judicial decision making, the U.S. Supreme Court, and public perceptions of law and courts. His work has appeared in the *American*

Political Science Review, American Journal of Political Science, Journal of Politics, Public Opinion Quarterly, and other outlets. His work has also been supported by the National Science Foundation. His current work focuses on legal change and the constraining capacity of law on the Supreme Court and the consequences of Supreme Court policymaking for public perceptions of judicial legitimacy and democracy.

Jon R. Bond is Professor of Political Science at Texas A&M University. He has published articles on presidential-congressional relations, congressional elections, and party polarization in the *American Political Science Review, American Journal of Political Science, Journal of Politics, British Journal of Political Science, Legislative Studies Quarterly,* and *Presidential Studies Quarterly,* among others, as well as numerous book chapters. He is coauthor of *The President in the Legislative Arena* (1990) and *Analyzing American Democracy: Politics and Political Science* (2013), and he is co-editor of *Polarized Politics: Congress and the President in a Partisan Era* (2000) and *Institutional Games and the U.S. Supreme Court* (2006). Dr. Bond, who received his PhD from the University of Illinois at Urbana-Champaign, was an American Political Science Association Congressional Fellow. He has served as co-editor of the *Journal of Politics* and as president of the Southern Political Science Association, and Pi Sigma Alpha, the national political science honor society.

Adam Bonica is Assistant Professor of Political Science at Stanford University. His research examines American political ideology, campaign finance, interest group politics, and judicial politics. The focus of his research has been the development of a methodology for measuring the ideology of political actors using campaign finance records. By leveraging a large-scale database of contributions made to campaigns at every level of American politics, the method is able to recover a unified set of ideological measures for a wide range of political candidates as well as thousands of political organizations and millions of individual donors. His work has appeared in the *American Journal of Political Science, Journal of Economic Perspectives, Legislative Studies Quarterly, Quarterly Journal of Political Science, Journal of Law, Economics, and Organization,* and *JAMA Internal Medicine.* Before joining the Stanford faculty, he was a fellow at the Center for the Study of Democratic Politics at Princeton University.

Jeffrey E. Cohen is Professor of Political Science at Fordham University. He is the author of thirteen books; *Going Local: Presidential Leadership in the Post-Broadcast Age* (2010) won both the 2011 Richard E. Neustadt Award from the Presidency Research Group of the American Political Science Association and the 2012 Goldsmith Award from the Joan Shorenstein Center on the Press, Politics and Public Policy, John F. Kennedy School of Government, Harvard University. Cohen, who received his PhD from the

University of Michigan, is the author of articles in academic journals such as the *American Political Science Review, American Journal of Political Science,* and *Journal of Politics.*

Alexander Curry, who has an MA from Brigham Young University, is a doctoral student in Communication Studies at the University of Texas at Austin. He is also a research associate at the Engaging News Project. His research focuses on political communication and online news, and he is particularly interested in sports and the role sports play in America's political landscape. His work has appeared in the *Journal of Computer-Mediated Communication* and the *Journal of Public Relations Research.* From 2005 to 2010, he served as a writer for California Governor Arnold Schwarzenegger.

Morris P. Fiorina is the Wendt Family Professor of Political Science at Stanford University and a senior fellow of the Hoover Institution. He received an undergraduate degree from Allegheny College (1968) and a PhD from the University of Rochester (1972), and taught at Caltech and Harvard before coming to Stanford in 1998. He has written widely on American politics, with special emphasis on the study of representation and elections. He has published numerous articles and written or edited twelve books: *Representatives, Roll Calls, and Constituencies; Congress – Keystone of the Washington Establishment; Retrospective Voting in American National Elections; The Personal Vote: Constituency Service and Electoral Independence* (coauthored with Bruce Cain and John Ferejohn); *Home Style and Washington Work* (co-edited with David Rohde); *The New American Democracy* (with Paul Peterson and Bert Johnson); *Divided Government; Civic Engagement in American Democracy* (co-edited with Theda Skocpol), *Change and Continuity in House Elections* (co-edited with David Brady and John Cogan), *Culture War? The Myth of a Polarized America* (with Samuel Abrams and Jeremy Pope), *Disconnect: The Breakdown of Representation in American Politics* (with Samuel Abrams); and most recently, *Can We Talk?: The Rise of Rude, Nasty, Stubborn Politics* (co-edited with Dan Shea). He has served on the editorial boards of a dozen journals in political science, political economy, law, and public policy, and from 1986 to 1990 served as chair of the Board of Overseers of the American National Election Studies. He is a member of the American Academy of Arts and Sciences, the American Academy of Political and Social Sciences, and the National Academy of Sciences. In 2006 the Elections, Public Opinion, and Voting Behavior section of the American Political Science Association awarded him the Warren E. Miller Prize for career contributions to the field.

Richard Fleisher is Professor of Political Science at Fordham University. His interests focus on American political institutions and processes. He has written or edited several books and has published articles in the *American Political Science Review, American Journal of Political Science,* and *Journal of Politics,* as well as other leading political science journals. He earned his PhD from the University of Illinois at Urbana-Champaign.

Danny Hayes is Associate Professor of Political Science at George Washington University. His research focuses on political communication and political behavior in American politics. He is the coauthor of *Influence from Abroad: Foreign Voices, the Media, and U.S. Public Opinion* (2013). His work has been supported by the National Science Foundation and has appeared in the *American Journal of Political Science, Journal of Politics, Perspectives on Politics, Political Communication, Politics & Gender,* and *Political Behavior,* among others. Since 2011, he has written for the *Washington Post* blogs Behind the Numbers, Wonkblog, and The Monkey Cage.

Marc J. Hetherington is Professor of Political Science at Vanderbilt University. He is the author of three scholarly books: *Why Trust Matters: Declining Political Trust and the Demise of American Liberalism* (2005), *Authoritarianism and Polarization in American Politics* (with Jonathan Weiler, 2009), and *Why Washington Won't Work: Polarization, Political Trust, and the Governing Crisis* (with Thomas Rudolph, 2015). In addition, he has published numerous articles in scholarly journals such as the *American Political Science Review, American Journal of Political Science, Journal of Politics, Public Opinion Quarterly,* and *British Journal of Political Science.* He was also the recipient of the Emerging Scholar Award from the American Political Science Association's section on Elections, Public Opinion, and Voting Behavior.

Gary C. Jacobson is Distinguished Professor of Political Science at the University of California, San Diego, where he has taught since 1979. He received his AB from Stanford in 1966 and his PhD from Yale in 1972. He specializes in the study of U.S. elections, parties, interest groups, public opinion, and Congress. He is the author of *Money in Congressional Elections, The Politics of Congressional Elections,* and *The Electoral Origins of Divided Government,* and he is the coauthor of *Strategy and Choice in Congressional Elections* and *The Logic of American Politics,* as well as more than 100 research articles. His most recent book is *A Divider, Not a Uniter: George W. Bush and the American People.* He has served on the Board of Overseers of National Election Studies (1985–93), the Council of the American Political Science Association (1993–94), the APSA's Committee on Research Support, as Treasurer of the APSA (1996–97), and as chair of the APSA's Elections Review Committee (2001–02).

Martin Johnson is the Kevin P. Reilly, Sr. Chair in Political Communication and Professor of Mass Communication and Political Science at Louisiana State University. He studies media, politics, public opinion, political psychology, and public policy. His book, *Changing Minds or Changing Channels: Partisan News in an Age of Choice* (coauthored with Kevin Arceneaux, 2013) investigates how the choices viewers make shape the influence of political media. It was the co-winner of the 2014 Goldsmith Book Prize awarded by the Harvard Kennedy School Shorenstein Center on Media, Politics, and Public Policy. He has published papers in the *American Journal of Political Science, Journal of Politics, Human Communication Research, British Journal of Political Science, Political Communication, Political Psychology*, and *Political Analysis*, among other scholarly venues. He is the former president of the Southwestern Political Science Association. He currently serves on the editorial board of *Social Science Quarterly* and previously served on the editorial board of the *American Journal of Political Science*. Before joining the faculty at LSU, he served as department chair and professor at the University of California, Riverside, and directed the Media and Communication Research Lab there. He earned his MA and PhD in political science from Rice University.

David Karol is Associate Professor of Government and Politics at the University of Maryland, College Park. His research focuses on parties, interest groups, political institutions, and American political development. He is the author of *Party Position Change in American Politics: Coalition Management* (2009), coauthor of *The Party Decides: Presidential Nominations before and after Reform* (2008), and coeditor of *Nominating the President: Evolution and Revolution in 2008 and Beyond* (2009). He has published articles in several journals and contributed chapters to edited volumes. He is a member of the editorial board of the *Journal of Politics* and the Council of the APSA Section on Political Organizations and Parties (POP).

Jennifer L. Lawless is Professor of Government at American University, where she is also the Director of the Women & Politics Institute. She received her PhD in political science from Stanford University in 2003 and her BA from Union College in 1997. Professor Lawless's research, which has been supported by the National Science Foundation, focuses on representation, political ambition, and gender in the electoral process. She is the author of *Becoming a Candidate: Political Ambition and the Decision to Run for Office* (2012) and coauthor of *Running from Office: Why Young Americans Are Turned Off to Politics* (2015) and *It Still Takes a Candidate: Why Women Don't Run for Office* (2010). Her work has appeared in academic journals including the *American Political Science Review, American Journal of Political Science, Perspectives on Politics, Journal of Politics, Political Research Quarterly, Legislative Studies Quarterly*, and *Politics & Gender* (of which she served as editor, 2010–13).

Thomas E. Mann is Senior Fellow in Governance Studies at The Brookings Institution and Resident Scholar, Institute of Governmental Studies, University of California, Berkeley. He held the W. Averell Harriman Chair at Brookings between 1991 and 2014 and was Director of Governmental Studies between 1987 and 1999. Before that, Mann was executive director of the American

Political Science Association. Mann earned his BA in political science at the University of Florida and his MA and PhD at the University of Michigan. He first came to Washington in 1969 as a Congressional Fellow in the offices of Senator Philip A. Hart and Representative James G. O'Hara. Mann has taught at Princeton University, Johns Hopkins University, Georgetown University, the University of Virginia, and American University; conducted polls for congressional candidates; worked as a consultant to IBM and the Public Broadcasting Service; chaired the Board of Overseers of the National Election Studies; and served as an expert witness in the constitutional defense of the McCain-Feingold campaign finance law. He is a recipient of the American Political Science Association's Frank J. Goodnow and Charles E. Merriam Awards. He and Norman Ornstein in 2008 published an updated edition of The Broken Branch: How Congress Is Failing America and How to Get It Back on Track. Their latest book, a New York Times best seller entitled It's Even Worse Than It Looks: How the American Constitutional System Collided with the New Politics of Extremism, was published in the spring of 2012. Mann and Ornstein were recently named by Foreign Policy Magazine among "100 Top Global Thinkers of 2012" for "diagnosing America's political dysfunction."

Seth E. Masket is Associate Professor and Chair of the Department of Political Science at the University of Denver. He researches and teaches on party organizations, state legislatures, campaigns and elections, and social networks. He is the author of *No Middle Ground: How Informal Party Organizations Control Nominations and Polarize Legislatures* (2009), and is writing a book on state party reform movements. His work has appeared in the *American Journal of Political Science*, *Journal of Politics*, *Quarterly Journal of Political Science*, and *State Politics and Policy Quarterly*, among other journals. He is a founder of and frequent contributor to the political science weblog, Mischiefs of Faction, and he writes a weekly online column for the *Pacific Standard*. He is also an occasional contributor to the *Washington Post*'s political science weblog, The Monkey Cage. He received his PhD in political science from UCLA in 2004. He also holds a master's degree in campaign management from the George Washington University's Graduate School of Political Management and a bachelor's degree in political science from the University of California, Berkeley.

Nolan McCarty is the Susan Dod Brown Professor of Politics and Public Affairs and Chair of the Department of Politics at Princeton University. He was formerly the associate dean at the Woodrow Wilson School of Public and International Affairs. His research interests include U.S. politics, democratic political institutions, and political game theory. He is the recipient of the Robert Eckles Swain National Fellowship from the Hoover Institution and the John M. Olin Fellowship in Political Economy. He has coauthored three books: *Political Game Theory* (with Adam Meirowitz, 2006), *Polarized America: The Dance of Ideology and Unequal Riches* (with Keith Poole and

Howard Rosenthal, 2006), and *Political Bubbles: Financial Crises and the Failure of American Democracy* (with Keith Poole and Howard Rosenthal, 2013). In 2010, he was elected a fellow of the American Academy of Arts and Sciences. He earned his AB from the University of Chicago and his PhD from Carnegie Mellon University.

Michael McDonald is Associate Professor of Political Science at the University of Florida and a nonresident senior fellow at the Brookings Institution. He produces widely used voter turnout rates for the country. He has been a redistricting consultant or expert witness in fourteen states. Along with his collaborator, Micah Altman, he created the award-winning open-source redistricting software, DistrictBuilder, which was used by advocates and redistricting authorities across the United States and Mexico. This software builds on the first open-source multi-criteria redistricting optimization tool, BARD, also developed with Dr. Altman. He is the author of numerous peer-reviewed articles, law review articles, book chapters, and opinion editorials in the popular press. He is the coauthor of *Numerical Issues in Statistical Computing for the Social Scientist* (with Michah Altman and Jeff Gill, 2003) and coeditor of *The Marketplace of Democracy: Electoral Competition and American Politics* (with John Sides, 2006).

Keith T. Poole is the Philip H. Alston Jr. Distinguished Professor in Department of Political Science at the University of Georgia. He received his PhD in political science from the University of Rochester in 1978. His research interests include methodology, political-economic history of American institutions, economic growth and entrepreneurship, and the political-economic history of railroads. He is the author or coauthor of more than sixty articles, as well as the author of *Spatial Models of Parliamentary Voting* (2005), a coauthor of *Analyzing Spatial Models of Choice and Judgment Using R* (with David A. Armstrong II, Ryan Baker, Royce Carroll, Christopher Hare, and Howard Rosenthal, 2014), *Political Bubbles: Financial Crises and the Failure of American Democracy* (with Nolan M. McCarty and Howard Rosenthal, 2013), *Polarized America: The Dance of Ideology and Unequal Riches* (with Nolan M. McCarty and Howard Rosenthal, 2006), *Ideology In Congress* (with Howard Rosenthal, 2007), and *Congress: A Political-Economic History of Roll Call Voting* (with Howard Rosenthal, 1997). Professor Poole has served on the editorial boards of *Social Science Quarterly*, *Journal of Politics*, *American Journal of Political Science*, and *Legislative Studies Quarterly*.

Elizabeth Rigby is Associate Professor of Public Policy and of Political Science at George Washington University, where she teaches courses in the Trachtenberg School of Public Policy on the role of politics in the policymaking process. Her research examines the interplay of politics, policy, and social inequality in the contemporary United States and has been published in a range of journals including the *American Journal of Political Science*, *Political Research*

Quarterly, Journal of Policy Analysis and Management, Policy Studies Journal, and *Health Affairs.* Professor Rigby holds a PhD (with distinction) from Columbia University. In addition, she received postdoctoral training in population health at the University of Wisconsin–Madison as a Robert Wood Johnson Health and Society Scholar and has served as an APSA Congressional Fellow on the minority staff of the Senate Finance Committee.

Howard Rosenthal is Professor of Politics at New York University; a Roger Williams Straus Professor of Social Sciences, Emeritus, at Princeton University; and a political economist and methodologist. His most innovative scientific contributions took place during the twenty-seven years he was a faculty member at Carnegie Mellon University. In the earliest years, motivated by CMU colleagues, he applied game theory and spatial theory to the study of coalitions, voting, turnout, and electoral strategy. The next project was methodological, expressed in the coauthored volume, *Prediction Analysis of Cross-Classification* (with David K. Hildebrand and James D. Laing, 1977). Subsequently, he collaborated on the well-known Romer-Rosenthal model of agenda control, on *Partisan Politics, Divided Government, and the Economy* (with Alberto Alesina, 1995) and on the theory of participation in elections and the provision of public goods. His most widely noted contribution was the development of the Poole-Rosenthal dichotomous choice scaling model, NOMINATE, which led to coauthored books such as *Polarized America: The Dance of Ideology and Unequal Riches and Political Bubbles* (with Nolan McCarthy and Keith T. Poole, 2006) and the contribution in this volume. In recent years, Rosenthal's research interests have included the intersection of politics and finance, resulting in papers on bankruptcy and on political intervention in credit markets, as well as the coedited volume *Credit Markets for the Poor* (with Patrick Bolton, 2005). His current empirical project in that area is the study of the impact of deregulation on the ownership structure of American electric utilities. For part of 2015, Rosenthal is a research scholar at Columbia University. He was previously a Sherman Fairchild Distinguished Scholar at the California Institute of Technology, a National Fellow at the Hoover Institution, a fellow of the Center for Advanced Study in the Behavioral Sciences, a fellow at the Russell Sage Foundation, and a fellow at the John Simon Guggenheim Foundation.

Boris Shor is a visiting assistant professor in the Department of Government at Georgetown University. His research interests include state legislatures, political polarization, representation, and health policy. Using roll-call voting data and candidate survey responses, he co-created the data project on state legislative ideology and polarization located at http://www.americanlegis latures.com, containing estimates of ideological positions of more than 20,000 individual legislators in all 50 states across the past two decades, plus more than 1,800 chamber-years of aggregate data. He is the coauthor of *Red State, Blue State, Rich State, Poor State* (Andrew Gelman, David Park, Joseph Bafumi, and Jeronimo Cortina, 2009) and has published work in the *American Political*

Science Review, American Journal of Political Science, American Politics Research, State Politics and Policy Quarterly, Political Analysis, and *Quarterly Journal of Political Science.* He has been a Robert Wood Johnson Scholar in Health Policy at the University of California, Berkeley, and a fellow at the Center for the Study of Democratic Politics at Princeton University. His research website is http://research.bshor.com.

Natalie (Talia) Jomini Stroud is Associate Professor of Communication Studies and Assistant Director of Research at the Annette Strauss Institute for Civic Life at the University of Texas at Austin. She directs the grant-funded Engaging News Project, which examines commercially viable and democratically beneficial ways of improving online news coverage. In 2014–15, she was a fellow at the Center for the Study of Democratic Politics at Princeton University. She is interested in how the media affect our political behaviors and attitudes, and how our political behaviors and attitudes affect our media use. Her book, *Niche News: The Politics of News Choice* (2011), explores the causes, consequences, and prevalence of partisan selective exposure and the preference for like-minded political information. *Niche News* received the International Communication Association's 2012 Outstanding Book Award. Her work has appeared in *Political Communication, Journal of Communication, Political Behavior, Public Opinion Quarterly, Journal of Computer-Mediated Communication,* and the *International Journal of Public Opinion Research.* She received her PhD from the Annenberg School for Communication at the University of Pennsylvania.

Sean M. Theriault is University Distinguished Teaching Professor in the Department of Government at the University of Texas at Austin. Professor Theriault is currently researching the distinction between ideological and war-making behavior in the U.S. Congress, has published three books: *The Power of the People: Congressional Competition, Public Attention, and Voter Retribution* (2005), *Party Polarization in Congress* (2008), and *The Gingrich Senators: The Roots of Partisan Warfare in Congress* (2013). He has also published numerous articles in a variety of journals on subjects ranging from presidential rhetoric to congressional careers and the Louisiana Purchase to the Pendleton Act of 1883. Before obtaining his PhD from Stanford University in 2001 (and his MA in political science in 2000), he attended the University of Richmond (BA, 1993) and the University of Rochester (MS in public policy analysis, 1996).

James A. Thurber earned his BA in political science at the University of Oregon and his MA and PhD at Indiana University. He is Distinguished University Professor and Director of the Center for Congressional and Presidential Studies at American University. He is editor of the journal *Congress and the Presidency.* His latest publications are *Rivals for Power: Presidential-Congressional Relations* (2013, 5th ed.) and *Campaigns and Elections, American Style* (with Candice Nelson, 2013, 4th ed.). He is the author and editor of numerous books and articles on American politics, including *Obama in Office* (2011), *Congress and the Internet* (with Colton Campbell, 2002), *The Battle for Congress: Consultants, Candidates, and Voters* (2001), *Crowded Airwaves: Campaign Advertising in Elections* (with Candice J. Nelson and David A. Dulio, 2001), *Campaign Warriors: Political Consultants in Elections* (2000), and *Divided Democracy* (1991).

Jonathan D. Weiler received his PhD in Political Science from the University of North Carolina at Chapel Hill, where he is a senior lecturer and director of undergraduate studies in the Curriculum in Global Studies. He is the author of two books: *Human Rights in Russia: A Darker Side of Reform* (2004) and *Authoritarianism and Polarization in American Politics* (with Marc Hetherington, 2009).

Gerald C. Wright received his PhD from the University of North Carolina at Chapel Hill. Before joining the faculty at Indiana University, he served as program director for political science at the National Science Foundation and taught at Florida Atlantic University and Florida State University. His research concentrates on public opinion, legislative behavior, and particularly the nexus of the two in representation. He has authored dozens of articles on these topics and is the coauthor of *Statehouse Democracy* (with Robert S. Erikson and John P. McIver, 1993), which has won enduring impact awards from both the Elections and Public Opinion and the State Politics and Policy sections of the American Political Science Association.

Antoine Yoshinaka is Associate Professor at the State University of New York at Buffalo. His research examines how institutions and the preferences of political actors influence political outcomes. Some of his recent work on congressional redistricting examines the various ways in which partisan mapmakers strategically allocate uncertainty across districts. His upcoming Cambridge University Press book, *Crossing the Aisle: Party Switching by U.S. Legislators in the Postwar Era*, is the first book-length treatment on the causes and consequences of legislative party switching in the United States. He received his PhD from the University of Rochester.

Foreword

A few months ago, the weblog The Monkey Cage commissioned and published a series of short essays on polarization, kicked off by an overview written by Nolan McCarty, which summarized the findings of an APSA study group (on which I and several others present at the May 2014 conference at American University that formed the basis for this book served).[1] I think Nolan fairly reflected majority views of polarization within the scholarly community. What followed in the ensuing days and weeks was a rich offering of the research perspectives of colleagues, many by participants in this conference. Lots of interesting work on polarization is being done, and our knowledge is increasing. Much of that work is discussed in this volume.

PROFESSIONAL DISCOMFORT WITH POLARIZATION

What I would like to address, however, is what I see as our professional discomfort with and reluctance to take seriously the widespread public views that our political system is dangerously broken. I understand and sympathize with that defensive posture, one I've embraced most of my professional life. I've spent decades in Washington explaining and defending the American constitutional system in the face of what I considered to be uninformed and ill-considered attacks on Congress and our way of governing.

After all, the problems our country confronts are immensely difficult, other democracies struggle as we do trying to deal with them, we've overcome similar periods of subpar performance and political dysfunction throughout our history, and our political system has adapted to new circumstances and self-corrected.

[1] McCarty, Nolan. 2014. "What We Know and Don't Know about Our Polarized Politics." Retrieved from http://www.washingtonpost.com/blogs/monkey-cage/wp/2014/01/08/what-we-know-and-dont-know-about-our-polarized-politics.

But there's something else going on here: How would we justify ourselves if we didn't contest the conventional wisdom of mere pundits and journalists? We have a positive political science to conduct and are properly critical of half-baked diagnoses and ungrounded normative speculations on how to cure our governing maladies.

But I believe these times are strikingly different from what we have seen in the past, and the health and well-being of our democracy is properly a matter of great concern. We owe it to ourselves and our country to reconsider our priors and at least entertain the possibility that these concerns are justified, even if for us uncomfortably so.

MOSTLY CONSENSUS VIEWS OF IMPORTANT DEVELOPMENTS

Let's start with some basics.

- The parties in Congress are as polarized – internally unified and distinctive from one another – as at any time in history. This holds for both the House and the Senate, and for most state legislatures. It also holds for an electorate that Gary Jacobson (Chapter 12 in this volume) reports was in the 2012 elections the most polarized ever (or at least since the start of ANES in 1952).
- The fit between ideology and party is unusually strong. As Hans Noel argues in his new book, *Political Ideologies and Political Parties in American History*, for perhaps the first time in American history, the two dominant ideologies have captured the two dominant political parties.[2] The path to polarization, he argues, originated neither among elected officials nor within the mass public, but instead developed over a long period of time, with key roles played by ideological thinkers and political activists with policy demands.
- Under divided government and split chamber control, the current Congress has ceased to operate as an effective legislative body. Deliberation and compromise are scarce commodities, not the coin of the realm. The contemporary Congress bears little resemblance to the "textbook Congress" or "the reform Congress" that followed. Individual members are no longer the most useful unit of analysis for understanding congressional behavior and policy-making. Parties are the key actors, and they respond more to their activist bases than to the median voter.
- Public approval of the performance of Congress and public trust in government to respond to their needs have plunged to record depths.
- Whereas a causal connection between inequality and polarization is uncertain, growing concerns about economic and political inequality are rooted in real increases in the concentration of income, wealth, and opportunities for political influence (see Bonica et al., Chapter 16, this volume).

[2] Noel, Hans. 2013. *Political Ideologies and Political Parties in America*. New York: Cambridge University Press.

MORE CONTROVERSIAL ARGUMENTS ABOUT POLARIZATION

These are not controversial assertions. Now on to the often more disputed aspects of the polarization story.

- The most important and problematic feature of today's polarization is its partisan character. To treat polarization as "mere sorting" is to trivialize, if not miss entirely, the biggest and most significant development in American politics in recent decades.
- That polarization reflects first of all the striking ideological differences between the parties, evident most sharply in the behavior of elected officials at national and state levels and among party activists, but also clearly evident among voters (see Part I of this volume). The level of constraint (consistency of policy preferences) in the ideological views of voters has increased markedly since Philip Converse described "The Nature of Belief Systems in Mass Publics" more than a half century ago.[3]
- Partisan polarization reflects more than sincere ideological differences, however. The rough parity between the parties fuels an intense competition for control of the White House and Congress. The stakes for control are particularly high because the ideological differences and policy demands between the vast party networks are large, and the chances of gaining or maintaining control are realistic because of the competitiveness of the parties. This leads to strategic agenda setting and voting – what Frances Lee calls partisan team play[4] – even on issues with little or no ideological content, an expansion of the permanent campaign into an institutionalized partisan messaging war in Congress, and a tribalism (what scholars often call affective partisan polarization) that is now such a prominent feature of American politics (see Theriault, Chapter 7, this volume).
- The linkage of party and ideology has given us "more responsible parties" and with it the promise of more clarity and accountability for voters. But when embedded in our constitutional system, it can be a formula for willful obstruction and policy irresolution. That is precisely the outcome Austin Ranney forecast in his prophetic dissent to the famous 1950 American Political Science Association Report entitled "Toward a More Responsible Two-Party System."[5] Ranney powerfully argued that more ideologically coherent, internally unified, and adversarial parties in the fashion of Westminster-style parliamentary democracy would be a disaster within the American constitutional system, given our separation of powers, separately

[3] Converse, Philip. 1964. "The Nature of Belief Systems in Mass Publics." In D. Apter, ed., *Ideology and Discontent*. New York: Free Press.
[4] Lee, Frances. 2010. *Beyond Ideology: Politics, Principles, and Partisanship in the U.S. Senate*. Chicago: University of Chicago Press.
[5] Ranney, Austin. 1950. "Toward a More Responsible Two-Party System: A Report of the Committee on Political Parties." *American Political Science Review* 44 (3): Part 2, Supplement.

elected institutions, and constraints on majority rule that favor cross-party coalitions and compromise.[6]

- This mismatch between our parties and governing institutions is made even more problematic by another feature of our contemporary politics: **the polarization is asymmetric.** Republicans have become a radical insurgency: "ideological extreme, contemptuous of the inherited policy regime, scornful of compromise, unpersuaded by conventional understanding of facts, evidence, and science; and dismissive of the legitimacy of its political opposition."[7]

The evidence of this asymmetry is overwhelming. Nolan McCarty, Keith Poole, and Howard Rosenthal provide the strongest evidence for this asymmetry among members of Congress with their use of overlapping cohorts in the first dimension of DW-NOMINATE scores.[8] They find that the ideological distance between the parties grew dramatically since the 1970s, but that it would be a mistake to equate the two parties' roles in contemporary political polarization. "(T)he data are clear that this is a Republican-led phenomenon where very conservative Republicans have replaced moderate Republicans and Southern Democrats."[9] The rise of the Tea Party moved the Republican Party even further from the political center.

This striking party asymmetry measured by congressional roll-call behavior is also present in state legislatures, as Part III of this volume demonstrates.

But the evidence for asymmetry goes well beyond roll-call voting. Changing Republican Party positions on taxes, Keynesian economics, immigration, climate change and the environment, health care, science policy, and a host of cultural policies are consistent with the same pattern. So too are the embrace of hard-ball strategies and tactics involving parliamentary-like opposition, the rise of the 60-vote Senate, government shutdowns, debt ceiling hostage-taking, and nullification efforts not seen since the antebellum South. Historian Gregory Kabaservice in *Rule and Ruin* traces the key intellectual and political developments in the transformation of the GOP from Eisenhower to the Tea Party.[10] In *The Party Is Over*, former Republican congressional staffer Mike Lofgren provides a rich and colorful insider's perspective on the radicalization of the Republican Party in Congress.[11] And Norm Ornstein and I in *It's Even*

---

[6] Ranney, Austin. 1951. "Toward a More Responsible Two-Party System: A Commentary." *American Political Science Review* 45 (Sept.): 488–499.

[7] Mann, Thomas E., and Norman J. Ornstein. 2012. *It's Even Worse Than It Looks: How the American Constitutional System Collided with the New Politics of Extremism.* New York: Basic Books. xiv.

[8] McCarty, Nolan, Keith Poole, Howard Rosenthal, and Chris Hare. 2012. "Polarization Is Real (and Asymmetric)." Retrieved from http://themonkeycage.org/2012/05/15/polarization-is-real-and-asymmetric

[9] Ibid. p. 3.

[10] Kabaservice, Gregory. 2012. *Rule and Ruin: The Downfall of Moderation and the Destruction of the Republican Party, from Eisenhower to the Tea Party.* New York: Oxford University Press.

[11] Lofgren, Mike. 2013. *The Party Is Over.* New York: Viking.

Worse Than It Looks document how the asymmetry developed from Newt Gingrich in the 1980s to the Young Guns in the present.

Finally, given the salience of the racial and cultural divides in the new party coalitions, it should not be surprising that asymmetric polarization has found its way to the public. Republican Party voters are more skewed to their ideological pole than Democratic Party voters are to theirs.

Polarization is indeed asymmetric, yet many political scientists, like most mainstream journalists and political reformers, refuse to even acknowledge or take seriously the case for this assertion. It makes us uncomfortable framing an argument that some will characterize as partisan, even if it more accurately captures the reality of the contemporary party system. We (as well as mainstream media) do the public a disservice to say less than we believe to be true and avoid research directions that might produce "unbalanced" results. Insisting on false equivalence in the media or the academy is no virtue.

One final point about polarization: Apart from the substantial minority of citizens who never vote and whose lives are fully detached from politics and public affairs, we are indeed a Red and Blue nation. Alan Abramowitz's characterization of the current era of electoral competition (Chapter 1 in this volume) is in my view dead on: intense two-party competition for control, increasing one-party domination of states and congressional districts, and consistency of election results across levels and over time.

AN OUTDATED LITERATURE?

Much of what we have written about parties and Congress does not fit contemporary conditions. As John Zaller, Seth Masket, and their colleagues from UCLA have theorized and demonstrated, parties are less collectives of election-minded politicians responding to the median voter than networks including interest groups, activists, and donors with clear policy demands.[12] The imprint of these networks on the public has weakened the argument that voters are mostly moderate, pragmatic, and independent (see also Karol, Chapter 3, this volume).

Districts voting for presidential and House candidates of different parties are vanishing (see Abramowitz, Chapter 1, this volume). So too are states with U.S. senators representing both parties. Divided party government is today a formula for inaction, not an opportunity for bipartisan legislating.

So there is no reason to be smug about our past research findings or certain that we have seen it all before. Plenty of evidence suggests we have a serious mismatch between our "more responsible parties" and our constitutional system, especially when one of those parties is hell-bent on replacing, not amending to fit current conditions, a century's worth of policy development.

[12] Bawn, Kathleen, Martin Cohen, David Karol, Seth Masket, Hans Noel, and John Zaller. 2012. "A Theory of Political Parties: Groups, Policy Demands, and Nominations in American Politics," *Perspectives on Politics* 10 (3): 571–597.

WHAT TO DO?

What we know from our research is that there is no easy way out of the mess we are in.

Change our institutions to fit our new-style parties? Beyond reining in the Senate filibuster, this would entail far-reaching constitutional reform that is likely to remain in the realm of intellectual debate.

Alter the electoral system to produce somewhat less polarized parties? Lots of ideas worth pursuing in the states, but short of major changes such as compulsory voting or some form of PR, the evidence suggests that they would produce at best modest results.

Encourage independent or third-party candidates appealing to a vast moderate center in American politics? Been there. Done that. A definite nonstarter.

More wishful thinking about delegation to nonpartisan or bipartisan groups? Enough already!

Perhaps more promising are approaches that focus directly on the parties as they exist within our constitutional system. These parties are deeply and asymmetrically polarized, each anchored in a worldview and coalitions of interests and activists, and likely to stay that way for some time to come. Under these conditions, unified party government seems an essential first step, one that can sustain itself in office long enough to put in place and begin to implement a credible governing program. The second is nudging the Republican Party back into a genuinely conservative, not radical party, one a little more pragmatic and a little less ideological, one that aspires to win presidential as well as congressional elections over the long haul. The third is dampening the intense and unrelenting competition for control of Congress and the White House, which is itself an historical anomaly.

With demographic changes continuing to unfold to the benefit of the Democrats, it is not hard to see them retaining and increasing their advantage in presidential elections. Controlling the other end of Pennsylvania Avenue is more challenging. Democrats might have an opportunity to regain unified control in 2016. But holding those majorities in 2018 would be an even more difficult task.

How about another run of unified Republican Party government, one that is not discredited like George W. Bush's by unpopular wars and a financial collapse, and finds its way to a politically and substantively sustainable program for governing? Some argue the best way to bring the Republican Party back to reality is to put it in charge and make it fully accountable for its actions. Others fear the policy consequences of unconstrained extremism.

Perhaps a more reliable way of bringing the Republican Party back into the mainstream is a few more decisive presidential elections defeats. That might create the conditions for the emergence of new Republican ideas less detached from reality and new efforts among some coalition partners to challenge extremist forces in primary elections.

I don't know what the answer is, or even if there is one. But I do know that in spite of a lot of terrific research, we still have work to do fully diagnosing our strikingly dysfunctional government and speaking forthrightly in the public what we believe to be true. This collection of research, with its broad scope and focus on partisan change, is a good start toward that goal.

Thomas E. Mann

Acknowledgments

We are grateful to Robert Dreesen, Senior Editor at Cambridge University Press (CUP), for his early and strong support, which assured the timely publication of *American Gridlock*. We thank the two production editors who worked on this publication, Josh Penney at the United States Cambridge office and Adam Hooper at the Cambridge office in the United Kingdom. We also thank our very efficient project manager, Sathish Kumar at Integra Software Services and Kevin Broccoli, our indexer.

We thank Rebecca Prosky at American University's Center for Congressional and Presidential Studies for her outstanding organization of the conference that led to this book and for her careful assistance in the production of *American Gridlock*. Barbara Romzek, Dean of American University's School of Public Affairs, gave us her support of this project from conception to completion. I also thank my friend, Neil Kerwin, colleague and president of American University who has been a strong supporter of the Center and its projects since its founding in 1979.

The authors in *American Gridlock* contributed original and thought-provoking scholarship on polarization for this book, and they all submitted in a timely manner, despite their many other worthy endeavors. The book is a collective effort, but as editors and authors we take full responsibility for any omissions or errors of fact and interpretation.

We dedicate this book to our families. Jim thanks Claudia, Mark, Lissette, Kathryn, Greg, Tristan, Bryan, and Kelsey for your gifts of love, joy, inspiration and support. Antoine thanks his family, in particular his wife Daniela and their daughter Clara, for their love, patience, and understanding during the time it took to write and edit this book. He also thanks his parents, Louise and Tsukasa, and in-laws, Paulo and Ester, for their support and affection.

Introduction

James A. Thurber and Antoine Yoshinaka

Partisan polarization among the public, activists, and elected officials characterizes American politics in the twenty-first century, and it is often seen as the major source of our governing problems (Schaffner 2011, Persily 2015). Republicans and Democrats are further apart ideologically than at any point in recent history, expressing highly negative views of the opposing party (Doherty 2014). The deleterious impact of partisan polarization cannot be exaggerated. It discourages compromise, produces gridlock, fosters mistrust, and ultimately hinders the functioning of governmental institutions. Lawmaking, representing, overseeing, executing laws, and adjudicating legal and constitutional disputes requires that individuals who might otherwise disagree come together and serve interests that go beyond their own. Failure to compromise results in gridlock, dysfunction, and partisan warfare. To paraphrase former House Speaker Sam Rayburn, we are not going along, let alone getting along!

It was not always thus. In fact, during much of the twentieth century, our national parties did not exhibit this sort of intense partisan polarization that we have seen emerge over the last generation or so. To understand how we got to where we are today, we must account for the rapid partisan change that the U.S. South has witnessed over the latter half of the twentieth century. Long gone are the days of the conservative southern Democrats (Dixiecrats) holding a more liberal northern caucus in check. Largely as a response to federal intervention in the civil rights arena, conservative southern Democratic voters started to migrate toward the GOP in the mid-1960s. Today's southern conservatives are well ensconced within the Republican Party. Southern Democrats in 2014 are largely liberal and nonwhite. The South has realigned politically. A similar, if not somewhat less acute, change occurred in reverse in other parts of the country such as the northeastern and the far west of the United States. With large swaths of the country realigning into one or the other party, each party's coalition has become much more homogeneous ideologically and in terms of policy preferences. To be liberal in 2014 is to be a Democrat; the same goes for conservatives and Republicans. Battles over the scope and size of the federal government have produced a wide policy schism between parties.

WHY WRITE THIS BOOK?

Although it is true that the literature on gridlock and polarization is extensive, it is also the case that it is quite disparate. What we wanted to present in this volume was the latest research encompassing the various strands in the literature into a single book that not only synthesizes our understanding of gridlock and polarization, but also pushes it forward with new questions, new data, and new answers. The book examines polarization among the American public (voters and non-voters), national and state political elites (Supreme Court Justices, legislators, executives, and party activists), and the media. Contributors are well-known scholars who have published extensively on topics related to polarization in government institutions, elections, public opinion, the media, and state politics.

The publication of this book coincides with a 114th Congress that pits a Republican House and Senate against a Democratic president entering his last two years in the White House. It follows the 113th Congress, which was one of the least productive in recent history in terms of total laws passed. As our federal government struggles to enact solutions to foreign, economic, and social problems that face the country, it is imperative to gain a better understanding of how polarization came to be, what contributed to its rise, and some of the reforms proposed to curb it. We posit that a government that fails to find solutions to broad-based issues, especially when majorities or intense minorities favor such solutions, deserves close scrutiny. It may be the case that conservatives often prefer to see non-governmental (e.g., market-based) solutions to societal problems, but the fact remains that a vast number of policies (or repeal thereof) advocated by those who generally identify as conservatives still require government to act: tax cuts, reforming pension schemes, or curbing the power of public sector unions are all examples of policies espoused by conservatives that require government action. Thus, our claim that polarization is a source of gridlock does not necessarily privilege one view of the role of government (e.g., liberal) over another (e.g., conservative).

American Gridlock could not be timelier, with the recent rise of the Tea Party as a block of recalcitrant lawmakers especially loathe to compromise, the slow disappearance of Democratic Party "Blue Dogs," the challenges of Barack Obama's presidency with split congressional chamber or divided party government since 2011 (Thurber 2011, 2013), many states that experience some of the same dysfunction we observe at the federal level, and a media landscape that continues to polarize. As Frances Lee (2009) points out in her excellent treatment of partisanship, what we see nowadays is the rise of teamsmanship, where beating the other side becomes the most important outcome regardless of the actual content of the proposals.

The 2014 Republican sweep of Congress, governorships, and state legislatures reveal some electoral foundations of partisan change. The South continues to realign, to be solid Republican territory (leading the Republican Party to become a Southern-based party), Democrats are making inroads in states with a large and increasing Latino population, and the political makeup of suburbs and exurbs continues to evolve. Nationally voters are "sorting" themselves into one party or the other based upon residential choice, their ethnicity, opinions, and values as shown most recently in the 2014 election (Balz 2014). Fiorina (2011) and Levendusky (2009) define "sorting" as the process by which a tighter fit is brought about between political ideology and party affiliation – something that continued in 2014. These trends are likely to persist and contribute to a growing divide between the parties. After the 2014 elections, Democrats have the lowest number of U.S. House seats, state legislative seats, and are tied for the lowest number of U.S. Senate seats since 1928. Republicans won 57 percent of all House districts in 2014, up from 54 percent in 2012, but measured by land area, House Republicans will represent 86 percent of the nation revealing a sustained political sort.

This book centers on the questions of voter, activist, and elite partisan change and polarization at the national level, the state level, and the media. By providing the latest research on the foundation, character, and impact of polarization the volume helps to better explain the functioning of democracy in the contemporary United States.

WHAT DO WE KNOW ABOUT POLARIZATION?

Polarization is a multifaceted phenomenon, yet much of the scholarship tends to examine only one aspect of it, which produces an extensive but somewhat disjointed literature. For instance, recent books by Barbara Sinclair (*Party Wars*, 2006), Sean Theriault (*The Gingrich Senators*, 2013), and Thomas Mann and Norman Ornstein (*The Broken Branch*, 2006, and *It's Even Worse Than It Looks*, 2013), all superb contributions, are focused almost exclusively on the U.S. Congress (see also Lee 2009; Oleszek 2014). Other studies such as the important works of Morris Fiorina (*Culture War*, 2006, and *Disconnect*, 2011), Alan Abramowitz (*The Disappearing Center*, 2011), and Matthew Levendusky (*The Partisan Sort*, 2009) are concerned with polarization – or lack thereof (Fiorina 2014) – among the general public.

Galston and Nivola (2006, 2008) show that the U.S. Congress is more ideologically polarized than a generation ago and that the rise of "safe" districts in the House of Representatives has resulted in the movement of Representatives to the ideological poles with fewer and fewer moderates in the middle. They also show that the gap between activists in both parties has widened in recent decades. They also maintain that the technological and regulatory changes in the past two decades resulted in a more politicized mass media. Additionally, political activists, the most ideologically oriented Americans, are making their voices heard through greater participation in every stage of the political process. A Pew Research Center survey in 2014 found that self-reported voting rates are higher among those on the right than the left, but higher among those on the left than in the middle (Doherty 2014). Campaign donations are roughly double the national average among ideologically consistent liberals (31 percent have donated money) and conservatives (26 percent).

Polarization in the media is the central concern of Markus Prior (*Post-Broadcast Democracy*, 2007) and Matthew Levendusky (*How Partisan Media Polarize America*, 2013), while books such as those by Jacob Hacker and Paul Pierson (*Off Center*, 2005), Nolan McCarty, Keith Poole, and Howard Rosenthal (*Polarized America*, 2006), and Jon Bond and Richard Fleisher (*Polarized Politics*, 2000) look primarily to the federal government for evidence of polarization.

With this extensive literature, perhaps writing this book would have been "a great idea 10 years ago," as a fellow political scientist reacted when we began this project. We disagree. We contend that by bringing together these various strands of scholarship – and more – in a single volume, *American Gridlock* will set itself apart from similar efforts that led to the publication of edited volumes on polarization (Frisch and Kelly 2013; Nivola and Brady 2006, 2008). *American Gridlock* makes significant empirical and theoretical contributions and advances in explaining ideological polarization in the Obama presidency, debt-limit debates, government shutdowns, immigration policy deadlock, conflict over the Affordable Care Act, partisan cable news, voter sorting, change in campaign finance, and party activist strategies. In short, this volume showcases the state of the art in the scholarship on partisan polarization, and it does so from multiple vantage points. And it does so with the most recent data, including data that were simply not available a decade ago (e.g., data on redistricting or state legislators). For example, we bring scholarship on state-level polarization into the broader conversation on polarization and gridlock.

POLARIZATION AND GRIDLOCK ON MAJOR POLICY ISSUES

While we have an academic interest in the study of polarization and gridlock, much of the popular discontent with our political leaders stem from various policy episodes that highlighted the wide gulf that separates the two parties on many important policy questions. For example, Republican concerns over the public debt, growing unfunded social programs, taxes, the increasing number of illegal immigrants, the role of the federal government in education, and the appropriate size of the federal government generally versus Democratic concerns about declining social mobility, stagnant wages, increasing inequality, global warming, the role of the federal government in improving education, and justice for immigrants have driven conflict and polarization between the two parties.

A prime example of this is the continued war over the budget and the debt. Partisan battles over the federal budget over the last 20 years are a prime example of the fundamental policy differences between the parities. Bipartisanship is rare if not nonexistent in Washington when it comes to tax increases and cuts in popular domestic programs. Both are needed to reduce the deficit and the debt, but the parties have taken increasingly extreme positions on their willingness to compromise on taxes and means testing in social programs. For example, a primary reason for the failure of the so-called supercommittee that was created in August 2011 to address the federal debt and deficits is the wide ideological gap between the two parties in the House and Senate. The supercommittee members could not bridge their ideological differences and find a common ground because of basic philosophical differences between the two parties. There is little common ground with regard to the primary issue of the size of the federal government and the revenues needed to pay for existing government programs. Mainstream Democrats believe government should play an important role in the economy and provide a safety net for the disadvantaged. They also want high-income people to pay more taxes to fund those programs. A majority of Republicans disagree. They want to limit government's many domestic administrative actions, characterizing a wide range of regulations as interference in markets. They disagree with many social safety net programs and they believe taxes are too high. They promise smaller government and no new taxes while cutting the deficit and reducing the debt. There is little chance that members of Congress can agree to compromise or ever get the votes from their party members to bridge that size-of-government chasm.

The ideological divide is most evident in the battle over the budget with Republicans' refusal to shift or fudge their no-tax pledge and Democrats' insistence on tying spending cuts to tax hikes. In the end, the basic policy divide is almost certainly the biggest single factor influencing the failure of passing a budget and appropriations on time. As long as the GOP leadership remains trapped in its commitment to never raise taxes, there will be no serious fiscal agreement. And any Republican who dared to stick his head out of the no-new-tax foxhole and hint at a willingness to consider revenues has been and will be barraged with friendly fire. It seems that Democrats are never going to agree to cuts in Medicare and Medicaid without significant GOP concessions on taxes. However, with enough political cover from President Obama, Democrats might reluctantly move on those entitlements in exchange for some new revenues, but as the 2016 election (as with the pre-election gridlock in the past) nears, Democrats' unwillingness to take on their own base over major federal spending programs only grows. This estrangement of the Democrats on the left and the Republicans on the right has spread like a contagion into many other narrow to broad policies from the Keystone XL Pipeline to the Affordable Care Act, immigration, investment in infrastructure, to most of the Obama programs passed in his first two years in office.

One of the most highly politicized policies is immigration reform. The intense partisan battles over immigration policy since the mid-1980s is another major example of the wide policy chasm between the two parties. Policy proposals to maintain or increase legal immigration while decreasing illegal immigration through enhanced border security have become a fundamental division between Democrats and Republicans. Each year seems to produce even greater partisan rancor. Illegal immigration is a highly controversial issue that divides the parties with proponents (primarily Republicans) of greater immigration enforcement arguing that illegal immigrants cost Americans jobs, cost taxpayers billions in social services, and jeopardize the safety of law enforcement officials and citizens along the Mexican border. Democrats would like to establish a "pathway to citizenship" for law abiding undocumented workers in the United States. "Standards for Immigration Reform" announced in January 2014 by congressional Republicans favor stepwise implementation (rather than a package approach) with border security and interior enforcement preceding "a pathway to citizenship" to legal status. These examples are indicative of the broad partisan differences between the parties.

The most recent major immigration reform enacted in the United States, the Immigration Reform and Control Act of 1986, made it illegal to hire or recruit illegal immigrants, but left the immigration system without a key component: a workable nonimmigrant visa system program for lesser-skilled workers to enter the United States. Following this 1986 law, almost 12 million undocumented workers came across the U.S. border. It was estimated that this undocumented workforce made up about five percent of the U.S. workforce. It was also estimated that about 70 percent of those undocumented workers were from the country of Mexico.

Comprehensive immigration reform had some bipartisan support in 2001 when President George W. Bush and the leadership of both parties of Congress were ready to pass significant immigration reform legislation. The immigration reform Bush proposed was put on hold after the terrorist attacks of September 11, 2001, and the two parties split on their approach to immigration reform. Immigration reform then became a hot partisan topic when President Barack Obama signaled interest in beginning a discussion on comprehensive immigration reform again in 2009. Obama's proposed comprehensive immigration reform plan had as one of its goals bipartisan support, but it failed because it could not bridge the widening divide between the parties. Republicans moved to the right (more security on the border with Mexico and expulsion of undocumented workers) and Democrats moved to the left (with a proposal for a clear path to legal citizenship for undocumented people in the United States).

Policy gridlock continues to evolve. The policy landscape has changed dramatically over the last 50 years. Whether it is the budget, annual appropriations, health care reform, immigration reform, carbon emissions, reauthorization of the Elementary and Secondary Education Act (No Child

Left Behind), or foreign policy (what to do about Ukraine, Syria, ISIS, and Afghanistan, for instance), the parties continue to diverge. They are representing constituencies that view the world through very different policy, ideological, and partisan lenses. These differences are helping to drive conflict, polarization, and gridlock between the two parties at the national and state level.

SUMMARY OF THE BOOK

The book is organized around five areas of research, Part I: Polarization among Voters and Activists; Part II: Polarization in National Institutions; Part III: Polarization in the States; Part IV: Polarization in the Media; and Part V: Implications and Conclusions. Recent advances in data collection and advanced statistical analysis, as well as multiple reforms of the redistricting process and primary elections are allowing scholars in this book to disentangle various explanations for extreme partisanship and present new explanations about the sources and impact of polarization. The book brings greater theoretical and empirical breadth and integration to the polarization literature by moving beyond a singular focus on Congress or the federal government to the judiciary, states, voters, activists, and the media.

Thomas E. Mann's summary of the state of polarization in 2004 has not changed significantly in the last decade:

Party polarization and parity have consequences; for policy (difficulty enacting reasonable, workable, sustainable policies that are congruent with public preferences and needs); for the policy process (demise of regular order in Congress, a decline of deliberation, a weakening of our system of separation of powers and checks and balances); and for the electoral process (limited scope of competition, evermore egregious partisan manipulation of the democratic rules of the game). (2004: 16)

This volume's Foreword by Mann can be viewed as a summary of the current state of polarization in U.S. politics and public policymaking (see also Layman, Carsey, and Horowitz 2006; Mann and Ornstein 2006, 2013, 2014). Mann argues that the parties in Congress and voters are more polarized than at any time in history, setting the foundation for the studies in this volume. Citing authors in *American Gridlock*, Mann describes how political polarization developed over decades from ideological thinkers and political activists with policy demands. He argues that the contemporary Congress bears little resemblance to the "textbook Congress" or "the reform Congress" that followed it (Mann and Ornstein 2006, 2013; Oleszek 2014). Parties are the key actors, and they respond more to their activist bases than to the median voter. This coincided with record lows in the public approval of the performance of Congress and public trust in government to respond to public needs. Mann concludes that the current Congress has ceased to operate as an effective legislative body with deliberation and compromise being supplanted by conflict and gridlock (Thurber 2013). His is quite the indictment.

Part I of the volume tackles the question of polarization among voters and activists. Chapter 1, "The New American Electorate: Partisan, Sorted, and Polarized," by Alan I. Abramowitz, considers the abundant evidence that the United States has entered a new era of electoral competition characterized by a closely divided electorate at the national level and one-party dominance in most state and congressional districts with a high degree of consistency in the outcomes of elections over time and across different types of election. Long gone are the days of large inter-election swings. The 2014 election adds more confirming evidence for his generalization. Abramowitz focuses on how party loyalty and straight-ticket voting have reached record levels, reflecting the growing strength of partisanship within the American electorate. He concludes that these trends are based upon a growing divergence between Democratic and Republican coalitions along racial, cultural, and ideological lines (Abramowitz 2011, 2012).

What can be done to reduce this divide? Among the frequently cited causes for polarization is the redistricting process of drawing district boundaries following each decennial census (and sometimes in-between censuses). Chapter 2, "Redistricting and Polarization," by Micah Altman and Michael McDonald discusses how the ideological polarization of members of the U.S. House of Representatives is affected by the sorting of incumbents into more ideologically compatible districts, the replacement of incumbents by more ideologically extreme successors, and the drawing of more ideologically extreme districts. States are responsible for drawing House of Representatives district boundary lines, and because in most states politicians are in charge of the process, it can create an obvious conflict of interest. The authors show that there are fewer competitive congressional districts following redistricting. They go beyond the extant literature by introducing a series of innovative public mapping projects that demonstrate how district maps can be drawn to foster competition without sacrificing other values, such as compactness or minority representation. However, they conclude that the prospects for redistricting reform are very limited.

Voters are not the only ones being polarized. David Karol argues in Chapter 3, "Party Activists, Interest Groups, and Polarization in American Politics" that partisan polarization cannot be understood without attention to the role of both activists and party-aligned interest groups whose policy preferences are both shaped by and shape the behavior of elected officials. This story thus goes beyond voters and elected officials. Activists and party-aligned interest groups advance their policy goals via candidate selection and the lobbying of elected officials. Activists and well-organized interest groups take cues from politicians, but their actions also reinforce and contribute to polarization in important ways. Karol shows that the polarization of Democrats and Republicans reflects the incorporation of new groups in each party's coalition since the 1970s. Karol finds that polarization is visible in many aspects of American politics from Congress, to the courts to state legislatures and the electorate, a common theme found among many chapters in this volume. The shared factor linking all of these settings is political parties. Political parties, unlike the elected branches of government or even the electorate, are not well-bounded entities. They consist of activists and groups, often with no formal role or place on the organization chart, but they play important roles in parties and polarization, as shown, for instance, by the Tea party movement.

Chapter 4, "Authoritarianism and Polarization in American Politics, Still?" by Marc J. Hetherington and Jonathan D. Weiler, argues that a personality-based, authoritarian-non-authoritarian, divide continues to structure party conflict and polarization in America. Theirs is, therefore, an argument for a psychological basis to partisan polarization, which centers on the worldview of voters as a major explanation. They argue that Barack Obama's ascendancy to the presidency has deepened the divide they identified as emerging in the early 2000s (Hetherington and Weiler 2009). The issue agenda, which is central to understanding personality-based polarization, has evolved in ways that have also deepened the divide, particularly with the emergence of immigration reform as a central concern. They note that the Tea Party represents the clearest embodiment of the authoritarian politics that defines the current political right, pushing a substantive issue agenda but also eliciting deeper-seated emotions about order and change in American politics. The authors maintain that politics have increasingly become organized around a fundamental "worldview/personality divide," with preferences on the most important issues of the day, such as race, feminism, immigration, gay rights, and the proper responses to terrorism, all, in large measure, driven by the same worldview/personality.

Closing Part I of the book and taking a different stance on the polarization of voters, Samuel J. Abrams and Morris P. Fiorina, in Chapter 5, "Party Sorting: The Foundations of Polarized Politics," contend that whether one looks at partisan, ideological, or issue cleavages, the American electorate shows no evidence of polarization – the middle has not shrunk. Rather, the American electorate has sorted, which has made political parties more internally homogeneous and more distinct from each other. Party sorting increases inter-party conflict and makes cross-party compromise more difficult, establishing the foundation of polarization and gridlock. They support their argument with data spanning the last 40 years.

The focus of Part II of the volume turns to our national institutions: the presidency, Congress, and the Supreme Court. Chapter 6, "Presidential-Congressional Relations in an Era of Polarized Parties and a 60-Vote Senate," by Jon R. Bond, Richard Fleisher, and Jeffrey E. Cohen, provides clear evidence that party control of Congress is the strongest determinant of presidential success. Majority party presidents win more roll call votes than do minority party presidents (Thurber 2011, 2013). Until recently, the effects of party control were similar in both chambers; however, that authors show that rising party polarization in Congress affects presidential success differently in the House and Senate. In the House, party polarization amplifies the effects of party control – as party polarization increases, majority party presidents win more and minority presidents win less. In the Senate, however, party polarization suppresses success rates. Still, majority presidents win more on average, but as party voting increases, success rates decline for both majority and minority presidents. They show that the increase in Senate cloture votes and the emergence of the minority party filibuster during the Bush and Obama presidencies is responsible for the changes they find in how party polarization conditions the effects of party control in the Senate (Theriault 2013). For instance, on non-cloture votes, the effect of polarization on presidential success rate in the Senate resembles that which they find in the House. This clearly shows the importance of institutional rules in the relationship between Congress and the president.

The 60-vote Senate is the subject of Chapter 7, "Party Warriors: The Ugly Side of Party Polarization in Congress" by Sean M. Theriault. The author makes a conceptual argument pertaining to the various dimensions to gridlock and conflict. All too often, these are treated as one and the same and fall under the topic of party polarization (Baker 2015). Theriault maintains that another dimension to party polarization is distinct from it and is in many ways a better term for our current situation. Theriault calls it "party warfare." The concepts are related, but he maintains that their distinction is critical to understanding the current congressional dynamics. Some legislators are simply "at war," and their opposition doesn't always stem from ideological differences; they are there to fight and win. He shows that the number of roll call votes caused by senators' amendments gives an insight into partisan warfare in the U.S. Senate and reveals a second dimension of party polarization.

In Chapter 8, "The Sources and Consequences of Polarization in the U.S. Supreme Court," Brandon L. Bartels examines polarization in the U.S. Supreme Court, primarily from the post–New Deal era to the present. He reveals how the ideological center on the Court has gradually shrunk over time and analyzes the sources and consequences of this trend. Polarization in the Supreme Court has generally increased over time, though this trend has ebbed and flowed. The most robust center existed during the Burger Court of the mid to late 1970s, consisting of arguably five swing justices. Bartels shows that while the center has shrunk over time on the Court, it still exists due to (1) presidents from Truman to George H.W. Bush not placing exclusive emphasis on ideological compatibility and reliability when appointing justices, (2) an increase in the incidence of divided government, and (3) the rarity of strategic retirements by the justices. Since President Clinton took office, the norms have shifted to strategic retirements by the justices and presidents placing near exclusive emphasis on ideological compatibility and reliability in the appointment process. He uncovers the existence of a "polarization paradox," whereby the incidence of 5–4 case outcomes has increased over time, but so has the incidence of unanimous outcomes. He explains this paradox by looking at whether the Court is deciding cases within its "volitional agenda" (politically salient issues) or "exigent agenda" (institutional maintenance), with the former causing more conflict than the latter. With just one swing justice (Kennedy) on the current Court, whoever is president (Obama and beyond) has the chance to create the first ideologically homogeneous majority-voting bloc since the Warren Court of the 1960s.

Part III of the volume moves us from the Beltway and ventures into lesser-known territory in the scholarship on partisan polarization: the states. Boris Shor in Chapter 9, "Polarization in American State Legislatures," reveals new measures of state legislative polarization that show that Democrats and Republicans continue to diverge, more quickly in some states than others. Levels of polarization in many states exceed that of Congress. He shows that no single factor explains state legislative polarization. He maintains that in many cases we can only rule out commonly argued causes such as primaries since they bear little connection to state-level polarization. He argues that specific forms of opinion polarization and income inequality can explain some of the state-level polarization. The consequences of state legislative polarization are only now beginning to be explored. Increasing unilateralism by governors appears to be one major cause of increased gridlock within the state legislatures. Shor concludes that major advances in our understanding of American polarization are more likely to come from further examination of the states rather than a singular focus on Congress.

Seth E. Masket in Chapter 10, "The Costs of Party Reform: Two States' Experiences," describes state attempts to rein in political parties through a series of reforms. It is an important chapter in that it shows how reform efforts can sometimes backfire. This chapter details with two such efforts: campaign finance reform in Colorado and cross-filing in California. While these reforms met with mixed success in limiting partisanship, they imposed other costs on the political system that generally worked against reformers' stated goals. Masket finds that Colorado's campaign finance reform in 2002, which sharply limited parties' donations and expenditures, did not curtail partisanship in the state, while making campaign contributions more difficult to trace. He also shows that cross-filing in California (1913–59) had the effect of limiting partisanship in the statehouse, but also created a corrupt environment dominated by lobbyists and business interests. He argues that strong party systems, while frustrating, tend to allow for greater accountability in elections. His chapter serves as a warning that weakening parties in order to reduce partisanship may be less effective than adapting current institutions to the presence of strong parties.

In Chapter 11, "The Policy Consequences of Party Polarization: Evidence from the States," Elizabeth Rigby and Gerald C. Wright analyze the policy consequences of polarization, asking whether we see different policy choices when parties are more (versus less) polarized. Their analysis is motivated by recent research suggesting a constraining effect of partisan polarization on redistributive policy, contradicting earlier expectations that greater benefits will accrue to the poor when parties are competitive and offer clear policy choices. To better understand these consequences, they capitalized on variation in both policy choices and party polarization over time and across the 50 states. They find that party polarization results in lower levels of redistributive policy across eight distinct forms of policy redistribution. This pattern was most pronounced for redistributive policies that are not indexed to inflation; thus, without new legislation, the real value of the policy decreases over time. They show that these policies, such as the minimum wage, are particularly impacted by polarization-induced gridlock. For redistributive policies that do increase in magnitude as inflation, incomes, or earnings rise, such as the corporate tax rate, they show polarization had more of an indirect effect, shifting the impact of party control of the state government. These distinct paths of influence for different types of policies illustrate both the importance of polarization for policymaking and the complexity of these relationships.

Our contributors to Part IV of the volume turn their attention to one major source of polarization in recent years, namely the American media landscape. In Chapter 12, "Partisan Media and Electoral Polarization in 2012," Gary C. Jacobson reveals that partisan divisions among Americans over issues, ideology, evaluations of leaders, and perceptions of political, economic, and scientific realities reached new extremes during Barack Obama's presidency. He shows that the 2012 electorate was more polarized along party lines than any in at least six decades. The electorate displayed the highest levels of party-line voting, lowest levels of ticket splitting, and widest partisan difference in presidential approval ever documented in American National Election Studies (ANES) going back to 1952. The proportion of both approvers and disapprovers of Obama who held these views "strongly" were both at all-time highs for a president pursuing reelection (Jacobson 2013). These trends coincided with the proliferation of partisan news and opinion outlets enabled by the spread of cable television, talk radio, and the Internet. Jacobson raises the question of how these two phenomena might be related. Using data from the 2012 ANES, he offers a unique perspective on this question by examining whether respondents attended to any of over thirty specific television, radio, newspaper, and Internet sources of news and opinion programs. He categorizes these sources as conservative, liberal, or mainstream, allowing his analysis of the relationship between the ideological and partisan leanings of the sources voters reported using and their political beliefs, attitudes, and behavior. He shows that most people who do attend to partisan media chose sources "that could be relied on to confirm rather than challenge their existing attitudes and opinions." Partisans showed a clear preference for sources of news and opinion that reliably fit their biases. This selective exposure in turn polarized the electorate even further. Jacobson concludes that the intense partisanship expressed in the 2012 election amplified partisan intransigence and gridlock in Washington during the 113th Congress, for Obama and the House Republican majority owed their elections to thoroughly disjunctive coalitions, with the most starkly opposed opinions and beliefs, of any modern Congress and administration on record.

In Chapter 13, "News as a Casualty: District Polarization and Media Coverage of U.S. House Campaigns," Danny Hayes and Jennifer L. Lawless analyze the effect of district polarization on local political news coverage with original data gathered by analyzing the content of local newspaper coverage from every congressional district during the 2010 midterms. Their analyses clearly show that district polarization affects the competitive context of House campaigns, which influences the attention congressional races receive from the news media, with lopsided districts seeing much less coverage than more evenly split districts. Importantly, competitiveness also affects the substance of local news coverage in U.S. House campaigns, with more substantive coverage found in more competitive races. This is true whether they examine the number of stories that mention both candidates, the number of issue mentions across the campaign's coverage, or the number of times the candidates' personal traits are discussed in the coverage. By linking polarization to competitiveness, and competitiveness to news coverage, they reveal that polarization impoverishes the news environment. These findings are consequential because a growing body of research suggests that a diminished news environment can depress citizens' political knowledge and engagement.

Chapter 14, "More a Symptom Than a Cause: Polarization and Partisan News Media in America," by Kevin Arceneaux and Martin Johnson, is an analysis of the emergence of partisan news media in the United States and an assessment of its effect on political polarization. The authors argue that the emergence of partisan news media is more a symptom of a polarized political system than a source. Political parties in the U.S. Congress polarized before the advent of partisan news media. The expansion of entertainment options on television and the Internet has limited the reach of both mainstream and partisan news. Although exposure to partisan news programs can polarize political attitudes, exposure to mainstream news can also polarize. News programs are polarizing, in part, because they communicate to the public the degree to which politicians are polarized along party lines. Consequently, if political elites were to become less partisan, the electorate would likely follow. They provide experimental evidence suggesting that partisan media may be more a symptom than a cause of polarization.

In Chapter 15, "The Polarizing Effects of Partisan and Mainstream News," Natalie Jomini Stroud and Alexander Curry show that strong partisans gravitate toward like-minded partisan media and that like-minded media use can polarize attitudes (similar to the Jacobson findings in Chapter 13). In some instances, however, the use of counter-attitudinal media can also polarize, which is an important counterintuitive finding. Using an experimental design with NBC, MSNBC, and Fox News coverage of the Keystone XL Pipeline's environmental impact, they show that media coverage affects attitudes and beliefs. Drawing from "inoculation theory," they show that like-minded news polarized attitudes and watching a combination of like-minded and mainstream news coverage did little to reduce polarization.

The last two chapters of the book offer an overview of the work by Keith Poole and his colleagues as well as the conclusion to the book. Chapter 16, "Congressional Polarization and Its Connection to Income Inequality: An Update," by Adam Bonica, Nolan McCarty, Keith T. Poole, and Howard Rosenthal, present new findings on political polarization in Congress and among elite political actors who work through Congress to affect public policy (also see McCarty, Poole, and Rosenthal 2006). They begin by describing the methodologies that enabled them to identify the emergence of political polarization in Congress. They confirm the findings of other authors in the book that polarization in Congress is the highest since Reconstruction. They show that polarization is not an artifact of roll call voting and that it also occurs in patterns of campaign contributions too. They link various threads of their research with the other chapters in this volume. They agree with Mann's Foreword to this volume that polarization in Congress is asymmetric, largely due to the Republican Party becoming more conservative. Their concluding analysis reveals that polarization and income inequality appear to be mutually causal.

We conclude *American Gridlock* in Chapter 17, "The Sources and Impact of Political Polarization," with a summary of common themes and a consensus of shared findings about the causes and consequences of polarization and partisanship. We comment on the implications of these findings and suggest future directions for research and reform.

We hope that readers of our volume will not only appreciate the synthesis of large segments of the literature, but that chapters will spawn new research questions and ideas. The juxtaposition of federal- and state-level research; the use of observational and experimental methods to estimate media effects; an emphasis not only on voters and legislators, but also on activists and Supreme Court Justices; a look at all three branches of the federal government – this amalgamation was done with an eye toward showcasing, in a single volume, these very diverse approaches and novel data that we hope will lead more scholars, pundits, practitioners, and students to engage with this very important question of polarization and gridlock in the United States.

REFERENCES

Abramowitz, Alan I. 2012. *The Polarized Public: Why American Government Is So Dysfunctional.* New York: Pearson.

Abramowitz, Alan I. 2011. *The Disappearing Center: Engaged Citizens, Polarization, and American Democracy.* New Haven, CT: Yale University Press.

Balz, Dan. 2014. "Dysfunction Is Washington's New Normal," *Washington Post.* December 14, A2.

Baker, Ross K. 2015. *Is Bipartisanship Dead? A Report from the Senate.* Boulder, CO: Paradigm Publishers.

Bond, Jon, and Richard Fleisher, eds. 2000. *Polarized Politics: Congress and the President in a Partisan Era.* Washington, DC: CQ Press.

Doherty, Carroll. 2014. "7 Things to Know about Polarization in America." Pew Research Center, June 12. Retrieved from http://www.pewresearch.org/fact-tank/2014/06/12/7-things-to-know-about-polarization-in-america/.

Fiorina, Morris P. 2014. "Americans Have Not Become Politically More Polarized." Retrieved from http://www.washingtonpost.com/blogs/monkey-cage/wp/2014/06/23/americans-have-not-become-more-politically-polarized/.

Fiorina, Morris P. 2011. *Disconnect: The Breakdown of Representation in American Politics.* Norman: University of Oklahoma Press.

Fiorina, Morris P., Samuel Abrams, and Jeremy Pope. 2006. *Culture War? The Myth of a Polarized America,* 2nd edition. New York: Pearson Longman.

Frisch, Scott A., and Sean Q. Kelly, eds. 2013. *Politics to the Extreme: American Political Institutions in the Twenty-First Century.* New York: Palgrave Macmillan.

Hacker, Jacob S., and Paul Pierson. 2005. *Off Center: The Republican Revolution and the Erosion of American Democracy.* New Haven, CT: Yale University Press.

Hetherington, Marc. 2005. *Why Trust Matters: Declining Political Trust and the Demise of American Liberalism.* Princeton, NJ: Princeton University Press.

Hetherington, Marc, and Jonathan Weiler. 2009. *Authoritarianism and Polarization in American Politics.* New York: Cambridge University Press.

Jacobson, Gary. 2013. "Partisan Polarization in American Politics: A Background Paper." *Presidential Studies Quarterly* 43 (December): 688–708.

Layman, Geoffrey C., Thomas M. Carsey, and Juliana Menasce Horowitz. 2006. "Party Polarization in American Politics: Characteristics, Causes and Consequences." *Annual Review of Political Science* 9 (June): 83–110.

Lee, Frances E. 2009. *Beyond Ideology: Politics, Principles, and Partisanship in the U.S. Senate.* Chicago: University of Chicago Press.

Levendusky, Matthew S. 2013. *How Partisan Media Polarize America.* Chicago: University of Chicago Press.

Levendusky, Matthew S. 2010. "Clearer Cues, More Consistent Voters: A Benefit of Elite Polarization." *Political Behavior* 32 (1): 111–131.

Levendusky, Matthew S. 2009. *The Partisan Sort: How Liberals Became Democrats and Conservatives Became Republicans.* Chicago: University of Chicago Press.

Mann, Thomas E. 2004. "Remarks at the 'Polarization of American Politics: Myth or Reality?' Conference," Princeton University, December 3.

Mann, Thomas E. and Norman J. Ornstein. 2014. "The Party of Now What?" *Washington Post,* November 9, B1 and B4.

Mann, Thomas E., and Norman J. Ornstein. 2013. *It's Even Worse Than It Looks: How the American Constitutional System Collided with the New Politics of Extremism.* New York: Basic Books.

Mann, Thomas E., and Norman J. Ornstein. 2006. *The Broken Branch: How Congress is Failing American and How to Get It Back on Track*. New York: Oxford University Press.

McCarty, Nolan, Keith T. Poole, and Howard Rosenthal. 2006. *Polarized America: The Dance of Ideology and Unequal Riches*. Cambridge, MA: MIT Press.

Masket, Seth, 2011. *No Middle Ground: How Informal Party Organizations Control Nominations and Polarize Legislatures*. Ann Arbor: University of Michigan Press.

Muirhead, Russell. 2014. *The Promise of Party in a Polarized Age*. Cambridge, MA: Harvard University Press.

Nivola, Pietro, and David S. Brady, eds. 2006. *Red and Blue Nation? Characteristics and Causes of America's Polarized Politics: Volume One*. Washington, DC: Brookings Institution Press.

Nivola, Pietro S., and David S. Brady, eds. 2008. *Red and Blue Nation? Volume Two: Consequences and Correction of America's Polarized Politics*. Washington, DC: Brookings Institution Press.

Oleszek, Walter J. 2014. "The Evolving Congress: Overview and Analysis of the Modern Era." In *The Evolving Congress*, prepared by Congressional Research Service, December. Library of Congress for the Committee on Rules and Administration, U. S. Senate. Washington, DC: U.S. Printing Office, 3–60.

Noel, Hans. 2013. *Political Ideologies and Political Parties in America*. New York: Cambridge University Press.

Persily, Nathaniel (eds.). 2015. *Solutions to Political Polarization in America*. New York: Cambridge University Press.

Poole, Keith T. 2013. *Political Bubbles: Financial Crises and the Failure of American Democracy*. Princeton, NJ: Princeton University Press.

Poole, Keith T., and Howard Rosenthal. 2000. *Congress: A Political-Economic History of Roll Call Voting*. New York: Oxford University Press.

Prior, Markus. 2007. *Post-Broadcast Democracy: How Media Choice Increases Inequality in Political Involvement and Polarizes Elections*. New York: Cambridge University Press.

Schaffner, Brian F. 2011. "Party Polarization," In Erick Schickler and Francis E. Lee, eds., *The Oxford Handbook of American Congress*. New York: Oxford University Press.

Sinclair, Barbara. 2006. *Party Wars*. Norman: University of Oklahoma Press.

Sinclair, Barbara. 1995. *Legislators, Leaders, and Lawmaking*. Baltimore: Johns Hopkins Press.

Theriault, Sean. 2013. *The Gingrich Senators: The Roots of Partisan Warfare in Congress*. New York: Oxford University Press.

Thurber, James A. 2014. "The Dynamics and Dysfunction of the Congressional Budget Process: From Inception to Deadlock," In Lawrence C. Dodd and Bruce I. Oppenheimer, eds., *Congress Reconsidered*. Washington, DC: CQ Press, 319–345.

Thurber, James A. 2013. "An Introduction to Presidential-Congressional Rivalry." In James A. Thurber, ed., *Rivals for Power: Presidential-Congressional Relations*. Lanham, MD: Rowman and Littlefield, 1–26.

Thurber, James A. 2012. "Agony, Angst, and the Failure of the Supercommittee," *Extensions* Summer: 1–10.

Thurber, James A. 2011. "An Introduction to an Assessment of the Obama Presidency." In James A. Thurber, ed., *Obama in Office*. Boulder, CO: Paradigm Publishers, 1–20.

PART I

POLARIZATION AMONG VOTERS AND ACTIVISTS

I

The New American Electorate

Partisan, Sorted, and Polarized

Alan I. Abramowitz

- The United States has entered a new era of electoral competition in the twenty-first century.
- The key features of the new era of electoral competition are a closely divided electorate at the national level, one-party domination of most states and congressional districts, and a high degree of consistency in the outcomes of elections over time and across different types of elections.
- These features of electoral competition reflect the growing strength of partisanship within the American electorate – party loyalty and straight-ticket voting have reached record levels in recent years.
- The partisan behavior of the electorate is based on a growing divergence between the Democratic and Republican electoral coalitions along racial, cultural, and ideological lines.

In the first two decades of the twenty-first century, the United States has entered a new era of electoral competition. This new era of competition has three main characteristics that distinguish it from the patterns of electoral competition that were evident for half a century following the end of World War II. First, there is a close balance of support for the two major political parties at the national level, which has resulted in intense competition for control of Congress and the White House. Second, despite the close balance of support between the parties at the national level, there is widespread one-party dominance at the state and local levels. Third, there is a high degree of consistency in the outcomes of elections over time and across different types of elections. These three characteristics are closely related. All of them reflect the central underlying reality of American electoral politics in the current era: an electorate that is strongly partisan and deeply divided along racial, ideological, and cultural lines (White 2003; Hood, Kidd, and Morris 2004; Abramowitz and Saunders 2006; Brewer and Stonecash 2007; Jacobson 2007; Hillygus and Shields 2008, ch. 5; Abramowitz 2013; Jacobson 2013).

COMPETITIVE ELECTIONS

Recent national elections in the United States have been highly competitive. Shifts in party control of both chambers of Congress and the White House have been fairly regular, and popular vote margins in presidential elections have been relatively close. Between 1948 and 1992, shifts in party control of the White House occurred quite regularly, with party control changing in 1952, 1960, 1968, 1976, 1980, and 1992. However, during these years, shifts in party control of the House of Representatives and Senate were more unusual, occurring only in 1952 and 1954 in the case of the House and only in 1952, 1954, 1980, and 1986 in the case of the Senate. Democrats controlled both chambers of Congress for 34 of the 40 years between 1954 and 1994. Since then, however, the House has changed hands three times – in 1994, 2006, and 2010 – and the Senate has changed hands five times – in 1994, 2001 (as a result of a party switch by one Republican senator), 2002, 2006, and 2014. Moreover, majorities in both chambers have generally been smaller than they were in many of the Congresses during the years when Democrats enjoyed uninterrupted control of the legislative branch.

Although swings in party control of the White House occurred frequently between the 1950s and 1990s, many of the elections during those years were decided by very large popular vote margins. In contrast, the popular vote margins in recent presidential elections have been fairly small. Of course, there have been closely contested presidential elections throughout American history, but there have also been many landslide elections in which one candidate defeated his opponent by a margin of 10 percentage points or more in the popular vote. In fact, during most of the twentieth century, landslide elections were the rule and not the exception. Of the 17 presidential elections between 1920 and 1984, 10 were won by a double-digit margin. But there hasn't been a landslide election since Ronald Reagan's drubbing of Walter Mondale in 1984.

Not only have the results of recent presidential elections been considerably closer on average than earlier ones, they have also been much more stable. It was not unusual in the earlier elections of the postwar era for the margin between the Democratic and Republican candidates to fluctuate widely from one election to the next. For example, the five elections between 1956 and 1972 included Republican landslides in 1956 and 1972, a Democratic landslide in 1964, and two closely contested elections in 1960 and 1968.

Table 1 presents data summarizing trends in competition in the 16 presidential elections between 1952 and 2012 by dividing them into four eras, each consisting of four elections: 1952–64, 1968–80, 1984–96, and 2000–12. For each era, the table displays the average popular vote margin of the winning candidate and the standard deviation of the margin of victory or defeat of the Democratic candidate. The data in this table show a striking pattern. The elections during the first era between 1952 and 1964 show both the largest

TABLE 1. *Competition in U.S. Presidential Elections since 1952*

Elections	Average Winning Margin (%)	Standard Deviation (%)
1952–64	12.5	17.3
1968–80	9.0	11.9
1984–96	9.8	12.1
2000–12	3.5	4.4

Source: uselectionsatlas.org

average margin of victory and largest standard deviation. Average margins of victory and standard deviations were somewhat smaller in the second and third eras. But the most dramatic change occurs in the most recent era. The four presidential elections between 2000 and 2012 have had by far the closest average margins of victory and by far the smallest variability from election to election of any of the four eras. In fact, the four most recent presidential elections had the closest popular vote margins and the least election-to-election variability in Democratic margin of any set of four consecutive presidential elections in the past century. To find a series of presidential elections with outcomes as close and as stable as these, one has to go back to the last quarter of the nineteenth century.

ONE-PARTY DOMINANCE OF STATE AND LOCAL ELECTIONS

Despite the competitiveness of recent presidential and congressional elections at the national level, there has been a marked decline in the competitiveness of elections at the state and local levels in many parts of the United States over the past several decades. There are far fewer swing states and congressional districts and far more strongly Democratic and Republican states and districts now than there were in the 1960s and 1970s. What is striking about the results of the 2012 presidential election at the state level is that, despite the closeness of the national popular vote, there were very few closely contested states. Only four states were decided by a margin of less than five percentage points: Florida, Ohio, Virginia, and North Carolina. On the other hand, 27 states as well as the District of Columbia were decided by a margin of at least 15 percentage points. Mitt Romney actually carried more states by landslide and near-landslide margins than Barack Obama, but the states that Obama carried had far more electoral votes than the ones that Romney carried.

The 2012 results continued the recent pattern of presidential elections that are decided by a narrow margin at the national level but by a landslide or near-landslide margin in many states. And that included some of the most populous and electoral vote–rich states in the country. Thus, President Obama carried California with its 55 electoral votes by a margin of 23 points, New York with its 29 electoral votes by 28 points, and Illinois with its 20 electoral votes by 17 points. Meanwhile, Mitt Romney won Texas's 38 electoral votes by a margin of 16 points.

This pattern of many deep red and blue states, including several of the nation's most populous states, represents a dramatic change from the pattern of electoral competition seen in close presidential elections during the 1960s and 1970s. In 1960 and 1976, when John F. Kennedy and Jimmy Carter won close, hard-fought battles for the White House, 20 states were decided by a margin by less than five percentage points. Moreover, in those elections every one of the nation's most populous states was closely contested, including California, New York, Illinois, and Texas. In 1976, states decided by less than five points accounted for 299 electoral votes, whereas states decided by 15 points or more accounted for only 66 electoral votes. In 2012, in contrast, states decided by less than five points accounted for only 75 electoral votes and states decided by 15 points or more accounted for 289 electoral votes.

Because there are so many deep red and blue states today, it is easy to predict which party's candidate will carry the large majority of states long before Election Day. A year before the 2012 presidential election, long before the Republican candidate was known, there was very little doubt about how at least 35 states would cast their electoral votes. That is because there is a very high degree of consistency in voting patterns at the state level from election to election. In the end, 48 of 50 states along with the District of Columbia supported the same party in 2012 as in 2008.

The decline in the number of competitive states since the 1960s and 1970s has been paralleled by a similar trend at the congressional district level. There are far more districts today that are dominated by one party and far fewer that are closely divided. This can be seen by comparing presidential election results at the House district level in 1976 and 2012. Despite the similarity in the national margins of victory in these two elections, the results at the congressional district level were very different. In 1976, only 26 out of 435 House districts were won by a margin of at least 20 percentage points in the presidential election, whereas 187 districts were won by a margin of less than five percentage points. In 2012, in contrast, 232 out of 435 House districts were won by a margin of at least 20 percentage points in the presidential election and only 47 were won by a margin of less than five percentage points.

Some political observers have attributed the recent decline in the number of competitive House districts to partisan gerrymandering. But a comparison of the partisan composition of House districts before and after redistricting in 1980–82, 1990–92, and 2000–02 did not find significant differences in the competitiveness of the districts. Most of the decline in district competitiveness actually occurred between redistricting cycles (Abramowitz, Alexander, and Gunning 2006). Similarly, an examination of redistricting of state legislative districts found that partisan gerrymandering had little impact on either competition or polarization (Masket, Winburn, and Wright 2012). Moreover, as we have seen, the same trend of declining competitiveness has occurred over this time period at the state level even though state boundaries are fixed. These trends clearly cannot be explained by clever line drawing to protect incumbents. In order to explaining declining party competition in states and congressional districts, one has to look to deeper trends in American society.

CONSISTENCY OF ELECTION RESULTS

The third major feature of the recent era of electoral competition in the United States has been a very high degree of consistency in the preferences of voters and, therefore, in the outcomes of elections at the state and local levels as well as at the national level. Not only have the election-to-election swings in the national popular vote been much smaller than in earlier time periods, but the outcomes at the local and state levels have been exceptionally stable. Thus, only two states – Indiana and North Carolina – switched sides between the 2008 and 2012 presidential elections. This was the smallest number of states switching sides in two consecutive presidential elections since the end of World War II. Moreover, the correlation between the Democratic share of the vote in 2008 and the Democratic share of the vote in 2012 across all 50 states and the District of Columbia was a remarkable .98. This was the strongest correlation between two consecutive elections in the postwar era. The Democratic share of the vote in 2008 almost perfectly predicted the Democratic share of the vote in 2012. And the correlation between the Democratic share of the vote in 2004 and the Democratic share of the vote in 2012, two elections eight years apart with totally different sets of candidates, was almost as impressive at .95. Correlations between the results of recent pairs of presidential elections were just as strong at the congressional district and county levels.

Recent elections have also been marked by an extraordinary degree of consistency in the outcomes of elections at different levels (Jacobson 2013). Thus, the correlation between the Democratic share of the presidential vote and the Democratic share of the vote for U.S. House of Representatives across all districts with contested House races in 2012 was .95. This was the highest correlation between presidential and U.S. House election results in the entire post–World War II era. As a result, only 25 out of 435 House districts were won by a candidate from the opposite party from the presidential candidate who carried that district. In the 113th Congress, only 16 Republicans represented a district carried by Barack Obama, and only 9 Democrats represented a district carried by Mitt Romney. This was the smallest number of districts represented by a member from the presidential minority party in any Congress since the end of World War II.

Although results of Senate elections have not been as consistent with presidential voting as the results of House elections, there has been a marked increase in recent years in the relationship between presidential and Senate election outcomes. As a result, the vast majority of U.S. senators now come from the same party as the winner of the most recent presidential election in their state. Thus, the 26 states carried by Barack Obama in 2012 were represented by 43 Democrats and 9 Republicans in the 113th Congress, whereas the 24 states carried by Mitt Romney were represented by 12 Democrats and 36 Republicans. In the 2014 midterm election, 33 out of 36 Senate contests were won by the candidate of the same party that carried the state in the 2012 presidential election.

The growing consistency of election results in recent years extends all the way from the presidential contest at the top of the ticket down to state legislative races. Thus, the party composition of state legislatures in the United States is now strongly related to the results of presidential elections. The correlation between the Democratic share of the presidential vote in 2012 and the Democratic share of state legislative seats in 2012 was an impressive .85. This was the strongest correlation between presidential and state legislative election results for any year since at least 1956. Since the 2010 midterm election, Republicans have controlled most of the nation's state legislative chambers. Nevertheless, in the 26 states carried by Barack Obama in 2012, Democrats controlled 37 out of 52 legislative chambers following the 2012 elections. In contrast, in the 23 states with partisan legislatures (Nebraska has a nonpartisan, unicameral legislature) carried by Mitt Romney in 2012, Republicans controlled 43 out of 46 legislative chambers following the 2012 elections. Altogether, more than 80 percent of partisan state legislative chambers in 2013 were controlled by the party whose candidate carried the state in the 2012 presidential election.

A STRONGLY PARTISAN ELECTORATE

The remarkable consistency in the results of recent presidential elections and between the results of presidential, congressional, and state legislative elections as well as the large number of deep blue and deep red states and districts can both be explained by the fact that the American electorate today is sharply divided along party lines. The results of all of these elections closely reflected the underlying strength of the parties in the states and districts, and the fact that while the nation as a whole is closely divided between supporters of the two parties, the large majority of states and congressional districts now clearly favor one party or the other. As a result, the outcomes of presidential elections and control of the House and Senate are determined by a few swing states and districts in which the outcome is in doubt – a group of states and districts whose number has been steadily decreasing.

The partisan divide was clearly evident in the results of the 2012 election at the individual level as well as at the state and district level. Thus, according to the national exit poll, 93 percent of Republican identifiers voted for Mitt Romney and 92 percent of Democratic identifiers voted for Barack Obama. This was the highest level of party loyalty in any presidential election since the beginning of exit polls in 1972, and it continued a pattern of strong partisan voting by Democratic and Republican identifiers in recent presidential elections. Data from the 2012 American National Election Study confirm this pattern: 91 percent of party identifiers, including leaning independents, voted for their own party's presidential candidate while only 7 percent defected to the opposing party's candidate. This was the highest level of party loyalty in any presidential election since the American National Election Studies (ANES) began asking the party identification question in 1952.

This recent pattern of strong party loyalty in presidential voting represents a dramatic change in the behavior of Democratic identifiers. According to national exit poll data, in the five presidential elections between 1972 and 1988, an average of 25 percent of Democratic identifiers voted for the Republican presidential candidate. Even in the one election won by the Democratic candidate during this time period – in 1976 – 20 percent of Democratic identifiers voted for the Republican candidate. In contrast, in the four presidential elections between 2000 and 2012, the average defection rate for Democratic identifiers was only 10 percent. The average defection rate among Republicans has also fallen over time, but much less sharply, from an average of 10 percent for the five elections between 1972 and 1988 to an average of 7 percent for the four elections between 2000 and 2012.

Independents made up 29 percent of the electorate, according to the national exit poll, and they divided their votes relatively evenly – 50 percent for Romney to 45 percent for Obama. But that 29 percent figure undoubtedly exaggerates the significance of the independent voting bloc since the exit poll does not ask independents whether they usually lean toward one party or the other. Based on data from the ANES and other surveys, however, we know that the large majority of self-identified independents lean toward a party and that these leaning independents vote very similarly to regular partisans (Keith et al. 1992). In fact, in recent elections, leaning independents have been more loyal to their party than weak party identifiers. In the 2012 ANES, 72 percent of independent voters leaned toward one of the two major parties, and only 9 percent of these leaning independents defected to the opposing party's presidential candidate as compared to 14 percent of weak party identifiers.

It is possible that the strong relationship between party leaning and vote choice among leaning independents is owing to vote choice influencing party leaning rather than party leaning influencing vote choice. That is, some independents may simply indicate that they lean toward the party whose candidate they plan to vote for in the current election. However, it is worth noting in this regard that there is a very strong relationship between party leaning and a vote for U.S. House and Senate as well as president. Thus, according to data from the 2012 ANES, 85 percent of independent Democrats voted for the Democratic House candidate in their district as compared with 79 percent of weak Democrat identifiers. Likewise, 91 percent of independent Republicans voted for the Republican House candidate in their district as compared with 90 percent of weak Republican identifiers. Similarly, in 2012, in states with Senate races, 88 percent of independent Democrats voted for the Democratic Senate candidate as compared with 87 percent of weak Democrat identifiers, and 86 percent of independent Republicans voted for the Republican Senate candidate as compared with 81 percent of weak Republican identifiers.

An even more critical piece of evidence concerning the partisanship of leaning independents involves their ideological orientations and policy preferences. According to data from the 2012 ANES, the ideological orientations and opinions of leaning independents on a wide range of policy issues closely resembled the opinions of their co-partisans. In fact, on most issues, independent Democrats were more liberal than weak Democrats, and independent Republicans were more conservative than weak Republicans. For example, 66 percent of independent Democrats supported the Affordable Care Act compared with only 56 percent of weak Democrats. And on the other side, 72 percent of independent Republicans opposed the ACA compared with only 61 percent of weak Republicans. These results suggest that the responses of most independent leaners to the party identification question are based not on their support for a particular candidate but on their underlying ideological and policy preferences. Leaning independents feel closer to one of the two parties because they feel closer to that party's ideological and policy positions.

Another sign of the strength of party loyalties in the American electorate can be seen in the extraordinarily high level of straight ticket voting in 2012. According to the national exit poll, 92 percent of Obama voters supported a Democratic House candidate, while 92 percent of Romney voters supported a Republican House candidate. Only 6 percent of Obama and Romney voters split their tickets by voting for a House candidate from the opposite party as their presidential candidate. Similarly, data from state exit polls showed that in most states with competitive Senate races, close to 90 percent of voters supported presidential and Senate candidates from the same party.

The high levels of party loyalty and straight ticket voting in 2012 extended a trend that has been evident in American elections for some time. Recent elections have seen consistently higher levels of party loyalty and straight ticket voting than elections from the 1970s and 1980s. Both increased party loyalty and increased partisan consistency in voting reflect the fact that over the past several decades, the party divide has become increasingly associated with other, deeper divisions in American society: a racial divide between a declining white majority and a rapidly growing nonwhite minority; an ideological divide over the proper role and size of government; and a cultural divide over values, morality, and lifestyles (Bafumi and Shapiro 2009; Abramowitz 2013, ch. 2–4).

THE RACIAL DIVIDE

Perhaps the most important of these three divides for the contemporary American party system is the racial divide (Black and Black 1987; Hood,

Kidd, and Morris 2004). It is so important because despite dramatic progress in race relations in recent decades, race and ethnicity continue to powerfully influence many aspects of American society, from housing patterns and educational opportunities to jobs and health care. And over the past 30 years, the impact of the racial divide on the American party system and elections has been increasing due to the growing racial and ethnic diversity of American society and the response to this trend among racially conservative white voters (Kinder and Kam 2009; Tesler and Sears 2010; Kinder and Dale-Riddle 2012).

The nonwhite share of the American population has increased steadily since the 1980s as a result of higher birth rates among nonwhites and high levels of immigration from Latin America and Asia. This demographic shift has altered the racial composition of the American electorate as well, although at a slower rate due to lower levels of citizenship, voter registration, and voter turnout among nonwhites (Frey 2008). Nevertheless, between 1992 and 2008, the nonwhite share of the electorate doubled, going from 13 percent to 26 percent. And contrary to the expectations of some conservative pundits and Republican strategists, that trend continued in 2012 with nonwhites – that is, African Americans, Hispanics, Asian Americans, and other nonwhites – making up a record 28 percent of the electorate according to both the national exit poll and the 2012 American National Election Study.

As the nonwhite share of the American electorate has grown in recent decades, the racial divide between the Democratic and Republican electoral coalitions has steadily widened. According to national exit poll data, between 1992 and 2012, the nonwhite share of Republican voters increased from 6 percent to 11 percent while the nonwhite share of Democratic voters increased from 21 percent to 45 percent. And this deep racial divide between the party coalitions was not confined to presidential voters. The racial divide was just as large among voters in the 2012 U.S. House elections.

The growing dependence of the Democratic Party on nonwhite voters has contributed to the flight of racially and economically conservative white voters to the GOP, thereby further increasing the size of the racial divide between the party coalitions. The effects of this trend were clearly evident in voting patterns in 2012. Among white voters, according to data from the national exit poll, the 2012 presidential election was a Romney landslide: Barack Obama lost the white vote by a margin of 20 percentage points: 59 percent to 39 percent. Moreover, according to data from the 2012 ANES, racial attitudes were strongly related to candidate preference among white voters. Among whites who scored in the lower third on a scale measuring racial resentment, only 23 percent voted for Mitt Romney. However, among whites who scored in the upper third on this scale, 78 percent voted for Romney.

No Democratic candidate before Barack Obama had ever won the presidency while losing the white vote by anything close to a 20-percentage-point margin.

Yet despite this enormous deficit among white voters, Obama won the national popular vote by a margin of almost four percentage points. He did this by winning 80 percent of the nonwhite vote to only 18 percent for Mitt Romney. According to the exit poll, Obama defeated Romney by 93 percent to 6 percent among African-American voters, 71 percent to 27 percent among Hispanic voters, and 73 percent to 26 percent among Asian-American voters.

THE IDEOLOGICAL DIVIDE

The growing dependence of the Democratic Party on nonwhite voters and the resulting flight of conservative whites to the Republican Party have also contributed to a growing ideological divide between the parties. Since at least the New Deal era, Democrats and Republicans have differed on the question of the proper role and size of government. In recent years, however, that ideological divide has widened due mainly to the rightward drift of the GOP (Mann and Ornstein 2012).

The sharp divide between the parties over the proper role and size of government was clearly evident during the 2012 campaign with Republicans, including the party's presidential nominee Mitt Romney, advocating cuts in taxes on upper-income households and corporations; sharp reductions in spending on a variety of social programs; elimination of many health, safety, and environmental regulations; and repeal of the health care reform law passed by Congress in 2010. On the other side, Democrats, including President Obama, were calling for tougher regulation of financial institutions and corporate polluters; increases in taxes on upper-income Americans to ensure adequate funding of federal programs; and full implementation of the health care reform law.

The sharp partisan divide over the proper role and size of government was very evident in the 2012 electorate, as can be seen in the data from the national exit poll displayed in Table 2. Thus, 74 percent of Obama voters favored a more active role for the government in solving societal problems while 84 percent of Romney voters felt that the government was already doing too many things that should be the responsibility of private individuals or businesses. Along the same lines, 84 percent of Obama voters wanted the recently passed health care law to be preserved or expanded while 89 percent of Romney voters wanted it to be partially or completely repealed. Finally, 83 percent of Obama voters favored increasing taxes on households with incomes of greater than $250,000 compared with only 42 percent of Romney voters.

THE CULTURAL DIVIDE

Economic issues weren't the only ones that divided Democrats and Republicans in 2012. Since the 1970s, a new set of issues have emerged in American politics

TABLE 2. *Liberalism of Obama and Romney Voters on Issues*

Issue	Obama Voters (%)	Romney Voters (%)	Difference (%)
Role of government	74	16	58
Health care law	84	11	73
Taxes	83	42	41
Abortion	84	40	44
Same sex marriage	76	26	50
Average liberalism	80	27	53

Source: 2012 National Exit Poll.

alongside the older issues of spending, taxation, and regulation – issues such as gay marriage and abortion that reflect deeply felt moral and religious beliefs and lifestyle choices (White 2003). Building on a growing alliance with religious conservatives of all faiths and evangelical Protestants in particular, the Republican Party has become increasingly associated with policies supportive of traditional values and lifestyles, including restrictions on access to abortion and opposition to same sex marriage and other legal rights for homosexuals. Meanwhile, the Democratic Party has gradually shifted to the left on these issues, with President Obama himself finally announcing his support for legalization of same sex marriage in 2012.

Today, the vast majority of Democratic candidates and elected officials, including President Obama, support a woman's fundamental right to choose whether to terminate a pregnancy as well as access to contraceptives under the new health care law. And an increasing number of prominent Democrats along with the president now support the right of same sex couples to marry along with protection from job discrimination and other legal rights for gays and lesbians. Certainly one of the most dramatic actions taken by President Obama during his first term was his decision to end the U.S. military's "don't ask, don't tell" policy and allow gays and lesbians to serve openly in the armed forces. It was a decision that was strongly opposed by most Republican leaders, including the party's 2008 presidential candidate, John McCain, and its 2012 standard bearer, Mitt Romney.

The 2012 election was supposed to be all about jobs and the economy. And those certainly were the top issues on the minds of voters as they went to the polls. Nevertheless, cultural issues played a significant role in the 2012 elections. At least two Republican Senate candidates, Todd Akin in Missouri and Richard Mourdock in Indiana, lost their races largely as a result of controversial comments about rape and abortion (Jaffe 2012). Meanwhile, voters in three states – Maine, Maryland, and Washington – passed referenda legalizing same sex marriage. It was the first time that same sex marriage had become law as a result of a vote of the people. In Florida, voters decisively defeated a proposed amendment to the state constitution aimed at restricting abortion rights, and in

Washington state and Colorado, voters for the first time passed referenda legalizing the sale and use of marijuana despite intense opposition by many conservative and religious groups.

The cultural divide was also clearly evident in the results of the 2012 presidential election (Jacobson 2013). According to the national exit poll, white born-again or evangelical Christians made up 26 percent of the electorate, and despite any reservations they may have had about supporting a Mormon, they voted for Mitt Romney over Barack Obama by an overwhelming 78 percent to 21 percent margin. On the other hand, those who described their religious affiliation as "something else" or "none" made up 19 percent of the electorate, and they voted for Barack Obama over Mitt Romney by an almost equally overwhelming margin of 72 percent to 25 percent. And voters who identified themselves as gay, lesbian, or bisexual made up 5 percent of the electorate, and they supported Obama over Romney by 76 percent to 22 percent.

The results in Table 2 show that on cultural issues, just as on economic issues, there was a sharp divide between Obama and Romney voters. Fully 84 percent of Obama voters wanted abortion to remain legal under all or most conditions, whereas 60 percent of Romney voters wanted abortion to be illegal under all or most conditions. Similarly, 76 percent of Obama voters favored legalizing same sex marriage in their own state compared with only 26 percent of Romney voters.

Even as support for same sex marriage has increased in the American public in recent years, data from the Gallup Poll shows that the divide between supporters of the two parties on this issue has remained very wide. Although support for same sex marriage has grown considerably among Democrats and independents, there has been little or no increase in support among Republicans. Thus, in a May 2012 poll, Gallup found that 65 percent of Democrats and 57 percent of independents, but only 22 percent of Republicans, supported making same sex marriage legal. This is not surprising and not likely to change soon since white evangelicals make up well over 40 percent of Republican voters across the nation, and the overwhelming majority of these evangelical voters view same sex marriage as contrary to fundamental religious beliefs.

Cultural issues also contributed to two other striking voting patterns in 2012 – the marriage gap and the generation gap. Unmarried voters and younger voters generally have more liberal views on cultural issues than married voters and older voters. This helps to explain why there was a large gap in candidate preference between married and unmarried voters regardless of sex and a large gap between voters under the age of 30 and those 65 or older. According to the national exit poll, 60 percent of married men and 53 percent of married women voted for Mitt Romney. On the other hand, 56 percent of unmarried men and 67 percent of unmarried women voted for Barack Obama. Similarly, 60 percent of those under the age of 30 voted for Obama while 56 percent of those 65 or older voted for Romney.

TABLE 3. *Diverging Electoral Coalitions, 1972–2012*

	Democratic Voters (%)		Republican Voters (%)	
	1972	2012	1972	2012
Nonwhites	17	42	3	12
White liberals	22	32	10	2
White moderates	43	21	42	18
White conservatives	18	6	45	68

Note: Respondents who opted out of the ideology question were coded as moderates.
Sources: American National Election Studies surveys.

DIVERGING ELECTORAL COALITIONS

Evidence examined thus far indicates that over the past several decades, growing racial, ideological, and cultural divisions within American society have resulted in a growing divide between the electoral coalitions supporting the two major political parties (Stonecash, Brewer, and Mariani 2003). This can be seen in Table 3, which compares the racial and ideological composition of the Democratic and Republican electoral coalitions in 1972 and 2012 based on data from the ANES. The results in this table show very clearly that in terms of race and ideology, the Democratic and Republican electoral coalitions are much more distinctive today than they were in 1972 – and the contrast would undoubtedly be even greater if we could go back further in time. Unfortunately, we cannot because the ideology question was not added to the ANES survey instrument until 1972.

In 1972, while conservative whites made up the largest single Republican voting bloc, they were less than half of all Republican voters, and they barely outnumbered moderate whites. In 1972, moderate plus liberal whites actually outnumbered conservative whites among Republican voters. In contrast, in 2012, conservative whites made up more than two-thirds of Republican voters, greatly outnumbering moderate and liberal whites combined. In terms of its electoral base, the Republican Party is much more conservative today than it was in 1972. And while nonwhites comprise a slightly larger proportion of GOP voters today than they did in 1972, they remain a very small minority of Republican voters despite the dramatic increase in the minority share of the overall electorate during these four decades. African Americans made up only 1 percent of Republican voters in 2012 compared with 23 percent of Democratic voters. Moreover, although nonwhite Republicans are somewhat more moderate than white Republicans, they are much more conservative than nonwhite Democrats. According to the data from the 2012 ANES survey, 66 percent of nonwhite Republican voters described themselves as conservative compared with only 15 percent of nonwhite Democratic voters. Nonwhite Republicans were only slightly less conservative than white Republicans, 77 percent of whom chose the conservative label. The presence of a relatively small group of rather conservative nonwhite Republicans has very little impact on the overall conservatism of the modern GOP base.

The Democratic electoral coalition has also undergone a makeover since 1972. In the case of the Democrats, however, the result has been to increase the influence of nonwhites and white liberals at the expense of moderate-to-conservative whites. In 1972, moderate-to-conservative whites made up about three-fifths of Democratic voters. In contrast, in 2012, moderate-to-conservative whites made up only about one-fourth of Democratic voters. Today's Democratic electoral coalition is dominated by nonwhites and white liberals. These two groups together made up only about two-fifths of Democratic voters in 1972. In 2012, they made up about three-fourths of Democratic voters. As a result of these changes, the center of gravity of the Democratic Party in the electorate has shifted considerably to the left of where it was in the 1970s.

HOW POLARIZED IS THE AMERICAN ELECTORATE?

The findings presented earlier in this chapter clearly demonstrate that the parties in the electorate today are sharply divided along racial, cultural, and ideological lines. But does this mean that the parties in the electorate are also polarized? According to Morris Fiorina and his coauthors, Americans today are better sorted by party than they were 30 or 40 years ago, but they are no more polarized than they were then (see Chapter 5, this volume). By this, Fiorina means that party identification today is more closely related to ideology, values, and specific issue positions than it was in the past. Democrats and Republicans are more likely to be found on the opposite sides of these divides in American politics, but they are not more polarized because the distribution of opinion remains unimodal. Most of us are found near the center, where we have always been found. The large majority of Americans, according to Fiorina, are moderate by nature. It is the elites and activists who are divided into polarized camps with few centrists, not the voters (Ansolabehere, Rodden, and Snyder 2006; Fiorina, Abrams, and Pope 2011; Levendusky and Pope 2011; Fiorina and Abrams 2012).

It is certainly possible for voters to become increasingly sorted but not increasingly polarized (Levendusky 2009). But as we shall see, the evidence from the American National Election Studies, the best available source of data on American public opinion over the past 60 years, does not support this conclusion. What these data actually show is that in practice sorting and polarization are so closely connected as to be almost indistinguishable. As the American electorate has become increasingly sorted by party, the distributions of ideological positions, policy preferences, and even candidate evaluations have become increasingly polarized with fewer

Democrats and Republicans found near the center and more found near the opposing attitudinal poles. However, this shift away from the center and toward the extremes has not always affected supporters of both parties equally. On some questions, such as ideology, polarization within the electorate (such as polarization in Congress) has been asymmetrical, with Republicans shifting further to the right than Democrats have shifted to the left.

ASYMMETRICAL POLARIZATION: THE CASE OF IDEOLOGY

Between 1972, the first time the ideology question was included in the ANES survey, and 2012, there was a rather dramatic change in the relative positions of Democratic and Republican voters on the seven-point ideology scale. These changes occurred very gradually, but the end result was quite substantial changes. The average Democratic voter moved from a mean location of 3.79, or just left-of-center on the scale, to a mean location of 3.36. Over the same time period, the average Republican voter moved from a mean location of 4.56 to a mean location of 5.31. As a result of these shifts, the distance between the average Democratic voter and the average Republican voter more than doubled, going from .77 units in 1972 to 1.95 units in 2012. However, 64 percent of this increase was due to the rightward movement of Republican voters.

The significance of these changes can be seen by directly comparing the distributions of Democratic and Republican voters on the ideology scale in these two years. These distributions are displayed in Table 4. Between 1972 and 2012, the proportion of Democratic voters placing themselves in the center of the scale or unable to place themselves on the scale fell from 52 percent to 41 percent, while the proportion placing

TABLE 4. *Distributions of Democratic and Republican Voters on Ideology Scale in 1972 and 2012*

Ideology	Democratic Voters (%)		Republican Voters (%)	
	1972	2012	1972	2012
Very liberal	16	28	2	1
Lean liberal	13	19	8	2
Moderate, none	52	41	44	22
Lean conservative	11	11	25	25
Very conservative	7	1	21	51

Note: Very liberal = 1, 2; lean liberal = 3; moderate, none = 4 or haven't thought about it; lean conservative = 5; very conservative = 6, 7.
Source: American National Election Studies surveys.

themselves on the left side of the scale increased from 29 percent to 47 percent. The change in the distribution of Republican voters on the ideology scale was considerably greater. Between 1972 and 2012, the proportion of Republican voters placing themselves in the center of the scale or unable to place themselves on the scale fell from 44 percent to 22 percent, while the proportion placing themselves on the right side of the scale increased from 46 percent to 75 percent.

As supporters of the two parties were moving apart over these 40 years, the shape of the overall distribution was also changing. The proportion of all voters placing themselves in the center of the scale or unable to place themselves on the scale fell from 49 percent in 1972 to 35 percent in 2012, while the proportion placing themselves at or close to the left or right poles of the scale – at 1, 2, 6, or 7 – increased from 23 percent in 1972 to 39 percent in 2012. In 1972, there were more than twice as many voters in the center or unable to place themselves on the scale as strong ideologues. By 2012, however, strong ideologues outnumbered those in the center or unable to place themselves.

The changing shape of the distribution of voters on the ideology scale can also be seen by comparing the standard deviation of the scale in 1972 with the standard deviation of the scale in 2012. The standard deviation of the scale is a direct measure of the intensity of disagreement over ideology within the electorate – the larger the standard deviation, the greater the intensity of ideological disagreement. As was true for the distance between the parties, the increase in the standard deviation of the ideology scale over these 40 years was very gradual but fairly steady and, ultimately, quite substantial. In 1972, the standard deviation of scores on the ideology scale was 1.15 units for all voters. By 2012, the standard deviation had increased to 1.46 units. This was an increase of 27 percent in the standard deviation of the ideology scale.

The evidence concerning changes in the locations of Democratic and Republican voters and in the overall distribution of voters on the seven-point ideology scale shows that party sorting and polarization have occurred simultaneously over this 40-year time period. During these years, Democrats have shifted to the left, Republicans have shifted even further to the right, and the overall distribution has shifted away from the center and toward the two poles of the scale. These shifts are very similar to those that have occurred among members of the U.S. Senate and House of Representatives during the same time period, although the shifts at the congressional level have been somewhat larger (see Chapter 16, this volume). Nevertheless, the evidence shows very clearly that for both voters and members of Congress, sorting and polarization are very closely connected. As Democrats and Republicans in the electorate and in Congress have moved to the opposite sides of the ideological divide, they have also moved away from the center.

THE RISE OF CONSTRAINT AND POLARIZATION
ON SOCIAL WELFARE ISSUES

The significance of increased sorting and polarization on the ANES ideology scale depends on how strongly voters' positions on this scale correlate with their positions on specific policy issues. Some early research on ideological identification suggested that this scale measured largely symbolic attitudes and was only weakly related to actual policy preferences (Conover and Feldman 1981). However, ideological identification is now strongly related to positions on a wide range of policy issues, especially social welfare policy issues. Moreover, opinions on social welfare policy issues have themselves become much more closely connected over time. In other words, to use the term coined by Philip Converse (1964) in his classic study of ideological thinking in the American public, voters' opinions on these issues have become much more constrained.

According to Converse, issue constraint is a key characteristic of ideological thinking: to the extent that opinions on different issues are shaped by an underlying world view or ideology, those opinions should be related. The fact that constraint was very weak in the American mass public in the 1950s showed, according to Converse, that ideology was largely confined to political elites and activists during that time period. The question for us is whether anything has changed in this regard since Converse conducted his pioneering research.

Unfortunately, we do not have public opinion data on issue questions that have been asked consistently since the 1950s. In fact, the issue questions used by Converse to measure issue constraint in the electorate were considered so flawed that they were abandoned shortly after he published "The Nature of Belief Systems in Mass Publics." Fortunately, we do have data on a series of four social welfare policy issues that, along with the ideology question, have been asked consistently in every presidential election survey since 1984. These issue questions, like the ideology question, ask respondents to place themselves on seven-point scales. The questions ask about government aid to improve the condition of black Americans, government vs. individual responsibility for jobs and living standards, reliance on government vs. private companies for health insurance, and the trade-off between government services and spending and taxes. As with the ideology question, I have assigned respondents who declined to place themselves on each of these questions to the middle position.

An analysis of the responses to these four questions along with the ideology question shows that even over a fairly limited time span of 28 years, issue constraint increased substantially within the American electorate. The average correlation among the four social welfare issue questions increased from .29 in 1984 to .50 in 2012, while the average correlation between the social welfare issue questions and the ideology question increased from .25 in 1984 to .47 in 2012. This means that in terms of shared variance, the

TABLE 5. *Distributions of Democratic and Republican Voters on Social Welfare Attitudes Scale in 1984 and 2012*

Social Welfare Scale Score	Democratic Voters (%)		Republican Voters (%)	
	1984	2012	1984	2012
Very liberal	8	8	1	0
Lean liberal	26	32	8	2
Moderate	52	45	43	17
Lean conservative	13	14	39	42
Very conservative	1	1	9	38

Source: American National Election Studies survey.

relationships between opinions on these questions were about three times stronger in 2012 than in 1984.

These findings indicate that ideological thinking was much more prevalent in the American electorate in 2012 than it had been in 1984. Moreover, issue constraint is an important indicator of ideological polarization. That is because higher levels of constraint mean that there is a larger proportion of voters with consistently liberal or consistently conservative opinions and a smaller proportion with a mixture of liberal and conservative opinions. The magnitude of this increase in ideological polarization can be seen in Table 5, which compares the distributions of Democratic and Republican voters on a social welfare issues scale based on responses to the four questions previously described. The full scale has values ranging from 1 (consistently liberal) to 25 (consistently conservative). This scale was recoded into a five-point scale with values ranging from 1 (most liberal) to 5 (most conservative).

The results displayed in Table 5 show that just as in the case of ideology, shifts in opinion on social welfare issues have been characterized by asymmetrical polarization. Between 1984 and 2012, the proportion of voters located in the center of the social welfare issues scale fell from 48 percent to 32 percent, while the proportion located close to the left or right poles of the scale rose from 10 percent to 23 percent. However, almost all of the increase in polarization during this time period was due to the growing conservatism of Republican voters. Democratic voters shifted only slightly to the left between 1984 and 2012 – the proportion of moderates fell from 52 percent to 45 percent, while the proportion of liberals rose from 33 percent to 40 percent. And there was no increase in the proportion of strong liberals among Democratic voters during these years. In 2012, just as in 1984, strong liberals made up only 8 percent of Democratic voters. In contrast, Republicans shifted dramatically to the right during these years – the proportion of moderates and liberals combined fell from 52 percent to 20 percent, while the proportion of conservatives rose from 48 percent to 80 percent and the proportion of strong conservatives rose from 9 percent to 38 percent.

SYMMETRICAL POLARIZATION: CULTURAL ISSUES

With regard to both ideology and social welfare attitudes, Republican voters have moved considerably further to the right than Democratic voters have moved to the left over the past several decades. This pattern of asymmetrical partisan polarization is similar to that found in Congress. Since the 1970s, analyses of roll call votes have found that Republicans in the Senate and especially in the House of Representatives have moved much further to the right than Democrats in either chamber have moved to the left. In the electorate, as in Congress, conservatives now greatly outnumber moderates and liberals among Republicans. In contrast, liberals do not greatly outnumber moderates and conservatives among Democrats. However, this pattern of asymmetrical polarization does not hold for all issues. When it comes to cultural issues such as abortion and gay rights, Democratic voters appear to be at least as far to the left as Republican voters are to the right.

In order to measure opinions on cultural issues, I created a scale combining two questions on abortion policy and two questions on gay rights. The abortion questions were the traditional four-point ANES abortion policy scale and a nine-point scale measuring support or opposition to abortion as a woman's choice. The gay rights questions asked about same-sex marriage and adoption rights. Opinions on these questions were rather closely connected with correlations ranging from .42 to .71 and an average correlation of .53. Scores on the cultural issues scale ranged from 1 (consistently liberal) to 15 (consistently conservative). I recoded the original scale into a five-point scale with scores ranging from 1 (very liberal) to 5 (very conservative).

Figure 1 displays the distributions of Democratic and Republican voters on the five-point cultural issues scale. It is clear that opinions on these cultural issues were quite polarized in 2012. Over half of all voters were classified as either strong liberals (34 percent) or strong conservatives (22 percent). Only 12 percent of voters were classified as moderates. There was also a sharp divide between the parties. On cultural issues, however, in contrast to social welfare issues, Democratic voters were somewhat further to the left of center than Republican voters were to the right of center. Sixty-six percent of Democratic voters were classified as liberals and 48 percent as strong liberals on cultural issues. On the other hand, 60 percent of Republican voters were classified as conservatives and 40 percent as strong conservatives.

While social welfare and cultural issues show different patterns of polarization, both types of issues are characterized by sharp differences between the two major parties. Moreover, there is a growing connection between these two types of issues. Voters in the liberal or conservative camp on social welfare issues are increasingly in the same camp on cultural issues. This can be seen by examining the trend in the correlation between location on the social welfare issues scale and opinion on the four-point abortion policy scale since 1984 – the abortion scale is the one cultural issue that has been

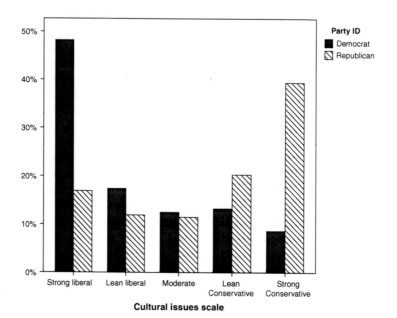

FIGURE 1. Distributions of Democratic and Republican Voters on Cultural Issues Scale in 2012
Source: 2012 American National Election Study.

included in ANES surveys over a lengthy period of time. The results show that the relationship between opinions on these two types of issues has grown steadily stronger with the correlation coefficients increasing from .01 in 1984 to .04 in 1988, .11 in 1992, .13 in 1996 and 2000, .18 in 2004, .23 in 2008, and .28 in 2012. As a result, opinions on these two types of issues are increasingly likely to reinforce one another and, therefore, to push voters in the same partisan direction.

GROWING AFFECTIVE POLARIZATION: EVIDENCE FROM CANDIDATE FEELING THERMOMETERS

The rise of partisan polarization within the American electorate over the past four decades has involved voters' feelings about the parties and candidates as well as their ideological and issue positions. In fact, the increase in affective polarization in recent years has been even greater than the increases in issue or ideological polarization. This can be seen in Table 6, which displays the trends in relative feeling thermometer evaluations of the Democratic and Republican presidential candidates between 1968 (the first time the feeling thermometer scales were included in the ANES survey) and 2012. The statistics shown in this table are the average difference between the feeling thermometer ratings of the

TABLE 6. *The Rise of Affective Polarization: Feeling Thermometer Ratings of Presidential Candidates, 1972–2012*

Year	Party Difference	Standard Deviation
1968	46.8	38.6
1972	54.5	47.9
1976	47.9	40.1
1980	55.5	43.7
1984	71.8	49.0
1988	67.6	46.6
1992	63.6	44.3
1996	69.0	47.1
2000	63.8	44.0
2004	91.4	56.7
2008	72.3	48.9
2012	105.2	62.3

Source: American National Election Studies survey.

candidates by Democratic and Republican voters and the standard deviation of the feeling thermometer difference scores for all voters. The former statistic measures the size of the divide between the parties, whereas the latter measures the overall divide in evaluations of the candidates within the electorate.

The results in Table 6 show that both the average difference between the relative thermometer ratings of Democrats and Republicans and the overall dispersion of these ratings by voters have increased substantially over this time period and especially since 2000, with the 2012 election setting new records for both measures. Moreover, the increase in affective polarization in recent years has been fairly symmetrical. Both Democrats and Republicans now favor their own party's presidential candidate over the opposing party's candidate much more strongly than in the past, especially in elections involving an incumbent. Thus, both the 2004 Bush-Kerry contest and the 2008 Obama-Romney contest produced very strong preferences by partisans for their own party's standard-bearer. In 2004, Republicans rated George W. Bush an average of 50 degrees higher than John Kerry, while Democrats rated Kerry an average of 41 degrees higher than Bush. Similarly, in 2012, Democrats rated Barack Obama an average of 55 degrees higher than Mitt Romney, while Republicans rated Romney an average of 50 degrees higher than Obama.

Contrary to claims by some scholars that affective polarization is distinct from ideological and issue polarization (Iyengar, Sood, and Lelkes 2012; Mason 2013), the increase in affective polarization in recent years is closely connected to the increase in polarization over issues and ideology during the same time period. Democratic and Republican voters prefer their own party's candidates more intensely than in the past because they prefer their own party's ideology and policy positions more intensely than in the past. Thus, the correlation between ideology and relative feeling thermometer ratings increased from .47 in 1984 to .66 in 2012. During the same time period, the correlation between location on the social welfare issues scale and relative feeling thermometer ratings increased from .53 to .72. In terms of shared variance, the relationship between ideology and relative feeling thermometer ratings nearly doubled in strength for these 28 years, while the relationship between social welfare attitudes and relative feeling thermometer ratings was about 1.8 times stronger in 2012 than in 1984.

The large increase in partisan polarization on relative thermometer ratings of the presidential candidates between 1984 and 2012 is especially impressive given that the choices presented to the voters by the two major parties appeared to be no more polarized in 2012 than in 1984. It would be difficult to find evidence that Barack Obama was a more liberal Democratic candidate than Walter Mondale, who had a consistently liberal voting record during his years in the U.S. Senate, or that Mitt Romney was a more conservative Republican candidate than Ronald Reagan, who was widely regarded as the leader of the conservative movement within the Republican Party prior to his election as president in 1980.

These results contradict the claim by Fiorina and his coauthors that more divided voter evaluations of political leaders today reflect more polarized choices, not more polarized voter positions (Fiorina, Abrams, and Pope 2011: 25–32). In fact, the difference in affective polarization between 1984 and 2012 can only be explained by a growing divide between Democratic and Republican voters on ideology and policy issues. Presenting polarized candidate choices to an overwhelmingly centrist electorate would be expected to produce mainly indifferent evaluations among voters. Only voters who are clearly on one side or the other of the ideological divide would be expected to have strong preferences between two candidates on opposite sides of that divide. Polarized evaluations of candidates or political leaders, such as those seen in 2012, require both polarized candidate choices and polarized voter positions on issues and ideology.

DISCUSSION AND CONCLUSIONS

America today is a polarized nation. Polarized politics in Washington is based on deep divisions in American society. There is no "disconnect" between political elites and the American public (Fiorina and Abrams 2012). Democratic and Republican leaders reflect the diverging characteristics, priorities, and values of the constituents who elected them. Today's Democratic electoral base is dominated by nonwhites and secular white liberals who view Republican politicians and voters as religious zealots, racial bigots, and defenders of multinational corporations and the wealthiest one percent of the population. The Democratic base is pro-government, pro-choice on abortion, and pro–gay marriage. In contrast, today's Republican electoral base is dominated by socially and economically conservative white voters who view the current Democratic president as an extreme liberal or socialist and his supporters as unpatriotic moochers who would rather live off of government handouts than work for a living. The Republican base is anti-government, anti-choice on abortion, and anti-gay marriage.

Because the two party bases are roughly equal in size and loyalty, elections tend to be highly competitive at the national level, which further fuels the intensity of partisan conflict. Every election is a battle for control of the White House and/or both chambers of Congress. Deeply rooted partisanship also explains the growing one-party domination of many states and congressional districts and the remarkable consistency in the results of elections over time and across different elected offices. The late House Speaker Tip O'Neill's famous remark that "all politics is local" has been turned on its head. Today, it is more accurate to say that all politics is national.

Deeply rooted partisanship and the close balance in support for the two major parties at the national level have also contributed to the frequency of divided party control of national government. This situation is made even more likely by the distinct advantages that each party has in different types of elections. Democrats appear to have a growing advantage in presidential elections due to the growing nonwhite share of the national electorate, which has contributed to the movement of several swing states into the Democratic column in recent years. However, Republicans continue to have an advantage in congressional elections due to the concentration of Democratic voters in urban districts in the House of Representatives and the over representation of sparsely populated Republican-leaning states in the Senate. As a result, we have had divided party government in Washington in one form or another for 25 of the past 33 years.

Even before the current era of polarized politics, divided party control was a fairly regular occurrence in American politics in the decades following World War II. But divided party government today has very different consequences. During the 1950s, 1960s, and 1970s, divided government could work fairly well because it was much easier to build bipartisan coalitions to pass legislation (Mayhew 1991). There were enough moderate-to-liberal Republicans and moderate-to-conservative Democrats that it was possible to build cross-party coalitions on at least some major issues. Today, however, there are almost no members in the middle in either chamber. As a result, divided party control almost inevitably leads to a politics of confrontation and gridlock. And with control of the two chambers at stake every two years, leaders of both parties in Congress often appear to be more concerned with posturing and positioning for the next election than with legislating and addressing pressing national problems.

The problems of governing in a polarized era have been compounded by the dramatic movement of the Republican Party to the right in recent years. As

Mann and Ornstein (2012) have argued (see also Mann's Foreword to this volume), polarization in Congress is not symmetrical – it is asymmetrical. Since the 1980s, the Republican Party in Congress, and especially in the House of Representatives, has moved much further to the right than the Democratic Party has moved to the left. The rise of the Tea Party movement has certainly contributed to this phenomenon, but the rightward shift of the GOP was already well underway before the first Tea Party demonstrations occurred in 2009.

Evidence that I have presented in this chapter and elsewhere (Abramowitz 2010) indicates that the growing conservatism of the Republican Party in Congress, and in many of the states, reflects the growing conservatism of the Republican electoral base and especially the more active segment of that base. The fundamental problem facing Republican leaders and strategists today is that the party's electoral base is gradually shrinking. The nation is slowly becoming more racially diverse, more secular, and more socially liberal, and these trends are making it more and more difficult for Republican candidates to compete in presidential elections. However, taking the steps that would be necessary to expand the party's appeal to nonwhites and socially liberal younger Americans would risk deeply offending large segments of the GOP base. This is something that few Republican elected officials appear willing to do at present, especially since few Republican elected officials need to appeal to these voter groups in order to hold onto their own seats.

The forces producing rising polarization in the American electorate appear far from spent. These include, most importantly, the growing racial and ethnic diversity of American society, growing secularism and the decline of traditional religion, and growing influence of partisan media (Prior 2007). Over the short-term, and perhaps over the medium-term, polarization within the electorate and among political leaders is more likely to increase than decrease. If this diagnosis is correct, and polarization is grounded in deep divisions in American society, rather than trying to reduce polarization by tinkering with electoral rules and procedures, which is unlikely to prove effective, political scientists and others concerned about the future of American democracy should focus on finding ways to help the political system to function in an age of polarization.

REFERENCES

Abramowitz, Alan I. 2013. *The Polarized Public: Why Our Government Is So Dysfunctional*. New York: Pearson Longman.
Abramowitz, Alan I. 2010. *The Disappearing Center: Engaged Citizens, Polarization, and American Democracy*. New Haven, CT: Yale University Press.
Abramowitz, Alan I., Brad Alexander, and Matthew Gunning. 2006. "Incumbency, Redistricting, and the Decline of Competition in U.S. House Elections." *The Journal of Politics* 68 (1): 75–88.

Abramowitz, Alan I., and Kyle L. Saunders. 2006. "Exploring the Bases of Partisanship in the American Electorate: Social Identity vs. Ideology." *Political Research Quarterly* 59 (2): 175–187.

Ansolabehere, Stephen, Jonathan Rodden, and James M. Snyder. 2006. "Purple America." *The Journal of Economic Perspectives* 20 (2): 97–118.

Bafumi, Joseph, and Robert Y. Shapiro. 2009. "A New Partisan Voter." *Journal of Politics* 71 (1): 1–24.

Black, Earl, and Merle Black. 1987. *Politics and Society in the South*. Cambridge, MA: Harvard University Press.

Brewer, Mark D., and Jeffrey M. Stonecash. 2007. *Split: Class and Cultural Divides in American Politics*. Washington, DC: Congressional Quarterly Press.

Conover, Pamela J., and Stanley Feldman. 1981. "The Origins and Meaning of Liberal/Conservative Self-Identifications." *American Journal of Political Science* 25 (4): 617–645.

Converse, Philip E. 1964. "The Nature of Belief Systems in Mass Publics." In David E. Apter, ed., *Ideology and Discontent*. New York: The Free Press, 206–261.

Fiorina, Morris P., Samuel J. Abrams, and Jeremy C. Pope. 2011. *Culture War? The Myth of a Polarized America*. 3rd ed. New York: Pearson Longman.

Fiorina, Morris P., Samuel J. Abrams, and Jeremy C. Pope. 2008. "Polarization in the American Public: Misconceptions and Misreadings." *The Journal of Politics* 70 (2): 556–560.

Fiorina, Morris P., and Samuel J. Abrams. 2012. *Disconnect: The Breakdown of Representation in American Politics*. Norman: University of Oklahoma Press.

Frey, William H. 2008. "Race, Immigration, and America's Changing Electorate." In Ruy Teixeira, ed., *Red, Blue, and Purple America: The Future of Election Demographics*. Washington, DC: Brookings Institution Press, 79–108.

Hillygus, D. Sunshine, and Todd G. Shields. 2008. *The Persuadable Voter: Wedge Issues in Presidential Campaigns*. Princeton, NJ: Princeton University Press.

Hood III, M.V., Quentin Kidd, and Irwin L. Morris. 2004. "The Reintroduction of the *Elephas Maximus* to the Southern United States: The Rise of Republican State Parties, 1960 to 2000." *American Politics Research* 32 (1): 68–101.

Iyengar, Shanto, Gaurov Sood, and Yphtach Lelkes. 2012. "Affect, Not Ideology: A Social Identity Perspective on Polarization." *Public Opinion Quarterly* 76 (3): 405–431.

Jacobson, Gary C. 2013. "How the Economy and Partisanship Shaped the 2012 Presidential and Congressional Elections." *Political Science Quarterly*, 128 (1): 1–38.

Jacobson, Gary C. 2007. *A Divider, Not a Uniter: George W. Bush and the American People*. New York: Pearson Longman.

Jaffe, Greg. 2012. "GOP's Akin, Mourdock Lose Senate Elections," *Washington Post*, November 7. Retrieved from http://articles.washingtonpost.com/2012-11-07/politics/35504534_1_republican-richard-mourdock-senate-seat-akin

Keith, Bruce E., David B. Magleby, Candace J. Nelson, Elizabeth A. Orr, and Mark C. Westlye. 1992. *The Myth of the Independent Voter*. Berkeley: University of California Press.

Kinder, Donald R., and Cindy D. Kam. 2009. *Us against Them: Ethnocentric Foundations of American Opinion*. Chicago: University of Chicago Press.

Kinder, Donald R., and Allison Dale-Riddle. 2012. *The End of Race? Obama, 2008, and Racial Politics in America*. New Haven, CT: Yale University Press.

Levendusky, Matthew S. 2009. *The Partisan Sort: How Liberals Became Democrats and Conservatives Became Republicans.* Chicago: University of Chicago Press.

Levendusky, Matthew S., and Jeremy C. Pope. 2011. "Red States vs. Blue States: Going beyond the Mean." *Public Opinion Quarterly* 75 (2): 227–248.

Mann, Thomas E., and Norman J. Ornstein. 2012. "Let's Just Say It: The Republicans Are the Problem." *Washington Post*, April 27. Retrieved from http://www.washingtonpost.com/opinions/lets-just-say-it-the-republicans-are-the-problem/2012/04/27/gIQAxCVUlT_story.html

Masket, Seth E., Jonathan Winburn, and Gerald C. Wright. 2012. "The Gerrymanders Are Coming! Legislative Redistricting Won't Affect Competition or Polarization Much, No Matter Who Does It." *PS: Political Science and Politics* 45 (1): 39–43.

Mason, Lilliana. 2013. "The Rise of Uncivil Agreement: Issue Versus Behavioral Polarization in the American Electorate," *American Behavioral Scientist* 57: 140–159.

Mayhew, David R. 1991. *Divided We Govern: Party Control, Lawmaking and Investigations, 1946–1990.* New Haven, CT: Yale University Press.

Prior, Markus. 2007. *Post-Broadcast Democracy: How Media Choice Increases Inequality in Political Involvement and Polarizes Elections.* Cambridge: Cambridge University Press.

Stonecash, Jeffrey M., Mark D. Brewer, and Mack D. Mariani. 2003. *Diverging Parties: Social Change, Realignment, and Party Polarization.* Boulder, CO: Westview Press.

Tesler, Michael, and David O. Sears. 2010. *Obama's Race: The 2008 Election and the Dream of a Post-Racial America.* Chicago: University of Chicago Press.

White, John K. 2003. *The Values Divide.* New York: Chatham House.

2

Redistricting and Polarization

Micah Altman and Michael McDonald

- We review how the ideological polarization of members of the House of Representatives (elite polarization) is affected by:
  - sorting of parties' incumbents into more ideologically compatible districts,
  - replacement of incumbents by more ideologically extreme successors,
  - the drawing of more ideologically extreme districts.
- We show there are fewer competitive congressional districts – having a near balance of Democrats and Republicans – following redistricting.
- We show that more competitive districts can be drawn without sacrificing other values, such as compactness or minority representation.
- We discuss the prospects for redistricting reform.

Increasing ideological polarization of American political elites ("elite polarization") has coincided with a marked increase of policy gridlock within the national government. Concerns with the government's ability to address major policy issues, even those with broad public support, have led many to search for causes for and solutions to a government so paralyzed that it cannot satisfy the basic democratic value of executing the will of its people.

Among the frequently cited causes for elite polarization is redistricting, the process of periodically drawing district boundaries to ostensibly align them with communities of interest, representational criteria, and neutral administrative goals, such as equalizing populations following a new decennial census. States are responsible for drawing House of Representatives district boundary lines; in

Authors are listed in alphabetical order. We describe contributions to the chapter using a standard taxonomy (Allen et al. 2014). Micah Altman and Michael McDonald were the lead authors, taking equal responsibility for revisions. Michael McDonald authored the first draft of the manuscript and was primarily responsible for the statistical analysis. Both contributed to the conception of the report (including core ideas and statement of research questions), to the methodology, to the project administration, to the data collection, and to the writing through critical review and commentary.

most states, politicians are in charge of the process, creating an obvious conflict of interest because redistricting affects their chances of reelection.

Redistricting's potential contributions to elite polarization emerge from the motives of individual politicians and political parties. District boundary lines may be manipulated to affect election outcomes by shoring up an otherwise competitive district (a district with a near balance of Democratic and Republican voters) by adding supporters of the party one wishes to advantage or subtracting the opposition. In redistricting, there are opportunities for bipartisanship that elude national policymaking: one incumbent's trash is another's treasure, whereby incumbents of different parties swap constituents unfavorable to their party, but support the other. If legislators reflect the will of their constituents, elite polarization increases when districts are made more ideologically homogeneous as reelection-seeking incumbents have less reason to moderate their positions to win over independents or the other party's supporters.

Reformers have amended the redistricting process in a handful of states to impose limitations, including most recently in New York through a 2014 constitutional referendum approved by voters. Among the technical innovations that quietly emerged during the last round of redistricting is public access to web-deployed redistricting software and data, which enabled greater public participation in the drawing of alternative redistricting plans (Altman and McDonald 2014a). The public approaches redistricting in a fundamentally different manner than politicians, particularly with respect to political goals such as partisan fairness and district competition (Altman and McDonald 2013, 2014b, forthcoming).These public plans thereby provide a benchmark comparison to plans fabricated by politicians to concretely assess how districts may be made more competitive through reform efforts and to what degree this may ameliorate polarization.

THE CAUSAL RELATIONSHIP BETWEEN REDISTRICTING AND POLARIZATION

Much has been written about the causes and consequences of political polarization, including by the contributing authors to this volume. Our purpose is not to rehash the extensive polarization literature. However, we do wish to provide context for redistricting's role. In Figure 1 we sketch how redistricting fits within theoretical frameworks explaining elite polarization of the House of Representatives. The linkage between redistricting and elite polarization is mediated through district partisanship, as visualized in Figure 1. The causal chain from redistricting to elite polarization has two necessary conditions. First, the ideological character of districts' constituencies must be related to the ideological character of their elected representatives. Second, redistricting must be able to affect districts' ideologies. We begin our discussion of the first-order causal connections with

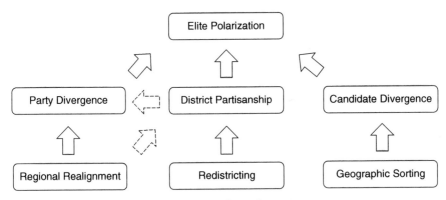

FIGURE 1. Causal Connections Affecting Elite Polarization

causes that directly affect elite polarization, and then with second-order causal connections affecting these first-order causal connections.

First-Order Connection: District Partisanship → Elite Polarization

With respect to the first condition, there are no reliable national survey measures for the ideology of districts' constituencies since sample sizes within districts are typically too small to develop reliable measures. Scholars frequently measure districts' ideologies using districts' partisanship, constructed from election results for statewide offices (McDonald 2014). Presidential election results are analyzed for national studies since this is the sole office elected nationally, thus providing a comparable metric across all congressional districts. We follow the scholarly norm equating district ideology with district partisanship.

The median voter theorem provides a theoretical basis to expect that district partisanship is a factor in representatives' ideologies. Downs (1957) formally shows how in plurality-win two-candidate elections, candidates who wish to win office will, in equilibrium, position their ideology such that it is the same as the district's median voter's ideology, in an electorate where all voters are distributed along a one-dimensional left-right ideological continuum. (This is, of course, a caricature of Downs' nuanced theory; we discuss complications and other motives subsequently.)

The logic is simple and, in the abstract, plausible. Consider a candidate whose primary motivation is to get elected. A candidate wins office by receiving 50 percent plus one of the votes. If voters prefer the candidate with the closest ideology, then without knowing what the other candidate will do, the first candidate is always best off positioning his or her ideology at the median voter. There are two cases to consider. Case one: if the second candidate positions at any point other than the median, the first candidate on the median is supported by all voters to the left or right (those with an ideology in the opposite direction from the median as the second candidate's position), as well as half of the voters between the median and the ideology of the second candidate. The first candidate wins and the second loses. Case two: if the second candidate also positions at the median voter, then voters are indifferent between the two candidates and they randomly choose between the two candidates. A first candidate who chooses a position other than the median is gambling that the other candidate will position him- or herself even further from the median. Why take this risk when there is a clear pathway to victory by positioning at the median?

The redistricting application is straightforward. The ideology of the median voter of a district is related to the proportion of voters on the left and right (i.e., Democrats and Republicans) who are assigned to a district. If more voters on the left or right are added to a district, the ideology of the median voter of the district will be a voter further to the left or right, respectively. Those in charge of redistricting thus have the ability to affect not only which party is favored to win a district, but, by manipulating the proportion of voters in a district on the left or right, the ideological character of the winning candidate as well.

To empirically demonstrate the relationship between district partisanship and elite polarization, which we will refer to again when we describe other causal pathways, we plot a measure of district partisanship against a measure of members' ideology in Figure 2. Our measure of district partisanship is the McCain share of the Obama and McCain 2008 presidential vote, or what is commonly called the two-party vote. A higher percentage thus describes a more Republican district. We might reasonably infer that district partisanship proxies constituents' ideology, with a more Republican district signaling a more conservative constituency. Our measure of members' ideology is Poole and Rosenthal's (2000) first DW-NOMINATE dimension, which places members' roll call votes on a left–right continuum, with higher values related to a more conservative roll call vote history. NOMINATE scores are endogenous to Congress, meaning that they are based on observable roll call votes that are the end product of the legislative process, and may not be true measures of members' ideology. If one cares about elite polarization within Congress, they serve as a static snapshot of the current Congress. We further identify Democrats with a *D* and Republicans with an *R*, and draw a simple linear regression line for each partisan type.

There are three important features of Figure 2: (1) the correlation between district partisanship and members' ideologies, (2) *party divergence* of members from different parties representing districts with similar partisanship, and (3) *candidate divergence* among members of the same party representing districts with similar partisanship. We first discuss the first feature and return to the two others.

Central to the argument that redistricting can affect polarization, and consistent with the median voter theorem (Downs 1957), there is a strong linear relationship

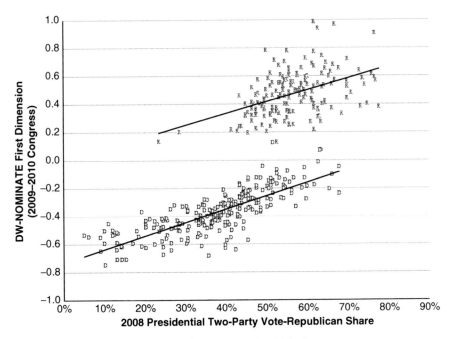

FIGURE 2. District Partisanship and Representatives' Ideology

between districts' partisanship and members' ideological voting patterns, with members from more Republican districts voting in a more conservative manner. Figure 1 is not controversial. This pattern of candidate convergence to the district ideology is presented in textbooks (Abramson et al. 2014) and confirmed by an analysis of all candidates' ideologies – incumbents, challengers, and open seat candidates – derived from members' ideological voting scores (Ryan and Lyons 2014) and candidate surveys (Erikson and Wright 1980; Ansolabehere, Snyder, and Stewart 2001; Stonecash et al. 2003). This convergence is evident in other legislative activities, such as bill sponsorship and roll call voting within specific issue domains that may be sensitive to constituency demographics (Hayes, Hibbing, and Sulkin 2010). Ansolabehere, Snyder, and Stewart (2001) find candidates more closely hew to district partisanship in the most competitive districts near 50 percent (this heteroskedastic dynamic is most apparent among Republican incumbents in Figure 1), although they also find that challengers to incumbents less closely converge to district partisanship than incumbents.

First-Order Connection: Party Divergence → Elite Polarization

A second feature that is illustrated by Figure 2 is a sizable ideological gap between the two political parties. An increasing ideological gap between the political parties is well documented and has grown so much that there is currently no overlap between the most conservative Democrat and most liberal Republican (McCarty, Poole, and Rosenthal 2009; see also Chapter 16, this volume). Contributing to this elite polarization is a decline in the number of incumbents who represent districts with a voter composition – measured in presidential vote – favoring the opposing party, a phenomenon that continues following the 2014 election. This decrease is a consequence of the sorting brought about through the sectional realignment of the South and Northeast. Before the recent rise in elite polarization, conservative Southern Democrats and liberal Northern Republicans filled the ideological center between the more extreme elements of their respective party caucuses. In recent decades, Southern Democrats either formally affiliated themselves with the Republican Party or a Republican claimed their seat following a retirement or electoral defeat (setting aside Southern Democrats representing minority communities). While regional realignment was most pronounced in the South, a mirrored dynamic occurred among liberal Republicans in the North. Redistricting may also affect sorting, when incumbents mismatched with an unfriendly constituency are drawn in a new, ideologically compatible district (Jacobson 2003; McCarty et al. 2009); we discuss this in greater detail later in the chapter. Parties have thus become more ideologically consistent (Fiorina and Pope 2010; Layman et al. 2010), which results in a further feedback mechanism whereby members of more ideologically homogeneous party caucuses provide their leaders additional powers to enforce party discipline, what is known as the conditional party government model (Rohde 1991).

A caricature of Downs (1957) portrays the median voter theorem as predicting candidates' full convergence to the median, framing divergence as a "failure" of the model (Ansolabehere, Snyder, and Stewart 2001: 153). Downs did not predict full convergence, as he could observe the obvious fact – even in 1957 – that in America's two-party system the parties' candidates were not ideological clones. Downs posited that parties would not adopt the median position within a district in order to distinguish themselves from one another and thereby present voters with tangible choices. But there are other compelling reasons for divergence. As evident from the distribution of districts across the X-axis in Figure 2, districts do not have the same partisanship, so candidates within party coalitions would be hard pressed to simultaneously adopt individual ideologies consistent with an overarching national party ideology (see contributions in Grofman, Blais, and Bowler 2009). There may be other reasons for this dynamic as well, such as candidates having intrinsic policy preferences of their own, being reputationally bound to their previous policy positions, being responsive to both more ideologically extreme primary and more centrist general election electorates within the same district (Brady, Han, and Pope 2007), or that entry costs deter politically moderate citizens who may wish to run for office (Grosser and Palfrey 2014).

First-Order Connection: Candidate Divergence → Elite Polarization

A third feature illustrated by Figure 2 is that within parties there is sizable variation of ideology even among members in districts with comparable district partisanship. This is more evident in the Senate, where senators who are of the same party and who represent the same state have different ideologies (Poole and Rosenthal 2000). It is also evident in how members from the same party replacing a retiring incumbent do not adopt the same ideology (Poole and Romer 1993; Stonecash, Brewer, and Mariani 2003; Theriault 2006). Indeed, these replacements have tended to adopt a more extreme position than their predecessor, thereby contributing to polarization with moderates being replaced by extremists (Bafumi and Herron 2010). Incumbents may also adapt to changing political environments by modifying their ideological voting over the course of their careers (Theriault 2006), with members moving toward their district partisanship (Stratmann 2000). It is for this latter reason that we draw a causal arrow from candidate divergence to elite polarization, although Figure 2 snapshot suggests there is much ideological variation among members representing districts with similar partisan composition, which is not necessarily contributing to ideological divergence of parties.

Second-Order Connection: Redistricting → District Partisanship

The second condition necessary for redistricting to affect elite polarization is that redistricting affects district partisanship. It may seem self-evident from observing the intense politics that surround redistricting, and the related problem of gerrymandering, that a causal connection between these two exists. Indeed, many scholars find redistricting affects partisan division of power among legislative seats (e.g., Tufte 1973; Cain 1985; Gelman and King 1994; Hirsch 2003), while others have proposed evaluation metrics on how much partisan gerrymandering may be constitutionally permissible (Grofman and King 2007). However, this second-order effect is challenged by competing explanations for changing district partisanship, particularly the number of competitive districts that, through the connection of district partisanship and members' ideologies, drive elite polarization.

Abramowitz, Alexander, and Gunning (2006) and McDonald (2006a) differ in their conclusions about whether redistricting results in fewer competitive districts. The measurement of competitive congressional districts using presidential elections lies at the heart of their divergent findings. Analyzing normalized two-party presidential vote,[1] Abramowitz et al. (2006) find an increase in competitive districts during the post-1990 census between the

---

[1] "Normalized two-party vote" is the vote share for a major party candidate expressed as a share of the two major parties' candidates, excluding minor party candidates. This vote share is then normalized, or simulating a hypothetical 50/50 election, by subtracting the difference between the

1988 Bush vs. Dukakis contest and the 1992 three-way Bush vs. Clinton vs. Perot contest (excluding Perot's votes since he was not a major party candidate). However, in analyzing the Bush and Dukakis vote in the pre- and post-redistricted districts, McDonald (2006a) finds a decrease in the number of competitive districts.[2]

We update McDonald's (2006a) analysis of the total number of competitive districts before and after redistricting for the most recent round of redistricting in Figure 3. The table reports the number of districts within two competitive ranges, 45–55 percent and 48–52 percent (the latter are included in the former). The vote between the two major party candidates (commonly referred to by scholars as the "two-party vote") is drawn from various issues of the *Almanac of American Politics*. The presidential vote shares are normalized by subtracting the difference between the leading candidate's vote share and 50 percent to simulate a hypothetical 50/50 election. To control for potential confounding campaign effects, statistics are calculated for the same presidential election, the one most recently occurred prior to a given redistricting.

Take, for example, the 2008 presidential election, whose results are reported for the 2010 and 2012 statistics. The statistics in Figure 3 show that for the most recent redistricting, there was a slight decrease of 4 districts within the wider competitiveness range and a decrease of 12 districts in the narrower competitiveness range. Despite the traditional reliance on a 45–55 percent to define competition elections (Mayhew 1974), McDonald (2006a) finds from a statistical analysis correlating presidential vote and candidate vote shares that the narrower range is more appropriate to measure competitive districts. Both numbers are near the lower bound evident in the last two redistricting cycles. In the larger picture, except for the 1980 cycle, there was a decrease in the number of competitive districts in the narrower range in the 1990, 2000, and 2010 redistricting cycles, and for the wider range there was also a decrease in 1990, 2000, and 2010 but an increase in 1980. Using Abramowitz et al.'s (2006) preferred measure, the 2012 normalized two-party vote, compared to the 2008 presidential vote, only strengthens these findings.[3] The preponderance of the evidence shows redistricting results in fewer competitive districts in the past three decades.

overall national two-party vote share and 50 percent from the two-party vote within a specific district.
[2] For similar findings in the decline in competition following a redistricting, see Swain, Borrelli, and Reed (1998) and McCarty et al. (2009: 673).
[3] An issue for the post-redistricting statistics is that some precincts are split by new districts, and the votes within these districts must be apportioned to the new districts (McDonald 2014). Using the 2012 presidential vote shares for the 2012 statistics, the number of districts is 84 within a 45–55 percent range and 29 within a 48–52 percent range. This alternative measurement provides stronger evidence for redistricting to result in a decrease in the number of competitive districts. Whereas the statistics reported in Figure 3 show a modest decrease of four in the number of competitive districts in the wider range between 2010 and 2012, the alternative measure shows a

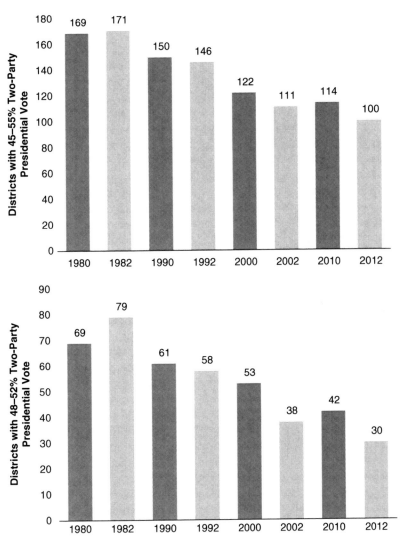

FIGURE 3. Competitive Districts Before (Dark) and After (Light) Redistricting, 1980–2012

Second-Order Connection: Geographic Sorting → District Partisanship

Redistricting can manipulate directly only district partisanship, but to what extent is manipulation possible? In states with a small number of districts – or just

30-district decrease. Similarly, whereas the statistics reported in Figure 3 show the narrower range has a 12-district decrease in competitive districts, the alternative measure has a 13-district decrease.

one – manipulation of district partisanship is neigh impossible. Even within larger states, scholars contest whether redistricting can affect district partisanship. The argument for minimal redistricting effects arises from research that argues Americans have residentially segregated themselves (Bishop and Cushing 2009). Such geographical sorting produces, so the argument goes, an increasing political homogenization of congressional districts (Abramowitz et al. 2006) that virtually locks in Republican majorities absent Democratic gerrymandering (Chen and Rodden 2014). The correlation between districts' partisanship and members' ideology evident in Figure 2 thus emerges organically from states' geographies, not through conscious redistricting manipulation.

Evidence for this "big sort" thesis is derived from county-level presidential election results from 1976 to 2004, which show that the number of landslide counties with a victory margin of 20 percentage points or more increased from 27 percent to 48 percent during this period (Bishop and Cushing 2009). Scholars have challenged these findings. Klinkner and Hapanowicz (2005), taking a longer view, show substantial up-and-down variation in the number of landslide counties between 1976 and 2004, with the rise between these two elections falling within the historical range from 1840 to 2004. Abrams and Fiorina (2012) object to the reliance on presidential election results, noting that presidential candidates are not all the same and, thus, polarization measured by presidential election results may be an artifact of the choices voters are presented with;[4] even if voters remained the same, two moderate candidates may produce different geographical distribution of votes than two extreme candidates. Utilizing an alternate measure freer from transitory campaign effects – party registration – there was a decrease in landslide counties from 1976 to 2004 (McGee and Krimm 2009).

The statistics presented in Figure 3 also do not conform to the big sort thesis, although we do not wish to take too much from statistics drawn from different presidential elections. There was a slight increase in the number of competitive districts between 2002 and 2010, in both the wider and narrower ranges. If ongoing geographical sorting of partisans is primarily responsible for a decline in competitive districts (Abramowitz et al. 2006), there should have been a decrease in the number of competitive districts over the last decade.

Second-Order Connection: Regional Realignment → District Partisanship

In Figure 1 we draw an arrow from regional realignment to party divergence, but the party divergence theory implicitly involves district partisanship. As Jacobson notes (2013: 548) "over the last several decades, changes in the preferences, behavior, and distribution of congressional voters have given the congressional parties more internally homogeneous, divergent and polarized

---

[4] Furthermore, Abrams and Pope (2012) argue that Americans are not polarized geographically; however, this critique is outside the scope of our analysis.

electoral bases ... The main source of this electoral transformation was the partisan realignment of the South." The representational anchor for Southern Democrats were their conservative constituents. If members had represented liberal constituencies, as Democratic members did elsewhere, they probably would not have been so conservative, likewise so with their Republican replacements (if regional realignment would have even occurred). Yet, party divergence is not typically presented laying bare these assumptions as Jacobson does, so we draw only dotted arrows from regional realignment to district partisanship to party divergence.

The regional realignment story, when framed as affecting district partisanship, has a potential interaction with redistricting. Southern Democrats attempting to stave off extinction were thwarted by the George Bush, Sr. Department of Justice following the 1990 redistricting. The Department of Justice ordered Southern Democratic–controlled state governments to maximize the number of African-American majority districts, a tactic that the U.S. Supreme Court would later find unconstitutional in the *Shaw v. Reno* cases. But the damage was done. Grofman and Handley (1998) find that without enough African-American constituents to buoy their electoral fortunes, some Democratic incumbents succumbed to mounting pressures of regional realignment.[5]

Full Causal Path: Redistricting → District Partisanship → Elite Polarization

As the preceding discussion should make plain, redistricting cannot be responsible for all elite polarization. Scholars find redistricting makes a contribution. Stonecash, Brewer, and Mariani (2003) examine changing district composition and conclude these changes produce more homogeneous districts that contribute to polarization. However, these scholars do not decompose the factors driving changing district demographics. Stronger direct evidence that redistricting affects polarization comes from studies that examine districts changed by redistricting. Carson et al. (2007: 878) find that "redistricting is one among many factors that produce party polarization." Their method examines the ideology of members elected from congressional districts that changed substantially following a redistricting. They find that these districts tend to be more extreme than others in their partisanship, and that members elected from these districts also tend to be more ideologically extreme. Using a similar approach to examine congressional districts that were changed by redistricting, Hayes, Hibbing, and Sulkin (2010) also find members' behavior is responsive to districts' change in terms of how they co-sponsor bills when their district becomes more competitive and how they vote in specific issue domains that may be of importance to certain constituents, such as rural constituents and farm policies. Members may modify their behavior in anticipation of constituency change wrought by redistricting (Boatright 2004),

---

[5] Today, with Democratic-controlled Southern state governments replaced with Republican-controlled state governments, the Voting Rights Act in some instances forced Republicans to draw Democratic districts where they may otherwise not wish to do so (Schotts 2002).

although it may take several election cycles for members to fully adjust to their new constituencies (Stratmann 2000).

Yet, there are limits to redistricting effects. Carson et al. (2007: 889) find that only 60 percent (or 261 of 435) of district boundaries substantially changed from the beginning to the end of the entire time span from 1962 to 2002. Others are more sanguine on the contribution of redistricting to polarization. McCarty, Poole, and Rosenthal (2009) argue that Carson et al. (2007) overstate redistricting effects since districts undergoing change are those found in the most polarized states.[6] McCarty et al. (2009: 667) examine two causes of polarization: the average distance between the ideologies of the two political parties (i.e., party divergence) and the congruence of ideology and district partisanship. They call the latter "sorting" (2009: 669) in how members may be arrayed along the continuum of district partisanship; in this context, sorting invokes the concept that members of the two political parties may be increasingly elected from districts more congruent with their party affiliation. The authors conclude from examination of detrended sorting effects across a redistricting that redistricting "can account for, at most, 10–15% of polarization since the 1970s."[7] These authors assert more forcibly in the popular press that "gerrymandering has nothing to do with political polarization."[8]

McCarty, Poole, and Rosenthal (2009: 672) set a high bar for redistricting to affect members' ideologies, in that members' behavior must have a "sharp increase" immediately following a redistricting, even though members may adjust their behavior prior to a redistricting (Boatright 2004) or gradually adjust their behavior over several election cycles after a redistricting (Stratmann 2000). Furthermore, McCarty et al.'s model is static. Redistricting may be used to shore up an incumbent mismatched with his or her district (Jacobson 2003), such that district constituencies are made to better match members' ideologies, particularly members of a party who represent districts that lean toward the other party as these are generally the most moderate of all incumbents (see Figure 1). Carson et al. (2007) directly explore this effect, while McCarty et al. (2009) infer it between changes in their estimated effects from one Congress to the next. A static model also cannot measure other potential

---

[6] It is also true that larger states are where more districts change vis-à-vis apportionment, and where voters can be most segregated in ways that would contribute to polarization.

[7] Elsewhere, McCarty, Poole, and Rosenthal (2009: 673) say that redistricting accounts for "less than 25% of the increase in polarization since 1973." Using their figures presented in Table 2 (p. 673), we calculate the effect from their OLS model to be 25.1 percent and 19.4 percent from their matching method. The 10–15 percent figure appears to be a detrended estimate that assumes a uniform increase in polarization in Congresses seated between 1973 and 2003. Their unspecified detrending method may wash out a curious feature of their estimates, that polarization due to sorting declines prior to a redistricting (consistent with Boatright 2004) and then increases sharply in all but one of six of their estimates.

[8] McCarty, Nolan, Keith T. Poole, and Howard Rosenthal. 2013. "Gerrymandering Didn't Cause the Shutdown," *BloombergBusiness*. Retrieved from http://www.bloombergview.com/articles /2013-10-09/gerrymandering-didn-t-cause-the-shutdown.

changes. If the conditional party government model (Rohde 1991) holds for how realignment contributed to elite polarization, vis-à-vis an increasingly homogeneous party caucus willing to give more powerful tools for leaders to enforce party discipline, then it stands to reason the reverse is true, too: making districts more competitive would lead to a more heterogeneous party caucus and a weakening of leaders' powers.

While these studies find redistricting affects elite polarization to varying degrees, some authors suggest that creating more competitive districts could, to the contrary, increase polarization. In the presence of competition, candidates must rely more heavily on party support, and thus may be more responsive to party leaders who demand party divergence. Cox and Katz (2002) note that incumbency advantage increased following the reapportionment revolution in the 1960s, when districts initially became less competitive. Engstrom (2013) notes that elite polarization has historically been higher when districts were more competitive. However, McDonald (1999) notes that the causal arrow may be reversed, that when voters polarize, an optimal gerrymandering strategy to take advantage of a less volatile electorate is to draw districts that only appear more competitive.

CAN REDISTRICTING BE REFORMED TO REDUCE POLARIZATION?

The preceding discussion primarily involves observational studies of the factors that drive elite polarization. If redistricting can affect district partisanship, then to what degree can redistricting reform lead to a greater number of competitive districts and a reduction in ideological polarization? This question can be answered through two methods. First, observational studies of states that adopt alternative redistricting institutions – particularly commissions, which are the preferred reform model (McDonald 2007) – reveal redistricting intervention effects. Second, alternative mapping by computer simulation or by humans reveals how alternative maps range across quantifiable measures such as compactness and district competitiveness.

Observational studies tend to find no measurable effect of redistricting institutions on polarization. Abramowitz et al. (2006) find redistricting commission states do not have a greater number of competitive districts. Ryan and Lyons (2014) similarly find commission states do not have a greater number of competitive districts – what they call "bipartisan districts" – or reduced elite polarization. Examining California, Kousser, Phillips, and Shor (2014: 25) bluntly find, "Neither the Citizens Redistricting Commission nor the top-two primary has halted the continuing partisan polarization of California's elected lawmakers or their drift away from the average voter in each district. If anything, polarization has increased and the quality of representation has declined."

A general problem with these analyses is that they do not deeply consider the causal mechanisms linking redistricting commissions' rules and membership to more competitive districts or moderation of elite polarization. Only two states, Arizona and Washington, explicitly have a redistricting criterion to draw competitive districts (McDonald 2007). California's commission is not required to draw competitive districts, so the theory is underdeveloped as to why the state's newly enacted citizen commission would reduce polarization. Likewise, Abramowitz et al. (2006) and Ryan and Lyons (2014) paint all commissions with a broad brush. We are not surprised that commissions are indistinguishable from legislatures if classification of commissions includes predominantly partisan or bipartisan commissions that may be politically motivated to draw partisan or bipartisan gerrymanders, both that theoretically should result in no uncompetitive districts (Owen and Grofman 1988).

Simulations help developing counterfactuals as to what outcomes are feasible within a state. The range of outcomes is profoundly affected by states' geographies. Idaho's bipartisan commission simply cannot draw one of the state's two congressional districts to be Democratic leaning or competitive, whereas Arizona's commission has more opportunities to draw both, by virtue of its larger size and more balanced partisanship, but is uniquely constrained by Latino voting rights concerns and other state constitutional redistricting criteria (McDonald 2006b). Observational studies by design treat states as equal cases, and scholars can offer only crude covariates at best to control for states' differing characteristics.

An alternative assessment methodology is to simulate what may happen within a state through alternative mapping. This approach has been used with human mappers to examine motives of the 1990s North Carolina redistricting (Gronke and Wilson 1999), to forecast the effects of California's 2000s redistricting reform (Johnson et al. 2005), to examine changing the rank-ordering of Arizona's criteria (McDonald 2006b), and to explore the use of alternative criteria in five Midwestern states (McDonald 2009), Virginia (Altman and McDonald 2013), Florida (Altman and McDonald forthcoming), and Ohio (Altman and McDonald 2014b). Scholars have also used automated methods to explore the range of potential redistricting plans. Automation was first proposed by Vickery (1961) and has been used to explore alternatives in four states in the 1960s (Nagel 1965), to probe racial gerrymandering intent in South Carolina (Cirincione, Darling, and O'Rourke 2000), to probe nationally the limits of creating competitive districts in the 2000s (McCarty, Poole, and Rosenthal 2009), and to probe through a case study of Florida's geographical constraints on partisan gerrymandering (Chen and Rodden 2014).

We created the first open-source automated redistricting algorithm, called BARD (Altman and McDonald 2011). Through our experience with automation, we came to a similar conclusion as Nagel (1965: 899): that automated algorithms are "useful for testing some policy proposals" by revealing alternatives for consideration. However, automated algorithms are deeply challenged by the well-established theoretical limits of integer optimization – what redistricting is in the abstract – and are susceptible to subtle implementation biases (Altman and McDonald 2010). In a nutshell, redistricting optimization algorithms are not guaranteed in a modest-sized state to find the global optimum of a scoring function (i.e., criteria) in a finite time. Because there are practically an infinite number of local optima, these algorithms tend to become trapped in local optima and are thus biased in unknown ways.[9] Alternative redistricting plans drawn by computers or humans can illuminate trade-offs among redistricting criteria, but the absence of a redistricting plan with a given scoring profile does not mean that a plan, or a host of similar plans, does not exist.

Some implementation issues arise out of simplifications that researchers make to their data. For example, McCarty, Poole, and Rosenthal (2009) employ a simulation approach to explore how geography constrains the number of competitive districts. These scholars draw districts out of counties. However, the largest counties in the United States can entirely contain several congressional districts. To address this issue, these scholars subdivide large counties into 1,000 person blocks, and "assume that each of these county blocks is identical" in terms of their political composition to the county (McCarty et al. 2009: 674). Thus, 9,546 identical blocks are created for Los Angeles County, where Obama won 70.6 percent of the two-party vote in 2008. McCarty et al. (2009: 674) assert without proof that this "homogeneity assumption biases towards finding a gerrymandering effect" because the simulation algorithm is unlikely to "produce either very conservative or very liberal districts" (2009: 675). This seems odd to us: the algorithm will produce roughly 13 Los Angeles County congressional districts; all will have exactly the same 70.6 percent Obama vote share. Similar patterns will be observed in other large counties that have two or more congressional districts. McCarty et al.'s (2009) data assumption is further at odds with the big sort thesis that Democrats gerrymander themselves by predominantly living in large counties (Bishop and Cushing 2009; Chen and Rodden 2014). To the contrary, McCarty et al.'s (2009) county homogeneity assumption biases against finding a gerrymandering effect.

Since redistricting algorithms may have subtle biases that affect conclusions, we wish to explore whether humans can draw plans that explore a broader range of outcomes across criteria of substantive interest, such as the number of competitive districts and compactness. Whereas humans may draw maps with biases, our intuition is that humans will begin their mapping from various starting points and employ complex heuristics that help them avoid trapping themselves in local optima, whereas the simple heuristics employed thus far research cannot. An observation of Mexico's experience with automated

---

[9] This is true when implementing algorithms to meet all U.S. legal redistricting criteria. An automated algorithm does exist to create equal population, contiguous, and compact (with a specific compactness scoring mechanism) (Olson 2010).

redistricting demonstrates humans are capable of beating a simulated annealing optimization algorithm (Altman et al. 2014). Working with our software development partner Azavea, we developed open-source web-accessible redistricting software called DistrictBuilder, which we deployed in several states to support advocates' efforts (Altman and McDonald 2014a). Florida's legislature developed a similar online tool to enable greater public participation. We present the results from three studies to date on Florida (Altman and McDonald forthcoming), Ohio (Altman and McDonald 2014b), and Virginia (Altman and McDonald 2013).

In Figure 4 we plot all legal redistricting plans that were publicly available in Florida, Ohio, and Virginia. We define legal plans as those where all geography is assigned to the correct number of congressional districts, that these districts have a population deviation of plus or minus 1.0 percent from the ideal equi-populous district (many plans have districts that deviate by one person), and there is a minimum number of minority-majority districts.[10] Publicly available redistricting plans are those either made available by the state legislature or developed through advocates' redistricting competitions that we supported. We plot the average compactness of districting plans along the horizontal axis, such that more compact districts have higher values,[11] and the number of competitive districts in the tighter plus or minus four percentage point range, using the 2008 two-party presidential vote, normalized to the candidates' national vote shares. We disaggregate precinct level presidential vote to the census block level to construct our statistics. This approach replaces McCarty, Poole, and Rosenthal's (2009) county-level homogeneity assumption with a precinct-level homogeneity assumption (a much smaller unit of aggregation), as is consultants' typical practice when constructing redistricting databases (McDonald 2014). We identify the adopted plan with a triangle; all other plans are identified by circles.

Figure 4 reveals that it is possible to create more competitive districts without sacrificing compactness in Florida, Ohio, and Virginia; indeed, the plan with the most competitive districts – and many other plans with a greater number of competitive districts – is more compact than the adopted plan.[12] In Florida, the adopted plan has one competitive congressional district out of 27, while a plan exists with eight competitive districts. In Ohio, the adopted plan has zero competitive districts out of 16, while the plan exists with eight competitive districts. In Virginia, the adopted plan has two competitive districts out of eleven while a plan exists with three

---

[10] We analyze plans with at least three majority-minority districts in Florida and one in both Ohio and Virginia.

[11] We use the Schwartzburg compactness measure. We normalize the values since the varying geography of these states does not make comparisons of scores across states meaningful.

[12] This is true for other criteria such as respect for political boundaries and partisan fairness; for space considerations, we do not present scatter plots of these other criteria (Altman and McDonald 2013, 2014a, 2014b).

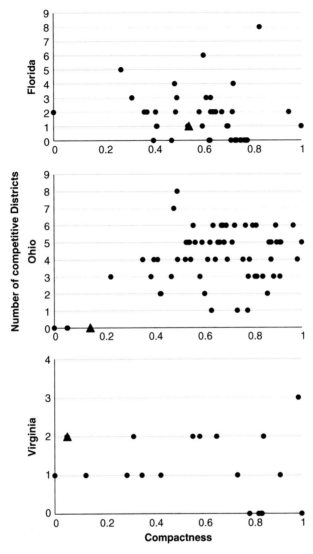

FIGURE 4. Competitive Districts and Compactness; All Florida, Ohio, and Virginia Publicly Available Legal Redistricting Plans

competitive districts. In all, the adopted plans have a total of three competitive districts out of 55, while plans with the maximum number of competitive districts have a combined 21 competitive districts. We do not know if it is possible to draw more competitive districts since those drawing plans may not have been trying to maximize district competitiveness; indeed, in Ohio and Virginia, many non-legislative map drawers participated in competitions where competitive districts were one criterion among others.

DISCUSSION: CAN REDISTRICTING REFORM SOLVE POLARIZATION?

Our analysis of alternative legal redistricting plans that include minority voting rights districts reveals that, compared to the adopted plans that have three competitive district out of 55, at least 21 competitive districts can be drawn in Florida, Ohio, and Virginia. McCarty, Poole, and Rosenthal (2009: 678), employing simulations with contiguity and compactness constraints, find that 80 competitive districts are possible nationwide (although the authors do not define their measurement of a competitive district). We cannot fully reconcile these two analyses since McCarty, Poole, and Rosenthal examine the entire country and our scope covers only three of the most closely contested battleground states. Furthermore, we do not believe that one should simply extrapolate our findings to all states; for example, there are clearly small uncompetitive states with one or two districts where redistricting can have little or no effect. Still, we believe that the opportunities for competitive districts, and a reduction in elite polarization, may be greater than the McCarty et al. analysis indicates.

Where we agree with McCarty, Poole, and Rosenthal (2009) is that not all congressional districts, and likely not even a majority, can be made competitive, and that redistricting is but one piece of a greater polarization puzzle. Further, even where districts could be made competitive, whether redistricting reform efforts leads to competitive districts depends on the manner in which the reform is implemented. Contrast the implementation of redistricting reform in California with the implementation of reform in Arizona.

As Kousser, Phillips, and Shor (2014) discuss, California's reform effort is likely to create competitive districts and to affect polarization only by happenstance. California has no explicit requirement for competitive districts, and the commission adopted only three congressional districts with a 2008 Obama two-party vote share between 48 percent and 52 percent. In contrast, in Arizona, the commission is explicitly tasked by the state constitution to draw competitive districts. Arizona's commission produced three congressional districts out of nine, which is a seemingly difficult task when also drawing two heavily Democratic Latino districts in this Republican leaning state (McDonald 2006b). Lumping Arizona and California under the same rubric of redistricting commissions is, perhaps, why scholars find these different institutions have no effect on district competition (Abramowitz, Alexander, and Gunning 2006; Ryan and Lyons 2014). (Similarly, Ohio advocates' redistricting competition balanced district competition against other criteria to a positive effect on district competition. See Figure 4 and Altman and McDonald 2014b.) If reformers wish to affect a political outcome, we recommend explicitly incorporating the intended outcome into the redistricting criteria.

Our analysis differs from some others such as McCarty, Poole, and Rosenthal (2009) in finding that redistricting reform can have a substantive effect on polarization. Redistricting is among the few inputs to elite polarization that are both measurable and readily subject to policy intervention. We believe redistricting institutions can be developed to proactively increase the number of competitive districts and thus reduce elite polarization.

It is possible that redistricting reform to increase competitive districts may have second-order effects beyond the direct effects of electing more moderate members. These secondary effects could act in the opposite direction; we note that increased district competition is historically correlated with greater ideological polarization (Engstrom 2013). However, we judge (following Engstrom) that historical correlation is a result of strong and polarized parties using biased districts with thin margins in attempt to maximize partisan advantage – and not a result of competitive districts *causing* polarization (McDonald 1999). Moreover, there are theoretical reasons to believe that the secondary effects will further decrease polarization. For example, if the conditional party model of government is correct (Rohde 1991), injecting the House of Representatives with more moderates will empower them to constrain the power of party leaders to enforce party discipline, which is among the primary drivers of elite polarization through party divergence. Based on the current evidence, we conjecture that the secondary effects will be neutral or positive – but note that these effects have yet to be systematically measured in the literature.

We recognize that there are many other reasons to embrace redistricting reform and competitive districts. With specific regard to competitive districts, they provide general election voters with the opportunity to hold members accountable as their districts are not so electorally safe, and it likewise allows voters to hold parties accountable as their majorities may be at risk. Members who represent competitive districts may not draw strong challengers if they represent their districts well (by being ideologically moderate); however, it is possible that a greater number of competitive districts can lead to a greater number of competitive elections, and higher associated campaign costs. Likewise, competitive elections may result in a greater number of voters being unhappy about the winner (Brunell 2008). We are reminded that any electoral reform is inherently a balance of competing values (Arrow 1951). Properly designed redistricting institutions may ameliorate elite polarization, although the effect may not be as large as advocates hope. As with all reforms, there may be unanticipated consequences. Still, if one is concerned about elite polarization, redistricting should be a reform option on the table.

REFERENCES

Abramowitz, Alan I., Brad Alexander, and Matthew Gunning. 2006. "Incumbency, Redistricting, and the Decline of Competition in U.S. House Elections." *The Journal of Politics* 68 (1): 75–88.

Abrams, Samuel J., and Morris P. Fiorina. 2012. "'The Big Sort' That Wasn't: A Skeptical Reexamination." *PS: Political Science & Politics* 45 (2): 203–210.

Abramson, Paul R., John H. Aldrich, and David W. Rohde. 2014. *Change and Continuity in the 2012 Elections.* Washington, DC: CQ Press.

Allen, Liz, Amy Brand, Jo Scott, Micah Altman, and Marjorie Hlava. 2014. "Credit Where Credit Is Due." *Nature* 508 (7496): 312–313.

Altman, Micah, Eric Magar, Michael P. McDonald, Alejandro Trelles. 2014. "Mexico's Experience with Automated Redistricting." Presented at the 2014 American Political Science Association Conference, Washington, DC.

Altman, Micah, and Michael P. McDonald. Forthcoming. "Paradoxes of Political Reform: Congressional Redistricting in Florida." In Seth McKee, ed., *Redistricting in the Sunshine State*, Gainesville: University of Florida Press.

Altman, Micah, and Michael P. McDonald. 2014a. "Public Participation GIS: The Case of Redistricting." Proceedings of the 47th Annual Hawaii International Conference on System Sciences, Computer Society Press.

Altman, Micah, and Michael P. McDonald. 2014b. "Redistricting by Formula: An Ohio Experiment." Unpublished Manuscript.

Altman, Micah, and Michael P. McDonald. 2013. "A Half-Century of Virginia Redistricting Battles: Shifting from Rural Malapportionment to Voting Rights and Participation." *University of Richmond Law Review* 47: 771–831.

Altman, Micah, and Michael P. McDonald. 2011. "BARD: Better Automated Redistricting." *Journal of Statistical Software* 42 (5): 1–28.

Altman, Micah, and Michael P. McDonald. 2010. "The Promise and Perils of Computers in Redistricting." *Duke J. Constitutional Law and Public Policy* 5: 69–112.

Ansolabehere, Stephen, James M. Snyder, Jr., Charles Stewart, III, 2001. "Candidate Positioning in U.S. House Elections." *American Journal of Political Science* 45 (1): 136–159.

Arrow, Kenneth. 1951. *Social Choice and Individual Values.* New York: John Wiley.

Bafumi, J., and M. C. Herron. 2010. "Leapfrog Representation: A Study of American Voters and Their Members of Congress." *American Political Science Review* 104 (3): 519–552.

Baldassarri, Delia, and Andrew Gelman. 2008. "Partisans without Constraint: Political Polarization and Trends in American Public Opinion1." *American Journal of Sociology* 114 (2): 408–446.

Bishop, Bill, and Robert G. Cushing. 2009. *The Big Sort: Why the Clustering of Like-Minded America is Tearing Us Apart.* New York: Houghton Mifflin Harcourt.

Boatright, Robert G. 2004. "Static Ambition in a Changing World: Legislators' Preparations for, and Responses to, Redistricting." *State Politics and Policy Quarterly* 4 (4): 436–454.

Brady, David W., Hahrie Han, and Jeremy C. Pope. 2007. "Primary Elections and Candidate Ideology: Out of Step with the Primary Electorate?" *Legislative Studies Quarterly* 32 (1): 79–105.

Brunell, Thomas L. 2008. *Redistricting and Representation: Why Competitive Elections Are Bad for America.* New York: Routledge.

Cain, Bruce. 1985. "Assessing the Partisan Effects of Redistricting." *The American Political Science Review* 79 (2): 320–333.

Carson, Jamie L., Michael H. Crespin, Charles J. Finocchiaro, and David W. Rohde. 2007. "Redistricting and Party Polarization in the US House of Representatives." *American Politics Research* 35 (6): 878–904.

Chen, Jowei, and Jonathan Rodden. 2014. "Unintentional Gerrymandering: Political Geography and Electoral Bias in Legislatures." *Quarterly Journal of Political Science* 8 (3): 239–269.

Cirincione, Carmen, Thomas A. Darling, and Timothy G. O'Rourke. 2000. "Assessing South Carolina's 1990s Congressional Districting." *Political Geography* 19 (2): 189–211.

Cox, Gary W., and Jonathan N. Katz. 2002. *Elbridge Gerry's Salamander: The Electoral Consequences of the Reapportionment Revolution.* Cambridge: Cambridge University Press.

Downs, Anthony. 1957. *An Economic Theory of Democracy.* New York: Harper and Row.

Engstrom, Erik J. Engstrom. 2013. *Partisan Gerrymandering and the Construction of American Democracy.* Ann Arbor: University of Michigan Press.

Erikson, Robert S., and Gerald C. Wright. 1980. "Elections and Policy Representation of Constituency Interests: The Case of the 1974 House Elections." *Political Behavior* 2 (1): 91–106.

Fiorina, Morris, Samuel J. Abrams, and Jeremy C. Pope. 2010. *Culture War? The Myth of a Polarized America*, 3rd ed. New York: Pearson Longman.

Gelman, Andrew, and Gary King. 1994. "Enhancing Democracy through Legislative Redistricting." *American Political Science Review* 88 (3): 541–559.

Grofman, Bernard, Andres Blais, and Shaun Bowler, eds. 2009. *Duverger's Law of Plurality Voting: The Logic of Party Competition in Canada, India, the United Kingdom and the United States.* New York: Springer.

Grofman, Bernard, and Lisa Handley. 1998. "Estimating the Impact of Voting-Rights-Act-Related Districting on Democratic Strength in the U.S. House of Representatives." In Bernard Grofman, ed., *Race and Redistricting in the 1990s.* New York: Agathon Press, 51–67.

Grofman, Bernard and Gary King. 2007. "The Future of Partisan Symmetry as a Judicial Test for Partisan Gerrymandering after LULAC v. Perry." *Election Law Journal* 6 (1): 2–35.

Gronke, Paul, and J. Matthew Wilson. 1999. "Competing Redistricting Plans as Evidence of Political Motives: The North Carolina Case." *American Politics Quarterly* 27 (2): 147–176.

Großer, Jens, and Thomas R. Palfrey. 2014. "Candidate Entry and Political Polarization: An Antimedian Voter Theorem." *American Journal of Political Science* 58 (1): 127–158.

Hayes, Matthew, Matthew V. Hibbing and Tracy Sulkin. 2010. "Redistricting, Responsiveness, and Issue Attention." *Legislative Studies Quarterly* 35 (1): 91–115.

Hirsch, Sam. 2003. "The United States House of Unrepresentatives: What Went Wrong in the Latest Round of Congressional Redistricting." *Election Law Journal* 2 (2): 179–216.

Jacobson, Gary C. 2013. "Partisan Polarization in American Politics: A Background Paper." *Presidential Studies Quarterly* 43 (4): 688–708.

Jacobson, Gary C. 2003. "Terror, Terrain, and Turnout: Explaining the 2002 Midterm Elections" *Political Science Quarterly* 118 (1): 1–22.

Johnson, Douglas, Elise Lampe, Justin Levitt, and Andrew Lee. 2005. "Restoring the Competitive Edge." The Rose Institute of State and Local Government, Claremont McKenna College.

Klinkner, Philip A., and Ann Hapanowicz. 2005. "Red and Blue and Déjà Vu: Measuring Political Polarization in the 2004 Election." *The Forum* 3 (2).

Kousser, Thad, Justin Phillips, and Boris Shor. 2014. "Reform and Representation: A New Method Applied to Recent Electoral Changes," *Social Science Research Network*, June 3. Retrieved from http://ssrn.com/abstract=2260083 or http://dx.doi.org/10.2139/ssrn.2260083.

Layman, Geoffrey C., Thomas M. Carsey, John C. Green, Richard Herrera, and Rosalyn Cooperman. 2010. "Activists and Conflict Extension in American Party Politics." *American Political Science Review* 104 (2): 324–346.

Mansbridge, Jane, and Cathie Jo Martin, eds. 2013. *Negotiating Agreement in Politics: Report of the Task Force on Negotiating Agreement in Politics*. Washington, DC: American Political Science Association.

Mayhew, David R. 1974. "Congressional Elections: The Case of the Vanishing Marginals." *Polity* 6 (3): 295–317. (2013).

McCarty, Nolan, Keith T. Poole, and Howard Rosenthal. 2009. "Does Gerrymandering Cause Polarization?" *American Journal of Political Science* 53 (3): 666–680.

McCarty, Nolan, Keith T. Poole, and Howard Rosenthal. 2006. *Polarized America: The Dance of Ideology and Unequal Riches*. vol. 5. Cambridge, MA: MIT Press.

McDonald, Michael P. 2014. "Calculating Presidential Vote in Legislative Districts." *State Politics and Policy Quarterly* 14 (2): 196–204.

McDonald, Michael P. 2009. *Midwest Mapping Project*. Fairfax, VA: George Mason University.

McDonald, Michael P. 2007. "Regulating Redistricting." *PS: Political Science and Politics* 40 (4): 675–679.

McDonald, Michael P. 2006a. "Drawing the Line on District Competition." *PS: Political Science and Politics* 39(1): 91–94.

McDonald, Michael P. 2006b. "Re-Drawing the Line on District Competition." *PS: Political Science and Politics* 39(1): 99–101.

McDonald, Michael P. 1999. "Representational Theories of the Polarization of the House of Representatives." *Legislative Studies Section Newsletter*, Extension of Remarks 22 (2): 8–10.

McGhee, Eric, and Daniel Krimm. 2009. "Party Registration and the Geography of Party Polarization." *Polity* 41 (3): 345–376.

Nagel, Stuart S. 1965. "Simplified Bipartisan Computer Redistricting." *Stanford Law Review* 71: 863–869.

Olson, Brian. 2010. "Redistricter: A Non-Gerrymandered Impartial Redistricting Program." Retrieved from http://code.google.com/p/redistricter/ (last visited Feb. 26, 2015).

Owen, Guillermo, and Bernard N. Grofman. 1988. "Optimal Partisan Gerrymandering." *Political Geography Quarterly* 7 (1): 5–22.

Poole, Keith T., and Thomas Romer. 1993. "Ideology, 'Shirking,' and Representation." *Public Choice* 77 (1): 185–196.

Poole, Keith T., and Howard Rosenthal. 2000. *Congress: A Political-Economic History of Roll Call Voting.* New York: Oxford University Press.

Rohde, David W. 1991. *Parties and Leaders in the Postreform House.* Chicago: University of Chicago Press.

Ryan, Josh M., and Jeffery Lyons. 2014. "The Effect of Redistricting Commissions on District Bipartisanship and Member Ideology." *Journal of Elections, Public Opinion and Parties* 25 (2): 234–263.

Shotts, Kenneth. 2002. "Gerrymandering, Legislative Composition, and National Policy Outcomes." *American Journal of Political Science* 45 (2): 398–414.

Stonecash, Jeffrey M., Mark D. Brewer, and Mark D. Mariani. 2003. *Diverging Parties: Social Change, Realignment, and Party Polarization.* Boulder, CO: Westview Press.

Stratmann, Thomas. 2000. "Congressional Voting over Legislative Careers: Shifting Positions and Changing Constraints." *The American Political Science Review* 94 (3): 665–676.

Swain, John W., Stephen A. Borrelli, and Brian C. Reed. "Partisan Consequences of the Post-1990 Redistricting for the U.S. House of Representatives." *Political Research Quarterly* 51 (4): 945–967.

Theriault, Sean M. 2006. "Party Polarization in the U.S. Congress: Member Replacement and Member Adaptation." *Party Politics* 12 (4): 483–503.

Tufte, Edward R. 1973. "The Relationship between Seats and Votes in Two-Party Systems." *The American Political Science Review* 67 (2): 540–554.

Vickrey, William. 1961. "On the Prevention of Gerrymandering," *Political Science Quarterly* 76 (1): 105–110.

3

Party Activists, Interest Groups, and Polarization in American Politics

David Karol

- Parties are more than their formal structures. They cannot be understood without attention to the role of both activists and party-aligned interest groups.
- The policy preferences of activists and interest groups are both shaped by and shape the behavior of elected officials. Sometimes activists and lobbies take cues from politicians, but their actions also reinforce and contribute to polarization in important ways.
- The polarization of Democrats and Republicans reflects the incorporation of new groups in party coalitions since the 1970s.

Polarization is visible in many aspects of American politics, from Congress to the courts to state legislatures and even the electorate. The common thread linking all of these settings is political parties. Polarization is a party story. Yet understanding American parties is a challenging endeavor. Parties, unlike the branches of government or even the electorate, are not well-bounded entities. Individuals and groups with no formal role or place on the organization chart play important roles in parties.

In this chapter, I argue that activists and interest groups are key elements of political parties. Activists and party-aligned interest groups work within parties to advance their policy goals via candidate selection and lobbying elected officials. Unlike the formal party structure and some elements closely linked to it, activists and interest groups are a force for polarization. I review delegate and donor surveys as well as trends in interest group campaign contributions revealing evidence of polarization among activists and lobbies. Elected officials' relationships with party activists and interest groups are not one-sided. Even more than highly informed voters, activists take cues from politicians, and interest group leaders are subject to pressure from elected officials. Still, evidence suggests that activists and party-linked interest groups promote polarization.

AMERICAN POLITICAL PARTIES: REVIVED AND POLARIZED

American political parties, once seen to be in terminal decline, have been reinvigorated in recent decades. In the same period that polarization emerged, party organizations have grown far better funded and staffed (Herrnson 2013). Mann and Corrado (2014) find that in the 1976 campaign, the Democratic National Committee (DNC), Democratic Senate Campaign Committee (DSCC), and Democratic Congressional Campaign Committee (DCCC) raised $52.8 million, $4.1 million, and $3.8 million, respectively (all sums are in 2012 dollars). By 2012, the DNC, DSCC, and DCCC raised $290.4 million, $145.9 million, and $183.8 million in 2012 dollars, respectively. The same trend is evident among Republicans. In the 1976 campaign, the Republican National Committee (RNC), National Republican Senate Committee (NRSC), and Republican National Congressional Committee (RNCC) raised $117.3 million, $7.2 million, and $49.2 million, respectively, in 2012 dollars. By 2012, the same organizations raised $390.2 million, $117.1 million, and $155.7 million.

Yet correlation is not causation. Scholars agree that the formal party structure is a "party in service" (Aldrich 1995) to candidates that does not focus on policy. Rather, it supports incumbents and recruits and funds the candidates who appear most electable. Thus, the enrichment of the party machinery is not a plausible driver of polarization. It is more likely that the strengthening of the national party apparatus and polarization both stem from the fragility of majorities in Congress in recent decades (Lee 2013). With control of Congress so uncertain, the incentive both to improve the parties' campaign operations and to behave like teams in government has grown.

Yet as Joseph Schlesinger (1984: 379) noted, where American political parties are concerned, "the formal structure is obviously not the real organization." Recognizing this, scholars have long viewed parties as networks (Schwartz 1990; Bernstein and Dominguez 2003) or "multi-layered" coalitions (Herrnson 2009). Yet some groups closely linked to the party apparatus, including consultants (Kolodny 2000), congressional staff (Bernstein and Dominguez 2003), and leadership PACs (Herrnson 2009) are also not plausible drivers of polarization. Consultants and staffers are careerists, and leadership PACs exist to increase the influence of their founder in the party. To find the roots of polarization, we need to look beyond the formal structure and groups that orbit closely around the party structure.

PARTY ACTIVISTS AND INTEREST GROUPS: INTENSE POLICY DEMANDERS WHO PROMOTE POLARIZATION

If we seek to understand parties' role in polarization, we must turn our attention to party activists and interest groups. If parties truly are candidate-centered organizations, then polarization is difficult to understand. Why would candidates take such divergent stands if electoral motivations were all? Recognizing that party activists are motivated in large part by policy concerns and that interest groups play an important informal role in parties makes the trend toward polarization far less mysterious. Formally party nominations are made in primaries. Often this process has been seen as "candidate-centered" since the traditional patronage-based party machines have faded, leaving aspirants for office to raise funds and build their own campaign organizations.

Yet studies show that in both presidential (Cohen et al. 2008a, 2008b) and congressional primaries (Dominguez 2011), endorsements from activists and interest groups as well as other elected officials are predictive of candidates' fortunes, holding constant candidate characteristics, early polling, and fundraising. Activists and groups control resources and influence voters. To win and retain the support of such "intense policy demanders" (Cohen et al. 2008b; Bawn et al. 2012), candidates make policy commitments, creating clearer divisions between the parties. These stands encourage activists and groups to join one party or the other. The concentration of groups with divergent preferences in the competing parties in turn increases pressures for polarization. Some incumbents change their positions on issues to remain in sync with their party (Karol 2009).

Surveys of party activists – be they convention delegates, donors, or campaign volunteers – reveal greater polarization vis-à-vis the public. By definition, activists are partisans, unlike a sizable minority of voters. Activists are also more likely than voters to self-identify as liberals when Democrats and conservatives when Republicans. Activists also are more apt to share their party's views on the full menu of issues and cluster around the extremes on survey questions offering a range of options.

These basic findings date back decades. Long before polarization developed, McClosky, Hoffman, and O'Hara (1960) found that delegates to the parties' 1956 national conventions were more consistently liberal or conservative and had more extreme preferences than their parties' voters. Subsequent delegate surveys also revealed preferences that fit far better in ideological categories than the responses of voters (Jennings 1992; Layman et al. 2010).

The same basic finding emerges from studies of campaign contributors. Brown, Hedges, and Powell (1980: 146) examined donors to presidential candidates in 1972, finding that "the views of this elite are substantially more structured than those of the general voting age population." More recent donor surveys reach similar conclusions (Francia et al. 2005; Bonica 2011; La Raja and Wiltse 2012), with Francia et al. noting that "the most active donors, in both parties, are the most ideologically extreme" (p. 762).

Numerous longitudinal studies show polarization increasing among activists in recent decades, whether the focus is convention delegates (Carmines and Woods 2002; Layman et al. 2010), donors (La Raja and Wiltse 2012), or campaign volunteers (Saunders and Abramowitz 2004). However the activist category is delineated, activists continue to take more consistently liberal or conservative stands than voters generally. Even scholars who differ both over what constitutes meaningful activism and the extent to which polarization is a mass phenomenon (Fiorina 2009; Abramowitz 2010) agree that the gap between activists and ordinary voters is substantial. Given some change at the mass level, whether one terms it polarization or simply "sorting," the persistence of the gap between activists and voters implies change in the activist stratum.

While it is useful to describe trends among activists, we would ultimately like to know how that change occurred. To what extent does polarization among activists stem from evolution in individuals' attitudes as opposed to compositional change via mobilization, demobilization, and generational replacement? Questions about the mechanism producing "issue evolution" and "party position change" at the elite and mass levels have long interested party scholars (Carmines and Stimson 1989; Adams 1997; Wolbrecht 2002; Karol 2009).

More fundamentally, we would like to understand activists' role in the broader process of polarization. At one extreme, activists' greater ideological consistency and more extreme attitudes might be seen as entirely a result of their greater political awareness. In this view, party activists have polarized, but changes in their own preferences are endogenous to others' actions and have no causal power of their own. Alternatively, activists may drive the process of polarization, compelling politicians to toe the party line and take more extreme views, prompting realignments among voters.

Turning first to the question of mechanisms, scholars find multiple processes underlying activists' changing views. A combination of ignorance and indifference allows many voters to live comfortably with inconsistencies between their party identification and policy views. By contrast, activists' far greater attentiveness to politics increases the psychological pressure on them to reduce dissonance between their policy preferences and their party identification. Some activists cared so strongly about particular issues that they changed parties. In many other cases, activists embraced the policies that had been adopted by their parties' politicians. Compositional change via replacement, mobilization, and demobilization also plays a role, but the speed of the shifts is such that change among existing activist populations is required to explain it.

Scholars find that activists have also influenced their parties' stands on issues. Carmines and Woods (2002: 374) note that activists polarized on the abortion issue well before the public, if not the politicians, and conclude, "[A]ctivists are crucial to the issue evolution process." In a similar vein, Layman et al. (2010: 334) report, "Granger causality tests show a causal effect of activist polarization on polarization in Congress" and that "changes in levels of abortion polarization among party activists and the parties in Congress cause changes in mass party polarization."

Studies that compare activists' views with the positions taken by politicians in roll calls or party platforms understate the effect of activism, however. This is the case because even activists do not care equally about all issues. For example, the fact that Republican politicians, including most prominently Ronald Reagan, were more pro-life than Democratic ones at a time when Republican convention delegates were not yet strongly pro-life (Carmines and Woods 2002) does *not* mean that politicians were entirely leaders rather than followers on this issue. One might reach that conclusion if one views party activists as an undifferentiated category.

Yet, just as there are "issue publics" among voters that care intensely about individual issues, there are segments of the activist stratum that are more focused on particular policies and interest groups with very narrow concerns. In the case of abortion, the Moral Majority and other early Christian right groups emerged in the late 1970s and supported Reagan strongly in 1980. Thus, the answer to the question of whether activists lead or follow politicians depends on whether we are discussing the activist category as a whole or the subset of activists and interest groups focused on an issue.

The answer to the question "Who leads and who follows?" also depends on whether the focus is on the most prominent politicians or the bulk of elected officials. Leading politicians are coalition managers (Karol 2009) who stake out early positions, welcoming new groups into their parties. These coalition group incorporation signals alter the composition of the party's base in ways that later constrain less prominent politicians. Cohen's (2005) study of the religious right at the grassroots reveals that traditional "country club" GOP elites were not comfortable with the influx of Christian right activists who reached their organizations in the 1980s. Yet Reagan's embrace of this group encouraged Christian right activists to become active in their local Republican Parties. Their growing presence was a new reality with which ambitious GOP politicians had to contend.

A similar development occurred earlier in the Democratic Party, which incorporated unions and African Americans in the New Deal years. Initially these groups were attracted to Franklin Roosevelt rather than the Democratic Party per se, but they increasingly became Democrats (Weiss 1983; Karol 2009). By the 1940s, these new Democratic constituencies had enough influence to veto possible vice-presidential nominees (Farrell 1994) and demand a platform favoring civil rights for African Americans (Cohen et al. 2008b).

Motivations for activism differ. In a classic study, Clark and Wilson (1961) delineated three broad categories: material, solidary, and purposive incentives. Material incentives (i.e., the desire for personal benefits such as patronage positions and government contracts) were most prominent in the nineteenth century before civil service reforms began to be enacted. A solidary motivation, or the desire for camaraderie, is common among activists of all stripes. Purposive activism, or the effort to affect public policy by electing candidates with congenial views, has always been a factor in party politics as well. Given the limited impact any individual's small donation of time or labor can make, these actions have always been hard to explain in a rationalist framework.

Certainly individual activists still seek benefits. One example is aspirants to ambassadorships, which presidents frequently award to fundraisers (Hollibaugh forthcoming). For fundraisers with such motives, the incentives are to side with the likely winner of the parties' nominations and with the candidate to whom they have the strongest ties. Like those who work on campaigns hoping for a staff position, such fundraisers are not a force for polarization.

Yet, while all of these motivations for activism remain, the balance among them may have shifted in ways that contributed to polarization. Polsby (1983) argued that reforms of the presidential nomination process weakened traditional parties and their pragmatic leaders empowering factions with extreme policy preferences. Aldrich (1995, 2011) contends that with the decline of machine politics due to civil service reform and other factors, the importance of ideologically driven activists has grown. Purposive motives still impel principled activism, whereas material incentives no longer attract campaign workers to the same extent. Similarly, to the extent that campaign finance laws have encouraged the rise of small donors by limiting individual contributions, the importance of purposive incentives for activism should grow, since small donors cannot realistically expect the personal benefits anticipated by bundlers.

This contention is plausible and some evidence supports it. Hinchliffe and Lee's (2014) finding that states which Mayhew (1986) coded as having stronger "traditional party organizations" in the postwar decades have less polarized legislatures even today is consistent with Aldrich's view. Enos and Hersh (forthcoming) find that canvassers for the Obama presidential campaign have strong ideological commitments and policy preferences that are not typical of Democratic voters.

Yet the decline of patronage and machine politics evident since the Progressive Era more closely coincides with the *depolarization* that occurred in Congress much of the twentieth century (Ansolabehere, Snyder, and Stewart 2001) rather than during the more recent polarization. Moreover, a look at the last strongholds of machine politics in the postwar decades – such as Cook County, Illinois; Philadelphia; the outer boroughs of New York City; and much of New Jersey – reveals legislators who mostly voted with their party with great regularity. Southern Democrats and Northeastern moderate Republicans more frequently broke ranks in Congress. La Raja and Wiltse (2012) find that the view that small, ideologically driven donors polarize parties is not supported empirically either. Polarization is evident among such donors vis-à-vis voters, but a notable increase in polarization among donors themselves is only evident since 2002. Since this shift lags developments in Congress by several years, these authors conclude that small donors were not driving the process.

There is reason to believe that activists help polarize parties, but the evidence is mixed. However, existing studies somewhat understate activists' role. Often activists' influence is seen as coming from candidate selection and lobbying. Yet polarization among party activists can fuel polarization in other ways. Two underappreciated ways in which activists' polarization can produce polarization among elected officials are via candidacy and incumbent perceptions of constituency.

Activists are an important part of the pool from which candidates are recruited. (Fox and Lawless 2010). Accordingly, a more ideologically homogeneous pool of activists will tend to promote polarization among elected officials. This change may not be attributed to activism, however. It is important to remember that yesterday's activist is tomorrow's candidate.

Another way that activists may contribute to polarization even without affecting candidate selection is by helping to shape elected officials' perceptions. Legislators often knowingly give greater weight to the concerns of a "subconstituency" (Fenno 1978; Bishin 2009) of core supporters and swing voters within their states or districts. Party activists and interest groups are prominent within subconstituencies. Yet scholars have also long known that elected officials' perceptions of constituency opinion may be skewed (Miller and Stokes 1963; Kull and Destler 1999; Miler 2010; Broockman and Skovron 2014). Such misperceptions are important because they can lead to legislators' voting against the wishes of their constituents inadvertently.

Party activists go to town meetings, attend party functions, and contact elected officials, making themselves more visible to elected officials than other citizens. Elected officials also devote much of their time raising money, often from donors who are party loyalists. Many members of Congress spend several hours a day attending fundraising events or "phone banking," even when they are in Washington.[1] While officials may realize on one level that the contributors, campaign workers, and other activists with whom they interact are not representative of the public or even the party-in-the-electorate, spending so much time among such people inevitably affects legislators' perceptions of constituency attitudes. This is true for members of Congress regarding their interactions with lobbyists (Miler 2010), and there is reason to believe the same biases emerge where activists are concerned. Polarization among party activists may exacerbate such skewed perceptions.

PARTIES, POLARIZATION, AND INTEREST GROUPS

My coauthors and I (Cohen et al. 2008a, 2008b; Karol 2009; Bawn et al. 2012) argue that the policies parties advocate are often traceable to the preferences of party-aligned interest groups. I contend (Karol 2009) that changes in party policies often result from *coalition maintenance* whereby a group develops

---

[1] "For Freshman in Congress, Focus Is on Raising Money," *Boston Globe*, May 12, 2013.

new policy preferences and the politicians of the party to which they are aligned adapt in order to continue to represent the group or *coalition group incorporation* in which politicians take new stands on issues in order to bring new groups into their party coalitions.

The era of polarization has been marked by the incorporation of new groups in both major parties. In other cases, while group-party linkages are very long-standing, social and demographic changes have made the groups a larger or smaller part of their party than they once were (Karol 2014b).

Newer Democratic constituencies include feminists, LGBT rights supporters, and environmentalists. Key feminist organizations active in campaigns include Emily's List, NARAL (formerly the National Abortion Rights Action League), and the National Organization for Women. The leading LGBT rights lobby has been the Human Rights Campaign. The two key environmentalist lobbies are the League of Conservation Voters and the Sierra Club. Labor unions remain strongly tied to the Democrats, but their numbers have greatly declined. Yet even in their reduced state, unions remain a crucial source of funds and "ground game" for Democrats (Dark 2001; Skinner 2007). Latinos have long leaned Democratic, but their growing numbers make them a larger component of the Democratic base than they used to be. African Americans remain the most loyal Democratic constituency, and the long-predicted realignment of Jews has yet to emerge, but the loyalties of elements of the New Deal coalition have greatly attenuated (white Catholics) or dissipated entirely (white Southerners).

The most dramatic change on the Republican side from an interest group standpoint is the arrival of the religious right. Different organizations that rallied this constituency have risen and fallen since the 1970s; the Moral Majority, the Christian Coalition, and Focus on the Family each had their day in the sun. Another important change has been the movement of gun rights supporters into the GOP. The key organization is, of course, the National Rifle Association, but other lobbies are active in this niche as well including Gun Owners of America. The Republican Party remains largely white, but has become dominant in the South and rural areas nationwide and has made great inroads among white Catholics.

Another phenomenon that has contributed to polarization is the rise of party-linked lobbies that police issue areas and seek to make politicians in their preferred party toe the line. These groups are not built on a social identity, but rather solely on a policy focus. Unlike traditional interest groups, such lobbies often dispense with any semblance of nonpartisanship. These groups are not entirely absent in the Democratic Party, but have been more prominent in the GOP in recent years, even prior to the advent of the Tea Party in 2009. These groups, of which the Club for Growth is the most prominent example, contribute to the pattern of "asymmetric polarization" (Saunders and Abramowitz 2004; Hacker and Pierson 2005; McCarty, Poole, and Rosenthal 2007) in which Republicans have polarized more than Democrats.

Although serious primary challenges to incumbents were uncommon during the polarizing decades and often driven by nonideological concerns (Boatright 2013), ideologically charged primary challenges have a demonstration effect. By targeting and occasionally helping to defeat an incumbent deemed insufficiently partisan or conservative, the Club for Growth, Tea Party organizations, and other conservative groups can influence the behavior of many other members of Congress.

Thus, looking at the number of cases in which such lobbies defeated incumbents or backed the winning candidate in an open-seat primary is likely to understate their impact. For example, Senator Orrin Hatch[2] (R-UT) moved to the right after seeing his long-time colleague Senator Robert Bennett unseated at the state Republican Convention in 2010. Hatch won renomination and reelection in 2012, but only after adjusting his voting record and forgoing the occasional ventures into bipartisanship for which he was once well known. Similarly, Senator Pat Roberts (R-KS) survived a Tea Party challenger in 2014, but only after adopting a more conservative posture.[3]

RECIPROCAL INFLUENCE BETWEEN PARTY POLITICIANS AND INTEREST GROUPS: THE PHENOMENON OF REVERSE LOBBYING

Much of the discussion of party group relations is based on the premise that groups have fixed policy preferences that politicians must take as givens. In many cases, that is a valid and useful assumption. Yet, much as politicians may influence activists, they may also affect the behavior of party-aligned interest groups. These processes are not identical; while activists may take cues from politicians whom they never meet, interest group leaders are subject to direct pressure from elected officials of the party with which they are aligned. Leaders of party campaign committees commonly enlist interest groups in efforts to recruit candidates (Herrnson 2009).

A more understudied process that contributes to polarization is politicians "reverse lobbying" interest groups on policy. In some cases, party leaders in Congress use these lobbies as whips to keep legislators from their caucuses in line, enhancing polarization. Scholars have identified the phenomenon of reverse lobbying, but they have focused on public policy (Weir 1995; Shaiko 1998) rather than parties and polarization.[4]

Yet there are multiple examples of this process in recent decades. In the fight over the Clinton health care reform plan of 1993–94, Democratic and

---

[2] "Sen. Orrin Hatch Survives Tea Party Challenge: How He Did It," *Christian Science Monitor*, June 27, 2012.

[3] "Where He Really Lives Aside, Sen. Pat Roberts Has Moved to His Right," *Rollcall.com*, February 10, 2014, and "Roberts Moves Right in Face of Tea Party Challenge," *Lawrence Journal World*, March 2, 2014.

[4] For a more thorough treatment of this phenomenon, see Karol (2014a).

Republican politicians guided the activity of aligned interest groups in important ways. Labor unions came to support the "managed competition" approach underlying the Clinton plan after seeing years earlier that Democratic leaders, including even Ted Kennedy, were no longer willing to advocate for a single-payer health care plan (Gottschalk 2000).

On the Republican side, the Chamber of Commerce initially expressed support for health care reform in principle, if not all the details of Clinton's plan.[5] Yet, in a dramatic reversal, the Chamber turned against the Clinton health care reform efforts following intense reverse lobbying by GOP members of Congress and activists. In a remarkable episode, U.S. Rep. John Boehner (R-OH) wrote to firms telling them to resign from the Chamber if it did not oppose the Clinton plan (Martin 1995).

Reverse lobbying was also important in the George W. Bush years. Sinclair (2006) reports that GOP leaders insisted that corporate lobbyists work for the passage of Bush's 2003 income tax cuts before congressional Republicans would bring up the narrower tax measures that were of greater concern to business lobbies.

GOP Senate Leader Mitch McConnell furnishes a still more recent example of polarizing reverse lobbying. In 2009, the Kentucky senator reportedly urged the National Rifle Association to oppose the nomination of Sonia Sotomayor to the U.S. Supreme Court.[6] McConnell asked the lobby if they would include the vote on Sotomayor among those used to calculate ratings for senators. The gun rights lobby had never taken a position on Supreme Court nominations, yet the NRA could help McConnell minimize defections among GOP senators and lower the ratings of Democratic senators from pro-gun states who were sure to support Sotomayor.

Certainly, party-aligned interest groups lobby politicians. In important cases, though, politicians have convinced their allied lobbies to take actions they would not have taken without guidance and even pressure. Party politicians did not convey the demands of their parties' "intense demanders" to voters. Rather, party leaders managed these groups in the interest of the party as a whole. In some cases, party leaders' reverse lobbying led to increased polarization. Once the Chamber of Commerce opposed the Clinton health care plan, it became more difficult for even moderate Republican members of Congress to remain open to reform. Similarly, the NRA's opposition to Sotomayor's nomination made it harder for GOP senators to support her.

[5] "Clinton Finds a Friendlier Chamber of Commerce," *New York Times*, April 14, 1993.
[6] While McConnell denied trying to influence the NRA, independent conservative observers, present at the meeting in question, reported otherwise. "NRA Threats Fail to Sway Senators on Sotomayor," *Washington Times*, August 2, 2009. See also "The NRA at the Bench," *New York Times*, December 26, 2012, and "The NRA's Party Stories," *Washington Post*, December 27, 2012.

POLARIZATION AND INTEREST GROUPS: EVIDENCE
FROM CAMPAIGN FINANCE

Interest groups have increasingly directed their campaign contributions to candidates from one party. This is less true for narrow economic interests that face no organized opposition in their quest for subsidies or favorable regulation. Such sectors can still employ the "access" strategy of supporting incumbents. Interest groups that represent one side of an active controversy, however, have increasingly aligned with the Democrats or Republicans. Wand (2007) finds that since 1994, business PACs, many of which once supported incumbents of both parties and backed the favorite in open-seat contests, have tilted more toward the GOP in open-seat races. They did so because they realized that Republican control of the House was really possible. This giving pattern led to fewer new legislators cross-pressured between their party and interest group supporters, contributing to polarization.

At the same time, newer party coalition components have become ever more closely aligned with Democrats and Republicans. Using data from the Center for Responsive Politics (CRP), which codes federal campaign contributions, I provide three illustrations of this important trend. In all cases the analysis begins in 1990, where the CRP time series begin, even though the trends I document were already well underway in the 1980s.

Environmentalism was not on the national political agenda during the New Deal and early postwar decades. Yet once the issue became politically salient in the 1960s, it has never gone away. Different controversies arise within this broad policy area, but more than four decades after the first Earth Day, environmental concerns still stir passionate debate. What has changed is that the divide on environmental issues has become increasingly partisan (Shipan and Lowry 2001). Democrats have embraced environmentalists while Republicans have represented economic interests that extract natural resources and oppose regulations (Gimpel, Lee, and Parrott 2014).

Figure 1 depicts the trends in contributions to congressional candidates by environmentalists as well as coal and oil and gas producers from 1990 through 2014. The figure reports the share of contributions from each sector going to Republican candidates. At the beginning of the period, there is already a clear difference between these groups. The bulk of environmentalist contributions already went to Democratic candidates in the early 1990s. By contrast, giving by the oil and gas and by the coal sectors was not one-sided initially; nearly 40 percent of their contributions were still going to Democrats at the beginning of this period.

Yet notable change is evident. Energy producers' Republican leanings have grown stronger while environmentalists have become even more closely aligned with Democrats. Oil and gas and coal producers who gave Republicans 62 percent and 59 percent of their contributions respectively in 1990 sent 87 percent and 95 percent to GOP candidates in 2014. Some traces of the access

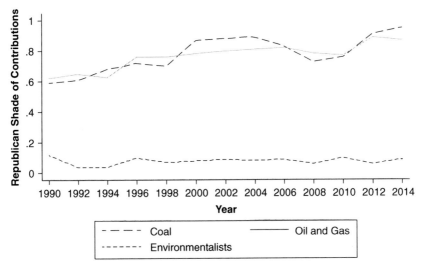

FIGURE 1. Republican Share of Contributions in Congressional Elections: Coal and Oil and Gas Sectors and Environmentalists Compared, 1990–2014

strategy of favoring incumbents and the party in power common to many lobbies are evident. The trend toward the Republicans was interrupted by the Democrats' brief resurgence on Capitol Hill after 2006.

Yet even taking party control into account, there is a clear shift. Oil and gas gave 63 percent of its contributions to Republicans in 1994 when they were still in the minority, while 68 percent of contributions from the coal sector went to Republicans in that cycle. In the 2008 cycle, after the GOP had returned to minority status, Republicans received 78 percent of the contributions from the oil and gas producers and 73 percent of those from the coal sector.

The shift among environmentalists is far less dramatic, if only because their giving was already so one-sided in the early 1990s, but their support for Republicans did decline from 12 percent in 1990 to 9 percent in 2014. Still the bulk of the polarization among donors who focused on environmental issues stems from energy producers' abandonment of a bipartisan strategy in favor of solid support for GOP candidates.

The increasing polarization among contributors focused on environmental issues is not unique. A similar trend marks giving patterns among those concerned with firearms regulation, another controversy that emerged in national politics during the late 1960s. In recent decades the parties have increasingly diverged on gun control (Karol 2009). This process has been gradual, and trends in campaign contributions reveal that interest group alignments have evolved in the past generation.

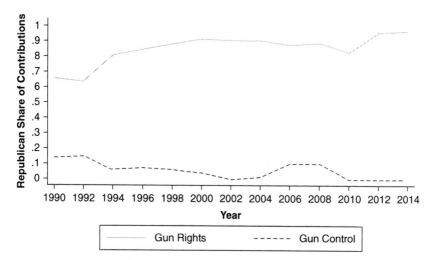

FIGURE 2. Republican Share of Contributions in Congressional Elections: Gun Rights and Gun Control Donors Compared, 1990–2014

By 1990, when the Center for Responsive Politics campaign contribution time series begins, Republicans were already associated with the gun rights cause. The NRA had made its first endorsement in a presidential race in 1980 when it backed Ronald Reagan. The gun rights lobby also supported George H. W. Bush in 1988.

Yet as Figure 2 reveals, even after those endorsements, gun rights advocates' giving patterns were not entirely partisan in congressional races. In another parallel to environmental issues, donor groups on the conservative side of the issue initially split their contributions between the parties, whereas the liberal lobbies overwhelmingly backed Democrats. In 1990, 66 percent of gun rights contributions went to Republican congressional candidates, as compared to only 14 percent of funds from gun control advocates.[7]

However, giving patterns among donors focused on firearms regulation have become far more partisan in recent years. By 2014, 97 percent of gun rights money was directed toward Republican candidates; remarkably, *none* of the contributions from the gun control groups went to Republican candidates after 2008.

The abortion issue is the longest-standing "social issue" after race and is the one most consistently associated with the "culture war" that underlies the contemporary party system. The growing partisan divide on abortion has received much attention (Adams 1997; Carmines and Woods 2002; Karol

---

[7] The gun rights side has typically been far better funded, and gun control advocates have been less successful in fundraising and organization building than environmentalists, but contribution data still is a useful gauge of group alignments.

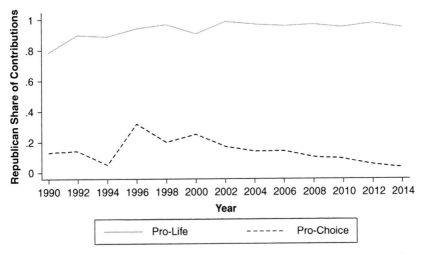

FIGURE 3. Republican Share of Contributions in Congressional Elections: Pro-Life and Pro-Choice Donors Compared, 1990–2014

2009; Layman et al. 2010). The roots of this important development are in the 1970s. As in the case of the environmental and gun issues, the parties were already diverging on the issue before 1990 when the CRP time series of campaign contributions begins.

Nevertheless, Figure 3, illustrating trends in campaign contributions by pro-life and pro-choice groups, reveals a growing gap. The share of pro-life contributions to GOP candidates grows. The percentage of pro-choice donations going to Republicans declines, although there is a spike upward after the GOP gained control of Congress in the mid-1990s.

In all three of these issue areas, increasing alignment between interest groups and parties is evident. In the cases of environmental and gun politics, Democrats, long the more ideologically diverse party, still received significant contributions from both sides of the debate in the early 1990s. During the last generation, however, this has diminished greatly, and Democrats now receive support from the environmentalists and gun control backers, while Republicans win backing from resource-extracting sectors and gun rights advocates. Already in 1990, abortion-related contributions were more polarized, but even in this issue area the concerned groups have lined up still more solidly behind their preferred party during the last 24 years.

CONCLUSIONS

Polarization is manifest in many different arenas within the American political system, as the authors of other chapters in this volume show. Yet to understand polarization, one must ultimately turn to parties themselves. A true appreciation of party dynamics requires moving beyond examination of the formal structure to focus on activists and interest groups tied to each of the parties.

Surveys of donors, convention delegates, and campaign workers all reveal levels of ideological coherence far exceeding those evident among even partisan voters. Moreover, disagreement between Democratic and Republican activists has grown substantially in recent decades. The older issues of taxation, the welfare state, and union rights that were so prominent in the New Deal and postwar decades have remained on the agenda. Yet they have been joined by a large set of "social" issues that have brought new constituencies into party coalitions.

The relationship between party politicians and activists and interest groups is not one-sided. These groups need each other, and they influence each other. Given their importance, these relationships will continue to engage scholars in years to come. For now, it is safe to say that the story of polarization is a partisan one and that we cannot understand parties without focusing on their activists and aligned interest groups.

REFERENCES

Abramowitz, Alan I. 2010. *The Disappearing Center: Engaged Citizens, Polarization and American Democracy*. New Haven, CT: Yale University Press.

Adams, Greg D. 1997. "Abortion: Evidence of an Issue Evolution." *American Journal of Political Science* 41 (3): 718–737.

Aldrich, John H. 2011. *Why Parties? A Second Look*. Chicago: University of Chicago Press.

Aldrich, John H. 1995. *Why Parties? The Origin and Transformation of Parties in America*. Chicago: University of Chicago Press.

Ansolabehere, Stephen, James M. Snyder Jr., and Charles Stewart III. 2001. "Candidate Positioning in U.S. House Elections." *American Journal of Political Science* 45 (1): 136–159.

Bawn, Kathleen, Martin Cohen, David Karol, Seth Masket, Hans Noel and John Zaller. 2012. "A Theory of Political Parties: Groups, Policy Demands and Nominations in American Politics." *Perspectives on Politics* 10 (3): 571–597.

Bernstein, Jonathan, and Casey B.K. Dominguez. 2003. "Candidates and Candidacies in the Expanded Party." *PS: Political Science and Politics* 36 (2): 165–169.

Bishin, Benjamin G. 2009. *Tyranny of the Minority: The Subconstituency Theory of Representation*. Philadelphia: Temple University Press.

Boatright, Robert. 2013. *Getting Primaried*. Ann Arbor: University of Michigan Press.

Bonica, Adam 2011, "Small Donors and Polarization." *Boston Review*, July 22.

Broockman, David, and Chris Skovron. 2014. "What Politicians Believe about Their Constituents: Asymmetric Misperceptions and Prospects for Constituency Control." Unpublished MS, University of California, Berkeley.

Brown, Clifford W., Roman Hedges and Lynda W. Powell. 1980. "Belief Structure in a Political Elite: Contributions to the 1972 Presidential Candidates." *Polity* 13 (1): 134–146.

Carmines, Edward G., and James Woods. 2002. "The Role of Party Activists in the Abortion Issue." *Political Behavior* 24 (4): 361–377.

Carmines, Edward G., and James Stimson. 1989. *Issue Evolution: Race and the Transformation of American Politics*. Princeton, NJ: Princeton University Press.

Clark, Peter B., and James Q. Wilson. 1961. "Incentive Systems: A Theory of Organizations." *Administrative Science Quarterly* 6 (2): 129–166.

Cohen, Martin. 2005. "Moral Victories: Cultural Conservatism and the Creation of a New Republican Congressional Majority." Ph.D. diss., University of California, Los Angeles.

Cohen, Marty, David Karol, Hans Noel, and John Zaller. 2008a. "The Invisible Primary in Presidential Nominations, 1980–2004." In William G. Mayer, ed., *The Making of the Presidential Candidates 2008*. Lanham, MD: Rowman & Littlefield.

Cohen, Marty, David Karol, Hans Noel, and John Zaller. 2008b. *The Party Decides: Presidential Nominations before and after Reform*. Chicago: University of Chicago Press.

Dark, Taylor E. 2001. *The Unions and the Democrats: An Enduring Alliance*. Ithaca, NY: Cornell University Press.

Dominguez, Casey B. K. 2011. "Does the Party Matter? Endorsements in Congressional Primaries." *Political Research Quarterly* 64 (3): 534–544.

Enos, Ryan, and Eitan Hersh. Forthcoming. "Party Activists as Campaign Advertisers: The Ground Campaign as a Principal-Agent Problem." *American Political Science Review*.

Fenno, Richard F. Jr. 1978. *Home Style: House Members in Their Districts*. Boston: Little, Brown.

Ferrell, Robert H. 1994. *Choosing Truman: The Democratic Convention of 1944*. Columbia : University of Missouri Press.

Fiorina, Morris P., with Samuel J. Abrams. 2009. *Disconnect: The Breakdown of Representation in American Politics*. Norman: University of Oklahoma Press.

Fox, Richard, and Jennifer Lawless. 2010. "If Only They'd Ask: Gender, Recruitment and Political Ambition." *Journal of Politics* 72 (2): 310–326.

Francia, Peter L., John C. Green, Paul S. Herrnson, Lynda W. Powell, and Clyde Wilcox. 2005. "Limousine Liberals and Corporate Conservatives: The Financial Constituencies of the Democratic and Republican Parties." *Social Science Quarterly* 86: 762–778.

Gimpel, James G., Frances E. Lee, and Michael Parrott. 2014. "Business Interests and the Party Coalitions: Industry Sector Contributions to U.S. Congressional Candidates." *American Politics Research* 42: 1034–1076.

Gottschalk, Marie. 2000. *The Shadow Welfare State: Labor, Business and the Politics of Health Care in the U.S.* Ithaca, NY: Cornell University Press.

Hacker, Jacob S., and Paul Pierson. 2005. *Off-Center: The Republican Revolution and the Erosion of American Democracy*. New Haven, CT: Yale University Press.

Herrnson, Paul S. 2013. "National Parties in the 21st Century." In Mark D. Brewer and L. Sandy Maisel, eds., *The Parties Respond: Changes in American Parties and Campaigns*. 5th ed. Boulder, CO: Westview Press, 131–160.

Herrnson, Paul S. 2009. "The Roles of Party Organizations, Party-Connected Committees, and Party Allies in Elections." *Journal of Politics* 71 (4): 1207–1224.

Hinchliffe, Kelsey, and Frances Lee. 2014. "Party Competition and Conflict in State Legislatures." Paper Presented at the 2014 Annual Meeting of the Midwestern Political Science Association.

Hollibaugh, Gary E. Jr. Forthcoming. "The Political Determinants of Ambassadorial Appointments." *Presidential Studies Quarterly.*

Jennings, M. Kent. 1992. "Ideological Thinking among Mass Publics and Political Elites." *Public Opinion Quarterly* 56 (4): 419–441.

Karol, David. 2014a. "Parties and Leadership in American Politics." Paper prepared for Conference on "Leadership in American Politics." Miller Center, University of Virginia. Charlottesville, Virginia, June 2–3, 2014.

Karol, David. 2014b. "Parties Revised and Revived: Democrats and Republicans in the Age of Reagan, 1980–2000." In Marjorie Hershey, ed., *CQ Guide to U.S. Political Parties.* Washington, DC: CQ Press.

Karol, David. 2009. *Party Position Change in American Politics: Coalition Management.* New York: Cambridge University Press.

Kolodny, Robin. 2000. "Electoral Partnerships: Political Consultants and Political Parties." In James A. Thurber and Candace J. Nelson, eds., *Campaign Warriors: Political Consultants in Elections.* Washington, DC: Brookings Institution Press.

Kull, Steven, and I. M. Destler. 1999. *Misreading the Public: The Myth of a New Isolationism.* Washington, DC: Brookings Institution.

La Raja, Raymond J., and David L. Wiltse. 2012. "Don't Blame Donors for Ideological Polarization of Political Parties." *American Politics Research* 40 (30): 501–530.

Layman, Geoffrey C., Thomas M. Carsey, John C. Green, Richard Herrera, and Rosalyn Cooperman. 2010. "Activists and Conflict Extension in American Politics." *American Political Science Review* 104 (2): 324–346.

Layman, Geoffrey C., Thomas M. Carsey, and Juliana Menasce Horowitz. 2006. "Party Polarization in American Politics: Characteristics, Causes, and Consequences." *Annual Review of Political Science* 9: 83–110.

Lee, Frances E. 2013. "An Irresponsible Two-Party System? Problems of Governance in a Time of Uncertain Majorities." Paper prepared for presentation at the Oxford Conference on Governing in Polarized Politics, Oxford University, April 17, 2013.

Mann, Thomas E., and Anthony Corrado. 2014. "Party Polarization and Campaign Finance." Report of the Center for Effective Public Management. Washington DC: The Brookings Institution.

Martin, Cathie Jo. 1995. "Stuck in Neutral: Big Business and the Politics of National Health Reform." *Journal of Health Politics, Policy and Law* 20 (2): 431–436.

Mayhew, David. R. 1986. *Placing Parties in American Politics.* Princeton, NJ: Princeton University Press.

McCarty, Nolan, Keith Poole, and Howard Rosenthal. 2007. *Polarized America: The Dance of Ideology and Unequal Riches.* Cambridge, MA: MIT Press.

McClosky, Herbert, Paul Hoffman, and Rosemary O'Hara, 1960. "Issue Conflict and Consensus among Party Leaders and Followers." *American Political Science Review* 54: 406–472.

Miler, Kristina C. 2010. *Constituency Representation in Congress: The View from the Hill.* New York: Cambridge University Press.

Miller, Warren, and Donald E. Stokes. 1963. "Constituency Influence in Congress." *The American Political Science Review* 57 (1): 45–56.

Polsby, Nelson W. 1983 *Consequences of Party Reform.* New York: Oxford University Press.

Saunders, K. L., and A. I. Abramowitz. 2004. Ideological Realignment and Active Partisans in the American Electorate. *American Politics Research* 32: 285–309.

Schlesinger, Joseph. 1984. "On the Theory of Party Organization." *Journal of Politics* 46 (2): 369–400.

Schwartz, Mildred. 1990. *The Party Network: The Robust Organization of Illinois Republicans*. Madison: University of Wisconsin Press.

Shaiko, Ronald G. 1998. "Reverse Lobbying: Interest Group Mobilization from the White House and the Hill." In Allan J. Cigler and Burdett A. Loomis, eds., *Interest Group Politics*, 5th edition. Washington DC: CQ Press, 259–267.

Shipan, Charles R., and William R. Lowry. 2001. "Environmental Policy and Party Divergence in Congress." *Political Research Quarterly* 54 (2): 245–263.

Sinclair, Barbara. 2006. *Party Wars: Polarization and the Politics of National Policy Making*. Norman: University of Oklahoma Press.

Skinner, Richard. 2007. *More than Money: Interest Group Action in Congressional Elections*. Lanham, MD: Rowman & Littlefield.

Wand, Jonathan. 2007. "The Allocation of Campaign Contributions by Interest Groups and the Rise of Elite Polarization." Unpublished MS, Stanford University.

Weir, Margaret. 1995. "Institutional and Political Obstacles to Reform." *Health Affairs* 14 (1): 102–104.

Weiss, Nancy. 1983. *Farewell to the Party of Lincoln: Black Politics in the Age of FDR*. Princeton, NJ: Princeton University Press.

Wolbrecht, Christina. 2002. "Explaining Women's Rights Realignment: Convention Delegates, 1972–1992." *Political Behavior* 24: 237–282.

4

Authoritarianism and Polarization in American Politics, Still?

Marc J. Hetherington and Jonathan D. Weiler

- A personality based, authoritarian-nonauthoritarian, divide continues to structure party conflict in America, providing it with the characteristics of polarization.
- Barack Obama's ascendancy to the presidency, in fact, has deepened the divide we identified as emerging in the early 2000s.
- The issue agenda, which is central to understanding personality-based polarization, has evolved in ways that have also deepened the divide, particularly with the emergence of immigration reform as a central concern.
- The Tea Party represents the clearest embodiment of the authoritarian politics that defines the current political right, pushing a substantive issue agenda but also eliciting deeper-seated emotions about order and change in American politics.

Our book, *Authoritarianism and Polarization in American Politics*, was published in 2009 (Hetherington and Weiler 2009). In it, we argued that politics had increasingly become organized around a fundamental worldview/personality divide. This was because people's preferences about many of the most important issues of the day – race, feminism, immigration, gay rights, and the proper responses to terrorism – are all, in large measure, driven by the same worldview/personality characteristic. We called that characteristic authoritarianism, although scholars have used many terms to describe those with the outlook we identified. Given the timing of our book's release, the most up-to-date data we could employ were gathered during the 2008 primary season. Much about politics has changed since then. Moreover, some of the new developments might suggest the critical change in the partisan divide that we identified then could have turned out to be more a blip in history than the durable worldview evolution we diagnosed.

Critics might, for example, identify the election of Barack Obama, the first African-American president, as evidence that the importance of race, the first layer of the process of worldview evolution that we argued was occurring, had been resolved. In addition, the issue agenda changed dramatically after Obama's election, with matters involving foreign wars and terrorism less pronounced than they were during the Bush administration. Because our original analysis had suggested the central importance of the September 11, 2001, terrorist attacks in forging the new worldview divide, the diminishing importance of such issues could, in turn, reduce authoritarianism's effect in structuring party conflict. Similarly, gay rights, another key issue we identified in defining the worldview divide, is perhaps on its way to resolution. Whereas Republicans worked hard to make it central to political contestation in the mid-2000s, they rarely make the issue salient in general election campaigns any longer because public opinion is moving swiftly in a tolerant direction.

Notwithstanding these developments, we believe authoritarianism remains central to post–George W. Bush American politics. If anything, the worldview divide that we identified in 2009 might be even deeper now. We posited that worldview evolution, once in place, would become difficult to displace. We still believe that is true. Although we were not systematic in our reasoning when we wrote our book, a few considerations seem, in retrospect, particularly important.

First, many of the issues that helped to create the divide are timeless. Degrees of comfort with new social norms and diversity in a population, as well as survival in the face of threats have been fundamental concerns in the history of humankind. Because people on either side of the worldview divide think about these issues differently, they are difficult for politics to resolve. Second, the specific issues that make the worldview divide salient can easily change from era to era without changing the fundamental nature of the divide. So, even if one issue diminishes in importance, a new issue that divides people along the same visceral lines as the old issue can replace it. Finally, political conflict about an issue that wasn't originally organized around authoritarian concerns can be reframed in ways that engage such worldview concerns, depending on whether enterprising political elites think the new frame benefits them. Health care reform, for one, can be framed as a complicated programmatic issue, or it can be framed as a gut-level symbolic issue. If framed in the latter way, as was apparently the case during the Obama years, it may engage the worldview divide, whereas it previously did not.

In this chapter, we first sketch a theoretical argument that suggests why the authoritarian-nonauthoritarian divide remains and why it will be difficult to displace. Second, we provide a narrative account of the first five or so years of the Obama presidency to provide qualitative evidence in support of our thinking. Finally, we turn to survey data gathered since the publication of our book to provide quantitative evidence that authoritarianism continues to play a central role in explaining what divides Republicans and Democrats.

MEET THE NEW BOSS, SAME AS THE OLD BOSS

Central to our theory of the import of authoritarianism in explaining polarization in American politics is a dynamic understanding of how a personality construct became so central to the political divide. In our 2009 book, we traced the issue agenda over several decades to explain how a "cluster of issues tied to an underlying disposition" (p. 64) became relevant to understanding political behavior and partisan identity.

Among the issues that emerged as salient over several decades in ways that formed and cemented the new divide were, in our estimation, (1) racial and ethnic difference; (2) crime and civil liberties; (3) the ERA, feminism, and family structure including, more recently, gay marriage; and (4) foreign policy, force, and diplomacy, including the war on terror. Over time, perceptions of these clusters of issues affixed themselves to identifiably partisan positions giving them political force and relevance. And as it happens, on all of these clusters of issues, the distinct positions the parties were staking out connected clearly to differences between authoritarians and nonauthoritarians.

In our book, we argued that these issues mattered more for changing the structure of political conflict over the past generation than did economic concerns, such as taxation and the size and role of government in the national economy. To be clear, we did not dismiss the importance of the latter issues for explaining political differences. But those differences between Democrats and Republicans were of much longer standing. It was the *emergence* of issue positions structured by authoritarianism that played the critical role in *transforming* the political landscape in recent years.

Most of the issues that were central to our original argument remain salient. Even if terrorism and foreign wars occupy less space on the issue agenda, they remain an international crisis away from becoming very salient again.[1] Furthermore, some of the issues we identified as important in structuring "worldview politics" have become more so. Consider the vexing problem of immigration, an issue we devoted only a brief chapter to because it was only beginning to emerge as a flashpoint between the left and right in 2007–08. Although many Republican elites would like to resolve it, they cannot because of the nature of the party's political base, causing the issue to occupy more and more attention with each passing election. We argue that a key reason that Republicans can't resolve the issue is because of the more authoritarian worldview that base Republicans today share.

This point is critically important to understanding the persistence of the present divide. Anyone who can use a calculator knows that the GOP, in the medium to long run, desperately needs to appeal better to racial and ethnic

---

[1] The language of "blame America first" to characterize Obama's putative approach to foreign policy has been widespread on the right in recent years. See, for example, Jennifer Rubin, "They Still Blame America First," *Weekly Standard*, September 23, 2010. Retrieved from http://www.weeklystandard.com/articles/they-still-blame-america-first.

minorities. Yet, party leaders have had little success convincing their followers that they must embrace immigration reform if they want to become the majority party. One reason for mass-level reticence is that the Republican base voters who party elites must convince to follow them are increasingly likely to score high in authoritarianism, with all the attendant concerns about difference that come along with that label. Because base Republicans in conjunction with their favored media personalities punish any Republican with national ambitions who floats a moderate line about immigration, Republican office holders rarely talk publicly about the virtues of a more moderate stance. As a result, the opinions of Republicans in the electorate do not moderate, and the issue remains a dividing concern.

A powerful cautionary tale in this regard took place in June 2014, when House Majority Leader Eric Cantor became the first such person in American history to lose a primary. The man who vanquished Cantor, Dave Brat, was an obscure economics professor at Randolph Macon College and a self-identified Tea Party candidate. In a low turnout election, with multiple issues at play – Brat railed against Wall Street, among other things – it is hard to assert definitively the precise causes of Brat's triumph. But his candidacy was given a significant boost by, among other things, the staunch advocacy of the well-known national radio host Laura Ingraham. Ingraham championed Brat largely because she saw Cantor as a sell-out on immigration. By any reasonable measure, Cantor was a hardliner on the issue. But he has, at times, supported negotiations that might include a (long and arduous) path to citizenship for some undocumented immigrants. This led to charges from Brat, greatly amplified by Ingraham, that Cantor supported "amnesty." That word threatens to become an albatross around the necks of Republican office seekers. In his summary of Brat's shocking win, another well-known conservative media personality, Todd Starnes, put the matter succinctly: "Here's the message from Virginia: You either stand with Americans or you stand with the invaders."[2]

What of this supposed post-racial society that elected an African-American president? Far from suggesting a post-racial society, the Obama presidency seems to have turned issues that were not racially charged before his election into racial issues. Take, for example, health care reform. We and others have shown that support for Bill and Hillary Clinton's health care reform was not a function of racial attitudes back in the 1990s, but Barack Obama's health care initiative, in contrast, was strongly related to racial attitudes (see Tesler and Sears 2010; Tesler 2012). The reason, apparently, is that Obama's race has racialized just about everything that people could possibly consider in the political world. Tesler provides perhaps the most telling manifestation. Through an innovative survey experiment, he showed that racial attitudes even structure Americans' evaluations of Bo, President Obama's dog.

---

[2] See Todd Starnes' tweet at https://twitter.com/toddstarnes/status/476521797924315136.

We also see evidence that the opposing worldviews that typify ordinary Republicans and Democrats today might now structure the debate about climate change, whereas it had nothing to do with it before. Indeed, until 20 years ago, there was no discernable difference between mass partisans on environmental issues, and as recently as 10 years ago, the statistically significant differences were not substantively large (McCright and Dunlap 2011). Today, the partisan differences on issues related to environmentalism, in general, and climate change, specifically, are enormous, with neither side able to understand how the other can possibly believe what it does. We believe and will show shortly that the worldview divide helps explain this recent development.

LATENT PUBLIC OPINION BECOMES MANIFEST[3]

Our treatment of what created the worldview divide is conventional. Ordinary citizens reflect the cues that political elites provide them. Since elites started to organize political choices around an increasing number of issues for which authoritarianism organized preferences, people's party choices began to reflect this worldview. Our thinking reflects that of John Zaller's (1992) *The Nature and Origin of Mass Opinion*. His work confirmed V. O. Key's (1966) central observation about public opinion from decades before: public opinion is like an echo chamber. The output bears an unmistakable relationship to the input. The key point here is that as long as "authoritarian issues" remain salient, this worldview will continue to structure party choices, which, in part, is central to understanding the polarized feelings that make the political system so difficult to manage these days (Hetherington and Rudolph 2015). If the issues that divided Republicans from Democrats were not as fundamental to people's worldviews, the feelings that partisans of one side have for the other would not be so negative.

Of course, it is possible that elites could find it strategically beneficial to resolve these issues, which would, in turn, displace the divide we identified in favor of another. By "resolve" an issue, we mean that elites could change their position on a given issue, which would, following Zaller's (1992) logic, cause their partisan followers to change their opinions on the issue and allow elites to forge a compromise across party lines, thus moving the issue off the agenda. We do not think this is likely, given the nature of the issues that are structured by authoritarianism. Zaller (2013) explains why. As part of his sweeping critique of his own seminal book, Zaller suggests that one important component of public opinion that *Nature and Origins* left out is what Key (1961)

---

[3] In his analysis of dreams, Freud said that latent content was the hidden symbolic meaning underlying the manifest content – those images that actually appeared in dreams. Mass publics might respond to overt appeals by politicians but, as scholars of motivated cognition suggest, do so according to deeper psychological motivations. How elites craft appeals to tap those deeper motivations is central to effective political persuasion.

characterized as latent opinion. Key suggested that, even if people's opinions about certain matters are not made manifest by political events at a particular point in time, people still have those opinions. Such opinions are about matters the public actually cares and feels strongly about. If politicians were to highlight the issues these opinions are connected to, thus making them manifest, it would be hard, perhaps impossible, for them to lead the opinions of their partisan followers as Zaller (1992) argues they are able to do on most issues. Put another way, strongly held opinions in the mass public, even if they remain latent, constrain what elites can say and do, and hence how much they can move public opinion.[4]

Another way to put this thinking is that some opinions are "stickier" than others. It might be relatively easy for elites to move public opinion on matters people care little about. But it is relatively hard on matters they care a lot about. This is important. Our original argument is premised on the fact that elite decision making created the worldview divide we now live with. Extending that argument into the future might suggest that, if elites took a new position on an issue, their partisan followers would simply adopt the new position. For example, Zaller's (1992) reasoning suggests that, if Republicans in Congress embraced comprehensive immigration reform, Republicans in the electorate would follow the cue and embrace it, too. If both parties agreed on the issue, consensus would develop, a compromise could be forged, and the issue would be resolved and disappear.

Of course, that has not happened, and Key's notion of latent public opinion explains why. It argues against elites' ability to change their followers' opinions on some issues because the costs of even attempting to are too high. If party elites believe that they cannot tread in an area because the electoral costs are too high, they will not try. As a result, public opinion in that issue area will remain the same. Resolution of that issue will not occur.

A few examples help to illustrate the point. Anti-government Republicans know they cannot wade into South Florida, home to a high percentage of older voters, arguing that it is necessary to cut Social Security benefits to present beneficiaries to make the system solvent for future generations. Regardless of whether that might be true, they know that they would pay with their jobs by championing such arguments. Similarly, Democratic elites would not descend on Detroit to argue that union protections had outlived their usefulness because, if they did, they surely would lose the next election. As these two examples make clear, we will never know whether such new cues would actually move the opinions of South Florida Republicans or Detroit Democrats, although it is a pretty good bet that they would not. Latent public opinion constrains what

---

[4] Zaller gives little ground in his essay as it relates to the role that partisan elites play in directing their followers to the "proper" position on issues of contestation, a process that is central to understanding the present state of polarization. Increasingly, homogeneous elite parties are fast producing increasingly homogeneous parties in the electorate (see Abramowitz 2010). This remains consistent with our original reasoning.

elites can say about certain matters. As a result, public opinion on these matters does not change.

The effect that latent public opinion has on political elites' position taking fits very nicely into the theory of worldview evolution that we described in our book. People tend to care deeply about the issues situated along the authoritarian/nonauthoritarian worldview divide because preferences on these issues are motivated by fundamental understandings of right and wrong. Unlike other more complicated political matters, people have strongly held opinions on them, which has important implications. For example, although Republican elites would likely love to be able to attract more Latino supporters by promising more open borders and more government benefits, for example, it is hard for them to do so because their authoritarian-minded base supporters are uncomfortable with the racial and ethnic diversity that more immigration would bring. Moreover, those who are more authority minded perceive illegal immigrants and their children as lawbreakers, another particular concern of the more authoritarian minded. As a result, Republican leaders cannot champion comprehensive reform efforts, including "amnesty," to deal with the millions of undocumented workers who are in the country and are unlikely to leave. In short, latent opinion among Republicans in the electorate on immigration is too strong for Republican elites to consider trying to change it.

With these considerations in mind, we trace forward from 2008 to the present evidence in political context and in public opinion data that show that the worldview evolution we identified years ago is as at least as strong today as it was then.

A NARRATIVE ACCOUNT OF THE CONTINUED IMPORTANCE OF AUTHORITARIANISM

Since President Obama's inauguration in 2009, the grounds of issue contestation have, in some ways, shifted. Immigration, already a fractious issue about which there was a growing partisan divide anchored in authoritarianism, has persisted as a politically relevant concern. Likewise, gay marriage, which became politically relevant in some states in 2004, has exploded on the national scene since the fall of 2008. Between 2004 and 2008, more than 30 states had amended their constitutions to enshrine marriage between one man and one woman as the only valid form of marriage. Beginning in 2008, when California became the second to last state to pass such a law, the pendulum swung dramatically in the other direction. Between Obama's first inauguration in 2009 and 2015, nearly 20 states had affirmed marriage equality, in the midst of a legal revolution that resulted in the June 2015 Supreme Court ruling making marriage equality the law of the land in all 50 states. Despite the ruling, simmering conflicts remain in a country that has grown more tolerant but remains bitterly divided over the issue.

In addition to these broadly cultural concerns, Obamacare has emerged as a central dividing line between Republicans and Democrats. And while it's not new that Republicans would be less inclined to support any broadly national system of health insurance coverage than Democrats, the nature and intensity of that opposition is an important illustration of how the worldview divide we've described has been deepened and extended.

In the discussion that follows, therefore, we look at three issue clusters that have become especially relevant since Barack Obama became president – gay marriage; immigration, and Obamacare. We are most interested in focusing on issues that have remained salient since 2009 and about which there have been enduring and intensifying partisan differences. For what we believe are obvious reasons, the questions of banking and mortgage bailouts have not had such enduring resonance. They remain part of a low simmer, but the GOP can hardly plausibly claim to be the party defending taxpayers from avaricious banks, and action on mortgage relief has been limp at best from Democrats. And both Tea Party adherents on the right and Occupy Wall Street activists on the left have complained loudly about what they perceive as the government's overly solicitous treatment of banks.

By contrast, the issues we consider most closely have been central and enduring features of partisan anger and disagreement since Obama took office. And as we will show in the next section, they have folded compellingly into the larger story of a personality-based political divide.

Immigration

In our book, we documented a dramatic chasm between low and high authoritarians on the question of immigration reform. At the time, a Republican president, George W. Bush, was pushing for comprehensive reform but facing stiff opposition from members of his own party who, we argued, were increasingly reflecting the preferences of their increasingly authoritarian base. It is quite clear that the Bush White House believed certain demographic realities – especially the growth of Americans coming from Spanish-speaking countries, particularly in swing states such as Colorado, New Mexico, and Nevada – required outreach to those groups of voters. But those political considerations ran headlong into a party base animated by unease with social change and uncomfortable with difference.

When President Obama took office, he attempted to restart the debate about comprehensive immigration reform that would include some path to citizenship for millions of residents currently residing illegally in the United States. For predictable partisan reasons, that effort did not get very far. But what's been interesting about immigration reform under Obama is that the president has, much to the chagrin of many of his supporters and immigration advocates, deported very large numbers of individuals – two million as of early 2014 – who have not been in compliance with American residency requirements. In spite of this fact, his Republican Party critics have repeatedly attacked him for his permissiveness in enabling law breaking and endangering U.S. national security. And when voices in the GOP have emerged to try to cobble together a deal that would combine some form of path to citizenship or indefinite residence, even combined with tougher action on the border, they've been met with the charge of "sell out" for enabling "amnesty."

The story of Marco Rubio is particularly relevant here. A Cuban American, Rubio was elected senator from Florida in the Republican wave of 2010. He was considered a Tea Party darling, a young, charismatic firebrand who was deemed well positioned to help modernize the party's demographic appeal while reflecting the preferences of the staunchly conservative grassroots. After Obama's victory in the 2012 elections, there were numerous GOP efforts to engage in soul-searching about why the controversial Obama, even presiding over a tepid economic recovery, could win a second decisive electoral and popular vote victory. Indeed, a widely publicized Republican National Committee "autopsy" concluded that the GOP was "out of touch" with a changing America and needed to be more inclusive. Increasingly, it recognized, it was becoming the party of older white Americans, weighed down by a message and approach that did not appeal to the young, to women, or to a more culturally diverse country.

After Obama's 2012 victory, some GOP leaders believed the time was right to pursue immigration reform. Because of his own background and because he was already being considered a front-runner for the 2016 GOP nomination, Rubio took the lead in trying to craft a conservative proposal that would nevertheless do more than merely beef up patrols and build a high-tech fence along the Mexican-American border. Instructively, Rubio's efforts failed utterly. He simply could not galvanize support among those in his party for his efforts. In the bargain, he severely damaged his own viability for president in 2016 despite his rock-solid conservative voting record and his own often hard-edged rhetoric about amnesty and reform. Likewise, many observers traced the flagging of Texas Governor Rick Perry's own presidential ambitions to his moderate statements on immigration reform in early 2012, even before his gaffe proneness became a central concern.

Williamson, Skocpol, and Coggins (2011) argue that immigration was an especially important issue for self-identified Tea Party adherents. There were multiple sources of concern: (1) that President Obama was planning to declare a mass amnesty in order to cultivate a significant new bloc of voters, (2) that immigrants receive undue government support, draining resources from already-strapped public coffers and deepening the gulf between hardworking Americans and free-loaders, and (3) a general anxiety about border security in a world run amok. Interestingly, worry about illegal immigrants "stealing" American jobs was not among the primary worries Tea Party supporters expressed about this group of people (Williamson, Skocpol, and Coggins 2011). As we will discuss further, that may be related to the way in which Tea Party supporters divide the world more broadly – into the deserving and undeserving. This construct is crucial to understanding their worldview and consistent with our understanding of the clear but complex ways that fear of change and antipathy to difference intersect among more authoritarian-minded individuals.

Gay Marriage

One of the most publicized moments of the 2012 Republican nomination fight took place during a debate in which Megyn Kelly showed a YouTube clip of a soldier, Stephen Hill. In the clip, Hill said that he'd had to hide who he was until the just completed repeal of Don't Ask, Don't Tell. Some in the assembled audience booed. More notable was the lack of reaction from any of the candidates present, none of whom wanted to speak up to defend a man who'd served his country in the armed forces. Additionally, Rick Santorum, who would go on to a surprisingly strong showing as Mitt Romney's main challenger for the nomination, specifically spoke out against Don't Ask, Don't Tell, decrying it as "social engineering" in the armed forces. To be clear, Santorum did not advocate allowing gay men and women to serve openly. Instead, he wanted everyone to revert to the policy that pre-dated DADT.

It is noteworthy that, as backdrop to this event, as many as 80 percent of Americans were telling pollsters they favored repealing DADT in favor of a policy that allowed gay service members to serve openly. This apparent disconnect between the GOP base and the electorate as a whole provides further evidence that Republicans have become more conservative over the past few decades and activist conservatives have come to comprise a growing share of the Republican Party (Abramowitz 2011). That development, Abramowitz contends, facilitated the rise of the Tea Party in 2009, a cohort of especially conservative Republicans who skewed older, more male, and more religious. The issue of DADT provides interesting insight into the internal dynamics of this increasingly conservative party. According to 2010 data, 44 percent of self-identified Republicans who were not Tea Party supporters opposed the end of DADT. By contrast, fully 71 percent of Tea Party Republicans did. The Tea Party is not co-terminous with the GOP,[5] but its staunch brand of conservatism is an increasing component of the Republican base. And in turn, it is especially heavily influenced by authoritarian disposition.

Without question, gay marriage is a more hotly contested issue than is DADT or its repeal. Interestingly, as public opinion has shifted dramatically in favor of same-sex marriage in recent years, the gap between Democrats and Republicans on the issue has widened, with Democrats now thirty points more favorably disposed toward gay marriage than Republicans. Especially

---

[5] When asked whether they oppose federal funding for clean energy research, only 32 percent of Republicans who don't support the Tea Party said they did. By contrast, 81 percent of Tea Party supporting Republicans did, a whopping 49-point spread (Abramowitz 2011: 22).

interesting here are the generational dynamics. According to a recent Pew poll, 61 percent of Republicans under 30 favor same-sex marriage. By contrast, only 22 percent of Republicans over 65 do.[6]

GOP party leaders, overwhelmingly, share the sentiments of the older Republicans. Of 55 serving senators who as of this writing have expressed support publicly for same-sex marriage, three are Republicans. Mark Kirk of Illinois expressed his support in part, he said, as a result of a near-death experience following a stroke, and Rob Portman of Ohio came out in support after acknowledging that he had a gay son. The third, Alaska's Lisa Murkowski, won her senate seat without receiving the endorsement of her state GOP. In the House of Representatives, of 182 members who have publicly endorsed same-sex marriage, exactly one is a Republican. As of this writing, no state Republican committee has come out in support of gay marriage. In sum, while public opinion is moving fast on the ground, especially among younger Republican voters, and the party's efforts to "modernize" itself and appeal to younger voters would likely benefit substantially from more explicit support for marriage equality, that position remains a fringe one among high-level GOP officials.

Obamacare

No issue has received more sustained and intense scrutiny nor been a more enduring focus of vitriolic disagreement among partisans in the past five years than the Affordable Care Act. Passed in March of 2010, after nearly a year of rancorous debate, repeated compromise, and negotiations, the final bill slipped through the Senate reconciliation process without a single Republican vote. And in the years leading up to the opening of the much-anticipated (and dreaded) federal and related state exchanges, acrimony has been the order of the day. While Obamacare is, on the one hand a bread-and-butter issue, it can be understood in terms of its symbolic dimensions, especially since it has repeatedly been characterized in apocalyptic terms as a threat to the very nature of American society as we know it. Invocations of "death panels" emerged as a mantra among Obamacare opponents. References to Obamacare as Stalinist and a government takeover of the economy have also been rife, both at the grassroots and among officeholders, with repeated dire warnings about its passage auguring "the end of America as we know it."

Notable about Obamacare, from the perspective of Tea Party supporters, is that it may be anathema less because it represents a generic expansion of big government, and more because of who its intended beneficiaries are perceived to be. As Williamson, Skocpol, and Coggins (2011: 32) report,

---

[6] "61% of Young Republicans Favor Same Sex Marriage," *Pew Research*, March 10, 2014. Retrieved from http://www.pewresearch.org/fact-tank/2014/03/10/61-of-young-republicans-favor-same-sex-marriage/.

"[T]he concerns of Tea Partiers ... should not be confused with blanket opposition to all federal social programs." They note that Tea Party supporters are favorably disposed toward Social Security and Medicare, by far the two biggest government programs. Media accounts have repeatedly highlighted the phenomenon of Tea Party supporters having themselves relied, at some point, on unemployment insurance, food stamps, or other government support programs.[7]

Perhaps this phenomenon can partly be explained by what Mettler (2011) has described as the "submerged state," the peculiar and opaque manner in which many Americans receive government largesse, obscuring who is and isn't a beneficiary of government assistance. This phenomenon may help to shed light on Tea Party opposition to certain kinds of "government handouts" to certain kinds of people. Williamson, Skocpol, and Coggins (2011: 33) suggest that while the distinction between "working and nonworking people is fundamental to tea party ideology, the empirical dividing line between those categories is not immediately clear."[8] Thus, they argue, the definition of "working" may be "an implicit cultural category rather than a straightforward definition" (2011: 33). The iconic image of a retiree at a town hall meeting during the raucous summer of 2009 screaming "[K]eep your goddamn government hands off my Medicare" (Rountree 2013: 47) reflects well the culturally complex – as opposed to empirically or logically straightforward – nature of Tea Party opposition to Obamacare.

As we've noted earlier, to the extent that a core feature of authoritarianism is opposition to change, especially when tethered to how that change might benefit certain disfavored groups, the link between Tea Party opposition to Obamacare and authoritarian influence on the GOP base is intriguing. As Williamson, Skocpol, and Coggins (2011: 34) put it, nonworking and suspect individuals "who have unduly profited from government programs" have "wrested control of the government from hardworking average Americans." And Obama has been the agent of that seizure of power, which they regard as fundamentally illegitimate. It is this usurpation, "rather than any absolutist

---

[7] Appearing on Glenn Beck's program on FOX in 2009, the noted actor Craig T. Nelson said he was considering no longer paying taxes because he didn't want to bail people out who didn't deserve it. Nelson complained: "They're not going to bail me out ... I've been on food stamps and welfare. Anybody help me out? No. No." As noted previously, such sentiments have been very widely reported in recent years. See the June 18, 2009, interview at https://www.youtube.com/watch?v=yTwpBLzxe4U.

[8] The most famous assertion of an "us-versus-them" mindset dividing the hardworking and deserving from the undeserving and "entitled" was, of course, Mitt Romney's leaked comments in 2012: "There are 47 percent of the people who will vote for the president no matter what. All right, there are 47 percent who are with him, who are dependent upon government, who believe that they are victims, who believe that government has a responsibility to care for them, who believe that they are entitled to health care, to food, to housing, to you name it. That that's an entitlement. And the government should give it to them. And they will vote for this president no matter what." They can be viewed at https://www.youtube.com/watch?v=M2gvY2wqI7M.

commitment to free-market principles," that may explain Tea Party opposition to Obamacare and other government programs. This is a story that would certainly be consistent with authoritarianism, as we understand it.

As a final consideration for now, it's also worth noting that, in spite of the initial reporting of the Tea Party as primarily concerned with a kind of libertarian agenda, numerous polls have found that members of the religious right comprise a majority of Tea Party adherents. Mike Lofgren, the long-time GOP congressional staffer who wrote a much-discussed dissection of the contemporary Republican Party in 2011[9], noted that a higher percentage of Tea Partiers than self-described Christian conservatives agreed with the statement "America has always been and is currently a Christian nation." Lofgren contended that this religious outlook, connected to the dominant influence of Christian Dominionism among important GOP leaders such as Rick Perry, Rick Santorum, and Michele Bachmann (each of whom vied for the presidential nomination in 2012), helped explain the resonance of the "death panel" charge. The charge itself, of course, originated with another GOPer associated with Dominionism, Sarah Palin. In our book, we noted that no single variable correlated with authoritarianism more strongly than belief that the Bible was the literal word of God. We do not contend, on this basis, that all those who score high in authoritarianism are religiously motivated, nor do we believe that all Christian conservatives score high in authoritarianism. But a shared sensibility between Tea Party support and Christian conservatism, anchored in an authoritarian worldview, does seem apparent.

Two Other Considerations

Though they are not policy issues or clusters, we consider two other developments significant to our discussion: (1) the emergence of a kind of factual know-nothingism that we believe is emblematic of the larger divide we discuss and (2) an inescapably racialized discourse around the president.

Factual Know-Nothingism

Specifically, important elements of the Republican Party have become increasingly hostile to what we can only describe as facts. One obvious example is anthropogenic climate change, about which there is a scientific consensus but about which the GOP, as a party, is openly derisive. In a 2014 debate among four Republicans candidates for one of North Carolina's United States Senate seats, every candidate spoke fervently against the idea. Indeed, one's political viability in the Republican Party is under threat if one affirms the validity of human-induced climate change. Another example was the bizarre

---

[9] Mike Lofgren, "Goodbye to All That: Reflections of a GOP Operative Who Left the Cult," *Truthout*, September 3, 2011. http://www.truth-out.org/index.php?option=com_k2&view=item&id=3079:goodbye-to-all-that-reflections-of-a-gop-operative-who-left-the-cult.

case of President Obama's birth certificate, about which there was a nearly three-year-long effort by significant elements of the GOP to expose as fraudulent, championed by, among others, a one-time (if brief) front-runner for the 2012 Republican presidential nomination, Donald Trump.

Likewise, in 2012, an obscure analyst, Dean Chambers, became an overnight sensation among conservatives for claiming that there was a systematic and deliberate effort by mainstream pollsters to "skew" the results of pre-election polls in favor of President Obama. Chambers' "methodology," such as it was, proved to be little more than a joke. And yet, for a few heady weeks in the fall of 2012, he enjoyed a meteoric ascent as a folk hero in conservative circles. The reality of the past five years is that we could go on and on with similar examples.

Two points are important to make here. The first is that we are not claiming that Democrats and liberals have no factual biases. Of course they do. And in the current political climate, there seems little doubt that both sides are especially dug in and particularly ungenerous in considering the perspectives and viewpoints of those they face across the political barricades. Those hunting for the liberal equivalent of the right's denial of climate change often invoke discussion of vaccinations, and their now (debunked) connection to autism. But the example proves the rule. There is no litmus test in Democratic circles mandating opposition to the widespread use of vaccinations. In fact, there is no mainstream Democrat in Congress pushing such an agenda. Furthermore, the evolution of opinion on that issue has progressed precisely in the way one would expect, in that fact-based premises were, in the end, determinative. First, there was widespread, if misguided, belief in a certain idea. Then more evidence came in undermining that belief. As a consequence, many changed their minds in conformity with the new information. Virtually no Democratic Party elites now espouse such views.

No such process has unfolded on the right in connection with climate change. Indeed, the more the evidence mounts that it is real, enduring, human-induced, and of profound consequence, the more the right digs in to deny that this is so.

The second point is that open defiance of knowledge by elites has itself become an important part of conservative identity. This is one reason why we've witnessed the fascinating development whereby better-educated conservatives are *more* consistently hostile to science than are less educated ones. As Gauchat (2012) has argued, hostility to science when it is connected to politicized issues has now become central to conservative identity. As it happens, this mindset is particularly strong among those who score high in authoritarianism.[10]

---

[10] Summarizing recent polling data about Tea Party members' distrust of scientists, the journalist Chris Mooney wrote: "It's one of the biggest trends in US politics over the last decade: A growing left-right split over the validity of scientific information." Retrieved from http://www.mother-jones.com/environment/2014/05/tea-party-climate-trust-science (May 20, 2014).

Racialized Discourse

President Obama's unique origin as the son of a white American woman and a black Kenyan man has been a source of fascination and consternation ever since he emerged on the national scene. As noted previously, one manifestation of the latter was a dogged effort over several years to "prove" he wasn't born in the United States and therefore was not a valid presidential candidate, despite the fact that he had one indisputably American parent. The "birther" movement aside, there has been an endless stream of statements about the president that resonate with political scientists' efforts to measure racial resentment by gauging how much Americans accept certain assertions about blacks' sense of their own victimization, their work ethic, and the validity of their grievances against American society.

Among GOP elites, there are too many incidents to mention, but a few are worth noting. In the fall of 2012, Sarah Palin criticized President Obama's failure to be forthcoming about the events in Benghazi, Libya, that resulted in the murder of the American Ambassador, Chris Stevens. Palin said the president's "shuck and jive with these lies"[11] must end. She later insisted she intended no racial connotations in the statement, but many critics thought the connection obvious.

Former Speaker of the House and 2012 presidential aspirant Newt Gingrich, perhaps trying to revive old welfare tropes in connection with a black and Democratic president, called Obama the "food stamp president."[12] Governor Mitt Romney himself, during the campaign, characterized an administrative change in Temporary Aid to Needy Families as a plan for welfare under Obama in which "you wouldn't have to work and you wouldn't have to train for a job. They just send you a welfare check."[13] Most observers considered this an extreme distortion of the change itself, but the telling fact was the appeal to a set of associations with a long provenance in American political culture, dating to the emergence of the race-based arc of issue evolution that Carmines and Stimson (1989) traced from the 1960s. Another Romney surrogate, John Sununu, a former Republican governor and White House Chief of Staff, variously called Obama "lazy and detached"[14] and said he needed to "learn how to be an American,"[15] a statement it's hard to imagine being made about,

[11] Kevin Cirilli, "Sarah Palin Defends 'Shuck and Jive,'" *Politico*, October 24, 2012. Retrieved from http://www.politico.com/news/stories/1012/82832.html.

[12] Ezra Klein, "Gingrich Says Obama Is the Food Stamp President. Is He?" *Washington Post*, January 18, 2012. Retrieved from http://www.washingtonpost.com/blogs/ezra-klein/post/gingrich-says-obama-is-the-food-stamp-president-is-he/2012/01/18/gIQA1Ino8P_blog.html.

[13] Tom Foreman and Eric Marrapodi, "Fact Check: Romney's Welfare Claims Wrong," *CNN*, August 3, 2012. Retrieved from http://www.cnn.com/2012/08/23/politics/fact-check-welfare/.

[14] Daniel Straus, "Romney Surrogate Sununu Calls Obama 'Lazy and Detached,'" *The Hill*, October 3, 2012. Retrieved from http://thehill.com/video/campaign/260321-romney-surrogate-sununu-calls-obama-lazy.

[15] "Sununu: Obama Needs to 'Learn How to Be an American,'" *Real Clear Politics* Video, July 17, 2012. Retrieved from http://www.realclearpolitics.com/video/2012/07/17/sununu_obama_needs_to_learn_how_to_be_an_american.html.

say, Bill Clinton. Returning to Gingrich, the former Speaker said in 2012 that Obama wasn't a "real president," and that "he doesn't do anything that presidents do, he doesn't worry about any of the things the presidents do."

In the same soliloquy, Gingrich mused: "You have to wonder what he's doing," Gingrich continued.

I'm assuming that there's some rhythm to Barack Obama that the rest of us don't understand. Whether he needs large amounts of rest, whether he needs to go play basketball for a while or watch ESPN, I mean, I don't quite know what his rhythm is, but this is a guy that is a brilliant performer as an orator, who may very well get reelected at the present date, and who, frankly, he happens to be a partial, part-time president.[16]

One might argue that in his reference to "rhythm," "basketball," and lack of work ethic, Gingrich had hit the racial resentment trifecta. But the larger point is that these statements – and this is an infinitesimal sampling – reflect powerfully the state of political discourse in recent years, the salience of a particular way of characterizing our first president of color, and fit well within a political landscape in which such appeals would find resonance with a substantial swath of American society, particularly those who score high in authoritarianism and who comprise a substantial proportion of self-identified Republicans.

QUANTITATIVE EVIDENCE OF THE CONTINUATION OF WORLDVIEW EVOLUTION

Beyond our qualitative analysis, we can also bring to bear survey-based evidence to suggest that authoritarianism continues to play an important role in structuring American politics. Since we can use more data points from YouGov surveys than ANES surveys, we use the former here. In addition, we focus all our data analysis that follow on white respondents only. Research subsequent to our book has demonstrated that the parenting battery designed to measure authoritarianism works well for whites, but not for racial minorities (Perez and Hetherington 2014). Specifically, racial and ethnic minorities score extraordinarily high in authoritarianism using this measure, but their scores do not correlate with the variables that they are supposed to correlate with. Only for whites are the relationships as they should be. Hence we focus on this group.

To measure authoritarianism, we follow many others in using the following four items, which ask people to express their opinions about desirable characteristics in children. Specifically, the questions are prefaced by the following paragraph:

[16] Jonathan Easley, "Gingrich Disparages Obama, Calls Him 'Not a Real President,'" *The Hill*, September 26, 2012. Retrieved from http://thehill.com/video/campaign/258689-gingrich-obama-not-a-real-president.

Although there are a number of qualities that people feel that children should have, every person thinks that some are more important than others. Listed below are pairs of desirable qualities. For each pair please mark which one you think is more important for a child to have:

1. Independence or respect for elders
2. Obedience or self-reliance
3. Curiosity or good manners
4. Being considerate or well behaved

Those who answer respect for elders, obedience, good manners, and being well behaved score at the scale's maximum. Those who answer independence, self-reliance, curiosity, and being considerate score at the scale's minimum.

We begin our exploration with the fundamentals: vote choice and party identification. Of course, 2010 was a particularly good year for Republicans in both Senate and House elections. The data in Figure 1 suggest that the loyalty of those scoring high in authoritarianism was a big reason why. In U.S. Senate elections, fully 78 percent of respondents who provided all four authoritarian responses to the parenting battery voted for Republican candidates. Nearly that percentage, 71 percent, who provided three authoritarian respondents did the same. The differences between the most and least authoritarian could hardly be

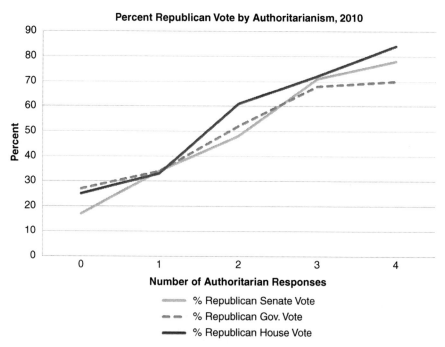

FIGURE 1. Percent Republican Vote by Authoritarianism, 2010

starker. A mere 17 percent of those who provided zero authoritarian responses to the parenting battery cast their Senate ballots for the Republican candidate. This means that, moving from most to least authoritarian, Senate voting behavior differed by about 60 percentage points.

The divide was similarly deep for House voting in 2010. At this level, a remarkable 84 percent of those scoring highest in authoritarianism voted Republican. In contrast, only 25 percent of those who scored at the minimum of the authoritarianism scale voted Republican, creating a 59-point difference between most and least authoritarian. The effect of authoritarian was somewhat smaller for gubernatorial voting. Here 70 percent of the most authoritarian and 27 percent of the least authoritarian voted Republican. The "across-the-range" difference is "only" 43 percentage points, a gap that seems small merely because the effect sizes for national political office voting were so large.

Authoritarianism's effect on voting was slightly smaller in 2012 than in 2010, but it was still very substantial. These results appear in Figure 2. As for Senate voting, 16 percent of those scoring at the minimum of the authoritarianism scale cast their ballot for the Republican, compared with 68 percent on the high end of the scale. Although the difference from minimum to maximum here is only 52 points in 2012 as opposed to 61 points in 2010, no

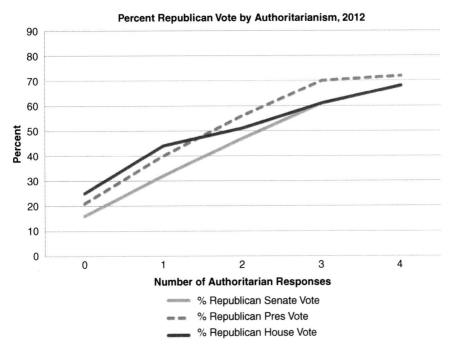

FIGURE 2. Percent Republican Vote by Authoritarianism, 2012

one would suggest that an effect of that size is not large. House voting followed a similar pattern. As in 2010, only 25 percent of nonauthoritarians voted Republican compared with 68 percent of authoritarians. Since so few gubernatorial races were on the ballot in 2012, we cannot estimate authoritarianism's effect on this level of voting with any precision.

Of course, 2012 featured a presidential race, and authoritarianism powerfully structured voting at this level as well. High-scoring authoritarians were overwhelming likely to vote Republican, with 72 percent of those providing four authoritarian responses and 70 percent of those providing three voting for Romney. Those scoring lowest in authoritarianism were even more overwhelmingly for Obama than those scoring highest were for Romney. Indeed, only 21 percent of those providing zero authoritarian responses voted for Romney. The difference from minimum to maximum in 2012 presidential voting checks in at a remarkable 51 percentage points.

Given authoritarianism's strong relationship with voting behavior, it should not be surprising that its relationship with partisanship remains robust as well since our original writing. Recall from Chapter 7 of our book that party identification and authoritarianism were uncorrelated as recently as 1992 and possessed only the faintest of correlations in 2000. A core feature of our theory of worldview evolution is the strengthening correlation between party and worldview. We see that process continuing through 2010 and 2012. Specifically, the five-point parenting battery is positively correlated with the seven-point party identification scale in both years at roughly 0.3 (0.33 in 2010 and 0.28 in 2012). This is a strong correlation when using survey data.

Presenting the differences in mean partisanship based on levels of authoritarianism allows a more visually compelling picture of what correlations of this size mean. We use the patchwork of data we have available from 1992 through 2012, which includes the four-item parenting battery. We map the seven-point partisanship scale onto a (0,1) interval, so differences in partisanship between entries can be interpreted as percentage point differences. The results appear in Figure 3. There was no difference in partisanship between the most and least authoritarian in 1992, and a difference of only 13 percentage points as recently as 2002. Focusing on the presidential election years, we see that 2004 saw a 22-percentage-point difference between the most and least authoritarian, with the difference growing to 29 points in 2008. In 2012, the partisanship difference reached 32 points. This is a very large difference on the most fundamentally important variable in the study of mass politics.

Not surprisingly, these differences also manifest themselves in terms of approval rating. The results of this analysis appear in Figure 4. In both 2010 and 2012, we find roughly a 50 percentage point difference between the most and least authoritarian in their approval of the first African-American president. In 2010, two-thirds of minimum scoring authoritarians continued to approve of the president during the doldrums following the Great Recession. Only

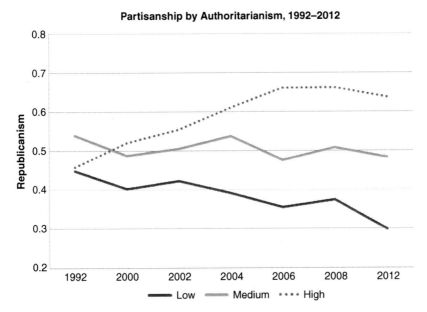

FIGURE 3. Partisanship by Authoritarianism, 1992–2012

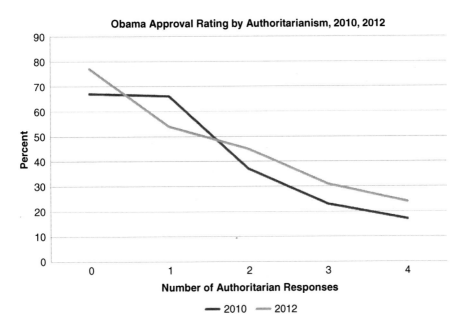

FIGURE 4. Obama's Approval Rating by Authoritarianism, 2010–12

17 percent of maximum scoring authoritarians did. The approval ratings of the least and most were 77 percent and 24 percent, respectively, in 2012.

Although Republican partisans were all but universally disapproving in both years, it is interesting to examine variation in Obama's approval rating by authoritarianism among Democrats. In 2012, for example, Obama's approval was 99 percent among those providing zero authoritarian responses to the parenting battery. Among the relatively small number of Democrats who provided four such responses, Obama's approval rating was only 64 percent.

Authoritarianism and the Issues

A detailed treatment of authoritarianism's relationship with all issues is beyond the scope of this chapter. But we want to highlight that its relationship to several issues we identified previously persists and that its relationship with other issue preferences seems to have emerged more recently. For this analysis, we rely on Vanderbilt's portion of the 2010 CCES survey. The dependent variables we explore in Figure 5 were all issues that Congress debated during the session leading up to the survey. Respondents were asked if they would have voted for or against the items had they been members of Congress themselves.

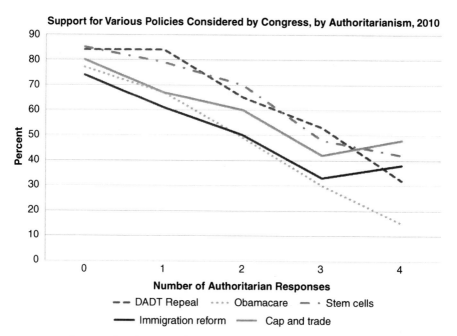

FIGURE 5. Support for Various Policies Considered by Congress, by Authoritarianism, 2010

We start this discussion with items that are familiar to those who read our book. Support for the repeal of the military's Don't Ask, Don't Tell (DADT) policy, a key item in the gay rights agenda, is strongly related to authoritarianism. Specifically, 84 percent of those who provided either zero or one authoritarian response to the parenting battery supported DADT repeal. Among those who provided four authoritarian responses, however, only 32 percent did. Put another way, those scoring highest and lowest were better than 50 points different in their support for the major item on the gay rights agenda that came before Congress in 2010.

The results for comprehensive immigration reform are also striking and supportive of our reasoning about why the GOP struggles with resolving this issue despite the clear case for potential electoral benefits. Not surprisingly, about three-quarters of those scoring at the authoritarianism minimum supported immigration reform. In contrast, only 38 percent of those scoring at the maximum did, and only a third of those who provided three authoritarian responses did. Such low levels of support among what has become the Republican base surely ties the hands of GOP elites who have an eye on diversifying the party. Also as expected, support for stem cell research is strongly a function of authoritarianism. Better than 70 percent of each category providing two or fewer authoritarian responses supports federal money for stem cell research. Yet fewer than 50 percent of those in each of the two categories providing three or four authoritarian responses do.

Finally we turn to two issues that we did not explore in our original work, but which now appear to be strongly associated with authoritarianism, namely Obamacare and environmentalism. The 2010 survey question makes no specific reference to Barack Obama or Obamacare, yet the support line for this item is steeper than any of the others. Whereas 77 percent of those scoring at the minimum of authoritarianism supported health care reform, only 15 percent of those scoring at the maximum did. This 62-percentage-point difference across authoritarianism's range is larger than for any of the other issues.

Support for cap and trade, an environmental vehicle introduced by conservatives two decades before but now championed mostly by those on the left, also produces remarkable results. Here, 80 percent of pure non-authoritarians provide support, whereas 48 percent and 42 percent of those providing four and three authoritarian responses, respectively, provide support. This is one of several issues for which those who score in the second highest category of authoritarianism provide more conservative preferences than those scoring at the maximum, a pattern we do not have a ready answer for.

Beyond cap and trade, we find further evidence for the importance of authoritarianism in understanding preferences about the environment. For example, in both the 2010 and 2012 CCES studies, there appeared a question asking people to rate the degree to which they thought climate change was a serious problem. In both years, the correlation between authoritarianism and these assessments was about −0.3, a strong relationship indeed. This issue area is particularly interesting to us. We suspect that there is nothing inevitable about a relationship between authoritarianism and preferences about environmental protection. When opposition to environmentalism in the larger political dialogue is couched in terms of skepticism about science, however, it will generate significant differences between those disposed to be comfortable with the messiness of scientific inquiry and those who tend to be skeptical of such things.

Authoritarianism and the Tea Party

Finally, we see manifestations of the divide in the rise of the Tea Party movement. When we were writing in the first years of the twenty-first century, this staunchly anti-government force did not exist. Yet, by the 2010 midterm elections, it had become a force to be reckoned with, providing passion and vigor to politics on the right. Of course, being anti-government does not make it authoritarian. However, Tea Party conservatives are particularly concerned about big government as it relates to racialized programs, but are not so concerned about big government when they, themselves, benefit from it. Perhaps not surprisingly, Parker and Barreto (2013) find that Tea Party identifiers were even more likely to score high in racial resentment than other white conservatives. This suggests that race, rather than broad anti-government sentiment, might be a key motivating factor behind the Tea Party movement.

We are by no means first to write about the authoritarian foundations of the Tea Party movement's attractiveness. Williamson, Skocpol, and Coggins (2011) and Arceneaux and Nicholson (2012) were first to the party, the latter more explicitly than the former. Here we find some evidence to suggest that evaluations of the Tea Party may be sharpening along authoritarian lines as time goes on. Specifically, we examine Americans' favorability of the Tea Party movement. We transformed both scales onto a (0, 1) interval again, so differences between categories can be interpreted as percentage point differences.

The results appear in Figure 6, with data drawn from both 2010 and 2012. In both years, the line is fairly steep. In 2010, the mean favorability score provided by those scoring lowest in authoritarianism was only .263, compared with .616 among those scoring at the highest end of the authoritarianism scale. Across its range, then, the effect of authoritarianism is about 35 percentage points. In 2012, the difference increases somewhat (43 percentage points), owing to the increasing negativity of those at the bottom of the authoritarianism scale. Whereas all the other categories remain statistically the same from 2010 to 2012, those providing zero authoritarian answers to the parenting battery dropped in their favorability toward the Tea Party by nearly 10 percentage points.

Taken together, all this seems to us to be strong evidence that the worldview divide we identified is at least as strong now as it was when we published our

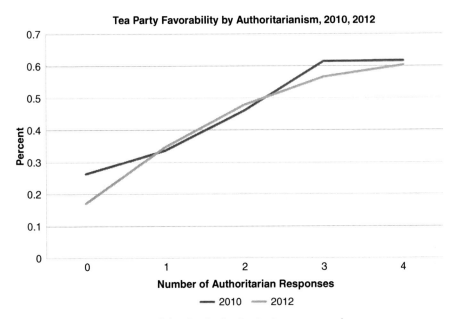

FIGURE 6. Tea Party Favorability by Authoritarianism, 2010 and 2012

book in 2009. Indeed, we believe there is much here to suggest that the divide has only continued to deepen and widen with time.

CONCLUSION

Although our work was very much an outlier in 2009 as far as research approach was concerned, we are no longer alone in identifying a partisan/ideological divide in public opinion based on fundamental personality differences in human beings. Our work is perhaps better considered as among the first in what is turning into something of a growth industry in political science. The labels are different, but what underlies the labels seems to be substantively similar to what we uncovered.

Gerber et al. (2010) tied Big Five personality characteristics to party identification. Although they found relationships between several of the Big Five and partisanship, their results are strongest for two of them: openness to experience and conscientiousness. Buttressing confidence in these results, other scholars have unearthed similar findings for these two of the Big Five (see Hibbing, Smith, and Alford 2013 for details). It is hard to miss in these renderings some of the characteristics that we identified in nonauthoritarians and those who score high in openness. Both are the types of people who, on average, will find themselves trying many different new dishes at Thai restaurants before attending an abstract art show at an edgy urban museum.

On the other side of the divide, those who score high in conscientiousness and those who score high in authoritarianism appear to share a lot in common. Both thrive on order and established conventions. We suspect that both would favor the tradition-mindedness of rural and some suburban areas. Indeed we suspect that some version of this construct is the underlying characteristic that explains why liberals and conservatives are decreasingly likely to live in the same areas (Bishop 2008). It is not that politics is sufficiently important to people for them to choose specific places to live. Rather, it is valuing things that are time-honored or edgy and different that is correlated both with residential decisions and political identities these days.

Several of the characteristics that divide authoritarians from non-authoritarians also crop up in the emerging biopolitics literature. This literature has identified a range of physiological differences between liberals and conservatives. Although the dependent variable, for the most part, in these works is ideology, not partisanship, the distinction between the two is much thinner now that the parties have become so much better sorted by ideology over the last decade or two (Fiorina et al. 2005).

Specifically, Hibbing, Smith, and Alford (2013) demonstrate and catalogue remarkable differences in gaze behavior, gag reflex, startle reflex, and much more. In situating their contribution to understanding politics, they explicitly point to its similarity to the authoritarian/nonauthoritarian divide. It is important to note that this literature is in its infancy, with many of its key findings resting on studies involving fewer than 100 nonrandomly selected subjects. However, we suspect the physiological differences that they unearth are likely to be replicated in future studies. If personality/worldview differences exist, it seems quite plausible that physiological differences would exist as well.

Finally, Jonathan Haidt (especially comprehensively in *The Righteous Mind*) and his collaborators have identified striking differences in the moral reasoning in which liberals and conservatives engage. Liberals tend to value the harm/fairness dimension of morality over others, whereas conservatives tend to weigh a range of competing moral considerations more evenly. We appreciate these findings, in particular, because they point out that, regardless of ideology or party identification, people try to think about the world in moral terms. Neither liberals nor conservatives are bad people. Neither has the market cornered on the correct approach to life. The key point is that they do not necessarily understand the other's way of thinking about politics. When certain issues become manifest, what is moral to one side may well be immoral to the other. Since so many of those issues are salient today, it is that difference in their reaction to circumstances that makes contemporary politics seem so difficult to navigate. As we have detailed in this chapter, we do not expect this type of conflict to disappear any time soon.

REFERENCES

Abramowitz, Alan. 2011. "Partisan Polarization and the Rise of the Tea Party Movement." Paper delivered at the Annual Meeting of the American Political Science Association, Seattle, Washington, September 1–4.

Abramowitz, Alan. 2010. *The Disappearing Center: Engaged Citizens, Polarization, and American Democracy*. New Haven, CT: Yale University Press.

Arceneaux, Kevin, and Stephen P. Nicholson. 2012. "Who Wants to Have a Tea Party?: The Who, What, and Why of the Tea Party Movement." *PS: Political Science and Politics* 45(4): 700–710.

Bishop, Bill. 2008. *The Big Sort: Why the Clustering of Like-Minded Americans Is Tearing Us Apart*. Boston: Mariner Books.

Carmines, Edward, and James Stimson. 1989. *Issue Evolution: Race and the Transformation of American Politics*. Princeton, NJ: Princeton University Press.

Fiorina, Morris, Samuel J. Abrams, and Jeremy C. Pope. 2005. *Culture War? The Myth of Polarized America*, 1st edition. New York: Pearson Longman.

Gauchat, Gordon. 2012. "Politicization of Science in the Public Sphere: A Study of Political Trust in the United States, 1974–2010." *American Sociological Review* 77(2): 167–187.

Gerber, Alan S., Gregory A. Huber, David Doherty, Conor M. Dowling, and Shang E. Ha. 2010. "Personality and Political Attitudes: Relationships across Issue Domains and Political Contexts." *American Political Science Review* 104 (1): 111–133.

Haidt, Jonathan A. 2013. *The Righteous Mind: Why Good People Are Divided by Politics and Religion*. New York: Vintage.

Hetherington, Marc J., and Thomas J. Rudolph. 2015. *Why Washington Won't Work: Polarization, Political Trust, and the Governing Crisis*. Chicago: University of Chicago Press.

Hetherington, Marc J., and Jonathan Weiler. 2009. *Authoritarianism and Polarization in American Politics*. New York: Cambridge University Press.

Hibbing, John R., Kevin Smith, and John Alford. 2013. *Predisposed: Liberals, Conservatives, and the Biology of Political Difference*. New York: Routledge.

Key, V. O. 1966. *The Responsible Electorate*. Cambridge, MA: Harvard University Press.

Key, V. O. 1961. *Public Opinion and American Democracy*. New York: Knopf.

McCright, Aaron M., and Riley E. Dunlap. 2011. "The Politicization of Climate Change and Polarization in the American Public's Views of Global Warming, 2001–2010." *The Sociological Quarterly* 52: 155–194.

Mettler, Suzanne. 2011. *The Submerged State: How Invisible Government Policies Undermine American Democracy*. Chicago: University of Chicago Press.

Mooney, Chris. 2014. "POLL: Tea Party Members Really, Really, Don't Trust Scientists." *Mother Jones*, May 20. Retrieved from http://www.motherjones.com/environment/2014/05/tea-party-climate-trust-science. Accessed on June 30, 2014.

Parker, Christopher S., and Matt A. Barreto. 2013. *Change They Can't Believe In: The Tea Party and Reactionary Politics in America*. Princeton, NJ: Princeton University Press.

Perez, Efren O., and Marc J. Hetherington. 2014. "Authoritarianism in Black and White: Testing the Cross-Racial Validity of the Child Rearing Scale." *Political Analysis* 22 (3): 398–412.

Rountree, Clark. 2013. *Venomous Speech: Problems in Political Speech on the Right and Left*. Westport, CT: Praeger Publishers.

Tesler, Michael. 2012. "The Spillover of Racialization into Health Care: How President Obama Polarized Public Opinion by Race and Racial Attitudes." *American Journal of Political Science* 56 (3): 690–704.

Tesler, Michael, and David Sears. 2010. *Obama's Race: The 2008 Election and the Dream of a Post-Racial America*. Chicago: University of Chicago Press.

Williamson, Vanessa, Theda Skocpol, and William Coggin. 2011. "The Tea Party and the Remaking of Republican Conservatism." *Perspectives on Politics* 9 (1): 25–43.

Zaller, John R. 2013. "What Nature and Origins Leaves Out." *Critical Review* 24: 569–642.

Zaller, John R. 1992. *The Nature and Origins of Mass Opinion*. Cambridge: Cambridge University Press.

5

Party Sorting

The Foundations of Polarized Politics

Samuel J. Abrams and Morris P. Fiorina

- A political cleavage illustrates polarization when the extremes grow at the expense of the middle.
- Whether one looks at partisan, ideological, or issue cleavages, the American electorate shows no evidence of polarization; the middle has not shrunk.
- The American electorate has sorted – the parties are more internally homogeneous and more distinct from each other.
- Party sorting increases inter-party conflict and makes cross-party compromise more difficult.

In the early years of the twenty-first century, the national media adopted a narrative promoted by a coterie of scholars, pundits, and politicos. According to the narrative, Americans were combatants in a culture war between red and blue states. Our country had become a 50/50 nation with no neutrals to mediate between the opposing sides. The United States of America had deteriorated into the Divided States of America. This narrative nicely met the media's concept of newsworthiness – division, polarization, battles, war! But to political scientists familiar with public opinion data, the narrative was puzzling.

If one thinks about polarization in partisan terms, the American public did not look much different than it had in the 1970s. As shown in Figure 1, the proportion of Democrats was a little smaller than in the 1970s and the proportion of Republicans a little larger. After 1984, there is almost no change. Rather than the middle – in this case, nonpartisans – having disappeared, it is slightly larger today than in the 1970s.

Similarly, if one thinks about polarization in ideological terms, the American public looked about the same as it did in the 1970s. The proportion of self-identified liberals – always the least popular label (Free and Cantril 1967; Ellis and Stimson 2012) – trails the proportion of conservatives, which with a few small exceptions, trails the modal category – moderates. Again, the middle has not disappeared.

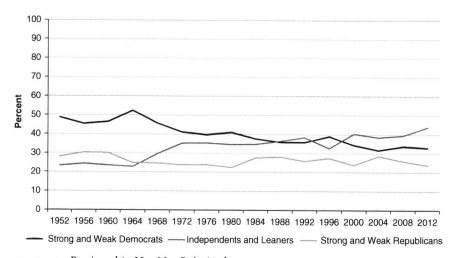

FIGURE 1. Partisanship Has Not Polarized
Source: Individual ANES files; all data has been weighted and uses FTF respondents only

If one thinks about polarization in terms of specific policy issues, the picture is less definitive because we do not have lengthy time series of data such as those previously described. But most data shows the American public clustering in the center, as on the seven-point scales included in the American National Election Studies (ANES) graphed in Figure 3.[1]

In sum, various academic databases provide little or no support for the polarization narrative. On the contrary, they show that the overall distribution of American public opinion has remained the same for more than a generation, despite the population turnover that has occurred during those decades.

POLARIZATION VS. SORTING

How could the polarization narrative become so widely accepted if there were no data to support it? The American electorate *had* changed in a very important way, just not in the way claimed by what Meyer (2014) calls the "polarization industrial complex." What the academic databases show is clear evidence of party sorting (Abramowitz and Saunders 1998; Levendusky 2009). To illustrate

---

[1] Abramowitz (2010: 38–39) recodes these scales and creates an index that shows some movement away from the center between 1984 and 2004. But as Broockman (2014) points out, this movement does not result from people adopting more extreme positions on the issues; rather, it reflects a somewhat higher correlation between issues. If one is slightly left of center on military spending, say, the likelihood that one is also left of center on health care is higher today than in 1984, a reflection of the party sorting that has occurred (Baldissarri and Gelman 2008).

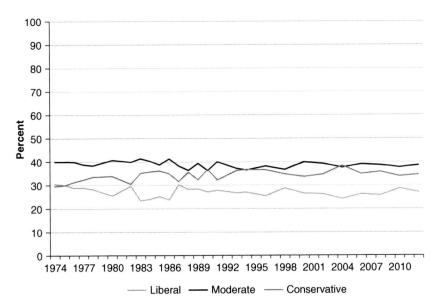

FIGURE 2. Ideology Has Not Polarized
Source: General Social Survey.

the difference between the two processes, consider two abstract examples. Figure 4 depicts a process of extreme polarization – the loss of the center to equal-sized extremes. At time 1, the electorate contains 50 unaligned moderates, a center-left Democratic Party with a moderate group and even a conservative faction, and a center-right Republican Party with the opposite configuration. But at time 2, the electorate has polarized: no moderates remain; everyone is now either a liberal Democrat or a conservative Republican. As Figures 1–3 show, that has *not* happened in the United States.

Figure 5, in contrast, is an abstract illustration of what *has* happened in the United States. At time 1, the situation is the same as that depicted in Figure 4, but at time 2, the electorate is better sorted. The marginal distributions of Republicans, Independent, and Democrats, Liberals, Moderates, and Conservatives remain the same as at time 1, but all conservatives are now in the Republican Party and all liberals are in the Democratic Party. The Democrats now are a decidedly liberal party and the Republicans a decidedly conservative party, with moderates hopelessly outnumbered in both.[2]

---

[2] How does sorting occur? Several types of conversion as well as replacement are implicated. Citizens can change their partisanship to match their ideology, or change their ideological position to match their partisanship (Layman and Carsey 2002). Moreover, since sorting takes place over time, liberals can leave the conservative party and vice versa, and newly enfranchised citizens can join the appropriate party.

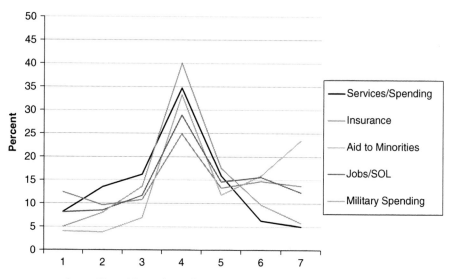

FIGURE 3. Issues Have Not Polarized, 2012
Source: ANES.
* "Haven't thought much about it" responses recoded as moderates.

	Democrats	Independents	Republicans
Time 1	50 Liberals 25 Moderates 25 Conservatives	50 Moderates	25 Liberals 25 Moderates 50 Conservatives
Time 2	125 Liberals	--------	125 Conservatives

FIGURE 4. Polarization

As we noted in an earlier piece (Fiorina and Abrams 2008: 577–578) one could refer to party sorting as partisan polarization, but we think that sorting more accurately describes the processes that have operated, and too often the modifier "partisan" is forgotten in discussions of partisan polarization, leading to confusion. A recent case in point is a major Pew Research Center report

	Democrats	Independents	Republicans
Time 1	50 Liberals 25 Moderates 25 Conservatives	50 Moderates	25 Liberals 25 Moderates 50 Conservatives
Time 2	75 Liberals 25 Moderates	50 Moderates	75 Conservatives 25 Moderates

FIGURE 5. Party Sorting

(2014) that provides a rich description of party sorting since the 1990s, but which created much confusion among political commentators because of its inaccurate title "Political Polarization in the American Public."[3] The critical distinction between the two processes involves the "middle." With polarization, increasingly distinctive partisan camps develop at the clear expense of the middle. With sorting, increasingly distinctive partisan camps do not necessarily entail a comparable decrease in non-partisans or those in the ideological or policy middle.[4]

To illustrate the process of sorting with a real political example, consider abortion. This issue often is viewed as highly polarizing. But while it clearly divides the political class (officeholders, candidates, activists, donors, interest group leaders), public opinion specialists long have recognized that the public is much less divided on the issue (Cook, Jelen, and Wilcox 1992). The best data comes from the General Social Survey, which has included the same abortion item for more than four decades. Figure 6 shows that there has been little movement on this issue during that period: in the aggregate the public looks about the same as it did in the 1970s. Three-quarters or more of the public favor legal abortion when the mother's health is threatened, the pregnancy results from rape, or there is a birth defect. When the reason for abortion is financial difficulty, the woman is unmarried, or the woman simply wants no more children, opinion is split. The average American believes abortion should be legal in slightly more than four of the six circumstances, and he and she have felt that way for four decades.

[3] An additional point of confusion among many commentators is that the data reflect the consistency of Americans' opinions rather than the extremity of their positions (Fiorina 2014). The report is clear on this point, but many readers have misunderstood the graphics.

[4] Obviously, the processes are not mutually exclusive. Both could operate simultaneously.

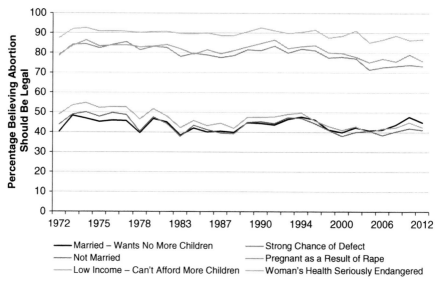

FIGURE 6. Should Abortion Be Legal? (GSS 1972–2012)
Source: General Social Survey.

Figure 7 shows how the public has sorted on the issue over that time span. The Supreme Court handed down the *Roe* decision in 1973, but for twenty years, partisans in the electorate were indistinguishable. In the early 1990s, however, they began to sort. Since then, Democrats have been more in favor of legal abortion than Republicans.

Figure 7 also shows two features commonly found in studies of party sorting. First, political elites sort before the larger electorate (Carmines and Stimson 1989; Levendusky 2009). In the case of abortion, Democratic and Republican activists were beginning to sort two decades before ordinary partisans began to diverge (Wolbrecht 2000; Sanbonmatsu 2002: 96–97). Second, sorting among ordinary partisans is much less complete than in the political class. The abortion planks adopted at the 2012 Democratic and Republican presidential nominating conventions could not have been more different. The Democratic plank said, essentially, "at any time, for any reason." The Republican plank said, "at no time, no exceptions." These positions are more distinct than those of ordinary partisans. In particular, Republican convention delegates who would score zero circumstances "should be legal" on this survey item are far more extreme than the average Republican partisan who would permit abortion in at least the three more serious circumstances.[5]

---

[5] In fact, in the 2012 American National Election Study, 21 percent of strong Republicans and 35 percent of not so strong Republicans think abortion should "always be a matter of personal choice."

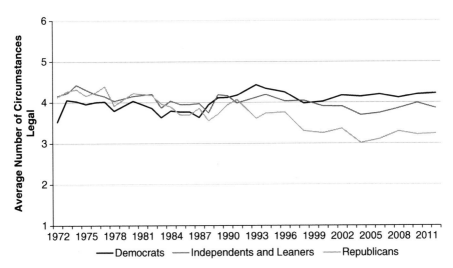

FIGURE 7. Partisans in the General Public Are Sorting on Abortion
Source: General Social Survey.
Note: Partisans include strong and weak identifiers.

Terminological discussion aside, we now turn to the central theme of this chapter. The party sorting that has occurred over the course of the past generation is the fundamental cause of the popular dissatisfaction with government and politics today. Dismayed citizens ask why politics is so nasty and vituperative. As one of us wrote in an earlier essay:

[T]he fundamental cause of today's climate of incivil politics is the sorting of politically active Americans into parties that have grown much more homogeneous than they were in the mid-20th Century. Particular interests (other than Wall Street) appear to receive protection from only one of the two parties. Particular values seem to be defended by only one of the two parties. And particular kinds of people seem to receive a sympathetic hearing by only one of the two parties. The consequence is that the actions considered by government bodies are more likely to present stark choices today than in some earlier, less polarized, more civil eras. In consequence, elections matter more. As the stakes rise, civility falls. (Fiorina 2013: 152–153)

And frustrated citizens ask why there is so much more political stalemate and government gridlock in Washington and many of our state capitals than in the living past of many of us.

[I]n the mid-20th Century period when politics seemed less contentious than today, the American parties were considerably more heterogeneous. The result was party platforms that were less divergent and more balanced among various interests, allowing greater room for compromise. (Fiorina 2013: 149)

In the body of this chapter, we develop these arguments and provide some empirical evidence.

MEASURING PARTY SORTING

Discussions of party sorting typically point to increasingly close relationships between partisanship and measures of ideology and positions on issues. Probably the most common reference is to the correlation between party identification and ideology. At mid-century, the Democratic Party had a conservative wing consisting primarily, but not entirely, of people in the south. The Republican Party had a liberal wing consisting primarily, but not entirely, of people in the northeast. Thus, the relationship between partisanship and ideology was muddled. But as the parties sorted, the relationship increased dramatically. The Pearson correlation between the ANES seven-point party ID and liberal-conservative scales doubled between 1972 and 2012, increasing from about 10 percent shared variance to nearly 40 percent. We will focus on those survey respondents who claim to be either Republicans or Democrats and who voted in the election that year – call them active partisans for short.[6] Within this sub-sample the relationship between partisanship and ideology increased linearly and had reached more than 50 percent shared variance by 2012 (Figure 8).[7] Another possible measure of party sorting is the distance between the average Democratic and Republican voter on the ideology scale. That measure, too, shows a significant increase (Figure 9). Interestingly, while the Republicans begin and end farther from the center point than the Democrats, on average partisans of both parties have moved exactly the same amount – .6 of a scale point – away from the center since 1972.[8]

Particular issue positions show similar correlation patterns than the ideology scale. Figure 10 shows the rising correlation trends between partisanship and three issue measures included in the ANES studies over the period that includes the lib-con scale. The three issue trends track the lib-con trend and are highly correlated with it.[9] Given its greater generality, we rely on the lib-con measure of party sorting in the remainder of this chapter.[10]

[6] We do not classify independent leaners as partisans. This common practice has little empirical basis and results in an overestimation of the strength of partisanship and an underestimation of voter volatility (Abrams and Fiorina 2014).

[7] The ANES measure of ideology allows respondents to deny any ideological leaning. In individual level analyses, common practice is to code these people as moderates so as not to lose data. There are fewer such people among active partisans, and the correlation between the two aggregate time series with and without such "don't knows" included is .996, so it makes no difference which one is used here.

[8] The more common finding is that of "asymmetric polarization" – Republicans moving toward their pole more than Democrats toward theirs. See, for example, Ura and Ellis (2012). Interestingly, Republicans perceive (correctly) that their party has moved rightward, but Democrats perceive their party's position as constant, even though, as the graph shows, the actual positions of partisans have moved leftward.

[9] The correlation between the lib-con measure and aid to blacks is .89, guaranteed job and standard of living .90, and government health insurance .86.

[10] The correlation and distance measures are extremely highly correlated as well (.98), so we will only use the more widely used correlation measure in the remainder of this chapter.

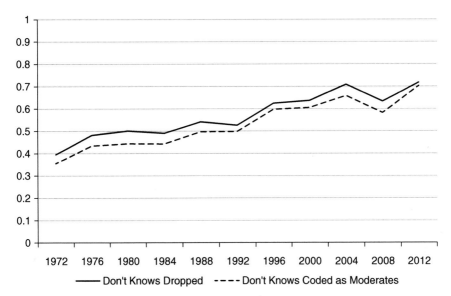

FIGURE 8. Correlation between PID and Ideology (Democrats and Republicans Who Voted)
Source: ANES.

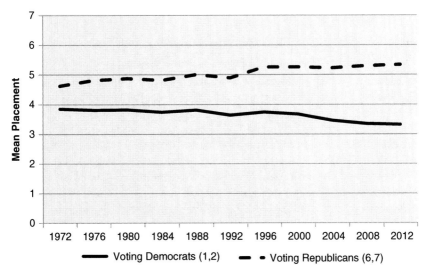

FIGURE 9. Symmetric Separation of Partisans on the Lib-Con Scale
Source: ANES.
Note: DKs dropped; 2012 data FTF only.

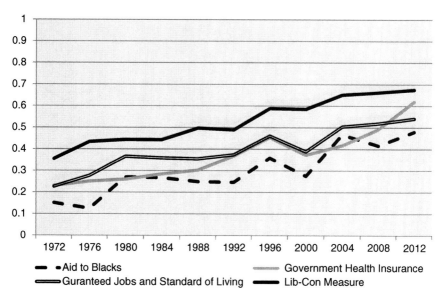

FIGURE 10. Correlations between Issues and with Party ID
Source: ANES.
Note: Figures are presented for the FTF respondents who are partisan voters. DKs in seven-point issue scales coded as 4. DKs in seven-point lib-con scale dropped.

PARTY SORTING AND ELECTORAL POLARIZATION: POLITICAL EVALUATIONS

In Chapter 12 in this volume, Gary Jacobson notes that in 2012 partisan differences in presidential approval ratings reached an all-time high (in ANES studies), eclipsing the previous high set in 2004. Despite his oft-quoted remarks about having gay friends in the red states and coaching little league in the blue states, President Obama turned out to be an even bigger divider than George W. Bush (Jacobson 2007). Party sorting likely provides a significant part of the explanation. To explain, consider a graphical representation of party sorting. In Figure 11 the top panel depicts two parties that are not well sorted. Some Democrats hold positions to the right of center (and to the right of some Republicans), and some Republicans hold positions to the left of center (and to the left of some Democrats). In the bottom panel, the parties are perfectly sorted, with all Democrats to the left of all Republicans.

If a Republican president adopts an agenda at the mode of his party, his policies will be farther away from more Democrats on average in the bottom panel than in the top; hence, more will disapprove and/or disapprove more strongly. The argument is symmetric for a Republican president. As parties

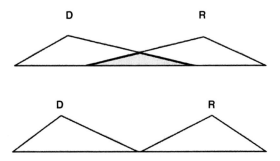

FIGURE II. Party Sorting

become more distinct, partisans in each party find that their positions are farther from those in the other party.

Jacobson also notes that partisan differences in evaluations of the presidential candidates reached an all-time high (in ANES studies) in 2012. That is, the difference between the ratings a voter gave to his or her party's candidate compared to the other party's candidate, were, on average, the highest in the time series. Again, this would be a simple reflection of the party sorting depicted in Figure 11. The argument is similar to that just offered for differences in presidential approval ratings. Assume the presidential candidate of each party takes a position near the party mode, something pretty much guaranteed by the contemporary nomination process and the need to protect oneself from charges of flip-flopping. In the top panel of the figure, some Republicans are actually closer to the Democratic mode than their own party's mode, and some Democrats are closer to the Republican mode than their own. *Ceteris paribus*, these unsorted partisans, will rate the other party's candidate higher than their own. But in the bottom panel, every partisan is closer to his or her own party's mode than to the other party's. When the parties sort, partisan differences in evaluating the candidates logically should increase.

PARTY SORTING AND AFFECTIVE POLARIZATION

Some recent research has concluded that "affective" partisan polarization has increased: Democrats and Republicans simply dislike each other more than a generation ago (Shaw 2012; Chapter 1, this volume). They are even less likely to want to date or marry someone from the other party today than in 1960 (Iyengar, Sood, and Lelkes 2012). Note that if human beings dislike others the more they disagree with them, the simple spatial models in Figure 11 would predict such an increase in affective polarization. The farther the average Democrat is from the average Republican, the greater the dislike. Clearly, however, citizens do not vote solely on the basis of ideological or policy distance as assumed in the simple spatial model. Their votes are a reflection of numerous considerations – beyond ideology and issues, there is partisanship, cultural images of the other party, the personal qualities of the competing candidates, and still others. So let us think about affective polarization more broadly.

In 1964, had a daughter come home from college and told her Democratic parents that she was engaged to a Republican, how might they have responded? They might very well have wondered, *Well, what kind of Republican?* A western conservative such as Barry Goldwater? A northeastern liberal such as Nelson Rockefeller? A midwestern moderate such as George Romney? Similarly, had a daughter come home from college and told her Republican parents that she was engaged to a Democrat, they might have wondered, *What kind of Democrat?* A union stalwart? An urban intellectual? A southern conservative? A western promoter of economic development? In the unsorted parties of the time, whatever kind of person you were, it was likely that there were people with similar characteristics and political views in the other party.

In the sorted parties of today (along with the crude stereotypes reinforced by a partisan media), parents might understandably react very differently. If a son comes home and announces his engagement to a Democrat, his Republican parents might think, *You want to bring an America-hating atheist into our family?* Similarly, Democratic parents might react to their son's engagement to a Republican, by thinking, *You want us to welcome an evolution-denying Bible thumper into our family?* In the sorted parties of today, it would be surprising if affective partisan polarization had not increased.

PARTY SORTING AND VOTING BEHAVIOR

According to ANES studies, more than one-quarter of self-identified Republicans voted for Democrat Lyndon Johnson rather than support their own candidate, Barry Goldwater, in 1964. Similarly, 40 percent of self-identified Democrats voted for Richard Nixon rather than support their own candidate, George McGovern, in 1972. No more. Today party loyalty is the rule. Self-identified partisans today vote almost unanimously for their own parties. Once common campaign organizations such as Democrats for Reagan are absent from today's electoral landscape.

Again, Figure 11 explains this development. If some members of each party find the candidate of the other party closer to their views, as in the top panel, they are more likely to vote for the other party's candidate as well. In the bottom panel, all members of the sorted parties rate their own candidate higher than that of the other party. Hence they are loyalists.

Finally, the decline in split ticket voting often is cited as evidence for a polarized electorate, but again it is a simple consequence of party sorting, although in a more complicated way. The decline of split-ticket voting reflects party sorting at both the voter and candidate levels. In Figure 12, consider a voter, V. This voter is closer to the Republican presidential candidate at R^P, than

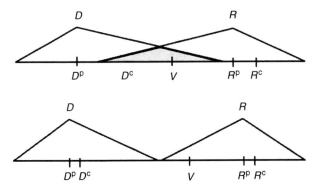

FIGURE 12. Party Sorting and Voting Behavior

to the Democratic presidential candidate at D^P. But she is closer to a moderate Democratic congressional candidate at D^c than to a very conservative Republican congressional candidate at R^c. Hence, the voter will split her ticket and vote Republican for president, but Democratic for Congress.

In the bottom panel, however, party sorting at the elite level means that there will be very little difference between the presidential and congressional candidates. Even a relatively moderate voter will be closer to both candidates of her party than to the candidates of the other party. Hence, she votes a straight ticket.

In light of the foregoing arguments, it is possible to hypothesize about the strength of the relationships between party sorting and the trends in political evaluations and behavior just cited. Because presidential candidates differ even within their own party, the relationship of party sorting with *candidate* evaluations should be weaker than the relationship of party sorting with *party* evaluations. For example, George McGovern was perceived to be more liberal than Bill Clinton, and George W. Bush more conservative than George H. W. Bush. Ronald Reagan in 1984 (but not 1980) was thought to be a more likeable person than Richard Nixon, and Barack Obama more likable than Al Gore. The party's images, however, should show less election-to-election variation because they capture the more stable underlying image of the party.

Similarly, because incumbent presidents are judged heavily on performance, party sorting should be less strongly related to presidential approval ratings than to party evaluations. Reagan and Clinton were widely thought to be successful presidents when they ran for reelection; Jimmy Carter, and George W. Bush not so much.

Finally, party sorting should have the strongest relationship with the decline in split-ticket voting for the simple reason that here party sorting operates on two levels – the voter level and the candidate level. Just as partisans in the electorate are more similar to each other than in the past, the presidential and

TABLE 1. *Party Sorting and ...*

	Pearson r
Presidential approval	.65
Republican candidate rating	.73
Republican Party rating	.90
Democratic candidate rating	.86
Democratic Party rating	.86
Split-ticket voting	.95
Republican presidential vote loyalty	−.08
Democratic presidential vote loyalty	.83

Source: ANES.

congressional candidates of their parties are more similar than in the past. Fewer Democrats will find themselves cross-pressured between a liberal presidential candidate and a conservative House candidate, and fewer Republicans will face the opposite choice.

How do the data match up with these expectations? Very well, in fact.

DATA

Table 1 lists the correlations between the lib-con measure of party sorting and the political evaluations just discussed. As hypothesized, the correlation with presidential approval is the lowest with the two trends showing about 40 percent shared variance. Research shows that there is clearly a partisan bias when evaluating presidential performance, but reality continues to intrude (Tilley and Hobolt 2011). Also as hypothesized, split-ticket voting shows the strongest relationship to party sorting; indeed, with 90 percent shared variance, the two trends are almost the same.

Candidates are more variable than parties, so as hypothesized, candidate ratings have a lower relationship with party sorting than do party ratings – but only for Republicans. Party sorting and Republican Party ratings share 80 percent plus of the variance compared to just over 50 percent shared variance between sorting and Republican candidate ratings. For Democrats, however, party and candidate ratings bear the same relationship to party sorting. Democratic candidates seem to be less distinguished from their party than Republican candidates.

On the other hand, party sorting has a strong positive relationship with Democrats' party loyalty in presidential elections, but no relationship at all with Republicans' loyalty in theirs. At first glance this might seem surprising, but an examination of the raw data shows why. With the exception of 1964, Republicans have always been extremely loyal to their presidential nominees. Indeed the 96+ percent support for Dwight Eisenhower in the 1950s has never been equaled, although Ronald Reagan came very close. As the parties sorted, Democrats came to behave more like Republicans always have.

CONCLUSION

Recently Thomas Mann (2014: 2; see also his preface to this volume) wrote, "To treat polarization as 'mere sorting' is to trivialize, if not miss entirely, the biggest development in recent decades." He provides a hyperlink to a column discussing an essay by Fiorina (2013). This is a misreading of our position. We do not believe that there is anything "mere" about the sorting process. Rather, we contend that to characterize the process as polarization contributes to a widespread misunderstanding that gets in the way of any effort to improve our politics, a goal we share with Mann.

Party sorting lies at the basis of our current political stalemate. When ideology and issues crosscut the party cleavage, party cohesion is difficult to maintain, and cross-party coalition possibilities expand. This was the case in mid-twentieth-century America. Today, ideology and issues reinforce the partisan cleavage rather than cut across it. This contracts the possibilities for constructing cross-party compromises. What to do? We cannot say, but our reading of American political history suggests that two kinds of developments can break partisan deadlocks.

The first is the development of a popular consensus so large that neither party can afford to ignore it. An example from the highly polarized Congresses of the late nineteenth century is the passage of the Interstate Commerce Act of 1887. Congress had tried and failed to pass railroad regulation since 1874, but a generally Democratic House and generally Republican Senate could not agree. In 1886, the U.S. Supreme Court invalidated state regulation of the railroads in its *Wabash* decision. This exogenous shift in the status quo left railroad operations completely unregulated, and both parties in Congress quickly decided that it would be electoral suicidal to go into the 1888 election without rectifying the situation.

The second possibility arises from the efforts of ambitious politicians who create new coalitions by raising issues that cut across existing party lines – they engage in party de-sorting, so to speak. Rand Paul's emphasis on privacy issues that unites some elements of the libertarian and liberal communities is an example. Other possibilities might lie in U.S. support for Israel, which seems to be losing ground in some parts of the Democratic base, and support for an interventionist stance in international affairs, which seems to be losing ground in some parts of the Republican base. Whether such issues have the "legs" to de-sort the parties seems doubtful, however. More likely would be the rise of new issues in response to global economic changes or foreign policy crises.

REFERENCES

Abramowitz, Alan I. 2010. *The Disappearing Center.* New Haven, CT: Yale University Press.

Abramowitz, Alan I., and Saunders, Kyle L. 1998. "Ideological Realignment in the U.S. Electorate." *Journal of Politics* 60 (3): 634–652.

Abrams, Samuel J., and Fiorina, Morris P. 2012. "Are Leaning Independents Just Deluded or Dishonest Weak Partisans?" Paper presented at the Conference on Revisiting Party ID, Rome, Italy.

Baldassarri, Delia, and Gelman, Andrew. 2008. "Partisans without Constraint: Political Polarization and Trends in American Public Opinion." *American Journal of Sociology* 114 (2): 408–446.

Broockman, David E. 2014. "Assuming Americans Are Reliably Ideological Can Mislead Studies of Representation." Retrieved from http://www.ocf.berkeley.edu /~broockma/broockman_artificial_disconnect.pdf.

Carmines, Edward G., and James A. Stimson. 1989. *Issue Evolution: Race and the Transformation of American Politics.* Princeton, NJ: Princeton University Press.

Cook, Elizabeth Addell, Ted G. Jelen, and Clyde Wilcox. 1992. *Between Two Absolutes.* Boulder, CO: Westview Press.

Ellis, Christopher, and James A. Stimson. 2012. *Ideology in America.* New York: Cambridge.

Fiorina, Morris P. 2014. "Americans Have Not Become Politically More Polarized." Retrieved from http://www.washingtonpost.com/blogs/monkey-cage/wp/2014/06 /23/americans-have-not-become-more-politically-polarized/.

Fiorina, Morris P. 2013. "Party Homogeneity and Contentious Politics." In Daniel M. Shea and Morris P. Fiorina, eds., *Can We Talk? The Rise of Rude, Nasty, Stubborn Politics.* New York: Pearson, 142–153.

Fiorina, Morris P., and Samuel J. Abrams. 2009. *Disconnect: The Breakdown of Representation in American Politics.* Norman: University of Oklahoma Press.

Fiorina, Morris P. and Samuel J. Abrams. 2008. "Political Polarization in the American Public." In Margaret Levi, Simon Jackman, and Nancy Rosenblum, eds., *Annual Review of Political Science*, vol. 11. Palo Alto, CA: Annual Reviews, 563–588.

Fiorina, Morris P., Samuel J. Abrams, and Jeremy C. Pope. 2006. *Culture War? The Myth of a Polarized America*, 2nd edition. New York: Pearson Longman.

Free, Lloyd A., and Hadley Cantril. 1967. *The Political Beliefs of Americans.* New Brunswick, NJ: Rutgers University Press.

Iyengar, Shanto, Sood, Gaurav, and Lelkes, Yphtach. 2012. "Affect, Not Ideology: A Social Identity Perspective on Polarization." *Public Opinion Quarterly* 76 (3): 405–431.

Jacobson, Gary C. 2007. *A Divider, Not a Uniter.* New York: Pearson Longman.

Layman, Geoffrey, and Carsey Thomas M. 2002. "Party Polarization and Party Structuring of Policy Attitudes: A Comparison of Three NES Panel Studies." *Political Behavior* 24: 199–236.

Levendusky, Matthew. 2009. *The Partisan Sort: How Liberals Became Democrats and Conservatives Became Republicans.* Chicago: University of Chicago Press.

Mann, Thomas E. 2014. "Admit It, Political Scientists: Politics Really Is More Broken Than Ever." *The Atlantic*, May 26.

Meyer, Dick. 2014. "Maybe Americans Are Not as Politically Polarized as Reported." Retrieved from http://www.theindychannel.com/decodedc/maybe-americans-are-not-as-politically-polarized-as-reported.

Pew Research Center for the People and the Press. 2013. "Political Polarization in the American Public." Retrieved from http://www.people-press.org/2014/06/12/political-polarization-in-the-american-public/.

Sanbonmatsu, Kira. 2002. *Democrats, Republicans, and the Politics of Women's Place*. Ann Arbor: University of Michigan Press.

Shaw, Daron. 2012. "If Everyone Votes Their Party, Why Do Presidential Elections Vary So Much?" *The Forum* 10 (3): Article 1.

Stonecash, Jeffrey M., Mark D. Brewer, and Mack D. Mariani, 2003. *Diverging Parties: Social Change, Realignment, and Party Polarization*. Boulder, CO: Westview Press.

Tilley, James, and Sara B. Hobolt. 2011. "Is the Government to Blame? An Experimental Test of How Partisanship Shapes Perceptions of Performance and Responsibility." *Journal of Politics* 73: 1–15.

Ura, Daniel Joseph, and Ellis, Christopher R. 2012. "Partisan Moods: Polarization and the Dynamics of Mass Party Preferences." *Journal of Politics* 74: 277–291.

Wolbrecht, Christina. 2000. *The Politics of Women's Rights: Parties, Positions, and Change*. Princeton, NJ. Princeton University Press.

PART II

POLARIZATION IN NATIONAL INSTITUTIONS

6

Presidential-Congressional Relations in an Era of Polarized Parties and a 60-Vote Senate

Jon R. Bond, Richard Fleisher, and Jeffrey E. Cohen

- Party control of Congress is the strongest determinant of presidential success – majority party presidents win more roll call votes than do minority party presidents.
- Until recently, the effects of party control were similar in both chambers. Rising party polarization in Congress affects presidential success differently in the House and Senate.
- In the House, party polarization amplifies the effects of party control – as party polarization increases, majority party presidents win more and minority presidents win less.
- In the Senate, party polarization suppresses success rates – majority presidents still win more on average, but as party voting increases, success rates decline for both majority and minority presidents.
- The rise in cloture votes and the emergence of the minority party filibuster during the Bush and Obama presidencies is responsible for the changes in how party polarization conditions the effects of party control in the Senate.
- Since cloture votes are unique to the Senate, excluding cloture votes provides a mix of Senate votes similar to the House – as party polarization increases on non-cloture votes, majority presidents win more and minority presidents win less, though the relationships are weaker than in the House.
- On cloture votes, polarization magnifies the effects of party control, but the pattern of success is a mirror image of the House – as party polarization increases, minority presidents win more and majority presidents win less.
- The simple arithmetic of which side of cloture the president is on explains why the relationships flip. Majority presidents usually favor invoking cloture, which requires 60 votes to win. Minority presidents usually oppose invoking cloture, which requires only 41 votes to win.

To achieve his goals, the president must persuade Congress to support his positions. It's a hard sell. The American system of "separated institutions sharing powers" (Neustadt 1960: 33) makes it difficult for any president to win support from Congress. Presidential success in Congress varies – some presidents win more than others – but President Obama seems to be having an especially hard time. In 2012, for example, Obama won only 15.5 percent of House roll call votes on which he expressed a position. That's pretty low, but not quite a record – President Bush barely holds on to this dubious distinction, winning only 15.4 percent of House roll calls in 2008. Are Bush and Obama just inept, or are these record low success rates in the House the result of systematic changes in Congress? If there have been systematic changes, are the effects the same in the Senate as well as the House? And if not, why?

In this chapter, we show that systemic changes associated with rising party polarization have altered presidential-congressional relations. Both chambers have become highly polarized in recent years, but the effects of party polarization on presidential success are different in the Senate and House. Senate rules permitting unlimited debate (i.e., filibusters) and the supermajority requirement to invoke cloture explain this difference. These rules protect minority rights of individual senators. Party polarization, however, has transformed the filibuster into a partisan tool that the minority party routinely uses to block legislation and nominees favored by the majority.

THE BASICS OF PRESIDENTIAL-CONGRESSIONAL RELATIONS

What explains variation in presidential success in Congress? Research initially focused on the president to explain presidential success. Richard Neustadt (1960; *v*), the dean of the behavioral study of the presidency, framed the question in terms of *personal* power – what the president "can do, as one man among many, to carry his own choices through that maze of personalities and institutions called the government of the United States." He downplayed the importance of party control of Congress, observing, "What the Constitution separates our political parties do not combine" (Neustadt 1960; 33). In the absence of strong parties to bridge the inevitable conflict between independent institutions, Neustadt argued that popular presidents who are highly skilled at bargaining and persuasion succeed, while unpopular, less skilled presidents fail.

Systematic quantitative tests did not find strong support for Neustadt's thesis. Research consistently finds that the effects of presidential popularity on success in Congress are small (Edwards 1989, 2003, 2009; Bond and Fleisher 1990, ch. 7; Bond, Fleisher, and Wood 2003). And presidents with reputations as highly skilled (e.g., Johnson and Reagan) did not win significantly more votes in Congress than should be expected, nor did reputedly unskilled presidents (e.g., Nixon and Carter) win significantly fewer votes (Fleisher and Bond 1983, 1992; Bond and Fleisher 1990, ch. 8; Fleisher, Bond, and Wood 2008; Cohen, Bond, and Fleisher 2013a, 2013b). Instead, the strongest and most consistent determinant of presidential success in Congress is party – support from members of the president's party is higher than that of members of the opposition (Edwards 1989), and the president wins more roll calls if his party has a majority (Bond and Fleisher 1990; Bond, Fleisher, and Wood 2003; Cohen, Bond, and Fleisher 2013a, 2013b). Although Neustadt's observation about the weakness of American parties was accurate, this pattern of robust party effects held even during the period of weak parties from the end of World War II to the 1970s. Furthermore, the effects of party on presidential success were similar in both chambers, although the advantage of majority control is somewhat smaller in the Senate (Bond, Fleisher, and Wood 2003; Fleisher, Bond, and Wood 2008).

Beginning in the 1980s, party voting in Congress began to rise. Party cohesion and polarization continued to escalate, so that by the dawn of the twenty-first century, we see what could be called the "polarized Congress." Party polarization has altered the relationship between party control and presidential success in Congress. The effects, however, are not the same in both chambers. In the House, party polarization amplifies the effects of party control: as partisanship increases, majority party presidents win more and minority presidents win less. In the Senate, party polarization suppresses success rates: majority presidents still win more than minority presidents do, but as party voting increases, success rates decline for both majority and minority presidents (Cohen, Bond, and Fleisher 2013a, 2013b).

How can we explain the consistently strong effects of party control on presidential success?

THE THEORETICAL BASES OF PARTY INFLUENCE IN CONGRESS

We have solid theoretical reasons to explain the strong influence of party on presidential support in Congress. Most obvious is simple arithmetic – majority presidents have more members on the floor with incentives to support their policy preferences than do minority presidents. Members of the same political party share a wide range of policy preferences because they must satisfy similar electoral coalitions. Hence, support for the president is higher among co-partisans in Congress because they and their constituents are more likely to agree with the president's positions than are opposition party members.

The degree of shared preferences among co-partisans varies over time (Rohde 1991; Aldrich, Berger, and Rohde 2002). Yet, the advantage of party control held even during the period of American politics when both party caucuses in Congress contained substantial numbers of cross-pressured members – conservative Democrats and liberal Republicans – who shared ideological ground with the rival party. Although defections were common, the president often got votes from cross-pressured co-partisans because they still had much in common with the president. When preferences differed, the cross-pressured faction was large enough that the president often had to compromise to get their support. Accommodating preferences of his cross-pressured co-partisans also helped attract support from cross-pressured members of the opposition (Bond and Fleisher 1990; Fleisher and Bond 2004).

In addition to shared policy preferences, co-partisans have similar political needs. Because members of the president's party must run for reelection on his record as well as their own, they have a political incentive to help him succeed. Simple arithmetic thus explains a good deal of why majority presidents win more votes in Congress than do minority presidents.

The advantage of majority party control, however, is not solely, or even mostly, arithmetic. A political party is more than a bundle of shared preferences. Rather, a party is a political institution with rules and procedures that channel and constrain behavior (Aldrich 2011). Parties have long been viewed as competing teams (Downs 1957). As a result, parties often take opposing positions on issues that have nothing to do with ideology – just because they are opposing teams (Lee 2009). Majority party agenda control is a central part of the two prevailing partisan theories of Congress – Conditional Party Government (CPG) theory (Rohde 1991; Aldrich and Rohde 2000) and Cartel theory (Cox and McCubbins 2005). With respect to presidential success, then, the primary advantage of majority party control is that the president's co-partisans control key levers of power in Congress, including committees, access to the floor, rules governing debate, and decisions about which amendments are considered. Thus, the issues on the congressional agenda and the presentation of choices to members are more likely to reflect the president's preferences when his party controls the chamber (Covington, Wrighton, and Kinney 1995).

HOUSE-SENATE DIFFERENCES

Although party control is a major determinant of presidential success in Congress, we do find chamber differences. In particular, the majority party advantage is generally smaller in the Senate than in the House, although a more accurate description is that the *minority party disadvantage* is smaller in the Senate than in the House (see Table 1). From 1953 to 2013, for example, the average advantage of majority status was about 39 percent more victories in the House and 24 percent more in the Senate. The smaller advantage in the

TABLE 1. *Presidential Success of Majority and Minority Presidents, 1953–2013*

	Majority Presidents	Minority Presidents	Majority Advantage
House	78.6%	39.3%	39.3%
Senate	77.8%	54.2%	23.6%

Source: Constructed by the authors from presidential roll calls identified in *Congressional Quarterly*'s annual Presidential Support Studies.

Senate, however, is mainly due to higher success rates of minority presidents. Majority party presidents win about three-fourths of the time in both chambers (78.6 percent in the House and 77.8 percent in the Senate). But minority party presidents win a majority of Senate votes on which they express a position (54.2 percent) compared to only 39.3 percent in the House.

Why are the effects of majority control different in the Senate? Students of Congress generally point to institutional differences to explain the smaller minority party disadvantage in the Senate. Because of longer terms and smaller size, the Senate traditionally was more collegial and less partisan than the House. Senate rules institutionalizing the privileges and prerogatives of individual senators reflect these traditions. The most important protection of individual prerogative in the Senate is the right of unlimited debate (filibuster) and Rule XXII requiring a supermajority to invoke cloture and close off debate. Research on Senate behavior in the 1950s suggested that part of the tradition was a norm that senators should rarely take advantage of these rules (Matthews 1960). Individual senators of both parties used the filibuster sparingly to draw attention to an issue, extract concessions, or to block legislation they felt strongly about. As long as filibusters were rare, Senate floor votes typically were decided by a simple majority as is the case in the House. As a result, success rates of majority presidents were similar in both chambers, but minority status was less of a disadvantage in the Senate because the president could often put together winning coalitions with the help of opposition party senators.

Party Polarization in the House and Senate

Party polarization has become a prominent feature of American politics in recent decades. The epicenter of party polarization is the U.S. Congress. Beginning in the 1980s, the number of moderate and cross-pressured members of both parties began to decline. By 2000, cross-pressured members – i.e., those closer to the mean of the other party than to their own party (Bond and Fleisher 1990) – had disappeared and moderates were an endangered species (Fleisher and Bond 2004). With the departure of moderate and cross-pressured members from Congress, each party caucus became more ideologically homogeneous and the party medians diverged.

Despite the tradition of lower partisanship in the Senate, trends in party voting are quite similar in both chambers (Bond and Fleisher 2000). Although relative partisanship varies considerably from year-to-year, presidents from Eisenhower to the senior Bush generally dealt with a Congress in which the Senate was somewhat less partisan than the House (see Figure 1). The three most recent presidents – Clinton, Bush, and Obama – faced a Congress in which Senate partisanship was not significantly different from the House.[1] In recent

---

[1] Difference of means tests for Nixon/Ford, Carter, Clinton, Bush, and Obama are not significant. We find significant differences for DDE ($t = -2.14, p = 0.05$), JFK/LBJ ($t = -2.95, p = 0.02$), RWR ($t = -2.52, p = 0.025$), and GHWB ($t = -2.28, p = 0.06$).

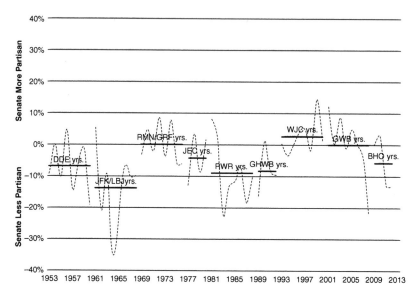

FIGURE 1. Difference in Party Voting in the House and Senate (% Senate Party Votes – % House Party Votes)

decades, two polarized parties have dominated policymaking in both chambers of Congress. How has party polarization changed the way the Senate responds to the president?

Party Polarization and the Emergence of the 60-Vote Senate

Although the formal rules have not changed, filibusters and cloture votes have increased precipitously. Filibusters have become so common that Senate scholars have begun to describe the institution as the "60-vote Senate" (Koger 2010). That is, because cloture has become the only tool to stop a filibuster, the contemporary Senate operates under a de facto 60-vote requirement to pass any controversial measure. Cloture votes are an imperfect indicator of filibusters – some filibusters have no cloture votes; others have multiple cloture votes. Nonetheless, cloture votes provide an indication of the increase in what Sinclair (2012: 265) calls "filibuster problems" – holds, threats to filibuster, and filibusters.

The escalation of cloture votes over time is well documented (Binder and Smith 2001; Koger 2010). Although the Senate adopted a supermajority cloture rule in 1917, it did not become the primary tool to limit obstruction until the 1960s (Koger 2010: 20–21). Because this chapter focuses on presidential success, we look at the trend from a presidential perspective. Figure 2 shows the mean percentage of Senate votes on cloture averaged by presidential administration, from Eisenhower through Obama's first term. Displaying the

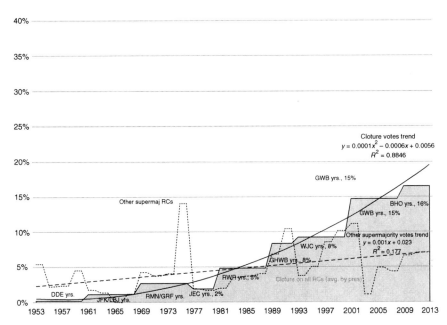

FIGURE 2. Mean Percentage of Cloture Votes by Presidential Administration

trend this way allows us to describe the overall escalation of cloture votes across presidential administrations. Cloture votes were rare during the Eisenhower years (0.2 percent of all conflictual Senate votes), and increased only slightly from Kennedy/Johnson through the Carter years (averaging about 1.8 percent). After the Carter years, we see an exponential rise: cloture votes more than doubled to an average of 4.8 percent during the Reagan presidency, then nearly doubled again to 8 to 9 percent during the senior Bush and Clinton presidencies, and nearly doubled yet again to averages around 15 to 16 percent during the Bush and Obama presidencies. The trend line on the figure summarizes this exponential increase in cloture votes. But there is no long-term trend for other types of supermajority votes (veto overrides, treaties, and constitutional amendments).[2]

Notable as this trend is, however, the overall rise in cloture votes underestimates the potential impact on presidential success. In recent years, cloture votes were more common on presidential roll calls than on Senate votes

---

[2] We estimate trends with Ordinary Least Squares (OLS) regression. The slope of the regression line summarizes the relationship. Steep slopes indicate that a small change in the independent variable (time, in this case) is associated with a large change (increase or decrease) in the independent variable, while flat slopes close to zero indicate weak relationships. The coefficient of determination (R^2) ranges from zero to 1.0. It is interpreted as the proportion of variance explained by the independent variable. The slope of the line for cloture votes rises sharply with an R^2 of .88, but the slope of the line for other supermajority votes is nearly flat with an R^2 near zero (.18).

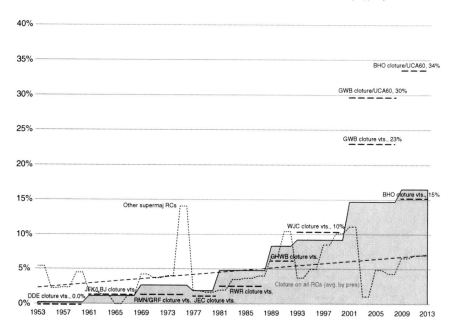

FIGURE 3. Mean Percentage of Cloture and Cloture-Related Votes on Presidential Roll Calls

overall. George W. Bush's presidency appears to be the watershed (see Figure 3). From Kennedy/Johnson to Carter, the proportion of cloture votes was roughly equal on presidential roll calls and overall. Even as cloture votes began to rise during the Reagan and senior Bush presidencies, they remained slightly less common on presidential roll calls. For the first time during the Clinton years, cloture votes were slightly more common on presidential roll calls than overall – an average of 10.3 percent on presidential roll calls compared to 9.2 percent overall. Then we see a surge during the Bush years. While cloture votes increased to an average of nearly 15 percent of all Senate roll calls, 23 percent of Bush roll calls were on cloture, more than 50 percent higher than overall. During Obama's first term, cloture votes dropped to an average of 15.2 percent of presidential roll calls, slightly below the 16.5 percent overall average. This drop, however, does not mean that the escalating trend of supermajority decision rules on presidential roll calls has slowed.

Indeed, the 60-vote threshold has begun to extend beyond cloture votes. In recent Congresses, party leaders have negotiated Unanimous Consent Agreements (UCAs) that set a 60-vote threshold to pass a bill or amendment (Smith 2014). Although the practice of setting a 60-vote threshold by UCA is a response to "filibuster problems," these votes are not the same as cloture. The number of votes required to win is the same, but 60 votes by UCA are not as partisan and the president wins more often. This type of supermajority vote first appeared on presidential roll calls in 2006 during Bush's second term. By the end of his presidency, Bush had expressed a position on 23 such votes, increasing the percentage of Bush roll calls with a 60-vote threshold to nearly 30 percent. Presidential roll calls requiring 60 votes by UCA became more common during Obama's first term (35 total). More than one-third of Obama roll calls (33.5 percent) were cloture or cloture-related votes. Since we observe no discernible trend in noncloture related supermajority votes (see Figure 2), the rise of cloture and cloture-related votes is solely responsible for the emergence of the 60-vote Senate.

The Minority Party Filibuster

Not only has the frequency of cloture votes changed during the recent period of partisan polarization, so has the nature of filibusters. Historically, the supermajority vote requirement to end a filibuster protected the prerogatives of individual senators. Party leaders did not use the filibuster in pursuit of party goals, and filibustering was not related to party control of the chamber (Wawro and Schickler 2006; Koger 2010). In recent Congresses, filibusters have become a tool the minority party uses to block objectionable presidential nominations (Bond, Fleisher, and Krutz 2009) as well as legislation.

Polarizing parties are in part responsible for the shift to 60 votes as the default threshold in the contemporary Senate. This is not to suggest that party polarization is the cause of more filibusters. Although some research finds evidence that partisanship contributes to more filibusters (Binder, Lawrence, and Smith 2002), Koger's (2010: 145) analysis of a more accurate count of filibusters over a longer period suggests otherwise. The key observation undermining the hypothesized link is that filibusters were rare during the first two decades of the twentieth century when Senate parties were about as highly polarized as they have been in recent decades.

The connection between increasing partisanship and the emergence of the 60-vote Senate, however, is clearer. Koger (2010, ch. 8) finds that the 60-vote Senate is mostly the result of developments that altered the relative costs of conducting and stopping filibusters. Although Senate rules have contained a procedure to end debate by supermajority vote since 1917, it was rarely used until the 1960s. The typical response to a filibuster was to wait it out and win through attrition. The dormant cloture rule was revived in the 1960s, and eventually replaced attrition as the primary method to end filibusters.

The shift from attrition to cloture had the unintended consequence of reducing the costs of obstruction. The informal system of "holds" allows senators to signal a threat to filibuster with a confidential communication to their party leader. Because holds are secret and the senator placing the hold does not have to be on the floor to object to a unanimous consent request, the costs of filibustering declined. Senators could exploit the supermajority threshold for almost anything and not have to worry about any negative consequences from colleagues, the news media, or voters. As the parties polarized, the number of minority party senators inclined to place a hold probably increased, and the likelihood that any would defect to support cloture declined.

Since holds are secret, we can't observe whether they come disproportionately from the minority party. There is, however, indirect evidence that filibusters have become a partisan tool the minority uses to block legislation and nominees favored by the majority. We have shown that while the exponential rise in cloture votes started during the Reagan presidency, cloture remained less common on presidential roll calls until Clinton. During George W. Bush's presidency, cloture votes were much more common on presidential roll calls. If the Bush presidency is the watershed for the minority party filibuster, then cloture votes on which the president expresses a position should be much more polarized than before Bush.

Let's define party polarization as highly unified parties voting on opposite sides of a floor vote. A simple measure polarization on a roll call vote is the distance between Democrats and Republicans. We calculate this as the absolute difference between the percentages of Democrats and Republicans voting "yea." This produces a polarization scale that ranges from 0 to 100. If the same percentage of Democrats and Republicans vote "yea," polarization on that vote is 0 (e.g., 65% − 65% = 0). If 100 percent of Democrats and 0 Republicans vote "yea" on a roll call vote, the parties are totally unified on opposite sides, and polarization is the maximum 100 percent (100% − 0% = 100). A 60–40 party division would be a distance of 20 percent (not very polarized at all), while a 90–10 split (or 100 − 20, 95 − 15, etc.) would be a distance of 80 percent (highly unified on opposite sides and polarized).

Figure 4 shows the percentage of highly polarized votes (i.e., polarization score of at least 80 percent) on different types of presidential roll calls (cloture, other supermajority votes, and majority decision rule). Polarization increased on all types of presidential roll calls, but the rise was most rapid on cloture votes. Before Reagan, there were few cloture votes, presidents rarely expressed positions on them, and none provoked a highly partisan vote. Beginning with the Reagan presidency, cloture votes on which the president expressed a position became increasingly partisan. The percentage of highly polarized cloture votes grew from zero to around one-third (31 percent) for Reagan, to nearly one-half (47 percent) for the senior Bush, to two-thirds (66.7 percent) for Clinton. Then for Bush and Obama, presidential cloture votes were highly polarized over 80 percent of the time, much more often than on other supermajority and majority rule votes. This evidence suggests that the institutionalization of the minority party filibuster occurred during the Bush presidency. How has this change affected presidential success in the House and Senate?

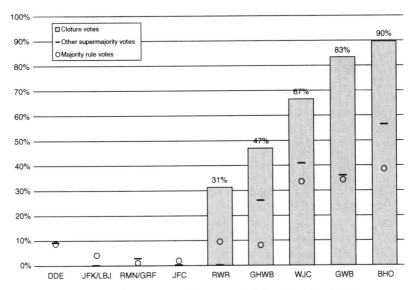

FIGURE 4. High Party Polarization on Cloture and Other Presidential Votes

PARTY POLARIZATION AND PRESIDENTIAL SUCCESS

We analyze how party polarization affects presidential success in the House and Senate from 1953 to 2012 – from Eisenhower through Obama's first term. We measure success with Presidential Success Scores (PSS) defined as the annual percentage of victories on presidential roll calls. Presidential roll calls are votes on which the president expresses a clear public position about what he does or does not want in the way of legislative action (*Congressional Quarterly*, 1953–2012).[3] Party polarization on a roll call vote is the distance between party positions as described earlier – maximum polarization is 100 percent of Democrats voting against 100 percent of Republicans; zero polarization occurs if the same percentage of both parties vote on the same side. Party polarization in Congress is the annual average level of polarization – distance between parties – on all conflictual roll call votes in the House and Senate.[4]

[3] We limit the analysis to votes with minimal conflict – at least 10 percent vote against the president. Excluding consensual presidential victories removes most minor and routine issues from the analysis. Votes that the president lost with more than 90 percent voting against him remain in the analysis because they are instances of important institutional conflict. This differs from the 20 percent threshold used in previous work (Bond and Fleisher 1990; Fleisher and Bond 2000).

[4] Other common measures of polarization are the difference between party means (or medians) of DW-Nominate scores (Poole and Rosenthal 1997), and the percentage of party votes (i.e., at least a majority of one party voting against a majority of the other party) in a year. These measures are highly correlated, and they produce similar results. The average level of polarization on conflictual votes is a superior measure for our study since it incorporates the two key aspects of the concept of polarization: high party unity and divergence. Averages above 65 percent indicate

Party control is whether the president's party has a majority of seats in the chamber.[5]

The other variable of interest is the size of the coalition needed for victory – simple majority or supermajority. Several procedures in Congress require a supermajority – veto overrides, treaty ratification, and proposal of a Constitutional amendment require support of two-thirds of senators present and voting; waiving the Budget Act and invoking cloture require support of three-fifths of the Senate. Of the various procedures requiring a supermajority, only cloture increases systematically over time (see Figures 2 and 3). To see if cloture votes are responsible for changes in the relationships in the Senate, we compare relationships on two subsets of Senate presidential roll calls – noncloture votes (majority and supermajority votes excluding cloture) and on cloture votes – to overall success.

Party polarization does not directly influence presidential success. Instead, polarization interacts with party control to influence presidential success indirectly (Bond, Fleisher and Wood 2003; Cohen, Bond, and Fleisher 2013a, 2013b). That is, majority presidents win more than do minority presidents, but how much more depends on the level of polarization.

Evidence that Party Polarization Operates Differently in the House and Senate

The interaction of polarization and party control operates differently in the House and Senate. Let's look at relationships in the House first. Figure 5 is a scatterplot of presidential success of majority and minority presidents at different levels of party polarization. This analysis shows that party polarization amplifies the benefits of majority control in the House, but the effects are not symmetrical. That is, as party polarization increases, majority presidents win more and minority presidents win less (a lot less). Regression lines summarize the relationships. The slope of the line for majority presidents is 0.29, indicating that a 10 percent increase in polarization is associated with about 3 percent more wins ($10 \times 0.29 = 2.9\%$). The slope of the line for minority presidents is negative and more than three times steeper (-0.97): if party polarization increases by 10 percent, minority presidents win nearly 10 percent fewer votes ($10 \times -0.97 = -9.7\%$). Thus, increasing party polarization in the House hurts minority presidents more than it benefits majority presidents.

---

many highly polarized votes with unified parties on opposite sides; averages below 35 percent indicate many fewer polarized votes.

[5] Coding majority control in the Senate in 2001 presents a dilemma. The initial party line-up was 50 Republicans and 50 Democrats/Independents, with Vice President Cheney breaking the tie to give Republicans control of the chamber. On June 6, Sen. James Jeffords (R-VT) switched to Independent, and handed control to the Democrats. In this analysis, we consider Bush as a minority president, but coding him as a majority president makes little substantive difference.

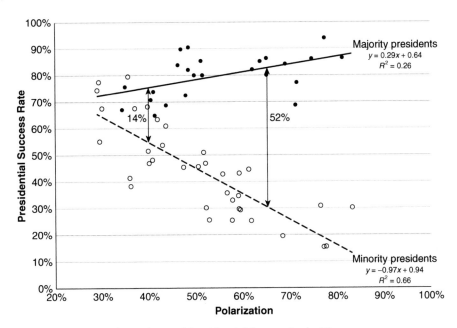

FIGURE 5. Party Polarization and Presidential Success in the House, 1953–2012

If polarization is low (at 35 percent), majority presidents win about 14 percent more than do minority presidents; if polarization is high (at 65 percent), the gap increases to 52 percent.[6] Notice that the gap in success rates almost disappears when party polarization is at a minimum (around 30 percent). It is no surprise that party control matters little if parties are not cohesive – both majority and minority presidents may get less support from their party, but they can attract support from the opposition.

Figure 6 presents the same analysis for the Senate. As we found in the House, party polarization suppresses success rates of minority presidents, although the effect is weaker – a 10 percent rise in party polarization is associated with about 2 percent fewer victories (10 × –0.18 = –1.8%). But party polarization in the Senate tends to suppress success rates of majority presidents as well – a 10 percent rise in party polarization is associated with about 2 percent fewer victories (10 × –0.19 = –1.9%). Because the rate of decline associated with rising polarization is nearly identical for both majority and minority presidents (slopes of .19 and .18), the gap in success rates of majority and minority presidents is about the same at all levels of polarization – majority presidents win 21 percent to 22 percent more votes.

[6] The increment from 35 percent to 65 percent polarization is roughly +/– one standard deviation from the mean.

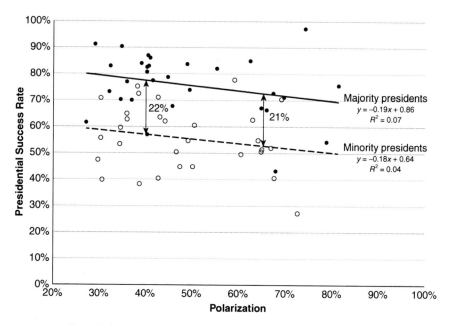

FIGURE 6. Party Polarization and Presidential Success in the Senate, 1953–2012

Evidence of the Effects of the Minority Party Filibuster

We have suggested that the rise in cloture votes and emergence of the minority party filibuster during the Bush and Obama presidencies is responsible for the changes in how party polarization conditions the effects of party control in the Senate. Since the filibuster and cloture are unique to the Senate, excluding cloture votes provides a mix of majority and supermajority votes similar to the House. If the rise of cloture votes is responsible for the changes in the Senate, then the relationships on noncloture votes in the Senate should look more like the House – that is, as party polarization increases on noncloture votes, majority presidents should win more and minority presidents should win less, although the relationships are likely to be weaker than in the House.

The results presented in Figure 7 support this expectation. On Senate votes other than cloture, increasing party polarization boosts the advantage of majority control, but effects are muted. In particular, if polarization increases 10 percent, majority presidents win almost 2 percent more noncloture votes (10 × 0.17 = 1.7%), and minority presidents win about 3 percent fewer (10 × –0.29 = –2.9%). Thus, on votes other than cloture, majority presidents benefit from polarization, but less than in the House – the gap in success rates of majority and minority presidents on noncloture votes increases from about 19 percent at low polarization to about 33 percent at high polarization, versus an increase from 14 percent to 52 percent on House votes.

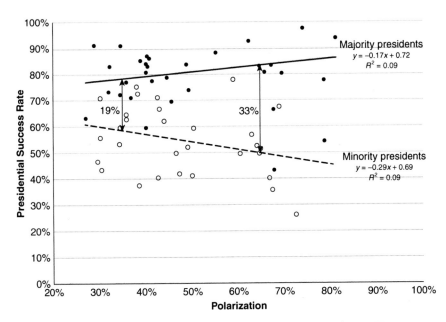

FIGURE 7. Party Polarization and Presidential Success on Noncloture Votes, 1953–2012

What about the relationship between party polarization and presidential success on cloture? If the supermajority requirement to invoke cloture has become a minority party tool used to block majority party policies, then polarization should magnify the effects of party control, but the pattern of success should be a mirror image of the House – that is, as party polarization increases, minority presidents should win more and majority presidents should win less. The analysis presented in Figure 8 supports these expectations. If party polarization increases 10 percent, majority presidents win about 7 percent fewer cloture votes (10 × −0.69 = −6.9%), but minority presidents win a whopping 16 percent more (10 × 1.65 = 16.5%). At high levels of party polarization, the gap between minority and majority presidents is 65 percent; at low levels of polarization, there is almost no gap (5 percent), although there are very few cases at this level.

Why is a 60-vote Senate so hard on majority presidents and so beneficial for minority presidents? It's just the simple arithmetic of which side of cloture the president is on. Majority presidents normally favor invoking cloture because they are trying to overcome opposition of a minority. If party polarization has transformed the filibuster into a tool the minority party uses for partisan objectives, then the number of cloture votes should rise and majority presidents will be compelled to take more positions supporting cloture. Minority presidents, on the other hand, tend to oppose invoking cloture. Building the

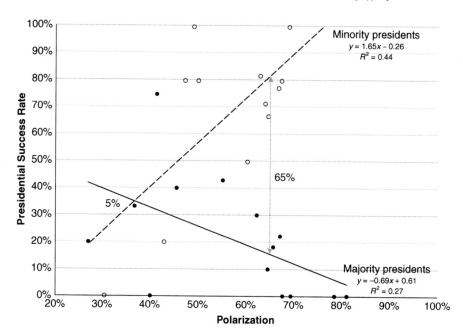

FIGURE 8. Party Polarization and Presidential Success on Cloture Votes, 1962–2012

supermajority coalition necessary to invoke cloture typically requires votes from the minority, but attracting minority votes is unlikely if parties are cohesive and if the filibuster has become a minority party tool. As a result, majority presidents' success rates on cloture decline. Success rates of minority party presidents, in contrast, increase because they usually oppose invoking cloture – it's a lot easier to win if you only need 41 votes that you can get from your own caucus.

Table 2 shows that majority and minority presidents behave as expected. Overall, majority presidents support invoking cloture more than 95 percent of the time, while minority presidents oppose invoking cloture about 74 percent of the time. Consistent with the speculation that the filibuster has become a minority party tool, the tendency of minority presidents to oppose cloture increased from 68 percent for presidents before Bush to 83 percent during the Bush and Obama administrations. The tendency of majority presidents to support cloture increased only slightly (about 3 percent) during Bush and Obama, but with 95.7 percent "yea" positions in the pre-Bush period, there is not much room for growth. Notice, however, that Bush and Obama expressed positions on 71 cloture votes, over 50 percent more than the 46 "yea" positions on cloture expressed by majority presidents before Bush.[7]

---

[7] This analysis understates the increase in presidential positions on cloture. There were more than twice as many years of presidential Senate majorities in the pre-Bush period (19 years

TABLE 2. *Presidential Positions on Cloture Votes*

	Majority Presidents Yea	Minority Presidents Nay
Pre-Bush Years	95.7% (44/46)	67.8% (40/59)
Bush/Obama Years	98.6% (70/71)	83.3% (30/36)
All Years	97.4% (114/117)	73.7% (70/95)

CONCLUSIONS

Thus, the inordinate difficulties that Presidents Bush and Obama have had are largely the result of party polarization in Congress. Both presidents surely made mistakes and fumbles that aggravated the inevitable friction with Congress. Yet it's unlikely that even masterful, flawless presidential bargaining and persuasion that Neustadt advocated could overcome the gridlock. Neustadt's observation that "[w]hat the Constitution separates our political parties do not combine" remains correct, but not because political parties are weak. Highly cohesive, polarized parties have replaced the weak, divided parties Neustadt described, yet the friction between institutions has turned into gridlock. Why? The Constitution created the system of separate institutions sharing power to protect minority rights and promote compromise – not to produce policies that everyone agrees on, but policies that everyone can at least live with. If highly cohesive, polarized partisans on either side refuse to compromise – if the minority is unwilling to live with anything proposed by the other side – the result is policy stalemate. Problems facing the nation remain unsolved, and the partisan battle rages on until the next election. Barring some catastrophic event that compels consensus, the solution resides with voters. A majority (53 percent) of Americans say that leaders should compromise rather than stick to their principles and get nothing done (Newport 2013), yet we keep electing leaders who refuse to compromise. Gridlock is likely to remain until the voters start voting for the type of leaders that they say they want.

from 1962, the first cloture vote with a presidential position in our data set, to 2000) than during the Bush and Obama presidencies (eight years).

REFERENCES

Aldrich, John H. 2011. *Why Parties? A Second Look.* Chicago: University of Chicago Press.

Aldrich, John H., Mark M. Berger and David W. Rohde. 2002. "The Historical Variability in Conditional Party Government, 1877–1986." In David W. Brady and Mathew D. McCubbins, eds., *Party, Process, and Political Change in Congress: New Perspectives on the History of Congress.* Palo Alto, CA: Stanford University Press.

Aldrich, John H., and David W. Rohde. 2000. "The Consequences of Party Organization in the House: The Role of the Majority and Minority Parties in Conditional Party Government." In Jon R. Bond and Richard Fleisher, eds., *Polarized Politics: Congress and the President in a Partisan Era.* Washington, DC: CQ Press.

Binder, Sarah A., Eric D. Lawrence, and Steven S. Smith. 2002. "Tracking the Filibuster, 1917 to 1996." *American Politics Research* 30 (July): 406–422.

Binder, Sarah A., and Steven S. Smith. 2001. *Politics or Principle?: Filibustering in the United States Senate.* Washington, DC: Brookings Institution Press.

Bond, Jon R., and Richard Fleisher, eds. 2000. *Polarized Politics: Congress and the President in a Partisan Era.* Washington, DC: CQ Press.

Bond, Jon R., and Richard Fleisher. 1990. *The President in the Legislative Arena.* Chicago: University of Chicago Press.

Bond, Jon R., Richard Fleisher, and Glen S. Krutz. 2009. "Malign Neglect: Evidence that Delay Has Become the Primary Method of Defeating Presidential Appointments." *Congress and the Presidency* 36 (3): 226–243.

Bond, Jon R., Richard Fleisher, and B. Dan Wood. 2003. "The Marginal and Time Varying Effect of Public Approval on Presidential Success in Congress." *Journal of Politics* 65 (February): 92–110.

Cohen, Jeffrey, Jon R. Bond, and Richard Fleisher. 2013a. "Placing Presidential-Congressional Relations in Context: A Comparison of Barack Obama and His Predecessors." *Polity* 45 (January): 105–126.

Cohen, Jeffrey, Jon R. Bond, and Richard Fleisher. 2013b. "The Implications of the 2012 Presidential Election for Presidential-Congressional Relations: Change or More of the Same?" In Amnon Cavari, Richard J. Powell, and Kenneth R. Mayer, eds., *The 2012 Presidential Election: Forecasts, Outcomes, and Consequences.* New York: Routledge.

Congressional Quarterly, Inc. Annually 1953–2012. "Presidential Support." *Congressional Quarterly Almanac.* Washington, DC: Congressional Quarterly.

Covington, Cary R., J. Mark Wrighton, and Rhonda Kinney. 1995. "A Presidency-Augmented Model of Presidential Success on House Roll Call Votes." *American Journal of Political Science* 39 (November): 1001–1024.

Cox, Gary W., and Mathew D. McCubbins. 2005. *Setting the Agenda: Responsible Party Government Theory in the U.S. House of Representatives.* New York: Cambridge University Press.

Downs, Anthony. 1957. *An Economic Theory of Democracy.* New York: Harper & Row.

Edwards, George C. III. 2009. *The Strategic President: Persuasion and Opportunity in Presidential Leadership.* Princeton, NJ: Princeton University Press.

Edwards, George C. III. 2003. *On Deaf Ears: The Limits of the Bully Pulpit*. New Haven, CT: Yale University Press.

Edwards, George C. III. 1989. *At the Margins: Presidential Leadership of Congress*. New Haven, CT: Yale University Press.

Fleisher, Richard, and Jon R. Bond. 2004. "The Shrinking Middle in the US Congress." *British Journal of Political Science* 34 (July): 529–451.

Fleisher, Richard, and Jon R. Bond. 2000. "Partisanship and the President's Quest for Votes on the Floor of Congress." In Jon R. Bond and Richard Fleisher, eds., *Polarized Politics: Congress and the President in a Partisan Era*. Washington, DC: CQ Press, chap. 8.

Fleisher, Richard, and Jon R. Bond. 1992. "Assessing Presidential Support in the House II: Lessons from George Bush." *American Journal of Political Science* 37 (May): 525–541.

Fleisher, Richard, and Jon R. Bond. 1983. "Assessing Presidential Support in the House: Lessons from Reagan and Carter." *Journal of Politics* 45 (August): 745–758.

Fleisher, Richard, Jon R. Bond, and B. Dan Wood. 2008. "Which Presidents Are Uncommonly Successful in Congress?" In Bert A. Rockman and Richard W. Waterman, eds., *Presidential Leadership: The Vortex of Power*. New York: Oxford University Press, 191–214.

Koger, Gergory. 2010. *Filibustering: A Political History of Obstruction in the House and Senate*. Chicago: University of Chicago Press.

Lee, Frances E. 2009. *Beyond Ideology: Politics, Principles, and Partisanship in the U.S. Senate*. Chicago: University of Chicago Press.

Matthews, Donald. 1960 [1973]. *U.S. Senators and Their World*. New York: W. W. Norton.

Newport, Frank. 2013. "Americans' Desire for Government Leaders to Compromise Increases: By 53% to 25%, say leaders should compromise rather than stick to principles." *Gallup Politics*, September 23. Retrieved from http://www.gallup.com/poll/164570/americans-desire-gov-leaders-compromise-increases.*aspx*. Accessed June 27, 2014.

Neustadt, Richard E. 1960: *Presidential Power: The Politics of Leadership*. New York: Wiley.

Poole, Keith T., and Howard Rosenthal. 1997. *Congress: A Political-Economic History of Roll Call Voting*. New York: Oxford University Press.

Rohde, David W. 1991. *Parties and Leaders in the Postreform House*. Chicago: University of Chicago Press.

Sinclair, Barbara. 2012. *Unorthodox Lawmaking: New Legislative Strategies in the U.S. Congress*. Washington, DC: CQ Press.

Smith, Steven S. 2014. *The Senate Syndrome: The Evolution of Procedural Warfare in the Modern U.S. Senate*. Norman: University of Oklahoma Press.

Wawro, Gregory J., and Eric Schickler. 2006. *Filibuster: Obstruction and Lawmaking in the U.S. Senate*. Princeton, NJ: Princeton University Press.

7

Party Warriors

The Ugly Side of Party Polarization in Congress

Sean M. Theriault

- Party polarization and legislative warfare are not the same thing. One implies ideology, whereas the other implies tactics.
  - The number of senators' amendments that result in roll call votes offers us insight into the warfare dimension. It appears to be related but not identical to polarization.
  - The lion's share of warfare, unlike polarization, can be attributed to relatively few senators.
- Public approval of Congress, even before the 2013 showdowns over the budget and debt ceiling, was at an all-time low. So, too, is comity in Congress.
- Pundits, politicians, and political scientists too frequently discuss these trends under the broad rubric of party polarization.
- This chapter teases out a dimension different from party polarization that I call "partisan warfare." While the concepts are, undoubtedly, related, I argue that their distinction is critical for understanding the current congressional dynamics.
- I show that roll call votes on senators' amendments can give us insight – though not perfectly – into the current partisan warfare in the Senate.

The 2013 double financial fiascos of the government shutdown and the near breaching of the debt ceiling caused unprecedented anger at the U.S. Congress by not just the American citizens, but also governments around the globe. In Mexico City, for example, the crises were known under the all-encompassing term of *berrinche* – literally translated as "spoiled little rich kids."[1] In a recent

---

[1] Quoted in *Damien Cave*, "Viewing U.S. in Fear and Dismay," *The New York Times*, October 15, 2013 (http://www.nytimes.com/2013/10/16/world/viewing-us-in-fear-and-dismay.html?_r=0, accessed on June 10, 2015).

poll, 78 percent of Americans wanted to "throw out [the] entire Congress and start over."[2]

After viewing a poll that would look rosy by this low benchmark, Senator John McCain (R-AZ) concluded that the only congressional supporters these days include "blood relatives and paid staff."[3] In an article titled "Our Broken Senate," Norman Ornstein, the dean of political pundits, argued that "the Senate had taken the term 'deliberate' to a new level ... In many ways, the frustration of modern governance in Washington – the arrogance, independence, parochialism – could be called 'The Curse of the Senate.'" He concludes that the problem with Congress is "the culture," and that "is not going to change anytime soon."[4]

This chorus of dysfunction is given its clearest voice as members of Congress are on their way out the door. When Senator Evan Bayh, whose father also served in the Senate, announced his retirement in 2010, he complained:

For some time, I've had a growing conviction that Congress is not operating as it should. There is much too much partisanship and not enough progress; too much narrow ideology and not enough practical problem-solving. Even at a time of enormous national challenge, the people's business is not getting done ... I love working for the people of Indiana. I love helping our citizens make the most of their lives. But I do not love Congress.[5]

Two years later, when Olympia Snowe announced that she would retire at the end of 2012, she commented, "Unfortunately, I do not realistically expect the partisanship of recent years in the Senate to change over the short term."[6]

When they were announcing their retirement from the Congress, it is my contention that Bayh and Snowe were criticizing the institution on two different, though related, dimensions. First, the members serving today are more ideologically polarized than their predecessors. Although Congress has always had both extreme conservatives and extreme liberals, today's Congress

---

[2] In a report released by Rasmussen on October 15, 2013 (see http://www.rasmussenreports.com /public_content/politics/general_politics/october_2013/78_want_to_throw_out_entire_congress_ and_start_over, accessed October 16, 2013).

[3] As quoted in Norman J. Ornstein, "Obama's Tactic Could Yield Political Results," *Roll Call*, February 8, 2012 (http://www.rollcall.com/issues/57_92/obama_tactic_could_yield_political_ results-212210-1.html, accessed on June 10, 2015).

[4] Norman Ornstein, "Our Broken Senate," *The American: The Journal of the American Enterprise Institute*, March/April 2008 (http://www.aei.org/publication/our-broken-senate/, accessed on June 10, 2015).

[5] Quoted in Lynn Sweet, "Sen. Evan Bayh Won't Run Again," *Chicago Sun Times*, February 15, 2010 (http://blogs.suntimes.com/sweet/2010/02/sen_evan_bayh_wont_run_again_c.html, accessed on June 10, 2015).

[6] As quoted in Paul Kane and Chris Cillizza, "Sen. Olympia Snowe Announces Retirement: Can the GOP Hold Her Seat?" *The Washington Post*, February 29, 2012 (http://www.washing-tonpost.com/politics/sen-olympia-snowe-announces-retirement-can-the-gop-hold-her-seat/2012 /02/29/gIQAlQoTiR_story.html, accessed on June 10, 2015).

seems to have more of them than it did before. As the members have become more ideologically polarized, the moderate middle has shrunk, which has impeded the compromises necessary for solving public policy problems.

Some may think that the growing ideological divide between the parties is reason enough to criticize the institution, but a second complaint seems to bother Snowe, Bayh, their fellow members, political pundits, and congressional scholars even more. That complaint, although it has its roots in party polarization, is combative in nature and requires more than what can be revealed in voting patterns on the floor. I call this second dimension "partisan warfare." The partisan warfare dimension taps into the strategies that go beyond defeating your opponents into humiliating them, go beyond questioning your opponents' judgment into questioning their motives, and go beyond fighting the good legislative fight to destroying the institution and the legislative process in order to serve not only your ideological goals, but also your electoral goals.

The rise of warfare within a polarizing Congress certainly suggests a link between the two. Indeed, polarization may be necessary for warfare, but it is not a sufficient cause of it. Parties that are divided over policy can have a serious and honest debate, which can even become heated. In the first half of the famous idiom, the opposing sides can "agree to disagree." Quite apart from the serious policy disagreement, though, the debate between the opposing sides can degenerate into a shouting match where the policy proscriptions are lost in a fight over legislative games where the combatants question the motives, integrity, and patriotism of their opponents. Under such a situation, the second half of the idiom – "without being disagreeable" – is never realized.

This partisan warfare dimension is harder to quantify, though it most certainly exists. What I call "partisan warfare" is what Barbara Sinclair (2006: 364) called "ugly politics" in a book titled *Party Wars*. She defined ugly politics as "politics descending to personal attacks that are inflammatory and untrue." Frances Lee (2009) loosened up this definition in recasting it as "beyond ideology" in her book of the same name. Lee argues that only so much of the divide between the parties can be understood as a difference in ideology. The rest of the divide – by some accounts, the lion's share of the divide – is motivated by some other goal. Lee (2009: 193) defines this behavior as "partisan bickering" and offers the following description:

If partisanship has roots in members' political interests, then political parties actually exacerbate and institutionalize conflict, rather than merely represent and give voice to preexisting policy disagreements in the broader political environment. In their quest to win elections and wield power, partisans impeach one another's motives, question one another's ethics and competence, engage in reflexive partisanship, and – when it is politically useful to do so – exploit and deepen divisions rather than seeking common ground.

I argue that it is this portion of the divide that causes the angst of those participants and observers of today's Congress. Lee restricts her evaluation of the combat that is beyond ideology to an examination of roll call votes, which is an appropriate first step. Partisan warfare, though, can operate in contexts beyond the yeas and nays on the floor. In fact, it is frequently other actions in the legislative and electoral processes that are better exhibits of partisan warfare.

More often than not, congressional scholars have opted to merge these two dimensions for a couple of reasons. First, they are clearly related. The distinction between party polarization and partisan warfare can easily be masked as the same or at least similar enough to collapse on to one dimension. Second, the second dimension of partisan warfare, especially in comparison to the first, is much harder to isolate, operationalize, and analyze. Nonetheless, real analytic leverage can be brought to our understanding of how the current Senate operates and how it is evaluated if these dimensions are pulled apart.

In this chapter, I tease out these two dimensions by examining the U.S. Senate. First, I argue that the Senate, because of its loose rules, provides for fertile ground to explore this second dimension. I also briefly outline the first dimension – party polarization in the Senate. In the second section, I present three anecdotes that clearly show behavior consistent with partisan warfare. In the third section, I undertake a more systematic examination of partisan warfare by examining senators' amendments that result in roll call votes. I find that the number of roll call votes on senators' amendments provides material for assessing partisan warfare, but that the measure needs to be refined to capture more fully this second dimension. Before concluding, I put both dimensions back together to assess the utility of separating partisan warfare from party polarization.

PARTY POLARIZATION IN THE U.S. SENATE

A surprising result from the polarization studies is not that the gap between the parties is bigger in the House (Fleisher and Bond 2004; Theriault 2008), it is that it is even as close as it is. Because the House is a majoritarian institution, good reasons exist for the parties to reveal distinctly different voting patterns. Ironically, instead of impeding the passage of legislation, party polarization in the House actually fosters it (Sinclair 2006). A clear distinction between the majority party and the minority party compels the majority party to endow its leaders with more power to pass the party's program (Rohde and Aldrich 2010).

The Fertile Ground of the Senate

When senators removed the motion to order the previous question from their rules in 1806, they began down a path that required senators to be more collegial if they hoped to pass bills. The 60-vote cloture requirement and the ability of any one single senator to virtually bring the entire institution to a halt compels senators to treat their institution more gingerly than representatives do the House, where the minority party has little recourse. Indeed, the one big difference between Asher's (1973) norms of the House and Matthews's (1960) folkways in the Senate is that the latter includes loyalty to the institution; there is no such House norm.

For these reasons, the Senate presents more fertile ground for examining the distinction between party polarizers and partisan warriors. Before turning to measures of the latter, I establish the bedrock for the former in the following section. I then turn to a more explicit consideration of the second dimension – partisan warfare.

The First Dimension of Party Polarization

The recent congressional elections have brought about the most polarized Congress since at least the early 1900s. I analyze Poole and Rosenthal's (1997) DW-NOMINATE data in this section to show how polarized the parties inside the Senate have become (see Chapter 16, this volume). These data, which are generated from all nonconsensual roll call votes, range from –1 for extremely liberal members to +1 for extremely conservative members.

The congresses after the 1964 election and into the 1970s were some of the least polarized in modern history. In the congresses during the Johnson administration, the Senate Republicans were less conservative than the Senate Democrats were liberal. By the time the Republicans took back the Senate in Clinton's first midterm election, though, the Senate Republicans became more ideologically extreme than the Democrats. In the 112th Congress (2011–12), the Republicans' votes were 32 percent more polarized than the Senate Democrats (see Figure 1). Such disparity in the parties gives credibility to the arguments offered by Hacker and Pierson (2005), Theriault and Rohde (2011), Mann and Ornstein (2012), and Theriault (2013) that the Republican members are primarily responsible for the growing divide between the parties in Congress.

Since Johnson's reelection in 1964, the Senate Democrats have become only 27 percent more polarizing – the Senate Republicans, on the other hand, have become more than 70 percent more polarizing. Both parties in the Senate are heading toward their ideological endpoint, but they are not moving at the same rate. For every step that the Senate Democrats are taking, the Senate Republicans are taking three steps!

PARTISAN WARRIOR ANECDOTES

While roll call votes provide a relatively easy way of measuring party polarization, measuring partisan warrior behavior is much more difficult, especially in a comprehensive and systematic fashion. Before engaging in that

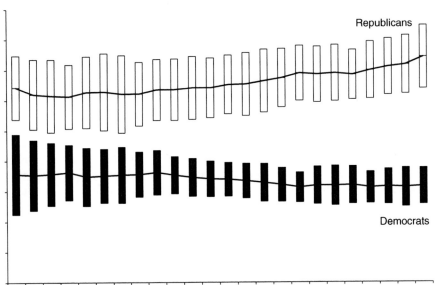

FIGURE I. Ideology by Party in the U.S. Senate, 89th–112th Congresses (1965–2012)

arduous task, I motivate the partisan warfare dimension with three recent anecdotes. In the following section, I offer a more systematical analysis.

Changing Positions – the Budget Commission

On December 9, 2009, Senators Kent Conrad (D-ND) and Judd Gregg (R-NH) introduced S. 2853, a bill to establish the Bipartisan Task Force for Responsible Fiscal Action. The bill had 29 cosponsors, including 12 Democrats and 17 Republicans. Over the next week, five more senators signed on as cosponsors (one Democrat and four Republicans). At introduction, President Barack Obama was skeptical of the proposed commission.

On January 20, 2010, Obama changed his mind and fully endorsed the idea of the commission. Within hours of Obama's announcement, John McCain (R-AR) and Jim Inhofe (R-OK) withdrew as cosponsors of the bill. The next day, Conrad and Gregg formally introduced the language of their bill as an amendment to the debt-limit bill, which was being debated on the Senate floor. On the same day, Mike Crapo (R-ID) and Sam Brownback (R-KS) withdrew as cosponsors. On the following day, Kay Baily Hutchison (R-TX) and John Ensign (R-NV) withdrew as cosponsors.

On January 26, Conrad and Gregg were able to get a majority, but not the 60 votes that the bill's unanimous consent agreement required for the underlying bill to be amended. Only 53 senators supported the commission; the only absent senator was Lisa Murkowski (R-AK), who remained a cosponsor of the proposal. The Democrats voted 37–23 in favor of the amendment; the Republicans voted 16–23 against the amendment. Those voting "no" included the six Republicans who withdrew as cosponsors of the bill as well as Robert Bennett (R-UT), who would withdraw as a cosponsor on the bill two days later. After its defeat in the Senate, Obama created a commission with weaker power through an executive order. It would come to be known as the Simpson-Bowles Commission.

Various reasons could explain why the seven Republicans voted against the amendment after signing on to the bill. Perhaps the easiest explanations are for Bennett and Hutchison, who were involved in tough primary fights that they would ultimately lose.[7] McCain, too, was involved in a tough primary, but he ultimately prevailed by 24 percentage points. Such obvious rationales do not exist for the remaining four Republicans. None of the others faced serious or imminent electoral reprisals. Given that 22 Democrats also voted against the amendment, something other than ideology motivated the 7 Republicans to withdrawal their support from the bill.

David Vitter and the "Saxbe Fix"

To protect the people from a corrupt system where members could create plush government jobs for themselves, the U.S. Constitution explicitly prohibits lawmakers from serving in an executive branch position for which they voted either to create or to increase the salary thereof. This restriction, called the Emolument Clause, has befuddled presidents and their potential appointees for years by erecting barriers for members to serve in the president's cabinet after they have voted to raise the cabinet secretaries' pay. The current workaround strategy was first used in 1973 when President Nixon wanted Senator William Saxbe (R-OH), who had earlier supported a pay increase for cabinet officials, to be his attorney general. Nixon asked Congress to pass a law reducing the attorney general's salary to the level it was before the raise that Saxbe supported. The reduced salary would last until the Senate term for which Saxbe was elected ended, at which point Congress would pass another law increasing the attorney general's salary to that of all the other cabinet officials. This workaround had passed muster by both the courts and Congress ever since.[8]

When Senators Hillary Clinton (D-NY) and Ken Salazar (D-CO) took their seats in the Obama cabinet in 2009, their pay was cut to what the secretaries of state and interior, respectively, made on the day before the term to which they were currently elected. As Clinton's Senate term would not have ended until

---

[7] Hutchison challenged incumbent Governor Rick Perry, but lost in the primary. Bennett was seeking reelection, though the convention process, which Utah uses, denied him renomination.

[8] President Jimmy Carter used the Saxbe Fix to install Senator Muskie as Secretary of State, and President Bill Clinton used it to install Lloyd Bentsen as Secretary of the Treasury.

2013, Salazar would first face the prospect of having his salary raised as a consequence of the second part of the "Saxbe Fix" when Salazar's Senate term would have ended in 2011. Majority Leader Harry Reid and Minority Leader Mitch McConnell worked out a unanimous consent agreement to pass a bill that would have increased Salazar's pay by $19,600 to $199,700, the same that all the other cabinet secretaries made with the exception of Clinton.

On May 23, 2011, David Vitter (R-LA) announced that he was placing a hold on the bill raising Salazar's pay until the Interior Department started "issuing new [deepwater drilling] permits at the same rate as before the Deepwater Horizon oil spill." Vitter argued that it was his "way of keeping the 'boot on the neck' of Interior until they get the job done."[9] Reid, who was blind-sided by the move, criticized Vitter's move: "It is wrong for Sen. Vitter to try to get something in return for moving forward on a matter that the Senate has considered routine for more than a century."[10] He vowed to keep fighting for Salazar's raise.

In a letter to Reid and McConnell the following day, Salazar asked them to "set aside any effort to address" the inequality in his pay. He feared that he needed to take the issue off the table because of Vitter's actions, which he thought constituted a bribe. A Vitter spokesperson retorted that charging Vitter of "bribery" would only "make my boss a Louisiana folk hero."[11] Vitter's response was a bit more temperate, "I'm glad the secretary has dropped his push for a pay raise ... Now I hope he starts earning what he already makes and properly issues new permits for much-needed drilling in the Gulf."[12] Salazar, until the day he retired in 2013, made nearly $20,000 less than the rest of the Cabinet.[13]

---

[9] From a Vitter press release (http://vitter.senate.gov/public/index.cfm?FuseAction=PressRoom .PressReleases&ContentRecord_id=1e453722-cbf2-c8f2-461c-11474e0559a6, accessed on December 18, 2011). The "boot on the neck" quote is the same one that Salazar used in reference to BP as it started cleaning up the Gulf.

[10] As quoted in Amanda Becker, "Reid Faults Vitter, Presses for Raise for Salazar," *Roll Call*, May 25, 2011 (http://www.rollcall.com/news/reid_faults_vitter_salazar_raise_gulf-205980-1.html, accessed on June 10, 2015).

[11] As quoted in Amanda Becker, "Reid Faults Vitter, Presses for Raise for Salazar," *Roll Call*, May 25, 2011 (http://www.rollcall.com/news/reid_faults_vitter_salazar_raise_gulf-205980-1.html, accessed on June 10, 2015).

[12] As quoted in Amanda Becker, "Reid Faults Vitter, Presses for Raise for Salazar," *Roll Call*, May 25, 2011 (http://www.rollcall.com/news/reid_faults_vitter_salazar_raise_gulf-205980-1.html, accessed on June 10, 2015).

[13] A Senate Ethics Committee, in dismissing a complaint by the Citizens for Responsibility and Ethics in Washington, chastised Vitter in a letter written by the chair Barbara Boxer (D-CA) and vice chair Johnny Isakson: "While the committee found that there was no substantial credible evidence that you violated the law or Senate rules, it did conclude that it is inappropriate to condition support for a Secretary's personal salary increase directly on his or her performance of a specific official act." Quoted in Darren Goode, "After Ethics Ruling, David Vitter Vows to Keep Blocking Ken Salazar's Pay Raise," politico.com, March 30, 2012 (http://www.politico.com /news/stories/0312/74689.html, accessed on April 22, 2012).

It has become common for senators to put holds on bills to force a presidential administration to take a particular action. It is not even that unusual for a hold to be placed on a bill that had cleared both the minority and majority leader. It is precisely because bills such as these get held up that the leaders circulate their unanimous consent agreements before they offer them on the Senate floor. What is extraordinary about Vitter's actions is the lack of senatorial courtesy with which they were carried out. The actions are even more out of step because they, in effect, punished a former senator, who was well respected on both sides of the aisle, as evidenced by his unanimous confirmation vote. Again, ideology does not seem to be the primary factor motivating Vitter's hold.

No Reindeer Games for the Gingrich Senators

The 112th Congress was difficult for most senators. Democrats were frustrated that the Republicans made legislating exceedingly difficult. The Republicans were frustrated that the Democrats would not consider important legislation passed by the House. Furthermore, they were frustrated that Obama was still in the White House and the Democrats were still a majority in the Senate.

Shortly after Thanksgiving in 2011, Senator Al Franken (D-MN), who is Jewish, decided that the Senate needed to institute a new tradition to ease tensions. In conspiring with Senator Mike Johanns (R-NE), he sent an email to his colleagues asking them to participate in a Senate version of Secret Santa. As Franken explained: "I remember one year [as a child] I picked this kid who used to intimidate me on the playground. Turns out after we got to know each other and we became friends. So, I thought Secret Santa would be a good way to cut through the partisan divide here in the Senate. And who knows, maybe it will create some unlikely friendships."[14] Franken and Johanns set the limit at $10 and picked December 13 as the date that they would exchange gifts.

The trick for the Secret Santa to work, though, was for the senators to participate. They did. At least 58 – and, perhaps, as many as 61 – senators offered their names up for the possibility of increasing comity (and, perhaps, comedy) in the Senate.[15] The participation rate varied by party. While at least 45 percent of the Republicans participated, 70 percent of Democrats did.[16] Secret Santa participation cannot be explained by ideology. The average DW-NOMINATE of the Republicans who did participate was 0.46 compared to 0.50 for those that did not participate. The difference was even smaller for

[14] As quoted in Jennifer Steinhauer, "Secret Santa in the Senate," *The New York Times*, November 30, 2011 (http://thecaucus.blogs.nytimes.com/2011/11/30/secret-santa-in-the-senate/, accessed on June 10, 2015).

[15] On the day of the drawing, 58 senators participated. On the day of the gift exchange, news accounts indicated that as many as 61 senators exchanged gifts. All news accounts said that either 21 or 22 Republicans participated. Through an extensive search of the Internet, including news articles, press releases, and blogs, 21 Republican senators and 29 Democratic senators could be identified.

[16] The proportions are statistically significantly different from one another ($p = 0.015$).

the Democrats. Participating Democrats had an average ideology of −0.35 compared to −0.37 for those who did not participate. Neither of these differences nears statistical significance.[17]

Not only was one senator unwilling to participate, but he ridiculed the entire enterprise. Pat Toomey (R-PA) scoffed at the gift exchange. When Ginni Thomas, wife of Supreme Court Justice Clarence Thomas, asked him on her radio show what he would give Majority Leader Harry Reid if he were to have participated, Toomey replied: "I would give him the inspiration to do a budget. I think I would try to inspire him to take responsibility that the majority party in the United States Senate ought to accept, which is to lay out to the American people just what they intend to do with American taxpayer dollars."[18] Perhaps if he had participated, he would have gotten lumps of coal from Senator Joe Manchin (D-WV). Instead, Manchin gave those lumps of coal, which were carved into a donkey and an elephant, to Senator Chuck Schumer (D-NY).[19]

A MORE SYSTEMATIC LOOK AT PARTISAN WARFARE

The anecdotes from the previous section help motivate the existence of this second dimension. I try to measure that dimension more systematically in this section by examining the number of roll call votes on senators' amendments. Admittedly, this metric cannot possible encapsulate the entirety of the second dimension of partisan warfare in the way that roll call votes can capture the first dimension of party polarization. Nonetheless, the metric can begin to scope out the distinction between party polarization and partisan warfare – or if you like "ugly politics" or the stuff that is beyond ideology.

Senators may have a variety of reasons for offering an amendment on the Senate floor. The most obvious reason is that they hope to move the bill closer to their preferred policy. Indeed, I suspect a good number of amendments on the Senate floor have exactly that purpose at heart. The debate on the Affordable Care Act (aka, Obamacare) presents other reasons why senators may offer amendments.

On March 24, 2010, Senator Coburn (R-OK) introduced an amendment that prohibited sex offenders from using the health insurance that was being established in Obama's health care reform package to pay for Viagra. Especially given that existing law explicitly forbade it, what senator would possibly vote against such an amendment? As it turned out, 55 out of 57 Democrats did.[20]

---

[17] $P = 0.55$ for Republican and $p = 0.47$ for the Democrats.

[18] See http://dailycaller.com/2011/12/24/sen-toomey-on-his-secret-santa-gift-for-sen-reid-video/#ixzz1pNuuuooo, accessed on March 17, 2012.

[19] To learn more about the gifts given and received, see Ann Gerhart, "Senate's Secret Santas Make Their Rounds," *The Washington Post*, December 13, 2011. Interestingly, the article was published in the Style section, not the front page.

[20] The floor mechanics on this amendment are a bit tricky. Instead of subjecting Democrats to an explicit vote on the amendment, Senate Max Baucus (D-Montana) offered a motion to table

During this particular debate, the Democrats were orchestrating a complex legislative maneuver that could lead to the passage of health care reform without explicitly overcoming a Republican-led filibuster. By passing the measure through the reconciliation process, the Democrats only needed a majority, but they could not change a word in the bill or the entire process might unravel. As such, the Republicans had the Democrats in the difficult position of voting down amendments that might otherwise seem constructive or reasonable.

In addition to voting down the prohibition of paying for sex offenders' Viagra, the Democrats defeated an amendment by Mike Crapo (R-ID) that would ensure that no individual making less than $200,000 would be subject to a tax increase as a consequence of the legislation. They also defeated an amendment by John Ensign (R-NV) to protect the damages in medical malpractice suits resulting from pro bono cases. By voting against each of these amendments, Democrats could be subject to campaign commercials arguing that they voted to give Viagra to sex offenders, to raise taxes on those making less than $200,000, and to subject pro bono health care providers to exorbitant malpractice lawsuits. No Democrat disagreed when Senator Max Baucus (D-MT) called Coburn's amendment "[a] crass political stunt aimed at making a 30-second commercial."[21]

In addition to sincerely trying to move policy closer to the sponsor's preferred policy, offering amendments on the Senate floor can have at least two other motivations. First, a senator can get his or her colleagues on the record for controversial policies that might divide their party leadership from their constituencies. Furthermore, so long as 20 senators agree, amendments must be disposed of through roll call votes, which can take up to a half hour to complete, rather than a 10-second voice vote. In comparison to the first – more earnest – reason for offering amendments, these later two reasons are a bit more nefarious.

Coburn's, Crapo's, and Ensign's amendments, while separating Democrats from Republicans, were not manifestations of how conservative the Republicans had become or how liberal the Democrats had become. These amendments highlighted warfare, not polarization. In an ideal world, warfare would be measured by the number of holds – or threats of placing holds – that senators make. Regrettably, holds are often secret. No reliable count exists. An examination of roll call votes from senators' amendments, nevertheless, can provide some insight into partisan warfare and obstructionism in the Senate.

Using roll call votes on amendments as a proxy for partisan warfare is legitimate so long as it correctly answers three questions. First, does it pass

---

Coburn's amendment. Fifty-five out of 57 Democrats voted for that motion, thus the amendment was tabled, which in this instance is equivalent to defeating the amendment.

[21] As quoted in Chris Casteel, "U.S. Sen. Tom Coburn's Viagra Amendment Fails," *NewsOK*, March 25, 2010 (http://newsok.com/u.s.-sen.-tom-coburns-viagra-amendment-fails/article /3449000, accessed on December 20, 2011).

the "face validity" test? In other words, are the senators whose amendments receive the most roll call votes the same senators that we think of as generals in the partisan war? Second, do amendments from senators in the minority result in more roll call votes than senators in the majority? Whereas majority party senators have the responsibility of governing, the minority party senators have the burden of trying to become the majority during the next election cycle. Third, are ideologically extreme senators more likely to offer amendments that result in roll call votes? If offering amendments were based on sincerely trying to move policy, senators from the middle of the ideological continuum should be the most active in trying to change policy. If, instead, senators at the ideological extreme are offering more amendments that result in roll call votes, then evidence will exist for the more nefarious reasons for offering amendments.

The Face Validity Test

From the 103rd (1993–94) to the 112th (2011–12) Congress, the Senate took 4,324 roll call votes on amendments, averaging approximately four roll call votes per senator in each congress. Some congresses resulted in more roll call votes than others. In the 104th Congress (1995–96), in the wake of the new Republican majority promising a more open and deliberative process, each senator's amendments resulted in an average of 6.5 roll call votes. In the 112th Congress, as Senate Majority Leader Harry Reid (D-NV) clamped down on the fully engaged death-by-amendment strategy, each senator's amendments only resulted in an average of two roll call votes. Reid blocked senators from even offering amendments by "filling the amendment tree."[22] The escalation in the war on the Senate floor is certainly a cause for the substantial drop in roll call votes on amendments in the last congress.

The partisan warfare proxy of roll call votes on amendments passes the face validity test. The list of senators whose amendments cause the most roll call votes reads like a who's who of partisan warriors in the Senate (see Table 1). In addition to his Viagra amendment in the 111th Congress contributing to his top rank, Coburn makes the list three times, as does John McCain (R-AZ). Democratic senators Barbara Boxer (D-CA), Ted Kennedy (D-MA), and Paul Wellstone (D-MN) make the list twice – each time while serving in the minority. Partisan warriors Jesse Helms (R-NC), Robert Byrd (D-WV), Jim DeMint (R-SC), David Vitter (R-LA), and Rand Paul (R-KY) are also prominently featured on the list.

A few names on the list are a bit surprising. Byron Dorgan (D-SD) and Dale Bumpers (D-AR) were never considered to be Senate malcontents.

---

[22] During the first 10 months of the 112th Congress alone, CRS counted 41 times when Reid blocked other senators from offering amendments (see http://www.coburn.senate.gov /public//index.cfm?a=Files.Serve&File_id=86a87020-75dc-4335-b192-ced34c6b8bd1, accessed October 25, 2013).

TABLE 1. *Senators Whose Amendments Cause the Most Roll Call Votes, 103rd to 112th Congresses (1993–2012)*

Rank	Congress	Senator	Roll Call Votes
1	111th	Tom Coburn (R-OK)	49
2T	110th	Tom Coburn (R-OK)	34
2T	110th	Jim DeMint (R-SC)	34
4	103rd	Jesse Helms (R-NC)	33
5	104th	Paul Wellstone (D-MN)	29
6T	108th	Robert Byrd (D-WV)	28
6T	104th	Tom Harkin (D-IA)	28
6T	103rd	John McCain (R-AZ)	28
9	111th	John McCain (R-AZ)	27
10T	112th	Tom Coburn (R-OK)	25
10T	104th	Byron Dorgan (D-ND)	25
10T	106th	Paul Wellstone (D-MN)	25
13	103rd	George Mitchell (D-ME)	24
14	111th	David Vitter (R-LA)	23
15	106th	Ted Kennedy (D-MA)	22
16T	104th	Barbara Boxer (D-CA)	21
16T	103rd	Hank Brown (R-CO)	21
16T	104th	Dale Bumpers (D-AR)	21
16T	112th	Rand Paul (R-KY)	21
20	104th	Bob Dole (R-KA)	20
21T	108th	Barbara Boxer (D-CA)	19
21T	109th	Ted Kennedy (D-MA)	19
21T	104th	John McCain (R-AZ)	19
21T	111th	John Thune (R-SD)	19

Furthermore, we could imagine party leaders being partisan warriors, but the inclusion of George Mitchell (D-ME) and Bob Dole (R-KS) on the list when they served as majority leaders suggests that this metric for measuring partisan warfare is not perfect.

Amendment Roll Call Votes in the Majority and Minority

If the number of amendment roll call votes is a valid indicator for partisan warriors, the minority party senators should be responsible for more votes than the majority party senators. During the 10 congresses since 1993, the minority party senators are responsible for two-thirds more amendment roll call votes than the majority party senators (see Table 2). Of the 10 congresses, the pattern reaches conventional levels of statistical significance eight times. It fails most explicitly in the 107th Congress (2001–12), when the Republican majority becomes a

TABLE 2. *The Difference between the Minority Party and the Majority Party Amending Activity, 103rd to 112th Congresses (1993–2012)*

Congress	Majority Party	Minority Party Average	Majority Party Average	Difference	Statistical Significance
103rd	Democrat	7.0	3.6	3.5	0.0030
104th	Republican	8.8	4.7	4.1	0.0008
105th	Republican	4.1	3.7	0.4	0.5591
106th	Republican	5.2	3.6	1.6	0.0760
107th	Democrat	3.4	4.7	-1.3	0.0750
108th	Republican	7.1	2.1	5.0	0.0000
109th	Republican	5.9	3.0	2.9	0.0006
110th	Democrat	5.2	3.2	2.0	0.0990
111th	Democrat	7.0	2.1	4.9	0.0003
112th	Democrat	2.9	1.4	1.5	0.0450
	103rd–112th	5.6	3.2	2.4	0.0000

minority only after Jim Jeffords (I-VT) resigns from the Republican Party six months into the Bush administration.

The trend of minority party senators causing more amendment roll call votes can be seen not only through a congress-by-congress analysis, but also through the congressional careers of a few senators (see Figure 2). Two Democrats – Frank Lautenberg (D-NJ) and Barbara Boxer (D-CA) – and two Republicans – John McCain (R-AZ) and Jon Kyl (R-AZ) – show how minority party status influences the number of roll call votes caused by their amendments. When Lautenberg served in the minority, the roll call votes caused by his amendments were four times greater than when he was in the majority; Boxer's amendments resulted in slightly less than three times as many roll calls when she served in the minority. McCain, perhaps indicative of his role as a "maverick," is active on the Senate floor while serving both in the minority and in the majority, though as a minority-party senator, his amendments are responsible for almost three additional roll call votes. His same-state colleague, Kyl, is responsible for almost twice as many amendment roll call votes when serving in the minority.

A more systematic test of this hypothesis can be performed through a fixed effects regression model that controls for both the senator and the congress. Such a test reveals that minority party status increases the number of roll call votes on senators' amendments by two. Considering that the constant is only 1.4, this effect is fairly large. Furthermore, the within R^2 of 0.13 suggests that a not insignificant amount of the variation within an individual senator's amending activity can be explained by his or her status in the minority party.

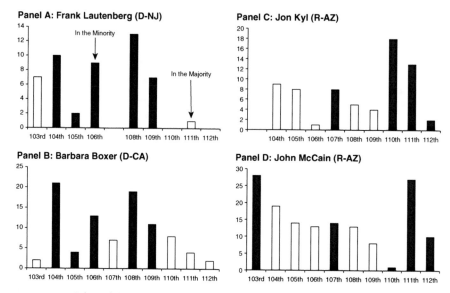

FIGURE 2. Selected Senators and Amending Activity in the Minority and Majority, 103rd to 112th Congresses

Amending Activity of Ideologically Extreme Senators

The number of roll call votes that come from senators' amendments passes the first two tests. The third test examines the differences in amending activity based on ideological extremism. If this third hypothesis is true, the two dimensions of party polarization and partisan warfare are correlated. In fact, the truer the relationship between ideology and amending activity, the less distinct the two dimensions become. At the extreme, if the amending activity is perfectly correlated with ideology, then the two dimensions collapse on to the one dimension that has received the bulk of the political science analysis.

Ideology, especially as mediated by the minority party status, has a marked effect on the senators' amending activity. For a Democrat going from a DW-NOMINATE score of 0.00 (moderate) to −1.00 (liberal), the predicted number of amendment roll call votes increases by 3 in the majority, but by 22 in the minority (see Figure 3, panel A). The differences for Republicans are not quite as dramatic (see Figure 3, panel B). Changing a moderate into an extreme conservative increases their amendments by 3 in the majority to 13 in the minority.

Nonetheless, the relationship is not perfect. The overall R^2 for the model is 0.23, which suggests that a good chunk of the amending activity is neither minority party status nor ideology.

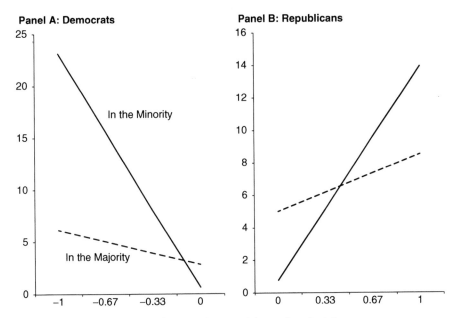

FIGURE 3. The Effect of Ideology on Senators' Amending Activity

A SECOND DIMENSION – PARTISAN WARFARE?

With the passing of three tests by the amendment roll call votes, in this section I present the two dimensions of party polarization as measured by DW-NOMINATE and partisan warfare as measured by roll call votes on amendments. The results from the tests as well as the argument itself suggest that partisan warfare will be easier to measure in the minority party. To see if warfare, like polarization, is an asymmetric phenomenon between the parties, I examine a recent congress for each party when they toiled in the minority. The two-dimensional depiction of party polarization and partisan warfare is presented in Figure 4. The axes are at the party averages for the respective parties. As such, the quadrants can roughly be thought of as a two-by-two table with data points populated within the "cells" of the table.

The Democrats were last in the minority in the 109th Congress (2005–06). They were particularly embittered because one of their own – John Kerry (D-MA) – had lost the presidential race to President Bush and by only one state. Furthermore, the Democrats lost four Senate seats, including the one held by their leader, Tom Daschle (D-SD). Democrats were particularly upset that Daschle's Republican counterpart, Bill Frist (R-TN), broke a long-standing Senate norm when he campaigned in the state of his leader counterpart.

The Democrats are scattered across the four quadrants relatively equally (see panel A of Figure 4). Six Democrats are partisan warriors. Thirteen

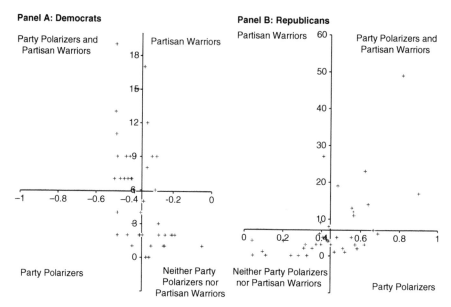

FIGURE 4. The Two Dimensions – Party Polarizers and Partisan Warriors

Democrats are party polarizers and partisan warriors, while 9 are partisan warriors, but not party polarizers. The remaining 15 are neither polarizers nor warriors.

Rather than showing the two dimensions in the 112th Congress (2011–12) when Senate Majority Leader Harry Reid (D-NV) exercised his prerogative of filling the amendment tree on so many occasions, I show the 111th Congress (2009–10) when the practice was relatively less prevalent. The bitter feelings from the 109th Congress crossed the aisle to the Republican side in the 111th Congress. One of their own, John McCain (R-AZ), was defeated in the presidential election and, shocking to most political observers, they lost their comfortable eight-seat margin to lose the majority. The Republicans were as spread out across the two-dimensional space as their Democratic counterparts were two congresses prior. Eight Republicans were both polarizers and warriors. Just three Republicans were warriors, but not polarizers. Twelve Republicans were polarizers, but not warriors. The remaining 18 Republicans were neither polarizers nor warriors.

This analysis of roll call votes on amendments suggests a few results. First, these roll call votes seem to be a good proxy for partisan warfare. The fact that Tom Coburn, the writer of the Viagra amendment, had 15 more amendment roll call votes than the second person on the list in the last 20 years in the Senate speaks to its power. The list of high amendment roll call vote senators suggests that it is not just the paramount of the list that receives face validity.

Furthermore, the data analysis suggests that it is exactly the senators who we would expect to be partisan warriors that are partisan warriors at least as defined by which senators' amendments result in roll call votes. Minority party members who are particularly ideologically extreme are the most likely to sponsor amendments that receive roll call votes.

Second, while party polarization seems to be widespread by the senators in both parties, the death-by-amendment strategy seems to be carried out explicitly by relatively few senators. In the 109th Congress, the five most liberal Democrats were responsible for 15 percent of the total Democratic party polarization. In contrast, the five Democrats whose amendments resulted in the most roll call votes, accounted for 31 percent of the Democratic total. The distinction between generals and foot soldiers was even bigger within the Republican Party in the 111th Congress. The five most conservative Republicans were responsible for 20 percent of the total Republican polarization. The five Republicans whose amendments resulted in the most roll call votes accounted for 47 percent of the Republican total. In fact, the top six had more amendment roll call votes than the other 35 Republicans serving in the Senate. The five-star general, Coburn, alone had 17 percent of the total, though he constituted just 2.5 percent of the Republican Conference. While party polarizers seem to abound in both parties, partisan warfare appears to be carried out by relatively few minority party members.

Third, though, this measure is not perfect for capturing this second dimension. The strong correlation between roll call votes on amendments and ideology suggests, in fact, that the two dimensions might not be that distinct. This analysis suggests that the measure needs to undergo further refinement in order to capture more vividly partisan warfare. In future research, I will examine the underlying voting behavior on these amendments. The moderates who are sponsoring more amendments, and thus being called "partisan warriors," may be doing so for nefarious purposes, but also for virtuous ones. If the underlying votes on their amendments are bipartisan, then it would be wrong to characterize their behavior as warfare rather than the normal legislative behavior practiced by actively engaged senators. If their amendments, however, do not receive support from the majority party, we will have more evidence for their partisan warfare behavior.

CONCLUSION

In this chapter, I have attempted to tease out a second dimension of party polarization in the U.S. Senate. Most scholars studying this phenomenon in Congress focus only on the ideological spread as witnessed by roll call voting. The disgust registered by not only the American public, but also the participants in the process suggests that something "beyond ideology" – in the words of Frances Lee (2009) – is going on.

While partisan warfare is a difficult concept to quantify, the quotes from Bayh and Snowe suggest something more than polarization is ruining their beloved Senate; and although more than ideology is motivating Coburn's Viagra amendment, no easily quantifiable metric can be gathered to measure warfare. In this chapter, I argue that the number of roll call votes caused by senators' amendments is a proxy that can be used systematically to understand partisan warfare in the Senate.

Vitter's attempt to "bribe" Secretary Salazar, the rejection of a bipartisan budget commission by one-time supporters, and the lack of across-the-board participation in the Secret Santa suggest that senators sometimes act not out of their ideological preferences, but out of their desire to win – and to win at almost any cost. The more comprehensive data analysis suggests a systematic explanation with partisan warfare at its roots can explain senators' actions in a way above and beyond their ideology. This analysis suggests that senator amendment activity may be used as the basis of getting at partisan warfare, but not without some refinement, which I hope to conduct in future research.

REFERENCES

Asher, Herbert B. 1973. "The Learning of Legislative Norms." *American Political Science Review* 67 (2): 499–513.

Fleisher, Richard, and Jon R. Bond. 2004. "The Shrinking Middle in the US Congress." *British Journal of Political Science* 34: 429–451.

Hacker, Jacob S., and Paul Pierson. 2005. *Off Center: The Republican Revolution and the Erosion of American Democracy*. New Haven, CT: Yale University Press.

Lee, Frances E. 2009. *Beyond Ideology: Politics, Principles, and Partisanship in the U.S. Senate*. Chicago: University of Chicago Press.

Mann, Thomas E., and Norman J. Ornstein. 2012. *It's Even Worse Than It Looks: How the American Constitutional System Collided with the New Politics of Extremism*. New York: Basic Books.

Matthews, Donald R. 1960. *U.S. Senators and Their World*. Chapel Hill: University of North Carolina Press.

Poole, Keith T., and Howard Rosenthal. 1997. *Congress: A Political-Economic History of Roll Call Voting*. New York: Oxford University Press.

Rohde, David, and John Aldrich. 2010. "Consequences of Electoral and Institutional Change: The Evolution of the Conditional Party Government in the U.S. House of Representatives." In Jeffrey M. Stonecash, ed., *New Directions in American Political Parties*. New York: Routledge.

Sinclair, Barbara. 2006. *Party Wars: Polarization and the Politics of National Policy Making*. Norman: University of Oklahoma Press.

Theriault, Sean M. 2013. *The Gingrich Senators: The Roots of Partisan Warfare in Congress*. New York: Oxford University Press.

Theriault, Sean M. 2008. *Party Polarization in Congress*. New York: Cambridge University Press.

Theriault, Sean M., and David W. Rohde. 2011. "The Gingrich Senators and Party Polarization in the U.S. Senate." *Journal of Politics* 73 (4): 1011–1024.

8

The Sources and Consequences of Polarization in the U.S. Supreme Court

Brandon L. Bartels

This chapter examines polarization in the U.S. Supreme Court, primarily from the post–New Deal era to the present. I describe and document how the ideological center on the Court has gradually shrunk over time, though importantly, it has not disappeared altogether. I provide an examination and discussion of both the sources and consequences of these trends. Key insights and findings include:

- Polarization in the Supreme Court has generally increased over time, though this trend has ebbed and flowed. The most robust center existed during the Burger Court of the mid-to-late 1970s, consisting of arguably five swing justices.
- Although the center has shrunk over time on the Court, it still exists due to (1) presidents from Truman to George H. W. Bush not placing exclusive emphasis on ideological compatibility and reliability when appointing justices, (2) an increase in the incidence of divided government, and (3) the rarity of strategic retirements by the justices. Since President Clinton took office, the norms have shifted more firmly to strategic retirements by the justices and presidents placing near exclusive emphasis on ideological compatibility and reliability in the appointment process.
- The existence of swing justices on the Court – even having just one swing justice – has kept Supreme Court outputs relatively moderate and stable despite Republican domination of appointments from Nixon to George H. W. Bush. The elimination of swing justices would likely lead to more volatile policy outputs that fluctuate based on membership changes.
- A "polarization paradox" exists: The incidence of 5-4 case outcomes has increased over time, but the incidence of unanimous outcomes has increased

I am grateful to Lawrence Baum, Sarah Binder, David Fontana, Jonathan Hack, Elizabeth Rigby, Richard Skinner, and Paul Wahlbeck for valuable feedback and suggestions. I thank Jonathan Hack for helpful research assistance.

as well. Polarization on the Court may be dependent on whether the Court is deciding cases within its "volitional agenda" (politically salient issues) or "exigent agenda" (institutional maintenance).

- A vicious circle exists between polarization on the Court and Supreme Court appointments. With just one swing justice (Kennedy) on the current Court, whoever is president (Obama and beyond) has the chance to create the first ideologically homogeneous majority voting bloc since the Warren Court of the 1960s. Constraints on this ability rest on divided party control of the Senate, the use of the filibuster by the minority party, and the majority's possibly using the "nuclear option" to eliminate the filibuster for Supreme Court nominations.

How many times have you heard it? "A closely divided Supreme Court ruled today that [*insert ruling on hot-button legal-political issue*]. Justice Kennedy joined the four [*liberal/conservative*] justices in the 5-4 outcome ..." This frequently reported event is a symptom of increasing polarization in the Supreme Court that has been occurring over time. The Court currently consists of four quite reliable liberal justices, four quite reliable conservative justices, and Justice Kennedy, the lone "swing vote" who generally tends to vote more conservatively than liberally but has voted with the liberals in several important cases. As other scholars have documented (e.g., Devins and Baum 2014), the current Court is arguably the most polarized Court in history. Republican and Democratic justices are now completely divided by ideology – all Republicans vote more conservatively than liberally, and all Democrats vote more liberally than conservatively. The polarizing change that occurred in Congress during the 1970s and especially the 1980s has also occurred in the Supreme Court. In short, the political center is disappearing, and Justice Kennedy is the last holdout.

It hasn't always been this way. Even as recently as about 35 years ago, as I will document, the Court consisted of a quite robust political center that included multiple – as many as four or five – swing voters at a given time. The political center on the Court has slowly disappeared, especially since the 1980s, which, not coincidentally, tracks the increase in polarization we have seen within and between the elected branches (Poole and Rosenthal 1984; Schlesinger 1985; Rohde 1991; Bond and Fleisher 2000; McCarty, Poole, and Rosenthal 2006; Devins and Baum 2014). The consequences of having zero swing voters relative to the status quo of one would be quite significant. If you think the Court is polarized now, wait until Justice Kennedy is replaced with a reliable liberal or conservative. That is probably not a hypothetical either. Such a move would have significant consequences, both for the nomination and confirmation processes (read: *World War III*) and the general nature and direction of judicial policymaking because the move from one to zero swing justices would represent a substantial and consequential increase in the degree of polarization on the Court.

In this chapter, I will expand on these issues by analyzing the sources and consequences of polarization on the Supreme Court. The time period on which I will focus consists of the Vinson Court and onward – that is, the 1946 to 2012 terms.[1] Not only does this time period contain a wealth of data from the Supreme Court Database (Spaeth et al. 2013), but more substantively, it also marks the early part of the post–New Deal era during which the Court increasingly began to shift its focus to civil liberties and civil rights issue vis-à-vis "famous footnote 4" from *U.S. v. Carolene Products* (1938) (see, e.g., Pacelle 1991). I will also explore the various normative and policy implications that result from some of the insights I uncover.

Hopefully this chapter will encourage further research on polarization in the judicial branch generally, including delving into the sources and consequences of this phenomenon. While polarization among elected elites and the American public has been studied quite extensively,[2] a similar level of scholarly inquiry of the judiciary has not occurred (see, though, Clark 2009; Devins and Baum 2014). Such lack of attention partly reflects a continuing emphasis on micro-level models of judicial decision making surrounding the influence of ideological, legal, and strategic considerations (e.g., Epstein and Knight 1998; Maltzman, Spriggs, and Wahlbeck 2000; Richards and Kritzer 2002; Segal and Spaeth 2002; Bailey and Maltzman 2008; Bartels 2009). And many of the extant macro-level analyses focus on external constraints imposed by Congress and the president (e.g., Spiller and Gely 1992; Segal, Westerland, and Lindquist 2011) or the public (e.g., Mishler and Sheehan 1993; McGuire and Stimson 2004) as opposed to polarization per se. As I will emphasize, the study of polarization in the Supreme Court represents a confluence of various compelling areas of study: judicial appointments, judicial decision making, separation-of-powers dynamics, and the nature of policy outputs generally. Connecting the dots between these areas is the key to producing stimulating explanations of polarization.

THE POLITICAL CONTEXT OF POLARIZATION: JUDICIAL APPOINTMENTS

The degree of polarization – and the resulting shrinking center – has its roots in the changing nature of Supreme Court appointments. The Supreme Court appointment process has always been political (Epstein and Segal 2005), but such political foundations themselves have traditionally encompassed multiple facets, including partisan and ideological compatibility and reliability, patronage, geographic considerations, and demographics (e.g., Epstein and

---

[1] See Devins and Baum (2014) for a broader historical sweep.

[2] On the distinction (and controversy) surrounding whether the mass public is polarized or merely better sorted, see Fiorina et al. (2006), Abramowitz and Saunders (2008), and Part 1 of this volume.

Segal 2005; Epstein et al. 2006; Baum 2012; Devins and Baum 2014). As a matter of fact, since FDR, who appointed justices based primarily on ideological/partisan compatibility with his New Deal agenda, presidential emphasis on non-ideological political considerations has come at the expense of ideological compatibility and reliability.

Dahl's (1957) landmark work on the Supreme Court as a policymaking institution essentially assumed that all presidents would appoint justices the way FDR did – on the basis of ideological compatibility, or choosing justices who would essentially vote in accordance with the president's preferences consistently over time. Combining this practice with the fact that the president, up to that point in time, appointed, on average, two justices per term, Dahl argued that the Supreme Court is essentially a partner in the extant political power structure, alongside the elected branches government, and can therefore serve as a powerful legitimacy-conferring mechanism for the policies produced by the elected branches. Dahl's theory and analysis provide a seemingly potent antidote to the "counter-majoritarian difficulty" – the democratic dilemma of how an unelected branch of government could legitimately invalidate laws passed by democratic majorities – and a glimmer of hope for popular constitutionalists (e.g., Tushnet 1999; Kramer 2004).

In terms of thinking through how judicial appointments connect to polarization and the shrinking center, we must understand the foundations on which Dahl's theory rests. First, as mentioned, presidents choose ideologically compatible and reliable justices. Second, there must exist a coherent "ruling regime" between the president and the Senate – implying unified government – and that the Senate defers and likely agrees with the president's choice. Third, fairly regular turnover – via death or retirement – must occur on the Court such that the president (and the ruling regime) is able to secure his ideological imprint on the Court through his appointments. If these conditions are met, the degree of polarization on the Court will be a function of the ideological extremity of the ruling regime and the degree of political turnover in the elected branches. If the parties were more ideologically extreme over time, then when Democrats are in power, they should appoint reliable liberals and when Republicans are in power, they should appoint reliable conservatives. As power changes hands between Democrats and Republicans, the Court will build up robust liberal and conservative blocs of justices. On the other hand, if the party in power is more ideologically moderate or heterogeneous, the Court may contain a more robust political center.

Dahl's theory provides an intuitive framework for understanding the conditions that explain increases in polarization over time. In the present era, someone may read this account and say, "That sounds about right." But the history that unfolded from the post–New Deal period all the way up until the 1980s provides events, practices, and conditions that contradict, to an extent, each of the three conditions that seem crucial to Dahl's theory. What happened?

During this period, presidents rarely chose justices *solely* on the basis of ideological compatibility and reliability. Once again, there is always a political reason for presidents appointing a particular justice, but pure ideological compatibility and reliability appeared to be lower than expected on the priority list for most presidents between Truman and George H. W. Bush. Presidents Truman and Eisenhower did not consistently choose justices based on ideological considerations. Truman actually chose mostly moderate to center-right justices (Vinson, Minton, and Clark) and even a Republican (Burton). Truman placed more emphasis on personal friendships and patronage than ideological compatibility. Eisenhower the Republican, of course, appointed two of the architects of the Warren Court revolution: Chief Justice Warren and Justice Brennan. Another of his appointments was Justice Stewart, who was a key swing vote during the Burger era but not a reliable conservative. While it could be said that Eisenhower was perhaps more moderate and did not prefer to appoint reliable conservatives, he did appoint Harlan and Whittaker, both of whom were indeed quite conservative. And it is well known that Eisenhower expressed regret over his appointments of Warren and Brennan. President Kennedy appointed Justice Goldberg, a liberal, and Justice White, a moderate who voted conservatively on some issues, liberal on others, and was another key swing vote during the Burger and Rehnquist eras. White was appointed more out of friendship and loyalty to Kennedy.

President Johnson was the perhaps the first since FDR to consistently appoint ideologically compatible justices in Fortas and Marshall (both reliable liberals), though he also emphasized personal friendship and loyalty, not to mention orchestrating perhaps both vacancies.[3] President Nixon appointed Chief Justice Burger and Justice Rehnquist, both reliable conservatives, but also Justice Blackmun, who started out as conservative but ended up becoming moderate and then quite liberal by the end of his career. Nixon also appointed Justice Powell, a southern Democrat who was a swing vote on the Court during the Burger era. President Ford appointed Justice Stevens, a moderate Republican who would eventually become the most liberal member of the Court. Coming out of Watergate, Ford emphasized qualifications and moderation over rigid ideological compatibility, though Ford is often characterized as a center-right president himself. No vacancies occurred under President Carter. President Reagan appointed Justices O'Connor and Kennedy, who would become swing votes, and Justice Scalia, a reliable conservative. Kennedy was perceived as a safe choice after the contentious confirmation process and rejection of Robert Bork and the controversial withdrawal of Douglas Ginsberg due to drug allegations. President George H. W. Bush

---

[3] In order to appoint Thurgood Marshall, whom Johnson wanted to make the first African-American Supreme Court justice, to the bench, LBJ appointed Justice Tom Clark's son, Ramsey Clark, to become U.S. Attorney General. Johnson then convinced Justice Clark to retire from the Supreme Court because his continued presence on the Court would pose too many conflicts of interest with his son.

appointed Justice Thomas – a very reliable conservative – but also Justice Souter, who started out moderate but became a reliable liberal vote in the 1990s until his retirement in 2009.

Starting with President Clinton (who appointed reliable liberals, Justices Ginsburg and Breyer), presidents have increasingly – and successfully – emphasized ideological compatibility and reliability as standards for selecting justices. As I will discuss later in this chapter, it is important to note that all six appointments starting with Ginsburg occurred under unified party control of the Senate and the presidency. President George W. Bush appointed reliable conservatives Chief Justice Roberts and Justice Alito, while President Obama appointed reliable liberals, Justices Sotomayor and Kagan. Obama also emphasized racial and gender diversity with his appointments, but it appears that ideological compatibility was the overarching consideration. One could argue, then, that the practice of presidents consistently appointing justices based purely on ideological compatibility and reliability grounds is a relatively recent phenomenon. Today, presidents place near exclusive focus on ideological compatibility and reliability.

It is important to understand how presidential reliance on pure ideological concerns is driven by the other two conditions underlying Dahl's theory – whether a coherent ruling regime is in place and nature of turnover and replacement on the Court. A president's ability to pack the Court with ideologues and shape the ideological balance of the Court will be constrained by the Senate and the level of scrutiny it places on the president's nominees. This becomes especially relevant when the Senate is controlled by the opposite party as the president, since the president may be inclined to moderate his or her appointments so as to avoid defeat in the Senate (e.g., Moraski and Shipan 1999). The post–New Deal era saw an increase in divided government generally and an increase in divided party control between the president and Senate. Thirty-two of the 70 years (46 percent) between 1945 and 2014 have seen divided party control between the president and Senate. To put that figure in some historical context, divided party control of the president and the Senate occurred in only 10 of the 68 years (15 percent) between 1877 (post-Reconstruction) and 1944. Thus, the concept of a coherent "ruling regime" between the president and the Senate with respect to Supreme Court appointments meant significantly more in the 1877–1944 period than it did from 1945 onward. Simply put, it means that presidents in this latter era were more constrained from placing an exclusive focus on ideological compatibility and reliability.

Ideological polarization in the Senate has also contributed to increasing Senate scrutiny of Supreme Court nominees. As the Warren Court inserted itself into some of the most hot button social and political issues of the day, the Senate placed an increasing focus on ideological considerations as early as the 1950s (Epstein et al. 2006). As the Senate became even more polarized since the 1980s, Senate scrutiny became even stronger. Robert Bork was rejected by the Senate in 1987, and Clarence Thomas, who faced sexual harassment allegations in the midst of his nomination process, was confirmed with just 52 votes. Interest groups and other elites have also factored very strongly into the equation leading to increased scrutiny in the appointment process (e.g., Caldeira and Wright 1998; Caldeira, Hojnacki, and Wright 2000; Devins and Baum 2014). In short, the president, senators, and policy demanders are intent on appointing ideologically like-minded justices to the bench. But the more the ideological interests of these actors diverge, the less freedom the president has in appointing a completely ideologically compatible justice.

The near-exclusive focus on ideological compatibility and reliability today is also driven by what many present-day ideologues widely agree were "mistaken" appointments. Conservative Republicans raise this concern most prominently, and justifiably so, given the liberal conversions undertaken by Republican-appointed Justices Blackmun (appointed by Nixon), Stevens (appointed by Ford), and Souter (appointed by George H. W. Bush). And two Reagan appointees – Justices O'Connor and Kennedy – became consummate swing justices during the 1990s and 2000s and cast crucial and pivotal liberal votes in several significant cases.

The nature and frequency of turnover on the Court also plays a role in the extent to which the president can place his or her ideological imprint on the Court and shift the Court's balance of power. A president only has the ability to alter the ideological balance of power on the Court if the person s/he is appointing is significantly more ideologically compatible with the president than the person s/he is replacing. In other words, a conservative president will not alter the balance of the Court if s/he appoints a conservative justice to replace an equally conservative justice. A conservative president can only alter the Court's ideological balance if he or she replaces a moderate or liberal departing justice with a strongly conservative justice. In the modern age of "strategic retirements," where justices choose to retire during the tenure of an ideologically like-minded president, the president typically trades in one ideologically compatible justice for another. Thus, given these realities, the only way for the president to alter the ideological balance on the Court is if an ideologically incongruent justice dies on the bench or is forced to retire due to bad health.

From Truman to George H. W. Bush, strategic retirements as I have described them are actually not as frequent as one might think. Chief Justice Vinson and Justice Jackson (appointed by Truman and FDR, respectively) died while President Eisenhower was in office. Though these justices were actually quite conservative on many civil liberties issues, when Eisenhower was given the opportunity to replace these Democrats, he appointed Earl Warren and John Harlan. I have discussed Chief Justice Warren, whom Eisenhower regretted appointing; as mentioned, Justice Harlan was a fairly reliable conservative until his retirement in 1971. Justices Minton (Truman appointee) and Reed (FDR appointee) also retired while Eisenhower was in office, giving Eisenhower four consecutive opportunities to replace Democrats with Republicans – and five straight opportunities if you count the replacement of Justice Burton (a Republican appointed by Truman) with moderate Potter Stewart. Though it is difficult to fully understand Eisenhower's views on many of the social issues that would eventually come before the Court, his choice of William Brennan to replace Justice Minton would certainly have long-term implications, as Brennan would remain a liberal bulwark on the Court until his retirement in 1990. Eisenhower used half of his opportunities to replace Democrats with Republicans (because of non-strategic retirements and deaths) in order to appoint the two primary leaders of liberal legal change in the 1950s and 1960s. Though again, with civil liberties not quite dominating the Court's agenda in the 1950s, Eisenhower could not have fully forecast the liberal legal change that was about to come via two of his appointments.

The eight years of JFK and LBJ generated just one out of four opportunities to replace a Republican with a Democrat – JFK replaced Justice Whittaker (who resigned due to disability) with Justice White, who was not a reliable liberal by any means and became a swing vote. On the other hand, Republican Presidents Nixon and Ford had four opportunities, out of five vacancies, to replace Democrats with Republicans. With Nixon making an issue of putting "law and order" justices on the bench during his 1968 presidential campaign, one would think he was looking to appoint reliable conservatives. He was half successful in the long term. He of course replaced Chief Justice Warren with Warren Burger, Fortas with Blackmun (after two previously failed attempts), Black with Powell (a southern Democrat), and then President Ford replaced Douglas with Stevens. Rehnquist replaced Harlan. Nixon certainly moved the Court rightward, and as I will show, the Court's policymaking reflected this change but not nearly as much as one might have forecast. With Blackmun's (and Stevens's) liberal metamorphosis and Powell's moderation, conservatives by the 1980s and 1990s were yearning for more reliable conservatives.

President Reagan's three appointments replaced Republicans with Republicans, though, as mentioned, two of those – Kennedy and O'Connor – turned out to be swing votes who cast their fair share of liberal votes in big cases, while the other – Justice Scalia – is the poster child for "reliable conservative." It is important to note that in retrospect, Reagan did not shift the ideological balance of the Court because his appointees roughly reflected the ideologies of the justices they replaced. O'Connor replaced the swing vote Justice Stewart; and O'Connor actually maintained a quite conservative voting record in the 1980s and then moderated beginning in the early 1990s. Kennedy replaced Powell, another center-right justice. And Scalia replaced Burger.

Perhaps the biggest blow to liberal hopes was the one-two punch of the health-induced retirements of Justices Brennan and Marshall – liberal icons in their own respects for substantial parts of the twentieth century – during the presidency of George H. W. Bush. In retrospect, Bush was half successful in transforming the Court – he replaced Thurgood Marshall with Clarence Thomas, who would become the most reliable conservative on the Court. But he replaced William Brennan with David Souter, who would become the third in the trifecta of Republicans-turned-liberals on the Court (alongside Blackmun and Stevens). Souter's liberal metamorphosis was surely the straw that broke the camel's back – perhaps for both conservatives and liberals. For conservatives, this was yet another in a long line of missed opportunities to pack the Court with reliable conservatives. Think of it this way: Since LBJ put Thurgood Marshall on the Court, Republican presidents (Nixon, Ford, Reagan, H. W. Bush; recall Carter had no appointments) had *ten straight appointments – six of which were opportunities to replace Democrats with Republicans.* Upon Justice Thomas's confirmation in 1991, the Court was staffed with eight Republican appointees, the lone Democrat being Justice White, whose voting record by then could be characterized as center-right.[4] It is no wonder that in the wake of this phenomenon (which conservative policy demanders would surely consider a missed opportunity, to say the least, especially in light of the increasing number of social issues on the Court's agenda), the rallying cry of conservative activists was, "No more Blackmuns, Stevenses, or Souters." Why not add to that list "O'Connors and Kennedys." One must remember, however, that different norms pervaded appointments in the 1940s through 1970s than they do today. Although all appointments are political in some way, it was not the norm in those days for ideological compatibility and reliability to be the most dominant consideration. Today, it is.

Starting with President Clinton, justices have strategically retired on a consistent basis so that the president can nominate a justice who is both ideologically compatible and reliable.[5] Thus, we have come full circle to Dahl's thesis, and the consequences for increased polarization are significant, as I will discuss later. The one lingering contradiction to Dahl's thesis is that since justices are staying on the bench for so long now, presidents rarely get two appointments per term. Since FDR transformed the Court, that trend held for about 30 years: Truman made four appointments in eight years. Eisenhower made five in eight years. JFK/LBJ made four in eight years (although as mentioned, LBJ orchestrated two retirements). Nixon/Ford made five in eight years. The "two-per-term" norm falters starting with Carter, who, as mentioned, did not make any appointments. Reagan made three in eight years. H. W. Bush did make two in four years, but Clinton and George

---

[4] The Court that decided the landmark abortion case, *Planned Parenthood v. Casey* (1992), consisted of eight Republican appointees. And the one Democrat on the Court, Justice White, dissented in *Roe v. Wade.* Yet the Court upheld the core of *Roe* that there exists a constitutional right for a woman to obtain an abortion. On the other hand, the Court lowered the level of scrutiny applied to abortion regulations, which gave states more latitude to impose restrictions on this right that did not pose an "undue burden" to a woman seeking to obtain an abortion.

[5] Note that Republican appointees Blackmun, Stevens, and Souter, each of whom retired under Democratic administrations, had become quite liberal well before their retirements.

W. Bush each appointed just two justices in their eight years as president. The 11-term span from the 1994 term through the end of the 2004 term marks the longest natural court – i.e., period of membership stability – since the 1820s. And Obama has appointed just two justices in his six years so far.

DOCUMENTING THE DISAPPEARING CENTER ON THE SUPREME COURT, 1946–2012

For a large share of the post-New Deal era, we have seen how (1) strictly ideological considerations in the appointment process took a back seat to other political considerations; (2) divided party control of the Senate and presidency often constrained the president's appointments; and (3) some justices transformed ideologically during their tenures. These practices and behaviors help tell a larger story of how polarization was held in check and how a robust ideological center was maintained on the Court. Multiple swing justices on the Court were capable of casting both liberal and conservative votes on highly salient issues of the day. Ideological polarization was relatively low for large chunks of this era, though it has increased as the middle has slowly dwindled in numbers. Measuring and documenting the degree of polarization on the Supreme Court is complicated by a small-n problem. Typically, polarization is defined by the ideological distance between the two parties (i.e., between the medians of each party) and the degree of intra-party ideological homogeneity (e.g., Rohde 1991; McCarty, Poole, and Rosenthal 2006; Devins and Baum 2014). Devins and Baum (2014) use Martin and Quinn's (2002) ideological scores to calculate (1) ideological distances between the Republican and Democratic median justices and (2) ideological homogeneity among both Republican and Democratic justices. Clark (2009) applies an existing measure from economics to tap ideological heterogeneity on the Court (using ideological preference scores).

In order to document the shrinking center and the degree of polarization more generally, I focus on the voting behavior of justices and specifically what I call a justice's "swing capacity," or a justice's willingness to join the majority – particularly in close votes (e.g., 5-4 or 6-3) – regardless of whether the case outcome is liberal or conservative. Thus, a justice with a high swing capacity should maintain a small difference in the percentage of times s/he is in liberal versus conservative majorities. Think about the theoretical connection to a truly pivotal (median) voter in a unidimensional policy space: The median voter should theoretically be in the majority 100 percent of the time, regardless of the direction of the collective outcome.

To examine the swing capacity concept, I analyze data consisting of all formally decided Supreme Court cases[6] spanning the 1946–2012 terms of the

---

[6] Formally decided cases are those that receive the full treatment of oral argument and an opinion from the Court. In the Supreme Court Database (Spaeth et al. 2013), these are cases for which the variable *decisionType* = 1, 6, or 7. I use citation as the unit of analysis.

Court. Collected from the Supreme Court Database (Spaeth et al. 2013), the data contain 7,400 cases and 66,335 justice-votes. This covers five Chief Justice eras: the Vinson, Warren, Burger, Rehnquist, and Roberts Courts. All of the years are reported with respect to the Court's annual *terms*, which range from October of the term year to September of the following year. For example, the 1946 term ranges from October 1946 to September 1947. For this analysis, I have subdivided the entire 1946–2012 terms into nine relatively cohesive time periods where there was a relatively low degree of membership change (or at least a relatively low degree of consequential membership change) but also contains a large enough number of cases to draw meaningful conclusions. I also try to keep the total number of eras relatively low. In some eras (e.g., Warren 1953–61), there is frequent membership change, but other eras are pure natural courts with no membership change (i.e., the last two Burger eras and the 11-term Rehnquist Court from 1994 to 2004).

Figures 1 and 2 present graphical representations of the swing capacity concept. Figure 1 presents the proportion of the time each justice is in the majority when the outcome is liberal and when it is conservative. These proportions are calculated for relatively close votes, which I limit to 5-4 and 6-3 outcomes.[7] Each graph is sorted by proportion in the liberal majority. Note that a high swing capacity occurs when the gap between the two bars (for liberal and conservative majority) is small, since that represents a justice's tendency to be in the majority regardless of whether the Court's ruling is liberal or conservative. On the other hand, a large gap between the bars represents a low swing capacity, since it indicates a justice's tendency to be in the majority contingent on whether the outcome is liberal or conservative. Figure 2 presents graphs of these gaps between the bars in Figure 1. Specifically, Figure 2 graphs the absolute difference between a justice's proportion in the majority for a liberal outcome and the proportion in the majority for a conservative outcome. Once again, smaller absolute differences represent higher swing capacities, and the graph is sorted from small differences to large ones. The asterisks in the graph indicate that a justice did not serve on the Court for the entire time period. The notes below each Figure include who replaced whom and the term in which the replacement occurred.

For the most part, Figures 1 and 2 paint a picture of generally increasing polarization over this time period. During the Vinson Court, Justice Clark became a solid swing vote once he joined shortly before the 1949 term. He joined liberal and conservative majorities over 80 percent of the time in close votes. To a lesser extent, Justices Minton and Reed also served as swing votes during the Vinson Court, both having joined liberal majorities just over 50 percent of the time and conservative majorities just over 80 percent of the time.

---

[7] More specifically, I define close votes as those where the difference in majority and minority votes is ≤ 3. This mostly captures 5-4 and 6-3 outcomes, but it can also encompass close outcomes when the number of participating justices is fewer than nine (e.g., 5-3 outcomes on an eight-member Court where a justice recuses him- or herself).

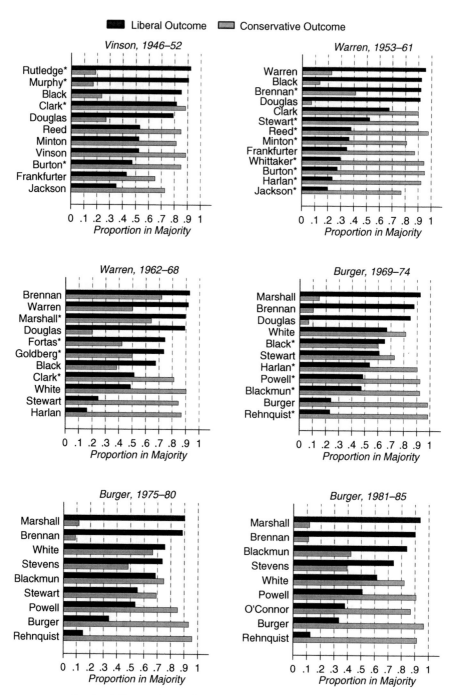

FIGURE 1. Justices' Proportions of Majority Votes for Liberal and Conservative Outcomes in Close Votes

Note: Asterisks indicate that a justice did not serve during the entire time span. Recall that years above are reported in the Court's terms, which begin in October of the term year and end in September of the following year. Time periods within which there were membership changes are reported below. "beg." = begins; "d." = died; and "r." = retired.

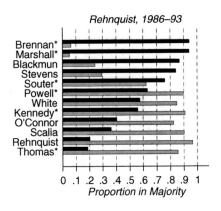

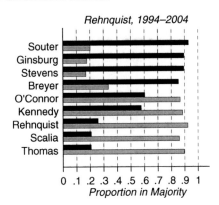

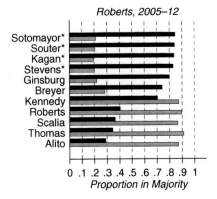

CAPTION FOR FIGURE I.(cont.)

Vinson: Clark (beg. 8/49) replaced Murphy (d. 7/49); Minton (beg. 10/49) replaced Rutledge (d. 9/49).

Warren 1953–61: Warren (beg. 10/53) replaced Vinson (d. 9/53); Harlan (3/55) replaced Jackson (d. 10/54); Brennan (beg. 10/56) replaced Minton (10/56); Whittaker (beg. 3/57) replaced Reed (r. 2/57); Stewart (10/58) replaced Burton (10/58).

Warren 1962–68: White (beg. 4/62) replaced Whittaker (3/62); Goldberg (r. 10/62) replaced Frankfurter (r. 8/62); Fortas (beg. 10/65) replaced Goldberg (be. 7/65); Marshall (beg. 10/67) replaced Clark (r. 6/67).

Burger 1969–74: Burger (beg. 6/69) replaced Warren (r. 6/69); Blackmun (beg. 6/70) replaced Fortas (r. 5/69); Powell (beg. 1/72) replaced Black (r. 9/71); Rehnquist (beg. 1/72) replaced Harlan (r. 9/71).

Rehnquist 1986–93: Scalia (beg. 9/86) replaced Burger (r. 9/86) [Rehnquist replaced Burger as Chief Justice, but Scalia's entrance was due to Burger's vacancy.]; Kennedy (beg. 2/88) replaced Powell (r. 6/87); Souter (beg. 10/90) replaced Brennan (r. 7/90); Thomas (10/91) replaced Marshall (r. 10/90); Ginsburg (beg. 8/93) replaced White (r. 6/93).

Roberts 2005–12: Roberts (beg. 9/05) replaced Rehnquist (d. 9/05); Alito (1/06) replaced O'Connor (r. 1/06); Sotomayor (beg. 9/09) replaced Souter (r. 6/09); Kagan (beg. 8/10) replaced Stevens (r. 6/10).

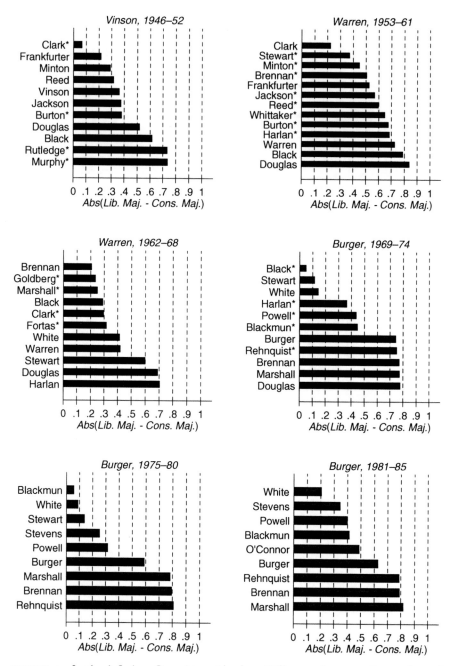

FIGURE 2. Justices' Swing Capacities: Absolute Difference between Proportion of Liberal Majority Votes and Conservative Majority Votes

Note: Asterisks indicate that a justice did not serve during the entire time span. Recall that years above are reported in the Court's terms, which begin in October of the term year and end in September of the following year. Time periods within which there were membership changes are reported below. "beg." = begins; "d." = died; and "r."= retired.

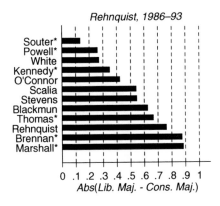

Rehnquist, 1986–93

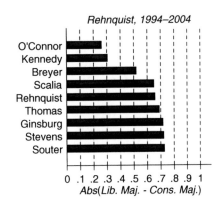

Rehnquist, 1994–2004

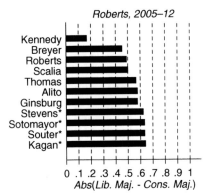

Roberts, 2005–12

CAPTION FOR FIGURE 2. (cont.)

Vinson: Clark (beg. 8/49) replaced Murphy (d. 7/49); Minton (beg. 10/49) replaced Rutledge (d. 9/49).

Warren 1953–61: Warren (beg. 10/53) replaced Vinson (d. 9/53); Harlan (3/55) replaced Jackson (d. 10/54); Brennan (beg. 10/56) replaced Minton (10/56); Whittaker (beg. 3/57) replaced Reed (r. 2/57); Stewart (10/58) replaced Burton (10/58).

Warren 1962–68: White (beg. 4/62) replaced Whittaker (3/62); Goldberg (r. 10/62) replaced Frankfurter (r. 8/62); Fortas (beg. 10/65) replaced Goldberg (r. 7/65); Marshall (beg. 10/67) replaced Clark (r. 6/67).

Burger 1969–74: Burger (beg. 6/69) replaced Warren (r. 6/69); Blackmun (beg. 6/70) replaced Fortas (r. 5/69); Powell (beg. 1/72) replaced Black (r. 9/71); Rehnquist (beg. 1/72) replaced Harlan (r. 9/71).

Rehnquist 1986–93: Scalia (beg. 9/86) replaced Burger (r. 9/86) [Rehnquist replaced Burger as Chief Justice, but Scalia's entrance was due to Burger's vacancy.]; Kennedy (beg. 2/88) replaced Powell (r. 6/87); Souter (beg. 10/90) replaced Brennan (r. 7/90); Thomas (10/91) replaced Marshall (r. 10/90); Ginsburg (beg. 8/93) replaced White (r. 6/93).

Roberts 2005–12: Roberts (beg. 9/05) replaced Rehnquist (d. 9/05); Alito (1/06) replaced O'Connor (r. 1/06); Sotomayor (beg. 9/09) replaced Souter (r. 6/09); Kagan (beg. 8/10) replaced Stevens (r. 6/10).

Figure 2 shows that Justice Frankfurter had the second highest swing capacity during the Vinson era, but his overall majority percentages in both liberal and conservative outcomes were lower than those for Minton and Reed. Chief Justice Vinson and Justices Jackson and Burton had moderate swing capacities, while Douglas, Black, Murphy, and Rutledge voted quite liberally and were rarely in the majority in conservative case outcomes. On the whole, the average swing capacity (vis-à-vis the absolute differences reported in Figure 2) during the Vinson era is 0.33,[8] which is actually quite low and suggests fairly low degree of polarization, especially starting in the 1949 term when moderates Clark and Minton replaced liberals Rutledge and Murphy. After this change, there were four justices on the Court with relatively high swing capacities (i.e., with differences in Figure 2 of around .3 or less).

The Warren Court from 1953 to 1961 was much more polarized than the Vinson era. Although the Court became increasingly liberal in this era, the close votes in this period broke liberal 54 percent to 46 percent. As seen in Figures 1 and 2, Justice Clark was again a solid swing vote in these close votes and was essentially the lone swing vote until Justice Stewart joined the Court at the beginning of the 1958 term. And Stewart's swing capacity (Figure 2) cannot be considered substantial, though he was in the majority in just over 50 percent of liberal outcomes and about 90 percent of conservative outcomes. The Court was quite polarized in this era, particularly in the latter half, with liberal justices Warren, Black, Douglas, and Brennan (once he joins) pitted against the more conservative Frankfurter, Whittaker, Burton, and Harlan. The liberals won out most of the time, though not by much. Outcomes of 5-4 were relatively frequent (around 20 percent, which is quite high historically, as I discuss in Figure 4) in the latter part of this period. Justice Clark was frequently the swing vote in such decisions, and was a pivotal vote on many of the close rulings that generated both liberal and conservative outcomes.

The "Second Warren Court" from the 1962–68 terms brought increasing liberalism and an increasing number of liberal justices on the Court. In close votes during this time period, 64 percent of outcomes were in the liberal direction. About 27 percent of outcomes were the result of close votes, which is the lowest rate out of the nine periods analyzed here.[9] Interestingly enough, the justices during this period with the highest swing capacity are liberals, those being Brennan, Goldberg (left before the 1965 term), Marshall (joined during the 1967 term), and Black. During this time, the Court was not polarized but lopsidedly liberal. The results suggest that only Stewart and Harlan joined the majority in close, liberal outcomes less than 50 percent of the time (White is just under 50 percent at 49 percent). Justices Clark and White can be considered swing votes to some extent, having joined liberal majorities about half the time

[8] This average is calculated as the median of the term-level median of justices' absolute differences between majority proportions in liberal and conservative outcomes.
[9] The rate of close votes for all other eras ranges between 35 percent and 40 percent.

and conservative majorities between 80 percent and 90 percent of the time. Since outcomes in these close votes were heavily tilted in the liberal direction, it is important to remember that in all votes during this period, all justices except for Harlan cast more liberal than conservative votes. Once again, for many votes, there was a high baseline capacity for a liberal majority given the solid liberal bloc that was on the Court at the time.

The first six terms of the Burger Court represent a marked contrast from the liberal Warren Court. As discussed, President Nixon was able to make four appointments in the first three years of his presidency; three of those were to replace liberal justices (Warren, Fortas, Black) with more conservative ones (Burger, Blackmun, Powell); the fourth was Rehnquist, who would be a very reliable conservative, replacing Harlan. By the 1971 term, the liberals, who held a robust majority during the second Warren Court, fell into the minority with just Marshall, Brennan, and Douglas carrying the torch during the early part of the Burger Court. While close outcomes leaned heavily liberal during the latter Warren era, the opposite held in the first years of the Burger Court, with 63 percent of close decisions garnering conservative outcomes. Ideological change on the Court also influences how the Court's agenda changes, with the Court taking a different mix of cases during this era compared to the Warren Court. While the Court made a significant right turn, this era also marks the beginning of the development of a fairly robust center. Justices Stewart and White became solid swing justices; in his last two terms on the Court, Justice Black also had a high swing capacity, as he became less liberal toward the end of his career. In close votes, both Stewart and White joined liberal majorities more than 60 percent of the time and conservative majorities 70 percent and 80 percent, respectively, of the time. This Court begins to see a more even distribution across the entire ideological spectrum, with reliable liberals who rarely joined conservative majorities, the swing justices as mentioned, and an increasing number of reliable conservatives, particularly Burger and Rehnquist, who rarely joined liberal majorities.

The Burger Court from the 1975–80 terms consisted of the most robust center on the Court during the entire 1946–2012 time period. First off, this era saw six consecutive terms without any membership change. In the close votes analyzed in Figures 1 and 2, 63 percent of case outcomes were conservative, though we do see several swing justices being willing to join liberal majorities. In fact, Figures 1 and 2 suggest that there were arguably five swing justices on the Court during this era – Blackmun, White, Stewart, Stevens, and Powell. All have swing capacities (Figure 2) of around .3 or lower (Powell is just over .3) and each joined liberal or conservative majorities 50 percent of the time or more (Stevens is just under 50 percent for conservative majorities). At the poles are Marshall and Brennan, who rarely joined conservative majorities, and Burger and Rehnquist, who rarely joined liberal majorities. The robust center that existed on the Court in this period is definitely unique for the entire time period examined.

The center begins to dissipate during the last years of the Burger Court (1981–85 terms), which on the whole maintains a similar conservative tenor compared to the previous era. Of closely divided outcomes, 61 percent were conservative. Justice Stewart retired and was replaced by Justice O'Connor before the 1981 term. Other justices who were swing votes in the prior era had low swing capacities in this era. For Blackmun and Stevens, this results from leftward ideological drift, with these justices now joining conservative majorities just 40 percent of the time and liberal majorities a little more than 80 percent and 70 percent of the time, respectively. Justice Powell's swing capacity also decreased, as he became slightly more conservative in this era. He still joined liberal majorities about 50 percent of the time, but he was also a reliable vote for conservative outcomes, joining conservative majorities 90 percent of the time. Whereas Powell was still an important swing vote, Justice White had the highest swing capacity in this era, joining liberal majorities over 60 percent of the time and conservative majorities over 80 percent of the time.

This story continues in the first part of the Rehnquist Court (1986–93 terms), which again maintained conservative levels compared to the prior era. In cases with close votes, about 64 percent were decided in the conservative direction. Justice White continued to be a key swing justice on the Court; note that Justice Powell served just one term in this era. The middle was essentially reconstituted by new justices who joined the Court during this era, such as Justices Kennedy (begins during the 1987 term) and Souter (who joins at the start of the 1990 term). Souter, appointed by George H.W. Bush, would eventually become a reliable liberal vote, but he started out as a swing vote, having joined conservative majorities just over 60 percent of the time and liberal majorities about 75 percent of the time. Justice Kennedy joined liberal majorities over 55 percent of the time, though he joined conservative majorities 90 percent of the time. The middle continued to dissipate while the ideological poles solidified, with Brennan (retired July 1990), Marshall (retired October 1991), and then former swing votes Stevens and Blackmun becoming fairly reliable liberals, and O'Connor, Rehnquist, and new Justices Scalia (begins in 1986) and Thomas (begins 1991) becoming quite reliable conservatives. In short, increasing ideological polarization begins to set in during this period, with reliable ideologues on the left and right but still enough swing justices who hold down the center and prevent extreme Supreme Court outcomes.

The 11-term natural Court from 1994 to 2004 represents the Court as we tend to think of it today: a fairly polarized Court, though with a genuine center that keeps the Court moderated in its policy outputs. The Court consisted of four reliable liberals (Ginsburg, Breyer, Stevens, and Souter; the latter two now becoming quite consistently liberal after being past swing justices), three reliable conservatives (Rehnquist, Scalia, and Thomas), and two center-right justices, O'Connor and Kennedy. Note that it is not until this era that O'Connor solidifies her swing justice status. Her first decade (or more) displayed fairly reliable conservative tendencies and a much lower swing capacity. During this era, however, Justices O'Connor's and Kennedy's swing capacities, from Figure 2, are .26 and .31, respectively. In close votes during this era, the Court ruled in the conservative direction 52 percent of the time – a sharp decrease from the prior four periods. Both Justices Kennedy and O'Connor voted with the majority in roughly 60 percent of liberal case outcomes, which is quite high, suggesting that these justices were willing to cast the swing votes in numerous closely divided liberal outcomes. They were also willing to grant the conservative side a significant number of victories in close votes, having each joined conservative majorities a little less than 90 percent of the time. The four reliably liberal and three reliably conservative justices maintained very low swing capacities (Breyer showing the highest among the reliable ideologues); none of them come anywhere close to crossing over to the other side 50 percent of the time. While the ideological poles continue to solidify, the center, although smaller than previous eras, is crucial in terms of moderating Court outputs. Both O'Connor and Kennedy showed a strong willingness to cross over to the liberal side, which means that no ideological bloc had a majority that could run the table in producing consistently liberal or conservative outputs.

Finally, we get to the Roberts era, which was more polarized than the prior era due to O'Connor's retirement and the entrance of Justice Alito – a reliable conservative. Additional replacements (Roberts replaced Rehnquist; Sotomayor replaced Souter; Kagan replaced Stevens) during this era did not change the ideological makeup of the Court because the replacements were ideologically similar to the departing justices. Thus, in this era, we see a straightforward pattern: four reliable liberals, four reliable conservatives, and Justice Kennedy as the lone swing vote. During this era, 60 percent of rulings in close votes broke in the conservative direction. With O'Connor gone, Justice Kennedy's swing capacity becomes even higher, at .17 (Figure 2). No other justice comes even close to that level of swing capacity. In close votes during this era, Justice Kennedy was in the majority a staggering 70 percent of the time when the Court's outcome are liberal. Kennedy continued to join conservative majorities at a high rate, just less than 90 percent of the time. During this era, Justice Kennedy is the lone swing vote and demonstrates among the highest swing capacities reported in Figure 2 across all eras. Once again, whereas the Court is arguably the most polarized it has been since 1946, Kennedy's swing vote status is crucial to moderating Supreme Court outcomes. As long as someone like Kennedy holds down the center in many cases, the Court's outputs will not necessarily reflect ideologically homogeneous voting blocs that hold majorities on the Court. It is interesting to note how the conservatives maintain higher crossover potential than the liberals during this era. Chief Justice Roberts joined liberal majorities in close votes roughly 40 percent of the time; Scalia and the other conservatives are not far behind that number. While parsing this differential is beyond the scope of this chapter, it likely has its roots in agenda change over time.

CONSEQUENCES OF POLARIZATION FOR SUPREME COURT
POLICYMAKING

Several patterns emerge on the Supreme Court in the post–New Deal period.
Polarization has generally increased, although with some ebbs and flows.
Especially in more recent times, we have seen ideological hardening on the left
and right and a shrinking center, but unlike in Congress, where the center has
virtually disappeared, a meaningful center still exists on the Court, and in a
small chamber such as the Supreme Court, it only takes one swing justice to
constitute a meaningful center. This center was quite large in parts of the Burger
era, leading Woodward and Armstrong (1979: 528) to conclude in their classic
work, *The Brethren*, that "the center was in control." Today, the center is
arguably still in control, but it is a center of one – Justice Kennedy. This
reality gives comfort to some people and agitation to others. Those who are
comforted by this reality, particularly liberals, see that the Court is still able to
produce a good share of significant liberal legal policy despite Republican
domination of Supreme Court appointments since President Nixon. In the
eyes of many conservatives, Kennedy's swing status signals a lack of
principled behavior. There is, of course, additional cause for concern. For
those bothered by the counter-majoritarian difficulty, having just one swing
voter seemingly exacerbates this dilemma. The fate of a significant share of
salient legal issues is left in the hands of one individual, Justice Kennedy, who is
the pivotal vote on many of these issues.

Figure 3 presents a general view of Supreme Court policy outputs since
the 1946 term.[10] Figure 3A presents the percentage of Court rulings that were
decided in the liberal direction; data and coding on liberal versus conservative
rulings come from the Supreme Court Database (Spaeth et al. 2013). The
solid line is a lowess, non-parametric line of best fit that tracks the general
trend over time. During the Vinson and Warren Courts, outputs are as
expected – fairly moderate during the Vinson Court, and then a significant
left turn during the Warren Court, particularly during the 1960s. The onset
of the Nixon-driven Burger Court and into the Rehnquist Court provided a
right turn in policymaking, but not as drastic of a right turn as might have
been expected given Republican dominance in appointments for almost 25
years (10 consecutive Republican appointments from Nixon to H. W. Bush).
On the whole, outputs were actually quite moderate from the Burger Court
onward, hovering around 45 percent. And this trend continued into the
Roberts Court.

What might give liberals even more hope and conservatives greater despair
are the patterns from Figure 3B, which plots the percentage of liberal rulings in
salient cases only. I use Epstein and Segal's (2000) measure of salience, based on
whether the Court's ruling was covered on the front page of the *New York*

---

[10] Portions of this section reflect similar discussions from Bartels and Johnston (2013), who report
and interpret very similar graphs as those contained in Figure 2.

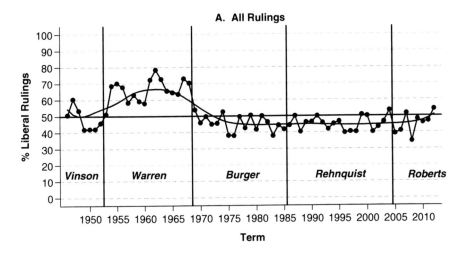

A. All Rulings

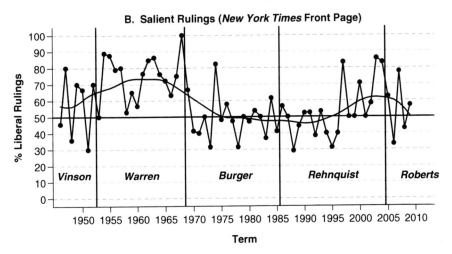

B. Salient Rulings (*New York Times* Front Page)

FIGURE 3. Supreme Court Liberalism, 1946–2012 Terms
Note: In each graph, the dots represent the percentage of liberal rulings in each term. The solid line is a nonparametric lowess smoother that gives a sense of the pattern over time.

Times the day after the ruling was issued. Data on salient cases are available from the 1946–2009 terms. In salient rulings, outputs were quite liberal in the Vinson and Warren eras and on average moderate during the Burger Court. The real surprise results are from the Rehnquist and Roberts Courts, where outputs in salient rulings during these periods were more liberal (52 percent) than conservative (48 percent). The long natural Court from the 1994–2004 terms seems to account for the greatest levels of liberalism, particularly the 1997–2004 terms, where 64 percent of the Court's 92 salient rulings were decided liberally.[11] And 57 percent of salient rulings were decided liberally during the first five terms of the Roberts Court.

Bringing various parts of this essay together, then, the trends from Figure 3 present some very important insights. First, as long as there is a genuine center on the Court – *even if there is just one swing justice* – the Court is capable of moderation, that is, generating a quite balanced mix of liberal and conservative outcomes. In highly salient cases, the so-called conservative Court during the contemporary era has been capable of producing its fair share of liberal rulings.[12] The existence of a middle, then, is desirable for those who prefer a balanced, moderate tenor to Supreme Court policymaking. It also implies greater stability in outputs generally, as seen in Figure 3A from the Burger Court onward, which is beneficial for lower courts, the other branches of government, and the states who have to comply with the Court's rulings. It is easier for these actors to deal with and anticipate a moderate and stable Court than one that is highly volatile in its outputs, switching from liberal to conservative whenever there is a membership change. On the other hand, when the center is quite small, like it is now with just Justice Kennedy, the small set of swing justices can seem to many like dictators – in many cases, whichever way they decide, the Court decides as well. This is disconcerting that on a Court that is not directly accountable to popular will in the first place, the non-democratic character of the Court is exacerbated by the fact that many rulings can come down to one or two justices. The existence of swing justices, though, depends on there being reliable liberals and conservatives on the Court. Reliable ideologues, if they want to have influence, must be willing to move to the center on occasion. The existence of ideologues on the extremes empowers swing justices to be pivotal on many issues in which the ideologues are sharply divided.

As for what influences the existence of a robust ideological center, the answer has been quite clear, at least from Truman to H. W. Bush: Presidents have not made ideological compatibility and reliability a dominant consideration in the nomination process. Placing this motivation as secondary has been the result of various political considerations, including, as mentioned, patronage, electoral reasons, and constraint by the Senate. Given these considerations, presidents during this era have appointed numerous justices who have served as genuine swing justices. In the conclusion, I will elaborate further on the implications of the new era of ideological compatibility and reliability as the primary motivations in presidents' appointments.

---

[11] The numbers of salient rulings begins to decrease in the 1980s, as the Court's caseload becomes smaller in general. While the number of salient rulings is in the mid-to-low double digits in the 1990s and very early 2000s, the number drops to the high single digits from 2003 onward.

[12] See the Supporting Information, Section A of Bartels and Johnston (2013) for some examples of highly salient liberal rulings in the contemporary era.

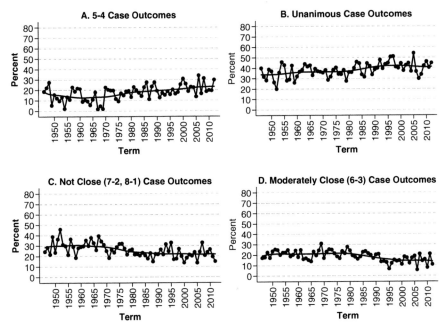

FIGURE 4. Percentage of Various Vote Splits over Time
Note: In each graph, dots represent the percentage of outcomes with the associated vote split for each term. The solid line is a nonparametric lowess smoother that gives a sense of the pattern over time.

POLARIZATION PARADOX?

What is the effect of polarization on the general degree of consensus/dissensus in vote splits over time?[13] One might think that with increasing polarization over time, the occurrence of closely divided (e.g., 5-4 and 6-3) rulings would increase while the occurrence of unanimous rulings would decrease. Figure 4 presents data on the degree of change in the occurrence of various vote splits over time. Figure 4A and 4B presents 5-4 and unanimous outcomes,[14] respectively, whereas Figure 4C and 4D presents "not close" (7-2 and 8-1) and moderately close (6-3) outcomes, respectively.[15] Although the patterns are subtle, Figure 4

[13] For an in-depth analysis of consensus and unanimity on the Court, see Corley, Steigerwalt, and Ward (2013).

[14] Figure 4A includes all cases decided by one vote, both 5-4 outcomes and the less frequent 4-3 outcome where seven members participated. Figure 4B includes all unanimous cases, most of which occur when all nine justices participate, but some include 8-0 outcomes where a justice recuses him- or herself or 8-0/7-0 outcomes where fewer than nine justices are on the Court because of a pending presidential appointment.

[15] "Not close" outcomes include instances where the difference between the number of majority votes and the number of minority votes is ≥ 4 and ≤ 7. Most of these outcomes are 7-2 or 8-1,

reveals what I refer to as a "polarization paradox." Whereas the occurrence of closely divided outcomes (5-4) increases over time, which is what we would expect given generally increasing polarization, the occurrence of unanimous opinions actually increases as well and is generally quite high. The occurrence of "not close" and "moderately close" outcomes actually decreases over time. What this suggests is that the distribution of vote splits has actually polarized over time – increases at the vote split extremes of unanimity and closely divided and decreases in not close and moderately close outcomes – but not in the way we would expect given a shrinking middle and more reliable ideologues.

Figure 4A shows that one-vote differences have occurred between just above 0 percent of the time (in the late Warren Court) to over 30 percent in the Roberts era. It is interesting that the highest occurrences of 5-4 outcomes occur in this contemporary era with just one swing justice and reliable ideologues on the left and right. There is some volatility in these rates during this era, ranging from a little more than 10 percent to just over 30 percent. Some of the lowest rates of 5-4 outcomes occurred during the Warren Court of the 1960s, which is actually not all that surprising since liberal justices had comfortable majorities on the Court. The Burger Court of the mid-to-late 1970s, where a robust center existed, experienced 5-4 rates of between 9 percent and 19 percent.

Rates of unanimity range from 20 percent to just over 50 percent and have slowly climbed over time. Although the average change over time is not drastic, it nonetheless begs the question of why we would see such high rates of unanimity in an age of increasing polarization (see Corley, Steigerwalt, and Ward 2013). Some of the highest unanimity rates have occurred in an era of quite high polarization, during the Rehnquist Court of the 1990s and into the Roberts Court period. The highest rate of unanimity (54 percent) actually occurred during the first term (2005) of Chief Justice Roberts' career; the 5-4 rate is also quite low that term, at 13.5 percent. Of course, Chief Justice Roberts made it widely known that his goal was to increase rates of unanimity in order for the Court to speak with one voice and enhance its legitimacy (e.g., Rosen 2007). Unanimity spiked upward in his first term, but it fell back to normal levels a few years later.

While I do not intend to provide a comprehensive answer to this "polarization paradox," I use one compelling perspective centering on Supreme Court agenda setting that provides insight as to why we see such a paradox. From the trends in Figure 4, it seems clear that even in a polarized era, the Court continues to maintain what Pacelle (1991) calls a "bifurcated agenda." According to Pacelle, underlying the Court's selection of the cases it will hear and decide on (at the certiorari stage) are two basic sub-agendas: (1) the *volitional agenda*, which contains the hot-button legal-political issues that

---

when all nine members participate. They also include, for example, 6-2 and 7-1 outcomes, for instances where fewer than nine justices participate. "Moderately close" outcomes include instances where majority votes minus minority votes is two (5-3) or three (6-3). The former instance rarely occurs.

are highly salient to the justices and that allow justices to pursue their policy goals; and (2) the *exigent agenda*, which contains cases on which the Court must settle legal questions, resolve lower court splits, and therefore manage the judicial hierarchy by giving clear signals to the lower courts and performing basic functions of institutional maintenance. Building on this view, Corley et al. (2013) provide empirical support to the notion that settling legal questions and creating national legal standards are very important considerations at the certiorari stage (see also Perry 1991). Moreover, Corley et al. provide important evidence from the 1989 term that unanimous rulings are just as likely as non-unanimous rulings to contain a lower-court split or a very important legal question, both of which are very important considerations at the certiorari stage. And cases in which there is a perceived need at the certiorari stage to settle a legal issue and issue a final ruling that applies to everyone tend to elicit quite high unanimity rates.

These are important explanations suggesting that polarization on the Court is actually bifurcated – it is alive and well within the volitional agenda but much less pronounced within the exigent agenda. The Court clearly has the capacity to engage in policymaking that has implications for the other branches of government, the states, and the American people. The justices have policy goals, and they presumably seek to have those goals achieved in certain legal areas. But the Court also has basic responsibilities concerning institutional maintenance. The Court sits at the head of the federal judicial hierarchy, and it is widely perceived to maintain judicial supremacy, meaning it has the final say on constitutional meaning for everyone. On the one hand, the Court is a political institution in the sense that it sometimes makes policy decisions on some of the most important issues in American politics. In these cases, the justices are quite polarized, just as many political elites in Washington are. But that's only part of the story of what the justices do, of course, invoking Pacelle's (1991) bifurcated agenda perspective and Corley et al.'s (2013) perspective on unanimity and consensus. The Court is also in the business of clarifying important legal questions for the lower courts and governments at the state and federal levels. For these cases, the Court is often able to speak in one voice – or at least a quite consensual voice. Surely this story does not constitute an exhaustive explanation of the polarization paradox as I have posed it. But it does suggest that polarization is not highly operative on every single case the Court decides. Polarization depends on the goals of the justices in how they are selecting cases and in which sub-agenda the case belongs – the exigent agenda or the volitional agenda.

CONCLUSION

The implications of the preceding discussion on Supreme Court polarization are numerous and leave room for many further examinations of this important concept. I conclude with a discussion of the implications for presidential nominations and Senate confirmation. As this chapter has implied, the linkage between the appointment process and polarization on the Court is a sort of vicious circle. The degree of polarization on the Court and in the Court's policymaking are driven by how presidents appoint and the Senate scrutinizes nominees, whereas whom the president nominates and how the Senate scrutinizes a nominee is driven in large part by the ideological makeup and polarization on a given Court. The implications are extremely tangible for the contemporary Court, which has four quite reliable ideologues on both the left and the right and a center of just one justice. Supreme Court vacancies in this context, particularly where the Senate is also very polarized, could trigger some unique events and actions in the appointment and confirmation process never before seen. I explain the situations as follows.

If either Justice Kennedy or a justice who is ideologically incongruent with the sitting president should die or retire, we will likely witness the most politically cantankerous appointment and confirmation process in history. I refer to this as the "blockbuster scenario." If such a scenario occurred, the president would have the opportunity to create the first ideologically reliable/ homogeneous majority coalition since the liberal coalition on the Warren Court of the 1960s. This could happen during an Obama presidency if, for example, Justice Kennedy or one of the reliable conservatives were to retire or die; President Obama would then have the chance to add a fifth reliable liberal (alongside Ginsburg, Breyer, Sotomayor, and Kagan), thereby creating a solid liberal majority on the Court. The same would hold if a Republican succeeds President Obama and Justice Kennedy or a liberal justice dies or retires. And as a matter of fact, the blockbuster scenario is actually guaranteed to occur because Justice Kennedy will have to vacate (via retirement or death) at some point. He will most likely strategically retire during a Republican administration (if he does not die before that, either during a Republican or Democratic administration), at which point a Republican president would have the opportunity to create a reliably conservative majority (alongside Roberts, Scalia, Thomas, and Alito). Given the nature of polarization on the Court at this point, the long-term ideological makeup of the Court and the nature of its policymaking will be extremely sensitive to which justice dies or retires and whether the justice who vacates is ideologically incongruent with the president.

No matter how this blockbuster scenario should occur, several additional factors will come into play: (1) whether the president's party controls the Senate; (2) whether the minority party would filibuster a president's nominee (in the event that the president's party controls the Senate); and (3) whether the majority party would use the "nuclear option" to rule out a filibuster and force a majority vote (in the case where the president's party controls the Senate).

Consider first the scenario where the president's party controls the Senate. Under this condition, the president will surely feel emboldened to nominate an ideologically reliable individual. The minority party in the Senate would certainly observe that the president would have the ability to create a solid majority voting bloc on the Court, and it would likely be tempted to filibuster the nominee in order to send a clear signal to the president to nominate someone more moderate. Thus, the next question is whether the majority party would invoke the nuclear option, which would eliminate the possibility of a filibuster, force a simple majority vote, and ensure that the president's nominee secures a seat on the Court, thereby creating an ideologically congruent and reliable majority coalition on the Court. In November 2013, Senate Majority Leader Harry Reid and the Democrats invoked the nuclear option to eliminate filibusters for most presidential nominations to the executive branch and the federal judiciary, *except for the Supreme Court*. Under this scenario, then, a war in the Senate would ensue over whether to eliminate the filibuster for Supreme Court nominations, as surely the minority would strongly consider the option of filibustering the president's nominee in this situation. This scenario, then, would bring to light all of the consequences of polarization across branches of government – in the Senate, between the Senate and the president, and pertaining to the Supreme Court.

Consider next the scenario where the president's party does not control the Senate. This process would be slightly more politically tame because in the Senate, the filibuster option would be off the table. Moreover, the president would be forced to back away from appointing a rock-solid, ideologically reliable nominee. The president would be constrained to nominate an individual who could secure at least 51 votes from the opposite party. This is a tall task indeed in an increasingly polarized Senate, and it would likely mean that the president would have to appoint a more moderate nominee. We have actually not seen a nomination and confirmation process under divided party control of the president and Senate since President George H. W. Bush nominated Clarence Thomas. The last six appointments (Ginsburg, Breyer, Roberts, Alito, Sotomayor, and Kagan) have occurred under unified party control of the president and Senate. And all have yielded quite reliable ideologues. With the Republicans regaining control of the Senate as a result of the 2014 midterm elections, this scenario could occur during the last two years of President Obama's time in office. Of course, appointments in the last two years have typically spelled trouble for the president (e.g., Epstein et al. 2006), leaving him or her in a very weak position where the Senate has an incentive to delay the process and wait until the next presidential election after which a more like-minded president may be elected.

I conclude by returning to the vicious circle between appointments and polarization on the Court. As this chapter has made clear, the consequences of increasing polarization on the Court with a center of one and reliable ideologues on the left and right will be quite substantial for the next Supreme Court appointment process, particularly under the "blockbuster scenario" previously described. Depending on which justice leaves and why (strategic retirement, death, non-strategic retirement due to health concerns), the next membership change could be extremely consequential for the long-term trajectory of Supreme Court policymaking. In the blockbuster scenario with unified party control of the presidency and Senate and the elimination of the filibuster, the president could secure the first ideologically homogeneous majority voting bloc since the Warren Court of the 1960s. The center would disappear altogether, but the question remains whether a sitting justice would step up and fill in the center gap, akin to how Justice O'Connor moved toward the center in the early-to-mid 1990s.

If the center does indeed disappear and the Court contains an ideologically homogeneous majority voting bloc, we will witness the most polarized Court in history, a Court that would be substantially more polarized than the Court of 2014 with a center of one. Recall that with a bifurcated agenda (Pacelle 1991; Corley, Steigerwalt, and Ward 2013), the Court would still likely maintain consensual decision making in cases where institutional maintenance concerns are prominent – that is, the exigent agenda. But a significantly more polarized Court could potentially alter the dynamics of case selection at the certiorari stage as well. It is clear that within the volitional agenda, a completely polarized Court with no center would be extremely consequential for the shape of policymaking, where an ideologically homogeneous majority voting bloc could simply run the table on hot-button legal-political issues. We would likely see more extreme policy outputs, providing a deviation from the patterns of moderation in Figure 3. What is most stunning is that this extreme polarization scenario just discussed will be triggered by just *one* membership change on the Court, a change that could occur as the result of chance (e.g., death) or the strategic retirement of Justice Kennedy.

REFERENCES

Abramowitz, Alan I., and Kyle L. Saunders. 2008. "Is Polarization a Myth?" *Journal of Politics* 70 (2): 542–555.
Bailey, Michael A., and Forrest Maltzman. 2008. "Does Legal Doctrine Matter? Unpacking Law and Policy Preferences on the US Supreme Court." *American Political Science Review* 102 (3): 369–384.
Bartels, Brandon L. 2009. "The Constraining Capacity of Legal Doctrine on the U.S. Supreme Court." *American Political Science Review* 103 (3): 474–495.
Bartels, Brandon L., and Christopher D. Johnston. 2013. "On the Ideological Foundations of Supreme Court Legitimacy in the American Public." *American Journal of Political Science* 57 (1): 184–199.
Baum, Lawrence. 2012. *The Supreme Court.* 11th edition. Washington, DC: CQ Press.
Bond, Jon R., and Richard Fleisher. 2000. *Polarized Politics: Congress and the President in the Partisan Era.* Washington, DC: CQ Press.
Caldeira, Gregory A., Marie Hojnacki, and John R. Wright. 2000. "The Lobbying Activities of Organized Interests in Federal Judicial Nominations." *The Journal of Politics* 62 (1): 51–69.

Caldeira, Gregory A., and John R. Wright. 1998. "Lobbying for Justice: Organized Interests Supreme Court Nominations, and United States Senate." *American Journal of Political Science* 42 (2): 499–523.

Clark, Tom S. 2009. "Measuring Ideological Polarization on the United States Supreme Court." *Political Research Quarterly* 62 (1): 146–157.

Corley, Pamela C., Amy Steigerwalt, and Artemus Ward. 2013. *The Puzzle of Unanimity: Consensus on the United States Supreme Court.* Stanford, CA: Stanford University Press.

Dahl, Robert A. 1957. "Decision-Making in a Democracy: The Supreme Court as a National Policy-Maker." *Journal of Public Law* 6 (2): 279–295.

Devins, Neal, and Lawrence Baum. 2014. "Split Definitive: How Party Polarization Turned the Supreme Court into a Partisan Court." *William & Mary Law School Research Paper, No. 09-276.*

Epstein, Lee, and Jack Knight. 1998. *The Choices Justices Make.* Washington, DC: CQ Press.

Epstein, Lee, René Lindstädt, Jeffrey A. Segal, and Chad Westerland. 2006. "The Changing Dynamics of Senate Voting on Supreme Court Nominees." *Journal of Politics* 68 (2): 296–307.

Epstein, Lee, and Jeffrey A. Segal. 2005. *Advice and Consent: The Politics of Judicial Appointments.* New York: Oxford University Press.

Epstein, Lee, and Jeffrey A. Segal. 2000. "Measuring Issue Salience." *American Journal of Political Science* 44 (1): 66–83.

Fiorina, Morris P., Samuel J. Abrams, and Jeremy C. Pope. 2006. *Culture War? The Myth of a Polarized America*, 2nd edition. New York: Pearson Longman.

Kramer, Larry D. 2004. *The People Themselves: Popular Constitutionalism and Judicial Review.* New York: Oxford University Press.

Maltzman, Forrest, James F. Spriggs II, and Paul J. Wahlbeck. 2000. *Crafting Law on the Supreme Court: The Collegial Game.* New York: Cambridge University Press.

Martin, Andrew D., and Kevin M. Quinn. 2002. "Dynamic Ideal Point Estimation Via Markov Chain Monte Carlo for the US Supreme Court, 1953–1999." *Political Analysis* 10 (2): 134–153.

McCarty, Nolan, Keith T. Poole, and Howard Rosenthal. 2006. *Polarized America: The Dance of Ideology and Unequal Riches.* Cambridge, MA: MIT Press.

McGuire, Kevin T., and James A. Stimson. 2004. "The Least Dangerous Branch Revisited: New Evidence on Supreme Court Responsiveness to Public Preferences." *Journal of Politics* 66 (4): 1018–1035.

Mishler, William, and Reginald S. Sheehan. 1993. "The Supreme Court as a Countermajoritarian Institution? the Impact of Public Opinion on Supreme Court Decisions." *American Political Science Review* 87 (1): 87–101.

Moraski, Bryon J., and Charles R. Shipan. 1999. "The Politics of Supreme Court Nominations: A Theory of Institutional Constraints and Choices." *American Journal of Political Science* 43 (4): 1069–1095.

Pacelle, Richard L. 1991. *The Transformation of the Supreme Court's Agenda: From the New Deal to the Reagan Administration.* Boulder, CO: Westview Press.

Perry, H. W. 1991. *Deciding to Decide: Agenda Setting in the United States Supreme Court.* Cambridge, MA: Harvard University Press.

Poole, Keith T., and Howard Rosenthal. 1984. "The Polarization of American Politics." *The Journal of Politics* 46 (4): 1061–1079.

Richards, Mark J., and Herbert M. Kritzer. 2002. "Jurisprudential Regimes in Supreme Court Decision Making." *American Political Science Review* 96 (2): 305–320.

Rohde, David W. 1991. *Parties and Leaders in the Postreform House.* Chicago: University of Chicago Press.

Rosen, Jeffrey. 2007. "Roberts' Rules." *The Atlantic,* January/February. Retrieved from http://www.theatlantic.com/magazine/archive/2007/01/robertss-rules/305559/.

Schlesinger, Joseph A. 1985. "The New American Political Party." *American Political Science Review* 79 (4): 1152–1169.

Segal, Jeffrey A., and Harold J. Spaeth. 2002. *The Supreme Court and the Attitudinal Model Revisited.* New York: Cambridge University Press.

Segal, Jeffrey A., Chad Westerland, and Stefanie A. Lindquist. 2011. "Congress, the Supreme Court, and Judicial Review: Testing a Constitutional Separation of Powers Model." *American Journal of Political Science* 55 (1): 89–104.

Spaeth, Harold J., Sara C. Benesh, Lee Epstein, Andrew D. Martin, Jeffrey A. Segal, and Theodore J. Ruger. 2013. "The Supreme Court Database, Version 2013 Release 01." Retrieved from http://supremecourtdatabase.org. Accessed on April 25, 2014.

Spiller, Pablo T., and Rafael Gely. 1992. "Congressional Control or Judicial Independence: The Determinants of U.S. Supreme Court Labor-Relations Decisions, 1949–1988." *RAND Journal of Economics* 23 (4): 463–492.

Tushnet, Mark. 1999. *Taking the Constitution away from the Courts.* Princeton, NJ: Princeton University Press.

Woodward, Bob, and Scott Armstrong. 1979. *The Brethren: Inside the Supreme Court.* New York: Simon and Schuster.

PART III

POLARIZATION IN THE STATES

9

Polarization in American State Legislatures

Boris Shor

- New measures of state legislative polarization show that Democrats and Republicans continue to diverge, although more quickly in some states than in others. Levels of polarization in many states exceed that of Congress.
- No one "smoking gun" explains state legislative polarization. In many cases, we can only rule out suspected causes such as primaries. However, interesting new evidence implicates specific forms of opinion polarization and income inequality.
- The consequences of state legislative polarization are only now beginning to be explored. Increasing unilateralism by governors appears to be one major implication of increased gridlock within the legislature.
- Major advances in our understanding of polarization are more likely to come from the states compared with Congress, given the tremendous institutional and preference variation in the former compared with the latter

INTRODUCTION

Most of the recent scholarly literature on Congress emphasizes trends that indicate rising party differences in roll call voting behavior (Poole and Rosenthal 1997; McCarty, Poole and Rosenthal 2006). These findings are generally based on measures of positions on the liberal-conservative continuum as revealed through roll call voting. Although various techniques for measuring the ideology of legislators have been developed, they all produce very similar findings. The measure of polarization I use in this chapter is the

This chapter emerges from work I did with Nolan McCarty. We acknowledge the support of the National Science Foundation, Award Nos. SES-1059716 and SES-1060092. The data in this chapter relies on the hard work of the following: Michelle Anderson, Michael Barber, Peter Koppstein, Chad Levinson, and Steven Rogers. Thanks to Project Vote Smart for making their NPAT data and questions available to me. I welcome comments and questions (boris@bshor.com). Any errors are my own.

difference in medians between Democrats and Republicans, with a larger gap indicating a greater level of polarization.[1]

Why do we care about polarization? Excessive levels of partisanship and ideological polarization have been shown to have a pernicious effect on many aspects of policymaking and governance (see McCarty, Poole, and Rosenthal 2006, 2013, and Barber and McCarty 2015 for a review of the evidence at the national level). As recent events in many state capitols attest, these problems are beginning to afflict policymaking at the state level. As a result, a robust public debate about how to reduce polarization and partisanship has emerged.

What about American state legislatures? Are they polarizing like Congress? It is important to quantify such trends because we want to know if polarization is leading to political gridlock and dysfunctional policy. We also need a barometer of polarization to find out whether institutional reforms such as opening up primaries, taking redistricting away from politicians themselves, setting term limits, and so forth can ameliorate this phenomenon. In addition, since there are fifty state legislatures, we might find answers to these questions more quickly and definitively than we can with Congress, of which we only have one.

While polarization in the states has not received the same attention as congressional polarization, our recent research has shown that state legislatures are quite polarized (Shor and McCarty 2011). Most state legislatures exhibit levels of partisan and ideological conflict that are at least as high as that of the U.S. Congress. Moreover, polarization has been rising in most – but not all – state legislatures. And just as it has in Congress, partisan conflict within state legislatures has become a central feature of policymaking – witness abortion policies in Texas, collective bargaining in Wisconsin[2], and the expansion of Medicaid in the states under the Affordable Care Act.

While the phenomenon of the polarization of state governments is intrinsically important, the states also provide a useful laboratory for evaluating the proposed reforms designed to mitigate polarization or its consequences at all levels. For example, suppose one wanted to evaluate the extent to which various features of the campaign finance system create biases toward the election of ideologues and partisans. Conducting such a study on the U.S. Congress faces any number of limitations. The basic structure of the federal campaign finance system changes very rarely. And when it does, the reforms are

---

[1] Scholars have used other measures as well, such as the "overlap" between the parties, which measures how many Democrats are more conservative than the most liberal Republican. A lower overlap score means less polarization. The use of medians is the most conservative measure as it is the least influenced by party outliers, those legislators with positions atypical of their party. The difference in means is influenced both by extreme and moderate party outliers, while the overlap measure is greatly influenced by moderate outliers (a single conservative Democrat can make the party overlap score large). Still, nearly every method designed to measure polarization is highly correlated with every other method, increasing our confidence in the validity of our measures. Aldrich and Battista (2002) find very high correlations as well.

[2] On the consequences of polarization in Wisconsin, see Gilbert (2014).

themselves a product of the partisan and ideological conflict that they are presumed to influence. The states, on the other hand, hold elections under a very diverse set of campaign finance rules, ranging from public financing in some states to trivial restrictions in others. Moreover, these rules change frequently. In principal, scholars could much more confidently evaluate the role of campaign finance in party polarization by leveraging both the variation in rules across and within states.

Clearly, the states are also ideal for evaluating proposed reforms of primary electoral systems, legislative districting, and convenience voting. Additionally, the states afford opportunities to examine the policy effects of partisan polarization. Do less polarized states manage their economies, governments, and disadvantaged citizens better than more polarized states? How might extreme partisanship impact opportunity for reform in education policy, public sector pensions, health policy, or any of the other salient areas of state policymaking?

TRENDS IN POLARIZATION

Unfortunately, the data necessary to use the states to study the causes and consequences of polarization has not been available. Prior to Shor and McCarty (2011), similar measurements of polarization at the state level were unavailable for two reasons: the lack of data on voting records and the lack of a metric for comparing across states. To address the first problem, legislative journals of all 50 states (generally from the mid-1990s onward) were either downloaded from the web or purchased in hard copy. The hard copy journals were disassembled, photocopied, and scanned. These scans were converted to text using optical character recognition software. To convert the raw legislative text to roll call voting data, we developed several data-mining scripts. Because the format of each journal is unique, a script had to be developed for each state, and each time a state changed its publication format. When our article initially came out in 2011, we covered roughly the period between 1996 and 2006, which effectively meant the legislators elected between 1994 and 2004. This included 16,732 unique state legislators and 1,378 chamber-years of data across the 50 states.

State legislative journals and votes have gradually become more accessible online, al-though that is rarely applied backward in time. New resources such as OpenStates aggregate these electronic archives and make accessing roll call votes much easier and less noisy than ever before. In part due to these new data sources, we have continued to update the data. Now our measures extend to 2014, meaning we now incorporate the legislators elected between 2006 and 2010. In all, our dataset currently covers 20,562 unique state legislators, with more than 1,800 chamber-years of data.[3]

---

[3] The aggregate and legislator level data is available for download at http://www.americanlegisla-tures.com.

The second issue is that we can only compare the positions of two legislators if they have cast votes on the same issues. If we assume that legislators have fairly consistent positions over time, we can compare two legislators so long as they both have voted on the same issues as a third legislator. But this issue poses special problems to the study of state legislators because two legislators from different states rarely cast votes on exactly the same issue. So to make comparisons across states, we use a survey of federal and state legislative candidates that asks similar questions across states and across time. The National Political Awareness Test (NPAT) is administered by Project Vote Smart, a nonpartisan organization that disseminates these surveys as voter guides to the public at large. Additional work needs to be done to process the raw NPAT data by merging identical questions and respondents across states and time. Then, by combining the data on roll call votes with the processed NPAT survey data from 1996 to 2014, we generate universal coverage of state legislators who have served in the states for which we have the roll call data. The technical details of how we combine these two data sources can be found in Shor and McCarty (2011).

We begin with a macro-level perspective on polarization. Figure 1 averages the distance between party medians over time and across chambers within states to get a sense of the average level of state legislative polarization. We are able to make direct comparison to Congress because congressional candidates answer the Vote Smart survey just as state legislative candidates do. Strikingly, the level of polarization in the U.S. House and Senate – the subject of substantial scholarly attention (McCarty, Poole, and Rosenthal 2006; Theriault 2008) is not an outlier. In comparison to Congress, the majority of state legislatures are less polarized, while many are actually more polarized. California is by far the most polarized state legislature, and Congress looks decidedly bipartisan by comparison (see Masket 2009 on the causes and consequences of polarization in this state.) On the other end, Rhode Island and Louisiana are the least polarized. In the former, Democrats are liberal, but so too are the Republicans. In the latter, the converse is true.

We also find that there is variation in polarization trends across states and chambers. Figures 2 further illustrates how heterogeneous states are with respect to polarization levels and trends. As with the U.S. Congress, all 99 state legislative chambers (Nebraska has a single chamber commonly referred to as the Unicam or Senate) are polarized. In 71 of those 99 chambers, the parties are getting more distant from each other. In 20 of them, the parties are roughly stable, not trending toward or away from each other. In eight chambers, the parties are actually depolarizing or getting closer. In most states, unlike in the U.S. Congress, the upper (Senate) chamber is typically more polarized than the lower (House or Assembly) chamber. On the other hand, the lower chamber is polarizing faster in more states than the upper chamber. It is not yet clear why these differences should exist.

FIGURE I. Comparison of Polarization Averaged across Chambers and Time for All Fifty State Legislatures
Note: Congress is included as the dashed line for comparison.

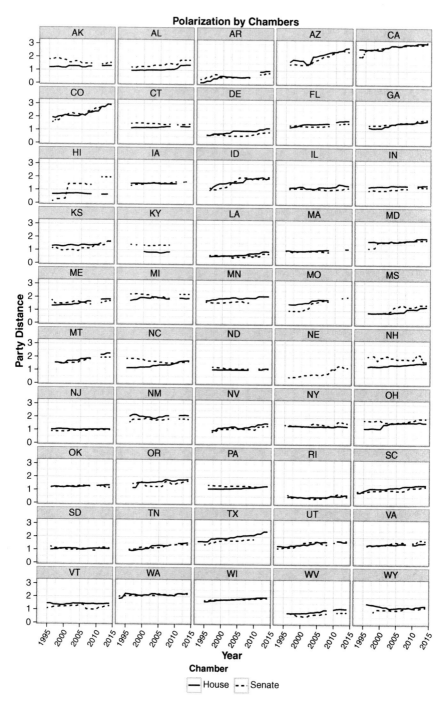

FIGURE 2. Difference in Party Medians
Note: Higher values indicate more polarization.

The top five fastest polarizing chambers, in order, are the Arizona Senate, the Missouri Senate, the Colorado Senate, the Arizona House, and the Idaho Senate.[4] The five fastest depolarizing (moderating) state chambers, in order, are the Alaska Senate, the North Carolina Senate, the North Dakota Senate, the New Hampshire Senate, and the Wyoming House. This is completely unheard of in recent years in Congress. At the same time, California retains its title as the most polarized state legislature in the country. It has even managed to move up a couple of notches in the past 20 years.

Asymmetric Polarization

Which parties are driving this polarization at the state level? Are both parties at fault, or is one becoming more extreme compared to the other? That is, is state legislative polarization symmetric or asymmetric? When we look at Congress over the past 20 years, we can clearly see that – in both the U.S. House and Senate – the Republican Party has gotten more extreme over time relative to the Democrats (although in the House, Democrats have polarized to a smaller degree as well). This is a familiar story of asymmetric polarization. In fairness, the move by Democrats in the liberal direction started earlier than the move by Republicans: the 1940s versus the mid-1970s. Still, in recent years, Congressional Republicans have unquestionably moved further and faster.

Looking at the state legislatures, Figure 3 shows the picture graphically, plotting party medians over time, separately for each chamber. On average, Republicans are polarizing faster than Democrats, but this varies across the states. In 72 of the 99 state legislative chambers, Republicans are getting more conservative over time, whereas in 62 chambers, Democrats are getting more liberal. In 20 chambers, Democrats are actually getting more conservative (e.g., depolarizing), while the converse is true only for 8 chambers for Republicans, where they are actually getting more liberal. In 17 chambers, Democrats are roughly stable, and the same is true in 19 chambers for Republicans.

But what the data clearly reveal is that states are wildly diverse. In some states, such as Arkansas and Colorado, Republicans are getting more extreme in recent time, while Democrats are not changing much. But in other states, such as Idaho, Mississippi, and Texas, the Democrats are largely responsible for the states' recent polarization. In California, the most polarized state, Democrats and Republicans are both polarizing, but the Democrats have moved further to the extreme. And finally, there are states such as Missouri and Nebraska, where both parties are polarizing roughly equally and simultaneously.

---

[4] The Hawaii Senate is also polarizing, but I have excluded listing it because there is only a single Republican in the chamber.

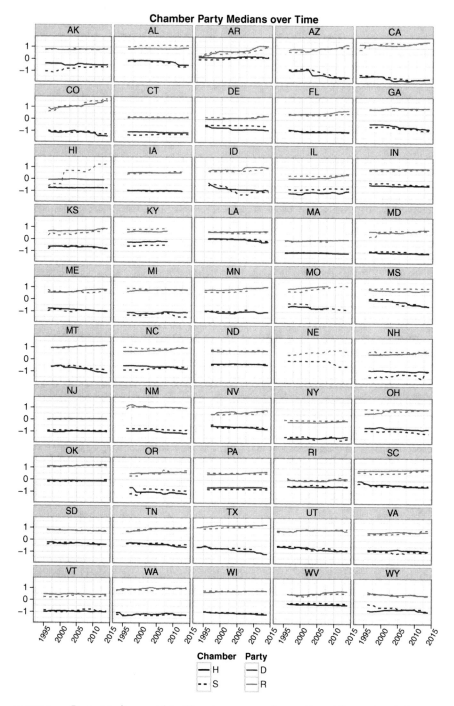

FIGURE 3. Party Medians within Chambers across States; Republicans Are Polarizing Faster in 10 More Chambers Than Democrats, and Depolarizing in 12 Fewer Chambers

The polarization story is similar in some ways in state legislatures as in Congress: Republicans are leading the charge to the ideological poles on average. But it's different, too: the average story obscures lots of differences across states. State polarization trends thus underline the usefulness of studying state legislatures as a laboratory for political observers: there is much variation to work with in trying to understand what causes what. And so we should look to state experiences to see whether reforms in areas such as redistricting, primaries, campaign finance, and so on do anything to mitigate polarization, and whether some reforms might have unintended consequences that make it worse.

CAUSES

A number of papers have utilized the Shor and McCarty (2011) data to investigate potential causes of polarization. I illuminate a few of these here.

Primary Institutions

One of the most popular electoral reforms concerns changing the ways in which parties nominate candidates for the general election. The idea that less partisan – and more open – primary elections would create the conditions for more moderate office holders was behind California's recent adoption of the "top two" primary system in which the top vote getters, regardless of party, move to the general election. Several studies have argued for a significant effect from nomination procedures (Gerber 1998; Bullock and Clinton 2011). However, these studies rely on either purely cross-sectional data or data from a limited number of states.

But our data provides an opportunity to evaluate empirically whether moving from closed partisan primaries to less partisan open primaries reduces polarization.[5] In McGhee et al. (2014), we use our data on state legislator positions to test whether states that use open primaries or shift to open primaries elect less extreme legislators (and by extension less polarized legislatures.) Our findings challenge the conventional wisdom as we find few strong relationships between the openness of a primary and the moderation of the legislators it produces.

Figure 4 shows our model predictions for the trends in legislator ideology for the five major primary systems we track. In all systems, legislators are getting more extreme over time: Democrats are becoming more liberal and Republicans more conservative. More open and nonpartisan systems, which are hypothesized to moderate candidates given the presence of independents and other-party identifiers, do not seem to have more moderate records than more closed systems.

---

[5] In *closed* primaries, only registered partisans may vote in their own party's primary. In *open* primaries, registered partisans as well as independents may vote in the primary of their choice.

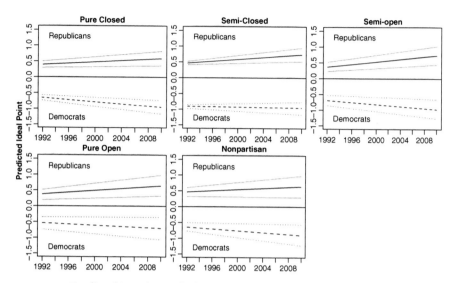

FIGURE 4. Predicted Legislator Ideology Trends Holding All Other Variables Fixed at Their Means, Including Fixed Effects

Note: Gray lines represent 95 percent error bounds. All systems appear to show polarizing trends over time, with little difference between them.

Our study, however, only considers opening primaries to independents and crossover partisans. Evaluations of more radical alternatives such as California's "top two" system have been limited, although our data is now being used to address this question in a new study (Kousser, Phillips, and Shor 2014). We show that despite the imposition of this radical primary reform (combined with the start of nonpartisan redistricting), candidates – and especially challengers – are no more moderate than they were prior to the reform. Shor-McCarty polarization measures for California in 2013 and 2014 show that polarization did not abate; it even accelerated in the upper chamber.

Term Limits

Congressional polarization is largely driven by replacement rather than adaptation. This is because – in Keith Poole's colorful phrase – members of Congress "die in their ideological boots" (Poole 2007: 435). Thus, polarization is for the most part driven by moderates leaving Congress, and being replaced by ideological extremists. This turnover is blunted to some extent by incumbency, which may shield long-serving moderates. An election loss (primary or general) or retirement eventually brings in someone new and who is more likely to be extreme.

Many states, unlike Congress, have term limit laws that mechanically increase legislator turnover. It stands to reason that term limit laws may accelerate underlying secular trends that favor increased polarization. Interestingly, the imposition of term limit laws began relatively recently, allowing scholars the opportunity to examine legislative voting behavior before and after these changes.

One such law can be found in Nebraska, where term limits were approved by voters in a 2004 initiative and began turning out members in 2006. Nebraska is an unusual state in that it hosts the only officially nonpartisan (both in the chambers and at the voting booth) and unicameral state legislature. Earlier work (Wright and Schaffner 2002) correctly noted the relatively unpolarized status of the two parties in the chamber, which they ascribed to the nonpartisanship rules.[6] New work by Masket and Shor (2015) shows that the rapid increase in Nebraska's polarization began around 2006. They document how state partisan leaders, especially Republican governor Dave Heineman and Democratic state party leadership, became extremely involved in candidate recruitment to replace term-out legislators. Ideological purity was newly emphasized as an important trait for these new candidates. Donors, who had previously given across party lines and with little regard for ideology, became far more exclusive in terms of party and ideology.

Public Financing

Many reformers regard the campaign financing system in the United States as a significant cause of legislative division. Individual private interests donate increasingly large (and often unlimited) amounts to individual candidates, party committees, and outside pressure groups. These donations are thought to insulate extremists from moderate public opinion.

If this logic holds, it is perhaps natural to suppose that public financing of campaigns should moderate polarization. Public financing for Congress, however, is a nonstarter given the deep partisan divisions over campaign finance. A number of states, however, have innovated and instituted varying degrees of public financing of state legislative campaigns. Hall (2014) uses a regression discontinuity design and the Shor and McCarty (2011) data to examine the evidence for this proposition. Hall finds a perverse result: states that institute public financing actually experience an *increase* in extremist legislators. This is because public funding undermines the incumbency advantage and enables ideological extremists access to campaign resources they previously had difficulty securing.

---

[6] Partisans are unofficially identified by media and individual party registration status.

Inequality

Nationally, there has been a great increase in both political polarization and income inequality since the early 1970s. McCarty, Poole, and Rosenthal (2006) document these trends and tie them together. Their argument is that rising income inequality is both a cause and an effect of polarization. When incomes grow unequally, there is a greater return to organizing political conflict over the central axis of attitudes toward government activism. At the same time, when Congress is polarized, redistributive policies that can ameliorate inequality are often very hard to pass given the presence of numerous veto points in the American separation of powers system.

What about the states? Until relatively recently, high quality data on income inequality has been lacking. This is partly due to well-known problems with income microdata, which is often either geographically censored (IRS), too sparse at lower levels of geographic detail (CPS), or top-coded at relatively low income levels (Census). New estimates of income inequality at the state level from Frank (2014) and Voorheis (2014) have finally tackled this problem.

In a new paper, Voorheis, Shor, and McCarty (2014) employ an instrumental variables approach to enable them to identify the causal effect of state income inequality on state legislative political polarization.[7] This identification strategy, which relies on an instrument for state income inequality generated from simulated state income distributions, rules out the possibility of reverse causality. We find that income inequality has a statistically significant, positive, and quantitatively large effect on political polarization. This effect appears to be slightly stronger for lower chambers, and for the period after 2000. We also find that the effect of income inequality on legislative polarization works mostly through the channel of state Democratic parties becoming more liberal.

Public Opinion

One of the enduring puzzles in the study of American politics is the juxtaposition of an increasingly polarized Congress with an apparently stable and centrist electorate (Fiorina and Abrams 2008). What about at the state level? I begin with directly comparing the distribution of legislator and district ideology throughout the country as a whole. This is displayed in Figure 6. Similar to the national story, state legislators are bimodally distributed, while individuals are distributed in a much more unimodal fashion. Aggregating nationally, state legislative polarization is clearly not merely a reflection of opinion polarization.

The next step is looking at some simple scatter plots comparing ideological polarization in the state legislatures with the variability of ideology as self-reported by survey respondents in three huge (tens of thousands of

---

[7] Garand (2010) shows that state level income inequality helps explain state opinion and U.S. Senate polarization, but does not address state legislative polarization.

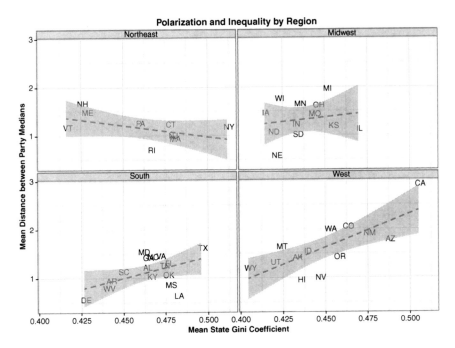

FIGURE 5.

respondents) surveys performed by the National Annenberg Election Study from 2000 to 2008. Figure 7 shows that states with more polarized electorates elect more polarized state legislatures. Moreover, this relationship appears to be getting stronger over time.

McCarty, Poole, and Rosenthal (2009) decompose polarization into two sources: sorting and intradistrict divergence. Polarization driven by the latter is the difference between how Democratic and Republican legislators would represent the same district. The former is the result of the propensity for Democrats to represent liberal districts and for Republicans to represent conservative ones. In Shor and McCarty (2011), we show that intradistrict divergence dominates sorting for state legislatures just as it does for Congress.

Yet this just moves the puzzle one step backward. Where does intradistrict divergence come from? How is that there is a large density of districts where the average voter is quite moderate, but the voting behavior of the representative is extreme? Similarly, why are legislatures so much more polarized than district medians? To answer these questions, we need to move the aggregation down one step to the district level. A new paper (Rodden et al. 2014) brings attention back to the distribution of ideology in the mass public with new data and an alternative theoretical approach. We marry state legislative ideology data with the 350,000 person "super survey" created by Tausanovitch and Warshaw (2013) to characterize the

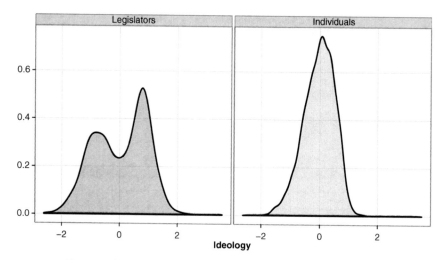

FIGURE 6. Density Plots of Legislator and District Ideology

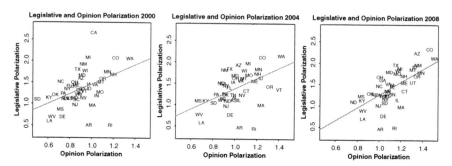

FIGURE 7. Opinion Polarization and Legislative Polarization Are Correlated, and This Is Increasing over Time
Note: Horizontal axis is the variation in self-reported ideology within states for a given National Annenberg Election Survey.

distribution of ideological preferences not only within states, but also across and within state senate districts.

Figure 8 from the paper confirms that state legislative polarization is highly correlated with between-district measures of opinion polarization. That is, states with greater variation of opinion across districts are indeed more polarized. Yet contrary to conventional wisdom, the relationship is actually stronger for *within-district polarization* than for between-district polarization.

The states with the highest levels of within-district polarization, such as California, Colorado, Arizona, and Washington, are those with the highest levels of legislative polarization. At the other end of the scale, states such as

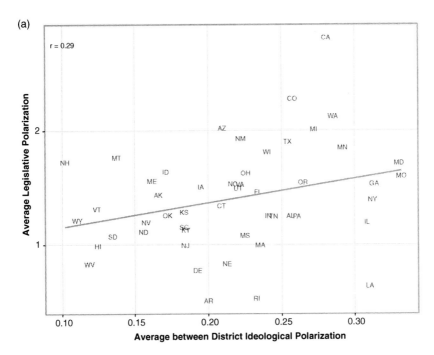

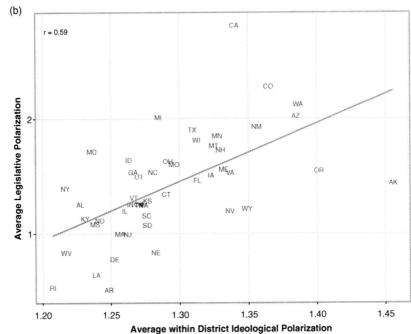

FIGURE 8. Legislative Polarization and Ideological Polarization

West Virginia and Louisiana have more internally homogeneous districts and are also far less polarized.

But why? Given the logic of the median voter, why would electoral competition in these pivotal but polarized districts generate such polarized legislative representation? The paper develops a simple intuition based on the idea that candidates must choose platforms in the presence of uncertainty over the median voter (Wittman 1983; Calvert 1985). The greater the uncertainty, the more candidates move toward their party's more extreme ideological preferences. The intuition is that when district opinion is unimodal, the median voter on election day will be largely predictable, constraining candidates. In contrast, when voters are more evenly distributed throughout the ideological spectrum or even polarized into a bimodal distribution, there is more uncertainty about the identity of the median voter on election day, and hence weaker electoral constraints on candidates' ideological positioning. In other words, when districts are moderate – but only as a consequence of internal divisions – they tend to elect more extreme legislators. This is because normal Downsian pressures to converge are balanced against the returns to turning out your own base. For example, this is seen in large legislative districts where red precincts in the outlying areas surround deep blue areas like college towns. They are moderate because they are deeply internally divided, with a balance between liberal and conservative voters. Many other districts are indeed filled with moderate and unimodally distributed voters. Aggregating everything together obscures the true heterogeneity of public opinion within American legislative districts.

CONSEQUENCES

Interest Group Environment

The constellations of interest groups vary markedly across states. In some, they are incredibly dense; in others, they are considerably less so. The same is true of diversity: interest groups are not all alike, and they vary substantially in composition across the states (Gray and Lowery 2000). These differences, in turn, influence state political dynamics and policy outcomes (Gray, Lowery, and Benz 2013).

What political factors determine interest group environments? New research in Gray et al. (2014) points out that polarization presents both opportunity and peril for interest groups, particularly nonprofits concerned with ideological rather than profit-based objectives. The benefits – and costs – to one side winning and another losing should be magnified in states with more polarized political systems. Indeed, for both 1997 and 2007, states with more polarized legislatures had increasingly dense interest group environments. But this effect extended only to nonprofits, rather than for-profit associations.

Unilateral Action

Despite the conventional wisdom in political science that executive power is dependent on persuasion, there is increasing evidence that presidents increasingly turn to unilateral action to accomplish their objectives. In particular, a difficult strategic environment for presidents, including divided government, is likely to increase the issuance of presidential executive orders (Deering and Maltzman 1999; Howell 2003). The logic should work the same way for state governors. They, too, are located in a complex separation-of-powers system with overlapping and sometimes ill-defined authority. And they, too, exert unilateral power at times. Although their power does not extend to national security matters as does the presidency, governors do have executive orders at their disposal. These orders have not attracted as much scholarly attention as have presidential directives.

Ferguson and Shor (2014) collect new data on gubernatorial executive orders, extending to nearly 600 state-years of data for all orders, and a smaller subset for orders deemed "significant."[8] This data is paired with state legislative polarization data. The key prediction is that governors facing a more gridlocked state legislature will turn to executive orders as an alternative route to lawmaking. The results of a multilevel Poisson model regressing executive order counts on this predictor, and a number of controls confirms this hypothesis.

CONCLUSION

Even as polarization increases in most American legislatures, so too does scholarly understanding of the phenomenon. Work continues on documenting the extent of polarization in the 50 states forward and backward in time. In addition, considerable new research is coming on line that tackles the possible causes of polarization, including new research on public opinion, income inequality, and institutional variation across the states. The smoking gun, however, remains elusive. No one cause has been identified as dominant, nor is there likely to be one. Scholars can only hope to chip away at individual explanations driven by theoretical expectations. Finally, a new and exciting body of work is starting to examine the consequences of polarization in politics and policy. More legislative gridlock is likely, for example, to lead to governors leaning on unilateral action.

A final caveat is in order. Unlike the U.S. Congress – which has been fairly closely divided in the past two decades – unified party government is a common reality in many states. When a single party holds both chambers of the legislature and the governorship, and is not burdened by supermajoritarian rules, polarization is far less "weaponized." Developments in California (which recently abandoned the two-thirds requirement to pass a budget via

---

[8] Cutting out, for example, symbolic actions.

initiative), Colorado, Michigan, and Wisconsin show that polarization need not slow down a unified party leadership intent on making far-reaching policy changes. These are likely to be exceptions to the rule, however.

REFERENCES

Aldrich, John H., and James S. Coleman Battista. 2002. "Conditional Party Government in the States." *American Journal of Political Science* 46 (1): 164–172.
Barber, Michael, and Nolan M McCarty. 2015. "Causes and Consequences of Political Polarization." In Nathaniel Persily, ed., *Solutions to Political Polarization in America.* Cambridge: Cambridge University Press.
Bullock, Will, and Joshua D Clinton. 2011. "More a Molehill Than a Mountain: The Effects of the Blanket Primary on Elected Officials' Behavior from California." *Journal of Politics* 73 (3): 915–930.
Calvert, Randall L. 1985. "Robustness of the Multidimensional Voting Model: Candidate Motivations, Uncertainty, and Convergence." *American Journal of Political Science* 29(1): 69–95.
Deering, Christopher J. and Forrest Maltzman. 1999. "The Politics of Executive Orders: Legislative Constraints on Presidential Power." *Political Research Quarterly* 52 (4): 767–783.
Ferguson, Margaret, and Boris Shor. 2014. "Unilateral Lawmaking in the American Governorship." Working paper.
Fiorina, Morris P., and Samuel J. Abrams. 2008. "Political Polarization in the American Public." *Annual Review Political Science* 11: 563–588.
Frank, Mark W. 2014. "A New State-Level Panel of Annual Inequality Measures over the Period 1916–2005." *Journal of Business Strategies* 31 (1): 241–263.
Garand, James C. 2010. "Income Inequality, Party Polarization, and Roll-call Voting in the US Senate." *The Journal of Politics* 72 (4): 1109–1128.
Gerber, Alan. 1998. "Estimating the Effect of Campaign Spending on Senate Election Outcomes Using Instrumental Variables." *American Political Science Review* 92 (2): 401–411.
Gilbert, Craig. 2014. "Legacy of Wisconsin's Polarization: No Consensus, Little Common Ground." *Wisconsin Journal-Sentinel*, May 13.
Gray, Virginia, John Cluverius, Jeffrey Harden, Boris Shor, and David Lowery. 2014. "Party Competition, Party Polarization, and the Changing Demand for Lobbying in the American States." *American Politics Research* 43 (2): 175–204.
Gray, Virginia, and David Lowery. 2000. *The Population Ecology of Interest Representation: Lobbying Communities in the American States.* Ann Arbor: University of Michigan Press.
Gray, Virginia, David Lowery, and Jennifer K Benz. 2013. *Interest Groups and Health Care Reform Across the United States.* Washington, DC: Georgetown University Press.
Hall, Andrew B. 2014. "How The Public Funding of Elections Increases Candidate Polarization." Working paper
Howell, William G. 2003. *Power without Persuasion: The Politics of Direct Presidential Action.* Princeton, NJ: Princeton University Press.

Kousser, Thad, Justin H. Phillips, and Boris Shor. 2014. "Reform and Representation: Assessing Californias Top-Two Primary and Redistricting Commission." Working paper.

Masket, Seth. 2009. *No Middle Ground: How Informal Party Organizations Control Nominations and Polarize Legislatures.* Ann Arbor: University of Michigan Press.

Masket, Seth E., and Boris Shor. 2015. "Polarization without Parties: The Rise of Legislative Partisanship in Nebraskas Unicameral Legislature." *State Politics and Policy Quarterly* 15 (1): 69–90.

McCarty, Nolan, Keith T. Poole, and Howard Rosenthal. 2013. *Political Bubbles: Financial Crises and the Failure of American Democracy.* Princeton, NJ: Princeton University Press.

McCarty, Nolan, Keith T. Poole and Howard Rosenthal. 2009. "Does Gerrymandering Cause Polarization?" *American Journal of Political Science* 53 (3): 666–680.

McCarty, Nolan, Keith T. Poole, and Howard Rosenthal. 2006. *Polarized America: The Dance of Ideology and Unequal Riches.* Cambridge, MA: MIT Press.

McGhee, Eric, Seth E. Masket, Boris Shor, Steven Rogers, and Nolan M. McCarty. 2014. "A Primary Cause of Partisanship? Nomination Systems and Legislator Ideology." *American Journal of Political Science* 58 (2): 337–351.

Poole, Keith, and Howard Rosenthal. 1997. *Congress: A Political-Economic History of Roll Call Voting.* New York: Oxford University Press.

Poole, Keith T. 2007. "Changing Minds? Not in Congress!" *Public Choice* 131: 435–451.

Rodden, Jonathan, Boris Shor, Christopher Warshaw, Christopher Tausanovitch, and Nolan McCarty. 2014. "Geography and Polarization." Working paper.

Shor, Boris, and Nolan McCarty. 2011. "The Ideological Mapping of American Legislatures." *American Political Science Review* 105 (3): 530–551.

Tausanovitch, Chris, and Christopher Warshaw. 2013. "Measuring Constituent Policy Preferences in Congress, State Legislatures, and Cities." *Journal of Politics* 75 (2): 330–342.

Theriault, Sean M. 2008. *Party Polarization in Congress.* Cambridge University Press.

Voorheis, John. 2014. "*State and Metropolitan Area Income Inequality in the United States: Trends and Determinants, 1968–2012.*" Working paper.

Voorheis, John, Boris Shor, and Nolan McCarty. 2014. "State Legislative Political Polarization and Income Inequality in the United States, 1993–2013." Working paper.

Wittman, Donald. 1983. "Candidate Motivation: A Synthesis of Alternative Theories." *American Political Science Review* 77 (1): 142–157.

Wright, Gerald C. and Brian F. Schaffner. 2002. "The Influence of Party: Evidence from the State Legislatures." *The American Political Science Review* 96 (2): 367–379.

10

The Costs of Party Reform

Two States' Experiences

Seth E. Masket

Several states have attempted to rein in or eliminate political parties through a series of reforms. This chapter details two such efforts: campaign finance reform in Colorado and cross-filing in California. While these reforms met with mixed success in reining in partisanship, they imposed other costs on the political system that generally worked against reformers' stated goals.

- Colorado's campaign finance reform in 2002, which sharply limited parties' donations and expenditures, did not curtail partisanship in the state, while it did make campaign contributions much more difficult to trace.
- Cross-filing in California (1913–59) did have the effect of limiting partisanship in the statehouse, but it also created a corrupt environment dominated by lobbyists and business interests.
- Strong party systems, while frustrating, tend to allow for greater accountability in elections.
- Our political system might be better served by seeking to adapt institutions to strong parties, rather than trying to conform parties to existing institutions.

American political discourse is suddenly filled with suggestions for political reform. A vast range of political activists, journalists, and politicians have reacted to increased concerns about party polarization and legislative gridlock in the nation's capital by proposing ideas that would do anything from marginally mitigating partisanship to eliminating parties altogether. Indeed, the very conference that spawned this edited volume began with an address by a university administrator describing polarization as a "tumor" and calling upon scholars to develop the T-cell therapy that would help beat back the disease. More recently, a U.S. Senator called for the national adoption of California's "top-two" primary system to encourage the election of more moderates (Schumer 2014), while the Bipartisan Policy Center released a report calling for, in part, more open primaries and increased participation in those contests (Bipartisan Policy Center 2014). Other reformers call for instant runoff voting, the abolition of the Electoral College, proportional voting, redistricting reform, campaign finance reform, and so forth, all in the name of reducing parties' influence on our political system.

In an upcoming book (Masket 2016), I examine several reforms enacted during the past century designed to rein in or eliminate parties at the level of an American state. I find that not only do these reforms tend to fail to curb the role of parties in the political system, but they usually inadvertently inflict harm on democracy in the process. This chapter has a similar focus. I examine two particular reform efforts – a campaign finance reform amendment in modern Colorado and a ballot reform change in early-twentieth-century California – both designed to curb the power of parties in state politics. The effects are different: the California reform may well have undermined parties, whereas the Colorado reform did nothing to curb parties and may have even strengthened them. But both reforms imposed considerable costs on their political systems, undermining transparency and accountability and arguably making politics far worse for voters. The chapter concludes with warnings about unintended but foreseeable consequences of many political reforms and questions the persistent drive to undermine political parties.

THE PRICE OF CAMPAIGN FINANCE REFORM

Changing the way our campaigns are financed has become a business unto itself, an ongoing crusade to rid politics of the scourge of money. For such reformers, money is an inherent evil in politics. Money, to them, buys influence, and thus those with more money have more influence and can bend government to their will. Political scientists, meanwhile, have generally had a very difficult time identifying any effect of campaign spending on the behavior of elected officials. To be sure, there are occasional examples of outright corruption – Rep. Duke Cunningham (R-CA) accepting a yacht in exchange for preferential treatment of a defense contractor, Governor Rod Blagojevich (D-IL) selling a U.S. Senate seat, etc. – but such examples are extremely rare and, notably, already illegal and punishable by prison time. The more typical transactions of campaign money generally do not seem to actually induce any changes in politicians' behavior. Indeed, the consensus finding is that money follows votes, instead of the reverse; donors give to candidates to reward desirable behavior rather than to induce it.

But what effects have we seen from various efforts to restrict campaign donations in the United States? One notable effect is that donations have become much harder to track. One of the basic and broadly supported principles motivating campaign law is that of transparency. Political leaders have strong disagreements over whether campaign donations or expenditures should be limited and by how much, but there is a widespread consensus that donations should be recorded and that this information should be available to the general public. Few are under the impression that voters will sit down at a computer on the eve of an election to review campaign finance disclosures and decide which candidate's supporters are more wholesome. But following a fire-fighting model, voters will rely upon reporters, watchdog activists, and rival campaigns to find donations that may appear to involve conflicts of interest. If a candidate advocating increased use of fracking for energy production is receiving millions of dollars from natural gas companies, it is presumably in the public's interest to know this. Furthermore, candidates, knowing that receiving funds from unsavory sources will eventually become news, will tend to avoid soliciting such support.

For decades, the federal government and most state governments have thus required that all donations to candidates above some modest threshold be recorded and made public. The federal government actually established such reporting requirements in the Tillman Act of 1907, but these disclosures were rarely enforced with much efficacy until the passage of the Federal Election Campaign Act in 1971. Most states have followed suit in the ensuing years.

Such disclosures are useful when the typical donation goes from an identifiable donor to an identifiable candidate. However, following the money becomes immeasurably harder when intermediaries are involved. Under such legislation as Colorado's Amendment 27, that's precisely what happened.

Amendment 27 was roughly a state-level analogue to the national Bipartisan Campaign Reform Act (BCRA) of 2002, also known as McCain-Feingold. Amendment 27, approved by two-thirds of Colorado's voters in 2002, established limits on what individuals and parties could donate to state candidates; no limits on party donations to candidates had existed previously. The amendment barred corporations and unions from donating to parties, and it lowered individual donations to parties from $25,000 to $3,000 (Fish 2002). The goal was to "reduce the impact special interests have on the political process and increase the influence of individual citizens" (Bender 2002). It was widely expected to have a devastating impact on the state's parties: "The reduction in donations would mean at least $4.7 million less for the state's Democratic Party this year and almost $1 million for the Republican Party, which is receiving the bulk of its funds from the national GOP" (Fish 2002, A2). According to Democratic Party chair Tim Knaus, "It means the end of parties as they currently exist. I don't know what the new party looks like, but I can tell you that we will not be able to pay the lease" (Ames 2002, 18A). Knaus expected he'd have to fire all but one employee under the new rules.

There was a loophole, however, embedded within section 527 of the U.S. Tax Code. Individuals could donate to new independent campaign organizations (dubbed 527s), which could in turn spend unlimited amounts of money on behalf of candidates so long as it did not explicitly advocate for the election or defeat of a candidate. The reform legislation could not change the fact that there were hundreds or thousands of individuals wishing to spend money to attempt to influence an election and plenty of candidates eager to receive it. All it could do was interrupt one conduit for that transaction.

How does a watchdog organization or journalist now track campaign money? Well, it's *possible* to examine the campaign disclosure records of a 527 organization to see who donated to it and how much they gave. But where did that money end up? Since a 527 can't coordinate directly with a candidate, it generally spends its money in a more dispersed manner. If it wants to boost voter turnout to help a particular campaign, it might hire a local campaign firm that specializes in voter turnout efforts, or it might hire a direct mail consultant to carpet-bomb several neighborhoods with turnout messages, or it might pay local radio or television stations to run advertisements. The 527 is supposed to report in its filings just which candidates are benefiting from these expenditures, but that's not terribly precise. If you're reminding voters to turn out for Barack Obama in 2012, after all, you're probably also encouraging them to vote for Democratic candidates for Congress and state legislature, too, even if you don't mention it explicitly. So figuring out which campaign benefited from the money isn't easy or obvious.

But it gets more complicated than that. One of the advantages that Colorado's innovative "Gang of Four" – a handful of wealthy liberals who channeled millions of dollars toward competitive state legislative races – had was that it often caught Republican candidates off guard. Few expected to see so much funding coming out of 527s in the 2004 election cycle. The Democrats maintained this imbalance by dismantling those 527s and creating new ones with different names for 2006. They did the same in subsequent elections, making it difficult for journalists or Republican strategists to know just where the next barrage of funds was coming from. What's more, they were coordinating all these donations across a vast web of liberal interest groups, labor unions, 527s, political action committees, independent expenditure groups, official party organizations, and individual donors. By 2010, the liberal umbrella organization AmericaVotes was coordinating spending across 37 different organizations. A diagram of these byzantine spending channels can be seen in Figure 1. A 2012 *Denver Post* profile of this network revealed some of the laborious work necessary to follow the money under such a campaign finance regime. Some of the records they sought were available electronically, but independent expenditure committees only make hard copies available, which had to be obtained from the Secretary of State's office (Crummy 2012). Karen Crummy, the author of the piece, estimates she spent roughly 100 hours examining these disclosures in order to map out the network.

Needless to say, this complexity runs strongly against the principle of transparency, and it makes a mockery of disclosure requirements. But campaign finance limits only incentivize this sort of activity. If you want a candidate to win, it makes far more sense to finance that candidate by means of 527s and super PACs – with unlimited spending capabilities and spotty disclosure requirements – than via limited direct donations.

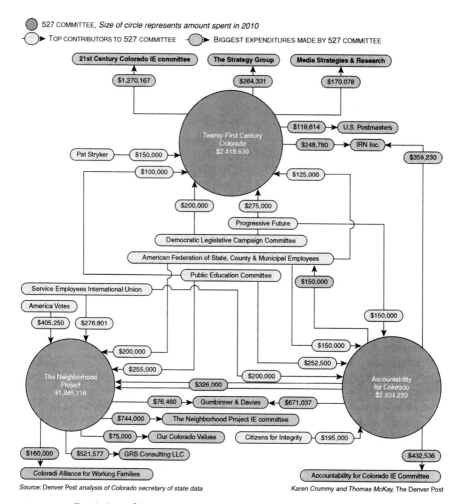

FIGURE I. Depiction of Campaign Finance in 2010 Colorado Democratic State House
Campaigns and Affiliated 527s
Source: Denver Post (Crummy 2012).

The situation is arguably worse thanks to the rise of 501(c)(4) charitable
organizations in politics. These groups are treated as nonprofits under the law
as long as less than half of their funds are used toward electioneering, meaning
that they are under no obligation to publicize their donors' names. Karl Rove's
Crossroads GPS is one such organization. It spent more than $70 million in the
2012 cycle with no real disclosure requirements. Many object to the lack of
transparency there, but what about disclosing the names of those who donate to
the 501(c)(4) run by the League of Conservation Voters? Many of those donors
may legitimately give with the expectation that their money will only be used for

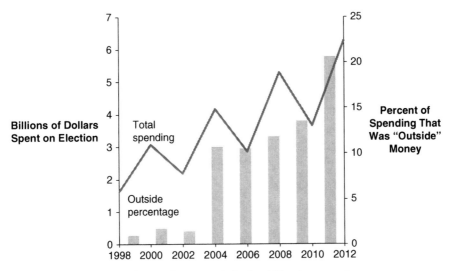

FIGURE 2. Spending and Outside Money in Federal Elections, 1998–2012
Source: OpenSecrets.org.

the social welfare functions of the group, such as raising awareness of environmental issues, and not on electioneering. Should their contributions be disclosed? It's possible that these groups provide legitimate public goods, but some donors would be less inclined to support them if it resulted in their name going onto a state or federal website. Yet this mix of charitable and more explicitly political work by 501(c)(4)s makes following the money all the harder.

Figure 2 demonstrates the growth of these alternative funding mechanisms over time. It shows two trends from 1998 to 2012. The first (the blue trend line) is the total spending on federal campaigns, including congressional and presidential. These spending figures include not just spending by the official campaign committees, but also "outside" spending, including that by 527s, PACs, party committees, independent expenditure groups, and others. While there are clear spikes in presidential years, the overall trend has been steadily upward, with spending increasing an average of 35 percent per election cycle, more than ten times the monetary inflation rate. Spending on the 2012 elections ($6.3 billion) was roughly double what it was in 2000 ($3.1 billion).

The second trend is marked by red bars, showing the percentage of all this spending that was "outside" money. By its nature, outside money is more difficult to trace. As described earlier, it is more challenging to figure out where the funds originated from and track them to where they ended up, and it can be difficult to know just which election they were intended to influence. The outside percentage has jumped sharply at two times. The first, and largest, jump came in 2004, when the percentage shot up from 1 to 11 percent of spending. This was in response to BCRA, which had recently banned much direct spending by parties and their ability to raise "soft money." Cut off from this source of funds, party actors responded by helping to develop 527s, dramatically increasing the proportion of federal funds that were difficult to trace. The other major jump in outside spending came in 2012, following the U.S. Supreme Court's 2010 decision in *Citizens United v. Federal Elections Commission*. As this decision relaxed some of BCRA's restrictions on campaign expenditures by corporations, unions, 527s, super PACs, and other entities, it is not surprising that it appears to have coincided with a rise in the outside spending percentage. As a result of all this, the 2012 election cycle saw more than one dollar in five spent on federal campaigning come through an outside path, making the donations difficult if not impossible to track.

Is there an alternative? Some reformers, concerned about the corrosive influence of money on politicians, have proposed floors on campaign spending rather than ceilings. That is, instead of creating limits on what candidates may spend or what donors may have, they propose that the government provide candidates with sufficient money to run a competitive campaign. While the Supreme Court's interpretation of the First Amendment precludes outright prohibitions of private campaign spending (*Buckley v. Valeo* 1976), the state can offer candidates ample public funds in exchange for a pledge to not spend their own funds.

Several states, in fact, have attempted such public funded, or "clean," campaigns for their state legislative elections: Maine, Connecticut, and Arizona. Miller (2013) finds a number of positive outcomes related to this experiment. For one, relieving candidates of the need to raise money frees up a great deal of campaign time. Candidates report using this time to walk precincts and meet with voters, theoretically placing them in greater contact with a wider range of their constituency than fundraising would. This has the effect of boosting voter participation in these down-ballot elections. Removing private funding from elections does not appear to moderate candidates, but it may have some other positive externalities. The lessons are not yet fully clear from a few states' relatively brief experiment with public funding. Nonetheless, it remains an option for those who see fundraising as an inherent conflict of interest for political candidates.

THE PRICE OF NONPARTISANSHIP

Much of the public finds political parties deeply frustrating entities. Indeed, a recent survey found that Americans see political parties as our most corrupt governing institution, with three-quarters of all respondents labeling them as corrupt (Transparency International 2013). Now, it's hard to know just what respondents meant by "corrupt" when responding to that question – they probably don't mean that the parties are behaving dishonestly in exchange for money – but it seems fair to take this as evidence that the public simply finds the parties loathsome.

This finding is neither novel nor unique to the United States. Indeed, in this same survey, respondents in two-thirds of the countries being studied labeled political parties as the most corrupt public institution. But it serves as a reminder that those political actors who wish to reform politics even for particularly self-serving ends can usually find willing allies in the American people if they frame their reform as curbing the power of parties.

While I have chronicled many cases in which anti-party reforms basically failed to mitigate partisanship, there is a notable exception to this trend. California's experiment with cross-filing in the first half of the twentieth century stands as an example of a reform that worked all too well (Masket 2009). The Progressives who wrote it into law widely felt that the two major parties were corrupt and interfered with the representative relationship between voters and elected officials (Mowry 1951). For four decades, cross-filing had a profoundly dampening effect on legislative partisanship in the Golden State, providing us with an opportunity to see just what a weak party system can look like. The answers, as we shall see, are far from encouraging.

Under cross-filing, written into the state constitution in 1913, California politicians running for partisan office (Congress, state legislature, and statewide constitutional offices) could run in as many party primaries as they wanted. A Republican member of Congress from California could run in the Republican primary, the Democratic primary, the Socialist primary, etc., and need only pay a modest filing fee for each contest. What's more, until 1952, the primary ballot contained no information about a candidate's party membership. Voters thus had very little idea about whom they might be voting for. As other research has found, in the absence of a party cue, voters tend to resort to other available cues about candidates, mainly incumbency (Schaffner, Streb, and Wright 2001). This proved true in California, as well, where incumbents overwhelmingly prevailed in all their primary contests, typically becoming the nominee of all the parties in a given race. Earl Warren, for example, was the gubernatorial nominee of both the Republican and Democratic parties in 1946. The general election was thus a mere formality, with a single candidate appearing with a hybridized party label (e.g., "Dem-Rep") next to his name.

The result of this fairly simple rule in the constitution was that local party activists lost all incentive to organize in primaries. You couldn't hold an incumbent accountable to a party agenda when so many other candidates from other parties were in the race and any anti-incumbent voting would be split so many different ways. Labor unions, business groups, and other interests largely fell silent during primaries. Incumbents faced few serious competitors in either primaries or general elections. Legislative partisanship largely collapsed.

In theory, this is the kind of environment for which many of today's reformers pine. Little divided the Democrats and Republicans in the state legislature. Legislators maintained friendships across party lines. The state capital was, by most accounts, a pleasant place in which to work. According to Assembly member Gordon Fleury, who chaired the chamber's Republican caucus in the late 1940s and early 1950s, "I ... never once took a vote on how we should vote. We just had lunch and had a couple of drinks" (Hicke 1987: 16). And, indeed, legislators tended to vote their districts; on average, more liberal districts were represented by more liberal legislators. So how did this work out?

This four-decade experiment ended up demonstrating the down side of weak party systems. Specifically, California during this period turned out to be profoundly corrupt. Industry lobbyists stepped in to provide the leadership that the parties no longer could. One such lobbyist was Artie Samish, who represented clients from the oil, banking, and entertainment industries, among others. He proudly detailed his methods in interviews and a book (Samish 1971), which was a boon for researchers but an albatross for him – such evidence was used to convict him of tax evasion in 1953, for which he served a three-year prison sentence (Rusco 1961).

Samish and his employees famously kept detailed records on members of the legislature, figuring out what each one was most in need of, whether that was financial support for reelection, a hotel room in Sacramento, a steady supply of bourbon, or female companionship. Samish would then use this knowledge to build bipartisan coalitions around bills important to his clients. This was usually only a handful of bills per session; a legislator could build a reputation as a good district representative the vast majority of the time, only deviating on those few bills Samish mentioned in exchange for the material rewards they desired. By such methods, Samish was able to delay California's adoption of daylight savings time by a decade on behalf of his motion picture industry clients, who were concerned that Californians wouldn't attend movies while it was still light outside.

But Samish was hardly the only corrupting influence within the state legislature. Organized business groups, representing oil companies, banks, and other industries, made no secret of bankrolling coalitions of legislators to get what they wanted, and most legislators appeared more than happy to abide. Roll call evidence from the early-twentieth-century California Assembly reveals bipartisan coalitions of legislators united by their fealty to some industry groups (Buchanan 1963). Even on the vote for Assembly Speaker – the very first vote of a legislative session and traditionally a party-line one in California, the U.S. House of Representatives, and most state legislatures – the chamber often broke down along bipartisan coalitional lines. In a telling example from 1946, the governor personally lobbied the chamber to pick one member as Speaker, and lobbyist Samish picked another. The chamber went with Samish's choice (Buchanan 1963: 28).

According to one story, members of the Assembly were at one point confronted with a bill concerning oil drilling that was perceived as favoring larger oil companies over smaller ones. The members, on the take from many different oil companies, were so desperate to avoid alienating their benefactors that they scrambled to get out of the chamber and be absent during the vote. The Speaker then announced his intention to put a "call" on the Assembly, preventing members from leaving the floor. In a near frenzy, escaping legislators shoved aside the Sergeant at Arms to leave the chamber, breaking the man's arm (Shaw 1988: 47–48). In another tale from the chamber, two novice lobbyists from Los Angeles banks drove to Sacramento with bags full of cash and announced upon entering the Assembly chamber, "We have the money. Who do we pay?" (Reinier 1987: 187)

Needless to say, this is not the ideal of representative democracy for which reformers have labored. But it is indeed what seems to happen when parties are forcibly removed from a legislature. Parties are hardly the antidote to lobbying and campaign spending – far from it. But they can channel those activities in a way that are more useful and accountable to voters.

California's experiences actually provide evidence for just this phenomenon. Partisan voting behavior began to return to the state legislature after 1952, when an initiative placing party labels on the primary ballot was approved by voters (Masket 2009). It quickly became much harder to cross-file successfully – primary voters could see who was in their party and who wasn't – and by 1959, the legislature banned cross-filing, which had largely fallen into disuse. It now made more sense for party activists to be involved in party nominations; they could channel resources toward preferred candidates with some chance of actually prevailing in a primary election.

One such political entrepreneur was Jesse Unruh, a promising Democratic Assembly member first elected from his Los Angeles district in 1954. By the late 1950s, he'd become a powerful and respected legislator, in large part due to his creative and very partisan channeling of campaign funds. He rarely faced a serious challenger at home, but he was nonetheless skilled at raising funds from donors throughout the state, and he would encourage donors to channel their funds to Democrats facing difficult reelection races. This had the effect of building a coterie of Democrats loyal to Unruh and willing to listen to his counsel on legislation in exchange for further campaign support. When his colleagues elected him Speaker in 1961 – a post he would hold until 1969 – he was able to transform their loyalty into a liberal agenda, passing a variety of bills on civil rights, housing, and education that helped define the state for the next generation (Cannon 1969; Boyarsky 2008).

Again, the money, the lobbyists, and the influence that had been present in Artie Samish's day were all still there in Unruh's. They were just being used in a different way. Under the partisan system, voters were no better able to observe the exchanges of favors and cash than they had been previously, but they could more easily observe the results – an expansion of the social welfare state. And they could judge those results at the ballot box. If they liked the way things were going, they could approve of all those exchanges by keeping Unruh's party in power. If they didn't, they could get a very different party by voting in the

Republicans (as they did in 1968). Under cross-filing, voters had no such mechanism; throwing the bums out meant handing the keys over to a new set of bums with the same priorities as the last one.

The system Unruh built is more or less running California today. The parties have continued to diverge, and the state's legislature is, by the best measures available, the most polarized partisan legislature in the country, far more so than the U.S. Congress (Shor and McCarty 2013). And it contains, according to a great many observers, a profoundly frustrating political system, where legislators' party loyalty often outweighs their desire to represent their constituents' needs. It features the most expensive state legislative races in the country and a well-heeled, highly entrenched lobbying industry. But that would be true whether the parties were strong or not.

To be sure, gridlock is related to polarization. California has had a harder and harder time passing a budget in recent decades in large part because the parties have been diverging on their economic principles. The gridlock in the Golden State is also due in part to budget rules requiring a two-thirds legislative vote for any tax increase. While Republicans are in the minority, they tend to maintain just over a third of the legislature, allowing them an effective veto on taxation, ensuring lengthy budget fights. (Notably, California garnered headlines for its newfound comity after Democrats secured a short-lived two-thirds majority in the 2012 elections [Nagourney 2013].) These sorts of anti-majoritarian rules tend to mix poorly with polarization. As modern state legislatures have demonstrated, one can have polarization without gridlock (Masket 2013). But super-majority votes, filibusters, and other such measures, when combined with polarization, produce stalemates in government.

But as California's example demonstrates, trying to fix polarization, even when successful, tends to produce all sorts of costly consequences. Accountability is undermined, transparency vanishes, elections lose their meaning, and voters have little understanding of just what is going on in their government. Perhaps gridlock can be mitigated, but at what cost? To allow for whose agenda to pass?

CONCLUSION

This chapter has focused on two examples of state-level reforms designed to mitigate partisanship – campaign finance reform in Colorado and cross-filing in California. Only the latter could be said to have succeeded in actually undermining partisanship. Both, however, offer important lessons about the costs of anti-party reforms.

If party reform efforts tend to impose costs on the political system in the form of lower turnout, more confusing and less meaningful elections, greater corruption, and declining accountability, what is the proper way forward? Must we resign ourselves to accepting hyper-partisanship as the law of the land and learn to love the government shutdowns, debt limit breaches, filibusters, and recall elections that seem to go along with it?

The situation is not necessarily that dire. There are at least some modest reforms that have shown promise in mitigating partisanship that lack some of the nastier side effects of the ones delineated in this chapter (Masket 2014). These could include ranked choice voting (which has shown some ability to boost turnout and limit factionalism) or media reform (by which coverage of local politics might be improved, giving voters the tools to punish ideological extremism), among other things. But we'd need to temper our expectations. Even the most highly successful reforms would only operate at the margins. The ideologies that separate our parties run deep in American history, and there has probably never been a more perfect alignment between our liberal-conservative ideological divide and our Democratic-Republican Party divide than there is right now (Noel 2013). To think that we could substantially undermine that by tinkering with election laws or by electing a "uniter" as president is wildly optimistic, at best.

The appropriate response may well be to adjust our institutions to meet our polarized parties, rather than depolarizing our parties to meet our institutions. That is, we know that polarization is not necessarily incompatible with governance. The 111th Congress (2009–10) governed during a highly partisan period in recent American history and yet still managed to produce landmark legislation on the economy, health insurance, student loans, and other areas. It did so, of course, because it enjoyed a relatively rare period of unified party governance. Seen in this light, the problems of the last few years aren't due to polarization so much as to a divided governing structure. Conversely, as described earlier, California has experienced polarization and unified party government for many years, but nonetheless faced great budgetary problems because of an unusual two-thirds vote requirement for passing budgets. Seen in this light, the problem wasn't polarization so much as supermajority requirements.

All this is to say that polarized parties – which, let's recall, are the norm in American history rather than the exception (Ansolabehere, Snyder, and Stewart 2001) – need not stand in the way of governance. Perhaps what is necessary is to allow majorities to govern by removing some of their impediments. Filibusters, debt ceiling votes, recall elections, supermajority requirements, and so forth, may certainly have their own justifications, but are they as valuable to us as the ability of a government to function? They are, after all, choices – sometimes aspects of state constitutions, sometimes laws, and sometimes just customs that have developed over the decades. They are hardly sacrosanct. And it is far easier to, say, eliminate the filibuster in a state legislature or even the U.S. Senate than it is to compel our parties to be more moderate, and with far fewer externalities.

But even as we consider all this, we shouldn't lose sight of the value that the party system offers our democracy. Despite the parties' unpopularity, they remain the greatest instruments for organizing elections, turning out voters, running government, and developing policy ideas and seeing them enacted that we've ever produced. At the very least, those who wish to weaken or abolish our parties should bear the burden of explaining why that is worth sacrificing.

REFERENCES

Ames, Michele. 2002. "'Big Money' Brouhaha No Laughing Matter – Both Sides Grit Teeth over Amendment on Campaign Finance." *Rocky Mountain News* (CO), 18A.

Ansolabehere, Stephen, James M. Snyder, Jr., and Charles Stewart, III. 2001. "Candidate Positioning in U.S. House Elections." *American Journal of Political Science* 45: 136–159.

Bender, Michael C. 2002. "Campaign-Finance Reform 'Answer to What Ails Politics.'" *Daily Sentinel* (Grand Junction, CO), September 22.

Bipartisan Policy Center. 2014. *Governing in a Polarized America: A Bipartisan Blueprint to Strengthen Our Democracy.* Retrieved from http://bipartisanpolicy.org /wp-content/uploads/sites/default/files/files/BPC%20CPR%20Governing%20in% 20a%20Polarized%20America.pdf.

Boyarsky, Bill. 2008. *Big Daddy: Jesse Unruh and the Art of Power Politics.* Berkeley: University of California Press.

Buchanan, William. 1963. *Legislative Partisanship: The Deviant Case of California.* Berkeley: University of California Press.

Buckley, V. Valeo. 1976. 424 U.S. 1 *Buckley v. Valeo.*

Cannon, Lou. 1969. *Ronnie and Jesse: A Political Odyssey.* Garden City, NY: Doubleday & Company, Inc.

Crummy, Karen E. 2012. "Spending by Super Pacs in Colorado Is the Dominion of Democrats." *Denver Post*, March 10.

Fish, Sandra. 2002. "Amendment 27 Would Change Funding Landscape – Parties, Candidates Would Have Millions Less If Limits Were in Effect This Year." *Daily Camera* (Boulder, CO), A2.

Hicke, Carole. 1987. *Oral History Interview with Gordon A. Fleury.* Sacramento: California State Archives.

Masket, Seth E. 2016. *The Inevitable Party.* Oxford: Oxford University Press.

Masket, Seth. 2014. "Mitigating Extreme Partisanship in an Era of Networked Parties: An Examination of Various Reform Strategies." Retrieved from http://www.brookings.edu/~/media/research/files/papers/2014/03/20-masket/masket_ mitigating-extreme-partisanship-in-an-era-of-networked-parties.pdf.

Masket, Seth. 2013. "Picking a State? The Stakes Are Getting Higher." *Al Jazeera America*, November 27.

Masket, Seth. 2009. *No Middle Ground: How Informal Party Organizations Control Nominations and Polarize Legislatures.* Ann Arbor: University of Michigan Press.

Miller, Michael. 2013. *Subsidizing Democracy: How Public Funding Changes Elections, and How It Can Work in the Future.* Ithaca, NY: Cornell University Press.

Mowry, George Edwin. 1951. *The California Progressives.* Chicago: Quadrangle Books.

Nagourney, Adam. 2013. "California Sees Gridlock Ease in Governing." *New York Times*, October 19, A1.

Noel, Hans. 2013. *Political Ideologies and Political Parties in America.* Cambridge: Cambridge University Press.

Reinier, Jacqueline S., ed. 1987. *Oral History Interview with Hon. Lloyd W. Lowrey.* Sacramento: California State Archives.

Rusco, Elmer Ritter. 1961. "Machine Politics, California Model: Arthur H. Samish and the Alcoholic Beverage Industry." Ph.D. diss., University of California.

Samish, Arthur H. 1971. *The Secret Boss of California: The Life and High Times of Art Samish.* New York: Crown Publishers.

Schaffner, Brian F., Matthew Streb, and Gerald C. Wright. 2001. "Teams without Uniforms: The Nonpartisan Ballot in State and Local Elections." *Political Research Quarterly* 54: 7–30.

Schumer, Charles E. 2014. "End Partisan Primaries, Save America." *New York Times,* July 22, A21.

Shaw, Stanford C. 1988. *Oral History Interview with Stanford C. Shaw.* Sacramento: California State Archives.

Shor, Boris, and Nolan McCarty. 2013. "Individual State Legislator Shor-McCarty Ideology Data." Retrieved from https://dataverse.harvard.edu/dataset.xhtml?persistentId=doi:10.7910/DVN/26805.

Transparency International. 2013. *Global Corruption Barometer 2013: Report.* Retrieved *from http://www.transparency.org/gcb2013/report.*

Yglesias, Matthew. 2009. "Gerrymandering and Polarization." *Thinkprogress.* Retrieved from http://thinkprogress.org/yglesias/2009/10/01/194566/gerrymandering-and-polarization/.

II

The Policy Consequences of Party Polarization

Evidence from the American States

Elizabeth Rigby and Gerald C. Wright

This chapter explores the policy consequences of polarization – asking whether we see different policy choices when parties are more (versus less) polarized. This analysis is motivated by recent research suggesting a constraining effect of partisan polarization on redistributive policy – and contradicting earlier expectations that greater benefits will accrue to the poor when parties are competitive and offer clear policy choices. To better understand these consequences, we capitalized on variation in both policy choices and party polarization over time and across the 50 American states.

- Across eight distinct forms of policy redistribution, we found that party polarization tended to result in lower levels of redistributive policy.
- This was most pronounced for redistributive policies that are not indexed to inflation (so without new legislation, the real value of the policy decreases over time). These policies, such as the minimum wage, are particularly impacted by polarization-induced gridlock.
- For redistributive policies that do increase in magnitude as inflation, incomes, or earnings rise, such as the corporate tax rate, polarization had more of an indirect effect – shifting the impact of party control of the state government.
- These distinct paths of influence for different types of policies illustrate both the importance of polarization for policymaking and the complexity of these relationships.

In recent decades, political parties in the United States have become more ideologically distinct (Rohde 1991; Aldrich 1995; Fiorina 1996; Poole and

This chapter draws from a larger project on Representation of the Poor in the American States, generously funded by the Russell Sage Foundation. We thank Ernesto Calvo, Jennifer Clark, and Martin Gilens for helpful feedback on earlier versions of this paper, and Boris Shor and Nolan McCarty for use of their data on state-level party polarization, as well as Caitlin Brandt and Dharani Ranganathan for valuable research assistance.

Rosenthal 1997). During the same time period, we have seen a parallel increase in income inequality (McCarty, Poole, and Rosenthal 2006), as well as the transformation of social welfare policy away from entitlements and cash assistance toward a work- and market-focused system of neoliberal reform (Pierson 2001; Korpi and Palme 2003; Hacker 2004; Schram, Fording, and Soss 2008; Allard 2009). Accounts of these political developments often draw linkages between these trends – describing how party polarization contributes to gridlock and policy drift that tends to disadvantage those with less power and organization (Hacker and Pierson 2010).

The most explicit examination of a relationship between party polarization and policy outcomes is found in McCarty (2007) and McCarty, Poole, and Rosenthal (2006), who describe a "dance of inequality" in which the upward trend in party polarization tracks alongside the declining real value of the minimum wage, as well as regressive shifts in estate and income tax policies. McCarty (2007, p. 243) concludes that "although the evidence about the effects of polarization on [social policy is] far from conclusive, it does seem to point strongly in the direction of a conservative effect of polarization on social policy." This suggests that party polarization is not ideologically neutral, but rather produces policies unfavorable to low-income citizens.

This view contradicts much of the previous thinking about the role of parties in the policymaking process. For decades, the conventional wisdom was that strong and competitive parties with defined issue bases would promote representation of less powerful citizens (Schattschneider 1942; Key 1949). In fact, Key (1949: 307) argued that "the have-nots lose in a disorganized politics." Along these lines, in the 1950s, political science decried the flabby character of Congressional parties, calling for stronger issue-based parties to better promote the ideals of representative democracy (APSA 1950). And then, supporting this expectation, other work found that class-based polarization in the states did lead to more generous welfare benefits (Jennings 1979; Dye 1984; Garand 1985; Brown 1995).

The logic of both arguments is reasonable. Polarization can lead to blocking and gridlock, which impedes policy change; it can also increase the likelihood that at least one party represents the poor. Therefore, further elaboration on the policy consequences of polarization is needed. Previous efforts in this area have been hindered by the near-exclusive focus on Congressional politics. The correlated trends among polarization, income inequality, and welfare retrenchment stymie efforts to tease apart the effects of polarization itself on the policymaking process. These time trends are further confounded with party control and composition patterns in Congress (Hacker and Pierson 2010), as well as with other dynamics such as the movement of issues onto (or off of) the federal agenda (Kingdon 1995; Jones and Baumgartner 2005). Thus, research linking polarization, inequality, and the retrenchment of social programs at the federal level may reflect more about recent developments in national politics than really serve to illuminate the way that party polarization shapes the policymaking process and its outcomes.

To provide another vantage point for assessing the policy consequences of party polarization, we draw on data capturing a range of redistributive policies enacted by the American states – a long-standing laboratory for research on American politics and policy. By comparing policymaking occurring concurrently across the 50 states, we have greater analytic leverage for examining the degree to which policy changes vary systemically across more or less polarized states. To do this, we pool data on the level of and change in eight state redistributive policies from 1998 to 2009. These redistributive policies range from the income eligibility a family must earn below to receive welfare benefits in the form of income or medical insurance, to minimum wage regulations, to the tax rates at which high-income individuals and corporations are taxed. We use fixed-effects models that include both state-fixed-effects to control for variation across states in both policy and politics and year-fixed-effects that account for national trends in each of the policies. This is a conservative estimation strategy based on an identification strategy that draws inferences only from the covariance between change in party polarization and redistributive policy effort *within* each state during the decade under study.

Our findings point to two ways that party polarization shapes states' redistributive policy effort. First, for policies based on non-indexed monetary values (i.e., a minimum wage such as $7.25), we identify a negative association between party polarization and redistributive policy in which the real value of these benefits declines over time more quickly in more polarized states. Second, for other redistributive policies those that are (explicitly or implicitly) indexed to inflation (i.e., a corporate tax rate of 4 percent of earnings) we find no direct relationship between polarization and policy change. Instead, we find an indirect association in which party polarization alters the importance of party control. As a result, in low polarization states we see significant differences in redistributive policy effort under Democratic versus Republican Party control. However, when party polarization is high, we find little difference – a pattern consistent with the notion of greater limits on majority party power in highly polarized party systems.

POLARIZATION AND POLITICS

Popular notions of party polarization typically focus on the increased potential for unproductive political conflict as well as the decreased potential for bipartisan compromise. Rivlin (2006: 3) articulated these concerns in a lecture entitled *Is America Too Polarized to Make Public Policy?*, in which she expressed her fear that "[w]e may blow the extraordinary opportunity that has been given the United States in this century to demonstrate that democracy can work in a diverse society – to show that our system can actually produce reasonable solutions to problems on which the public has differing views."

Hacker and Pierson (2005) noted the ability of majority parties in polarized systems to enact extreme policies not representative of the median voters. Further, Galston and Nivola (2006) concluded that polarization poses a risk to public trust, as well as to government's ability to generate effective policy solutions, particularly for redistributive entitlement programs.

Others, however, point toward the potential benefits of polarization. Hetherington (2008) found that elite polarization had some beneficial effects for the political engagement of the public by stimulating participation and engagement at the mass level among ideologues, moderates, and non-ideologues alike. Brooks and Geer (2008) linked Hetherington's findings to the earlier notion of responsible parties (APSA 1950) and concluded that the "benefits of polarization seem clear: a polarized system provides a chance for those competing for power to make a clearer case for why they should be given power. Of course, the other side can point to the risks associated with that position as well" (p. 38). Similar positive consequences of polarization were found by Aldrich and Battista (2002), who examined data from 11 states and concluded that competitive party systems breed highly polarized legislative parties and that these two traits lead to more representative committees. Similarly, Brady, Ferejohn, and Harbridge (2008) found policy responsiveness in budgetary allocations – even in a polarized Congress.

POLARIZATION AND REDISTRIBUTIVE POLICY

The notion that party polarization might align with differences in economic interests across socio economic classes is long-standing. Confirming Madison's (1961) observation that economic differences provide the most likely source of political factions, recent research has documented the relationship between increasing Congressional polarization and other changes in American's socio-political and socio economic characteristics. For example, Stonecash, Brewer, and Mariani (2003) highlight the increasing importance of income in shaping mass partisanship and vote choice, while McCarty, Poole, and Rosenthal (2006) link this income-party stratification with the upward trend in income inequality and lower turnout among the poor. These trends together have produced larger numbers of both rich and poor Americans – with each group more concentrated in one of two polarized political parties (Stonecash 2000). In fact, Garand (2010) finds greater ideological polarization at both the mass and elite level in states with greater income inequality.

This class-based polarization of the electorate can have important implications for political conflict. As parties are generally presumed to represent the interests of their base constituencies, income stratification contributes to the parties pursuing very different redistributive policies (Powell 1982). Because the primary ideological dimension that divides the two major parties captures, roughly speaking, the conflict between rich and poor (McCarty, Poole, and Rosenthal 2001), as polarization increases we are likely to see greater conflict in American policymaking. Drawing on descriptive time trends at the federal level, McCarty, Poole, and Rosenthal (2006) document the inverse relationship between congressional polarization and social policies such as the minimum wage, income taxes, and estate tax rates. They conclude that as "polarization increased through the last quarter of the twentieth century, policies moved in a less redistributive way when it was a matter of either taxing the income or the estates of the top brackets or improving the wages of the bottom brackets" (p. 175).

McCarty (2007) explains that it is not surprising to find polarization effects in the domain of social welfare policy – particularly since social programs are so rarely indexed to inflation. Without automatic increases in benefits or eligibility standards, the real value of non-indexed programs declines every year. Therefore, when polarization impedes policy changes to counteract this downward drift, it serves to inhibit the generosity of welfare programs over time (Hacker and Pierson 2010).

POLARIZATION AND GRIDLOCK

The dispersion of authority in American policymaking institutions provides the basis for our expectation that polarization produces less public policy. Systems of separation of powers and bicameralism require reasonable levels of consensus to pass new legislation (Krehbiel 1998; Binder 2003). However, under conditions of polarized parties, one pivotal actor is likely to face a wide ideological chasm between himself and the pivotal actor in the other party. As a result, this expands the "gridlock region," which represents the range of policy options unable to be enacted since, for each option, at least one pivotal actor is likely to prefer the status quo (Brady and Volden 1997; Krehbiel 1998). This effect is documented by McCarty (2007) and McCarty, Poole, and Rosenthal (2006), who compare the rate of congressional enactment of Mayhew's (1991) key legislation in more-versus-less polarized time periods. Similarly, Binder (2003) finds that greater issue partisanship (which could proxy polarization) negatively affected the likelihood of a high-profile agenda item becoming law.

We wish to distinguish between the potential for polarization to produce gridlock and the question of whether polarization-induced gridlock produces an ideological bias in policy outcomes. Hacker and Pierson (2010) suggest that it does – describing how polarization magnifies conservative policy drift via partisan stalemate. The potential for a de facto conservative bias stems from concern that gridlock can stall repeated action on social policies that require updating to hold their value or maintain their effectiveness in a changing society and economy, as well as to limit the possibility for enacting new policy expansions. However, gridlock may also serve to protect current social policies, such as Medicaid and Medicare, by limiting the success of those wishing to dismantle them. This protective role for parties in defending social welfare programs against efforts to cut back benefits has been illustrated in cross-national work in which gridlock serves as a buffer for the social welfare state in the face of neoliberal reform efforts (Pierson 1996; Bonoli 2001; Korpi and Palme 2003).

POLARIZATION AND PARTY CONTROL

Conflicting expectations regarding the ideological impact of gridlock and its role in linking polarization and policy outcomes do not refute the clear status quo bias in social welfare politics. Yet, they do challenge explanations that rely on gridlock alone to explain the policy consequences of polarization. We believe that additional insight can be gained by focusing more directly on partisan dynamics in understanding the policy consequences of polarization. Our call for additional focus on partisan politics is ironic since polarization is nothing but a measure of party positioning. Yet, we emphasize this point in response to the current literature, which often confuses gridlock with other (admittedly related) constructs, such as divided party control. For example, McCarty, Poole, and Rosenthal (2006) examine states' welfare benefits under united versus divided control – using the finding that benefits were less generous and more likely to erode due to inflation under divided control as evidence of the negative relationship between polarization-induced gridlock and social welfare benefits.

We believe it is important to distinguish between the concepts and effects of party control and polarization. For example, Kousser's (2008) analysis of the effects of polarization on policy gridlock in California reveals no direct link between polarization and gridlock. Instead, he reports an indirect effect in which divided government leads to even greater gridlock when parties are more polarized. Similarly, Jones (2001) distinguishes between divided control, party seat share, and polarization in his examination of major legislative proposals at the federal level – identifying distinct and interactive effects of each.

This conditioning or interactive role for polarization – to magnify or minimize the effects of party control rather than determining the direction of policy change – suggests that party control may have distinct effects when parties are more-versus-less polarized. Substantial literature illustrates the potential for more extreme policy changes under unified party control (e.g., Brady 1978; Brady and Stewart 1982; Aldrich, Berger, and Rohde 2002). When parties are further away from each other in terms of policy preferences (i.e., more polarized), unified parties have an incentive to expend political capital to enact policy changes in their preferred direction when they have the chance (Sinclair 2006, 2008). Consistent with this policy prediction, Schultz (1999) models the effects of polarization on monetary policy and concludes that when polarization is high, policy is driven by the preferences of the winning party such that policy outcomes fall some distance from those preferred by the median voter. This may also be the case for redistributive policy, for which party control has been found, in more recent (and polarized) years, to play a key role in shaping the generosity of states' social policy choices (Barrilleaux, Holbrook, and Langer 2002; Fellowes and Rowe 2004).

At the same time, party polarization increases the incentives for the minority parties to coordinate their efforts and use the power of obstruction to block the majority party's policy priorities. By definition, polarization places the two political parties far away from one another in terms of policy preferences with little shared middle ground to craft bipartisan policy solutions. Given the many veto points in American policymaking, the enactment of new legislation requires reasonable levels of consensus between and within the parties (Krehbiel 1998; Binder 2003). These veto points provide opportunities for minority parties to block the majority party's policy proposals – particularly when those proposals are far from the minority party's ideological ideal point and fall within the "gridlock region" described earlier (Brady and Volden 1997; Krehbiel 1998). As a result, less policy is likely to pass – leading to greater continuity and status quo bias (Pierson 2000; Bonoli 2001), as well as fewer policy gains accruing to the majority party.

As already discussed, there are plausible reasons to believe that polarization could magnify or minimize the impact of party control on policy outcomes. However, by relying on studies of congressional polarization to draw conclusions about the policy consequences of polarization, much of the previous research is unable to tease apart the influence of polarization itself from that of concurrent patterns of partisan control (as discussed both by McCarty, Poole, and Rosenthal 2006 and by Hacker and Pierson 2010). For this reason, we turn to the American states as a laboratory for examining this question, as described in the next section.

EMPIRICAL STRATEGY

To investigate the policy consequences of polarization, we capitalize on variation in the level of party polarization and in redistributive policy effort among the states. We pool data on party polarization, redistributive policy choices, and the political context for all 50 states across 12 years (1998–2009). Employing fixed-effects models (state- and year-fixed-effects), we are able to isolate the relationship between change in states' party polarization and the degree to which they change their redistributive policy effort in subsequent years. Specifically, we focus on a range of state redistributive policies in order to capture alternative policy tools – including benefit programs, market regulations such as the minimum wage, and tax policies. This broad focus allows us to assess the generalizability of our findings, as well as identify ways that the policy consequences of polarization may differ for different types of redistributive policies. Two distinctions seem most relevant to the question at hand. First, we include redistributive policies that primarily target the poor (typically providing benefits), as well as those focused on the rich (typically

TABLE 1. *Redistributive Policies by Target Population and Index Status*

	Target Population: Low- and Moderate-Income	Target Population: Higher-Income
Not indexed/monetary	TANF eligibility Tax credit (100%) Minimum wage	
Indexed/rate	SCHIP eligibility	Tax charge (500%) Top marginal tax rate Capital gains tax rate Corporate tax rate

taxes to secure revenue). Second, we include redistributive policies that are indexed for inflation and those that are not. Social benefit programs are rarely indexed to inflation and so do not receive automatic increases in benefits or eligibility standards. As a result, their real value declines each year (relative to inflation). If polarization impedes policy change, then it can fuel this "policy drift" away from generous social provision (McCarty 2007; Hacker and Pierson 2010). In contrast, many other policies are indexed to inflation explicitly or implicitly – by using a rate or percent of income formula.

Table 1 lists the eight redistributive policies we examine – arrayed along these two criteria: whether targeted at the poor versus wealthy and whether indexed to inflation or not. Reflecting the patterns evident in most American policymaking, policies targeted to the wealthy are more likely to be indexed to inflation (often because they are designed as rates or formulas in the tax code) than are those targeted to the poor (McCarty 2007; Mettler 2011).

These eight measures are:

- **TANF eligibility.** The Temporary Assistance to Needy Families (TANF) program provides income support to very low income families. This traditional welfare program allows states to set the eligibility limit, which sets the scope of the program with higher values indicates state decisions to make more people eligible for TANF. We use the real value of the maximum monthly income in which a family of three would be eligible for TANF. This value ranges from $270 to $1,895 and averages $884 (sd = 340) across the state-years under study. On average, this value has declined $84 during this time period – although this varies from a decrease of $721 to an increase of $820. These data were drawn from the Urban Institute's Welfare Rules database (http://anfdata.urban.org/wrd/).
- **SCHIP eligibility.** The State Children's Health Insurance Program (SCHIP) provides health insurance to children in low- and moderate-income families. The SCHIP eligibility limit is also set at the state-level, but typically as a percent of the federal poverty line (FPL), which is implicitly indexed to

inflation though regular increases in the FPL. This eligibility level varies from 114 percent to 431 percent (M = 219, sd = 52). During the time period under study, it increased by 27 percentage points; yet we saw real variation across states ranging from a decrease of 162 percentage points to an increase of 243 percentage points. These data were drawn from the Kaiser Family Foundation, State Health Facts dataset (www.statehealthfacts.org).

- **Minimum wage.** The federal minimum wage sets a floor on wage income and many states choose to establish a minimum wage above the federal wage. We use the real value (adjusted for inflation and presented in 2010 dollars) of the minimum wage in effect in each state-year, which ranges from $2.03 to $8.69 (M = $6.55, sd = $.99). Over this time period, the real value increased $.75 – although this ranges from a decline (through policy drift) of $.85 to a real increase of $3.09. These data were drawn from the U.S. Employment Standards Administration of the U.S. Department of Labor which compiles the state and federal minimum wages for each year.
- **Tax credit for those at 100 percent FPL.** This measure captures the state income tax credit/burden levied on a family of three earning 100 percent of the federal poverty line. In some states, this family would be charged income taxes while in others it would not. Additionally, many states have enacted Earned Income Tax Credits or refundable Child Tax Credits that produce a tax credit payable to low-income families when they file their income taxes. In most states, a family at 100 percent of FPL would receive a credit averaging $53 but ranging all the way up to $1,832. Yet, in other states, the same family would be charged a tax as large as $613. We indicate the charges as negative values in the dataset. During the time period under study, the tax credit value increased an average of $187 dollars. These values were simulated for a single adult with two children using the TAX SIM program provided by the National Bureau of Economic Research (NBER).
- **Tax charge for those at 500 percent of FPL.** This measure captures the size of the state income tax bill for a family of three living at 500 percent of the FPL (about $100,000 in 2014). It averages $3,391 but ranges from 0 (in states with no income tax) to $6,950. Over this time period, this charge decreased $30 on average – but as with the other policy measures this average masks tremendous variation across states that ranges from a decrease of $1,199 to an increase of $614. These data were simulated using the same TAX SIM model described above.
- **Top marginal tax rate.** This is the tax rate applied to the top income bracket in the state. It ranges from 0 to 10.75, mean = 5.16, sd = 2.91. During this time period, the top tax rate decreased .08; but this ranged from a decrease of 3.45 to an increase of 4.38. These rates are provided by NBER.
- **Capital gains tax rate.** This rate represents the maximum state tax rate on long-run investment gains. This rate ranges from 0 to 10.75, mean 4.85, sd = 2.85. Over this time period, states capital gains tax rates decreased .23,

including decreases as high as 7.67 to an increase of 4.38. As with the previous measure, it is reported by the NBER.

- **Corporate tax rate.** This rate characterizes the extent to which states tax corporations and businesses. The state corporate tax rate varies from 0 to 12 percent (M = 6.64, sd = 2.84). Over this time period, the corporate tax rate decreased an average of .33, although this included a decrease as large as 8.64 to increases up to 2.65. These data were drawn from Cordes (2010) and the Tax Foundation website.

The descriptive statistics for these policy measures, as well as for the other measures described below are presented in the Appendix at the end of this chapter.

To measure state party polarization, we use data from Shor and McCarty (2011) and Chapter 9 (this volume). We pool the individual-level ideal points generated by Shor and McCarty (2011) for all Democratic and Republican state legislators in office in each year. The ideological position of the Democratic Party is proxied by the mean value of the Democratic legislators, with the same calculation used to estimate the position of the Republican legislators. The distance between these two means is used to describe the level of party polarization in the state. This polarization measure averages 1.30 (sd = .43) across these 600 state-years, with a range from .47 to 3.10. Between 1997 and 2008, this measure of party polarization increased .12 (or about a third of a standard deviation) on average. Yet, this masks a good deal of variation ranging from a decrease in polarization of –.53 to an increase of 1.08.

We also include a measure of party control that captures the strength of the Democratic party on a scale ranging from zero (Unified Republican Control) to three (Unified Democratic Control). Calculated with data provided by Klarner (2003), this measure averages 1.50 (sd = 1.07). The use of state-fixed-effects accounts for many of the time-invariant characteristics of states (i.e., policy history, political culture, region). Yet, we also include a few economic and political variables to control for aspects of the state context known to predict redistributive policy effort. Specifically, these are the real value of the state per capita income in $1,000s (M = 35.87, sd = 5.65), the unemployment rate (M = 6.46, sd = 12.30), income inequality (M = .40, sd = .02), and the relative voter turnout between the wealthy and poor (M = 1.66, sd = .28).

FINDINGS: THE POLICY CONSEQUENCES OF POLARIZATION

Table 2 presents the results of our first set of fixed-effects models. Here we are testing for a direct relationship between changes in state party polarization and changes in state redistributive policy effort. We see a negative coefficient for party polarization for all eight policies. However, it only reaches statistical-significance for three policies: (1) TANF eligibility, which is expected to be $110

TABLE 2. *Polarization and Policy Change, Direct Effects*

	(1) TANF Eligibility	(2) SCHIP Eligibility	(3) Minimum Wage	(4) Tax Credit (100%)	(5) Tax Charge (500%)	(6) Top Tax Rate	(7) Cap Gains Tax	(8) Corporate Tax
Per capita income	14.55*	2.69*	-0.01	3.84	-12.61	0.02	-0.05	-0.05
	(4.93)	(1.02)	(0.02)	(5.63)	(6.73)	(0.02)	(0.04)	(0.03)
Unemployment rate	-16.17	-3.29	-0.09*	-19.92*	20.87	0.05	0.04	-0.01
	(8.28)	(1.84)	(0.04)	(9.95)	(11.89)	(0.03)	(0.06)	(0.06)
Income inequality	-420.63	362.38*	0.70	73.60	-1,178.61	-4.24	-1.80	17.67*
	(597.63)	(138.01)	(2.67)	(751.85)	(897.83)	(2.21)	(4.68)	(4.49)
Relative vote	46.17	-6.95	-0.42*	31.18	-11.75	-0.01	0.00	-0.03
	(26.77)	(6.19)	(0.12)	(34.20)	(40.84)	(0.10)	(0.21)	(0.20)
Dem Party control	-17.17*	3.63*	0.06	-0.99	14.36	0.08*	0.10	-0.03
	(7.15)	(1.59)	(0.03)	(8.81)	(10.53)	(0.03)	(0.06)	(0.05)
Party polarization	-109.81*	-15.38	-0.51*	-123.69*	-102.15	-0.02	-0.16	-0.47
	(48.78)	(12.01)	(0.22)	(60.68)	(72.46)	(0.18)	(0.38)	(0.36)
Constant	774.64*	14.42	8.44*	46.50	4,277.34*	6.00*	7.01*	2.26
	(331.48)	(75.23)	(1.44)	(406.60)	(485.55)	(1.20)	(2.53)	(2.43)
Observations	600	550	600	600	600	600	600	600
State fixed-effects	X	X	X	X	X	X	X	X
Year fixed-effects	X	X	X	X	X	X	X	X
R-squared (R^2)	0.19	0.19	0.32	0.13	0.04	0.06	0.04	0.06

* $p < .05$

lower (se = 48.79) if polarization is one-unit higher; (2) the minimum wage, which is expected to be $.51 lower (se = .22) in a state with one-unit greater polarization; and (3) the tax credit for the poor, which is expected to be $124 lower (se = 60.68). These three policies are three of the four that are not-indexed for inflation and represent all three of the non-indexed policy targeted to low-income groups. It seems that this type of redistributive policy – non-indexed and targeted to the poor – is quite susceptible to greater decreases (or fewer increases) when state parties are more polarized. That is, the poor receive less via these policies through the impact of polarization on policy drift as characterized by Hacker and Pierson (2010).

Table 3 presents the results from our second set of fixed-effects models. Here we present just the key variables of interest: Democratic Party Control, Party Polarization, and the interaction of these two variables. However, these models include the state- and year-fixed-effects, as well as the four control variables reported in the previous analysis. Again we find a pretty consistent pattern of coefficients – with negative coefficients for seven of the eight interactions. However, only four of the interactions reached statistical significance indicating that party control has less of an impact on redistributive policy when parties are more polarized. This challenges the idea that polarization would magnify the importance of party control but instead suggests that polarization makes it harder for the majority party to govern and enact their policy priorities. We find this indirect effect of polarization – via shifting the importance of party control – for four redistributive policies: SCHIP eligibility, taxes charged at 500 percent of FPL, top marginal tax rate, and capital gains tax rate. These are four policies for which we found no direct effect for polarization.

Figure 1 plots the four significant interactions for two states: one under unified Democratic control (top solid line) and one under unified Republican control (bottom dashed line) by a range of party polarization that includes values within one standard deviation (.4) from the mean (1.3). Although the estimates and confidence intervals vary somewhat across the four policies, we find a very similar pattern. Specifically, under low levels of party polarization, we see a deviation in the predicted policy generosity under Democratic versus Republican Party control – with Democratic Party control leading to higher SCHIP eligibility limits, and higher taxes. However, under higher levels of party polarization, we see no significant difference in redistributive policy effort by party control. Our analyses do not explore the mechanisms driving this interactive effect, but it is consistent with the idea that polarization produces a minority party holding distinct policy priorities that do not overlap with the majority party agenda. This minority party has strategic reasons to exploit its powers to block and obstruct legislation for which the party prefers the status quo. As a result, majority parties are less able to secure their policy priorities under high levels of party polarization.

TABLE 3. *Polarization and Policy Change, Indirect Effects*

	TANF Eligibility	SCHIP Eligibility	Minimum Wage	Tax Credit (100%)	Tax Charge (500%)	Top Tax Rate	Capital Gains Tax	Corporate Tax
Dem Party control	0.87	24.21*	-0.10	34.89	141.61*	0.37*	0.58*	0.10
	(23.27)	(5.44)	(0.11)	(30.30)	(35.77)	(0.09)	(0.19)	(0.18)
Party polarization	-75.50	0.96	-0.63*	-95.17	-0.98	0.20	0.23	-0.37
	(49.82)	(12.53)	(0.23)	(64.88)	(76.60)	(0.19)	(0.40)	(0.39)
Control X polarization	-13.29	-15.02*	0.11	-26.30	-93.28*	-0.21*	-0.35*	-0.09
	(16.32)	(3.80)	(0.08)	(21.25)	(25.06)	(0.06)	(0.13)	(0.13)

* $p < .05$

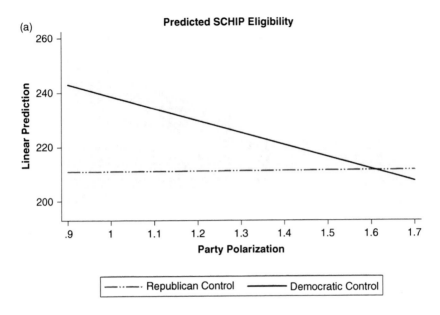

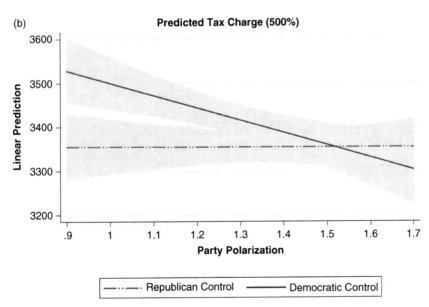

FIGURE 1. Predicted Policy, by Party Control and Polarization

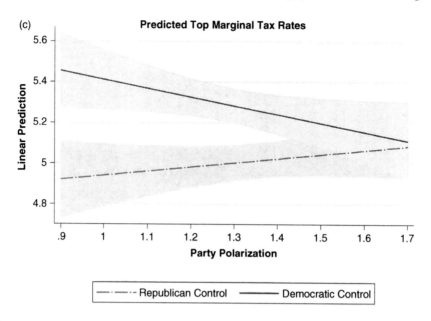

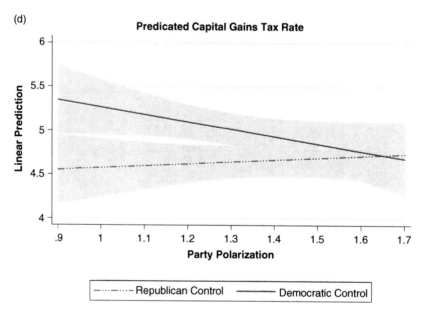

FIGURE 1. (cont.)

CONCLUSION

Despite the broad attention to party polarization, its increasing prominence, and its political causes and consequences, there has been little attention to the policy consequences of increased party polarization. This chapter reviewed a range of literature that highlights the importance of polarization-enhanced gridlock – particularly among non-indexed policies and others that need to be regularly reviewed and renewed. However, it also identified a range of reasonable expectations regarding the ideological bias of this policy impact. To empirically investigate these competing expectations, we turned our attention to the U.S. states, which vary greatly in terms of party polarization and patterns of redistributive policy generosity and change.

In general, our findings support those who expect polarization to produce a regressive or conservative shift in the generosity and stringency of redistributive policy effort. However, this operated in two different ways. First, for three of the eight policies examined, we found a direct negative association consistent with conservative policy drift theorized by Hacker and Pierson (2005, 2010) and McCarty (2007) among others. However, for four of the other policies examined, we instead identified an indirect association in which party control is less predictive of redistributive policy effort when party polarization is high. For only one of the eight redistributive policies examined, corporate tax rates, did we find no association (direct or indirect) between polarization and policy generosity.

REFERENCES

Aldrich, John A. 1995. *Why Parties? The Origin and Transformation of Political Parties in America.* Chicago: University of Chicago Press.
Aldrich, John H., Mark M. Berger, and David W. Rohde. 2002. "The Historical Variability in Conditional Party Government, 1877–1994." In David W. Brady and Mathew D. McCubbins, eds., *Party, Process, and Political Change in Congress: New Perspectives on the History of Congress.* Stanford, CA: Stanford University Press, 17–35.
Aldrich, John H., and James S. Coleman Battista. 2002. "Conditional Party Government in the States." *American Journal of Political Science* 46 (1): 164–172.
Allard, Scott W. 2009. *Out of Reach: Place, Poverty and the New American Welfare State.* New Haven, CT: Yale University Press.
APSA. 1950. "Toward a More Responsible Two-Party System: A Report of the Committee on Political Parties of the American Political Science Association." *American Political Science Review* 44: 1–99.
Barrilleaux, Charles, Thomas Holbrook, and Laura Langer. 2002. "Electoral Competition, Legislative Balance, and American State Welfare Policy." *American Journal of Political Science* 46 (2): 415–427.
Binder, Sarah. 2003. *Stalemate: Causes and Consequences of Legislative Gridlock.* Washington, DC: The Brookings Institution.

Bonoli, Giuliano. 2001. "Political Institutions, Veto Points, and the Process of Welfare State Adaptation." In Paul Pierson, ed., *The New Politics of the Welfare State*. Oxford: Oxford University Press, 238–264.

Brady, David, and Joseph Stewart, Jr. 1982. "Congressional Party Realignment and Transformations of Public Policy in Three Realignment Eras." *American Journal of Political Science* 26:333–60.

Brady, David, John Ferejohn, and Laurel Harbridge. 2008. "Polarization and Public Policy: A General Assessment." In Pietro S. Nivola and David W. Brady, eds., *Red and Blue Nation? Consequences and Correction of America's Polarized Politics*, vol. 2. Washington, DC: Brookings Institution, 185–216.

Brady, David, and Craig Volden. 1997. *Revolving Gridlock*. Boulder, CO: Westview Press.

Brady, David W. 1978. "Critical Elections, Congressional Parties and Clusters of Policy Changes." *British Journal of Political Science* 8: 79–99.

Brooks, Deborah J., and John G. Geer. 2008. "Comment on Chapter One." In Pietro S. Nivola and David W. Brady, eds., *Red and Blue Nation? Consequences and Correction of America's Polarized Politics*, vol. 2. Washington, DC: Brookings Institution, 34–39.

Brown, Robert D. 1995. "Party Cleavages and Welfare Effort in the American States." *American Political Science Review* 89: 23–33.

Dye, Thomas R. 1984. "Party and Policy in the States." *The Journal of Politics* 46: 1097–1116.

Fellowes, Matthew C., and Gretchen Rowe. 2004. "Politics and the New American Welfare States." *American Journal of Political Science* 48 (2): 362–73.

Fiorina, Morris. 1996. *Divided Government*, 2nd edition. Boston: Allyn and Bacon.

Galston, William A., and Pietro S. Nivola. 2006. "Delineating the Problem." In Pietro S. Nivola and David W. Brady, eds., *Red and Blue Nation? Characteristics and Causes of America's Polarized Politics*, vol. 1. Washington, DC: Brookings Institution and Hoover Institution, 1–48.

Garand, James C. 2010. "Income Inequality, Party Polarization, and Roll-Call Voting in the U.S. Senate." *The Journal of Politics* 72: 1109–1128.

Garand, James C. 1985. "Partisan Change and Shifting Expenditure Priorities in the American-States, 1945–1978." *American Politics Quarterly* 13: 355–391.

Hacker, Jacob S. 2004. "Privatizing Risk without Privatizing the Welfare State: The Hidden Politics of Social Policy Retrenchment in the United States." *American Political Science Review* 98 (2): 243–260.

Hacker, Jacob, and Paul Pierson. 2005. *Off Center: The Republican Revolution and the Erosion of American Democracy*. New Haven, CT: Yale University Press.

Hacker, Jacob S., and Paul Pierson. 2010. "Winner-Take-All Politics: Public Policy, Political Organization, and the Precipitous Rise of Top Incomes in the United States." *Politics and Society* 38 (2): 152–204.

Hetherington, Marc J. 2008. "Turned Off or Turned On? How Polarization Affects Political Engagement." In Pietro S. Nivola and David W. Brady, eds., *Red and Blue Nation? Consequences and Correction of America's Polarized Politics*, vol. 2. Washington DC: Brookings Institution, 1–33.

Jennings, Edward T. 1979. "Competition, Constituencies, and Welfare Policies in American States." *American Political Science Review* 73: 414–429.

Jones, Bryan D., and Frank R. Baumgartner. 2005. *The Politics of Attention: How Government Prioritizes Problems.* Chicago: University of Chicago Press.

Jones, David R. 2001. "Party Polarization and Legislative Gridlock." *Political Research Quarterly* 54 (1): 1251–41.

Key, Jr., V. O. 1949. *Southern Politics in States and Nation.* New York: Knopf.

Kingdon, John. 1995. *Agendas, Alternatives, and Public Policies.* Boston: Addison Wesley Press.

Klarner, Carl. 2003. "The Measurement of Partisan Balance of State Government." *State Politics and Policy Quarterly* 3 (3): 309–319.

Korpi, Walter, and Joakim Palme. 2003. "New Politics and Class Politics in the Context of Austerity and Globalization: Welfare State Regress in 18 Countries 1975–95." *American Political Science Review* 97 (3): 425–446.

Kousser, Thad. 2008. "Does Partisan Polarization Lead to Policy Gridlock in California?" Working paper, *Public Policy Institute of California.* San Francisco: PPIC.

Krehbiel, Keith. 1998. *Pivotal Politics: A Theory of U.S. Lawmaking.* Chicago: University of Chicago Press.

Madison, James. 1961. "Federalist #10." In Clinton Rossiter, ed., *The Federalist Papers.* New York: New American Library, 71–78.

Mayhew, David. 1991. *Divided We Govern: Party Control, Lawmaking, and Investigations, 1946–1990.* New Haven, CT: Yale University Press.

McCarty, Nolan. 2007. "The Policy Effects of Political Polarization." In Paul Pierson and Theda Skocpol, eds., *The Transformation of American Politics: Activist Government and the Rise of Conservatism.* Princeton, NJ: Princeton University Press, 223–255.

McCarty, Nolan M., Keith T. Poole, and Howard Rosenthal. 2006. *Polarized America: The Dance of Ideology and Unequal Riches.* Cambridge, MA: MIT Press.

McCarty, Nolan, Keith T. Poole, and Howard Rosenthal. 2001. "The Hunt for Party Discipline in Congress." *American Political Science Review* 95 (3): 673–687.

Mettler, Suzanne. 2011. *The Submerged State: How Invisible Government Policies Undermine American Democracy.* Chicago: University of Chicago Press.

Pierson, Paul. 2001. "Coping with Permanent Austerity: Welfare State Restructuring in Affluent Democracies." In Paul Pierson, ed., *The New Politics of the Welfare State.* New York: Oxford University Press, 410–456.

Pierson, Paul. 2000. "Path Dependence, Increasing Returns, and the Study of Politics." *American Political Science Review* 94 (2): 251–267.

Pierson, Paul. 1996. *Dismantling the Welfare State? Reagan, Thatcher and the Politics of Retrenchment.* Cambridge: Cambridge University Press.

Poole, Keith T., and Howard Rosenthal. 1997. *Congress: A Political-Economic History of Roll Call Voting.* New York: Oxford University Press.

Powell, Bingham. 1982. *Contemporary Democracies.* Cambridge, MA: Harvard University Press.

Rivlin, Alice. 2006. "Is America Too Polarized to Make Public Policy?" Presented at the APPAM Spring Conference, Park City, Utah.

Rohde, David. 1991. *Party Leaders in the Post-Reform House.* Chicago: University of Chicago Press.

Schattschneider, E. E. 1942. *Party Government.* New York: Reinhardt and Company.

Schram, Sanford F., Richard C. Fording, and Joe Soss. 2008. "Neo-liberal Poverty Governance: Race, Place and the Punitive Turn in US Welfare Policy." *Cambridge Journal of Regions, Economy and Society* 1: 17–36.

Schultz, Christian. 1999. "Monetary Policy, Delegation and Polarization." *The Economic Journal* 109: 164–178.

Shor, Boris, and Nolan McCarty. 2011. "The Ideological Mapping of American Legislatures." *American Political Science Review* 105 (3): 530–551.

Sinclair, Barbara. 2008. "Spoiling the Sausages? How a Polarized Congress Deliberates and Legislates." In Pietro S. Nivola and David W. Brady, eds. *Red and Blue Nation? Consequences and Correction of America's Polarized Politics*, vol. 2. Washington, DC: Brookings Institution and Hoover Institution, 55–87.

Sinclair, Barbara. 2006. *Party Wars: Polarization and the Politics of National Policymaking*. Norman: University of Oklahoma Press.

Stonecash, Jeffrey M. 2000. *Class and Party in American Politics*. Boulder, CO: Westview Press.

Stonecash, Jeff, Mark Brewer, and Mack Mariani. 2003. *Diverging Parties: Realignment, Social Change and Party Polarization*. Boulder, CO: Westview Press.

APPENDIX

TABLE A. *Descriptive Statistics*

	N	M	sd	Min	Max
Party polarization					
Polarization	600	1.30	0.43	0.47	3.10
Change 1997–2008	50	0.12	0.24	−0.53	1.08
Redistributive policy					
TANF eligibility	600	883.55	339.99	269.91	1,895.14
SCHIP eligibility	600	219.19	52.01	114.28	430.76
Minimum wage	600	6.55	0.99	2.03	8.69
Tax credit (100%)	600	52.37	415.93	−613.39	1,831.91
Tax charge (500%)	600	3,391.05	1,830.07	0.00	6,950.38
Top marg tax rate	600	5.16	2.91	0.00	10.75
Cap gains tax	600	4.85	2.85	0.00	10.75
Corporate tax	600	6.64	2.84	0.00	12.00
Change TANF eligibility	50	−83.93	258.40	−720.90	819.73
Change SCHIP eligibility	50	26.94	55.86	−161.53	243.26
Change minimum wage	50	0.75	0.81	−0.85	3.09
Change tax credit (100%)	50	187.22	310.49	−167.47	1,213.34
Change tax charge (500%)	50	−30.17	394.88	−1,198.91	614.32
Change top marg tax rate	50	−0.08	1.04	−3.45	4.38
Change cap gains tax	50	−0.23	1.68	−7.67	4.38
Change Corporate Tax	50	−0.33	1.62	−8.64	2.65

	N	M	sd	Min	Max
State context variables					
Dem Party control	600	1.50	1.07	0.00	3.00
Per capita income	600	35.87	5.65	24.29	57.09
Unemployment rate	600	6.46	12.30	2.30	93.84
Income inequality	600	0.40	0.02	0.36	0.46
Relative voter turnout	600	1.66	0.28	1.15	2.89

PART IV

POLARIZATION IN THE MEDIA

12

Partisan Media and Electoral Polarization in 2012

Evidence from the American National Election Study

Gary C. Jacobson

After widening for several decades, partisan divisions among ordinary Americans over issues, ideology, evaluations of leaders, and, in notable instances, perceptions of political, economic, and scientific realities, reached new extremes during Barack Obama's presidency. These trends coincided with the proliferation of partisan news and opinion outlets enabled by the spread of cable television, talk radio, and the Internet, raising the question of how these two phenomena might be related. The 2012 American National Election Study (ANES) offered a unique perspective on this question by asking, along with its usual battery of political questions, whether respondents attended to any of 34 specific television, radio, newspaper, and Internet sources of news and opinion programs. These sources are distinguishable as conservative, liberal or mainstream, allowing the analysis of the relationship between the ideological and partisan leanings of the sources voters reported using and their political beliefs, attitudes and behavior. The results of this analysis support several conclusions:

- As expected, most people who do attend to partisan media chose sources that could be relied on to confirm rather than challenge their existing attitudes and opinions; partisans showed a clear preference for sources of news and opinion that reliably fit their biases.
- Modal opinions, beliefs, and behaviors varied strongly with variations in the use of partisan media. Media choice was strongly related to voters' assessments of Barack Obama, the Affordable Care Act, gun control, and climate change, as well as their to comparative affect toward Obama and Romney and their parties, their presidential choice, and their expectations about who would win the White House.
- These relationships were not merely an artifact of voters selecting congenial partisan media; even after controlling statistically for the effects of a variety of variables that would predict selective exposure to partisan media, actual exposure continued to have a significant effect on attitudes, beliefs, and

reported behavior. The conservative media were particularly influential in this regard. Voters' use of partisan and ideologically slanted media outlets thus contributed appreciably to (as well as reflected) the high levels of partisan polarization of opinions of the presidential candidates, parties, and issues in 2012.

• The effects of partisan media use varied in ways that systematically echoed variations in the emphasis of partisan messages and thus were most pronounced on issues where conservative and liberal media took clear and emphatic contrary positions – particularly regarding Obama.

• The intense partisanship expressed in the 2012 election amplified partisan intransigence and gridlock in Washington during the 113th Congress, for Obama and the House Republican majority owed their elections to the most thoroughly disjunctive coalitions, with the most starkly opposed opinions and beliefs, of any modern Congress and administration on record.

Partisan divisions among ordinary Americans, after steadily widening for several decades, reached new extremes during Barack Obama's presidency. The electorate that returned Obama to the White House in 2012 was more polarized along party lines than any at least six decades. Voters displayed the highest levels of party-line voting, lowest levels of ticket splitting, and widest partisan difference in presidential approval ever documented in American National Election Studies going back to 1952. The proportion of both approvers and disapprovers of Obama who held these views "strongly" were both at all-time highs for a president pursuing reelection (Jacobson 2013a). The ideological divergence between the party coalitions was matched only by 2008 in the ANES time series.[1] Partisan differences in placement of the presidential candidates and political parties on the 100-degree feeling thermometer scales, displayed in Figure 1, also reached record levels in 2012.[2]

Although scholars continue to debate the trend's breadth and causes (Fiorina, Adams, and Pope 2006; Bishop 2008; Fiorina and Adams 2009; Hetherington and Weiler 2009; Levendusky 2009; Abramowitz 2010; Jacobson 2011a; Baumer and Gold 2010), it is clear that the American people have in recent decades become increasingly divided along party lines in their opinions on issues, ideologies, evaluations of leaders, and, in notable instances, perceptions of political, economic, and scientific realities (Kull, Clay, and Lewis 2003; Gaines et al. 2007; Jacobson 2010; Bradberry and Jacobson 2013b). Widening partisan divisions in the public have coincided with the proliferation of partisan news and opinion outlets enabled by the spread of cable television, talk radio, and the Internet, raising the obvious question of how these two phenomena might be related. The question has inspired a number of important studies (e.g., Mutz 2006; Prior 2007; Jamieson and

---

[1] Based on mean self-locations by partisans on the seven-point ANES liberal-conservative scale.

[2] The feeling thermometer is a scale ranging from 0 (coldest) to 100 (warmest), with 50 degrees as the neutral point.

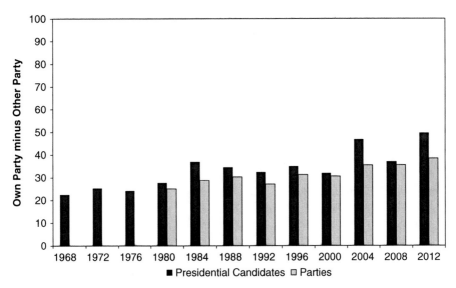

FIGURE 1. Partisan Differences in Thermometer Ratings of Presidential Candidates and Parties

Capella 2008; Iyengar and Hahn 2009; Stroud 2011; Arceneaux and Johnson 2013; Levendusky 2013) that point to several general conclusions. First, the multiplication of media options fragmented the audience for national news. Some people deserted the once-dominant network news in favor of entertainment shows; others migrated to partisan information sources on cable and later the Internet; the audiences for national network news shrank. Second, selective exposure is pervasive; most people who do attend to partisan media chose sources that can be relied on to confirm rather than challenge their existing attitudes and opinions. Third, exposure to ideologically slanted messages tends to reinforce the prior opinions in ways consistent with theories of motivated cognition and reasoning (Kunda 1990; Lodge and Tabor 2001; Tabor and Lodge 2006).

Together, these conclusions suggest that partisan media amplify as well as cater to partisan divisions in the public. My purpose in this chapter is to examine the contribution of partisan media outlets to the unusually high levels of partisan polarization observed in the 2012 electorate. The combination of selective exposure and reinforced biases poses tricky questions of causation, however. As we shall see, it is easy to document the remarkably strong relationship between the partisan and ideological thrust of media sources and the typical political attitudes and opinions of their audiences in 2012. But whether this relationship is simply the result of selective exposure, or whether the tendentious messages to which people expose themselves actually influence their attitudes, opinions, and beliefs, is a more difficult question to answer.

Experimental and panel studies have found evidence that such messages do alter opinions (Jones 2002; Arceneaux and Johnson 2013; Levendusky 2013), although these studies are necessarily limited in scope, focusing as they do on only a few partisan sources and often on unrepresentative populations. The 2012 ANES study I examine here provides much greater coverage of the range of real-world media outlets that people report using, but it cannot, as an observational study, unambiguously identify causal effects. The data leave no doubt that polarized political attitudes, opinions, and beliefs strongly reflect partisan media consumption. But they also provide at least strong circumstantial evidence that ideologically-biased media – particularly on the right – contributed appreciably to (as well as reflected) polarized opinions of the presidential candidates, parties, and issues in 2012.

THE DATA

The 2012 ANES Time Series Study (American National Election Study 2013) combined the traditional ANES sample interviewed face-to-face with a separate sample interviewed via the Internet. The two samples include 4,314 respondents who reported voting in the presidential election (1,361 in the face-to-face sample, 2,953 in the Internet sample), and these are the subjects of my analysis. Uniquely in 2012, the survey asked respondents whether they watched any of 34 specific television programs, listened to any of 15 radio programs, read any of four national newspapers in print or on the Internet, or visited any of 15 websites. For my analysis, I classified those sources whose primary focus is political news and opinion into three categories: conservative, liberal, and mainstream, based on their public reputations. In cases where a source had multiple outlets (for example, newspapers with Internet versions, television news programs with websites, or commentators with more than one venue), they were counted as a single source.[3] Table 1 lists the sources classified by ideological leanings and ordered, in the second column, by the number of respondents (out of the 4,185 voters responding to this part of the survey) who said they used each one.

Table 1 also displays the partisan composition of the audiences for each source; independents who said they leaned toward a party are considered partisans.[4] I also divided Republicans into those who said they supported or leaned toward supporting the Tea Party and those who did not.[5] Tea Party Republicans, comprising a majority of the Republican coalition (55 percent in

---

[3] I also combined NPR's *Morning Edition* and *All Things Considered* into a single NPR category.
[4] Partisan leaners were actually more loyally partisan in their voting behavior than weak partisans in this survey.
[5] The ANES measured Tea Party support with a three-part branching question patterned on the party identification question; as with party identification, weak and leaning Tea Party supporters held similar views and reported similar behaviors, so Republicans in both groups are classified as Tea Party supporters for this analysis.

TABLE 1. *Partisanship of Audiences for Television, Radio, Print, and Internet News and Opinion Sources*

		Republicans				
	Weighted N	Tea Party	Other	All	Independents	Democrats
National average	4,185	23.2	18.9	42.1	7.9	49.9
Conservative Sources						
Fox News	961	51.3	20.0	71.3	4.0	24.7
Bill O'Reilly	561	68.2	17.4	85.6	3.4	10.9
Sean Hannity	520	74.3	14.9	89.2	3.7	7.2
Greta Van Susteren	348	69.9	14.9	84.8	3.3	11.9
Mike Huckabee	313	77.8	15.3	93.1	3.2	3.7
Bret Baier	277	74.6	10.5	85.1	3.1	11.9
Rush Limbaugh	382	73.0	13.7	86.7	3.8	9.5
Glenn Beck	219	75.0	15.6	90.6	3.1	6.3
Wall Street Journal	178	42.8	18.4	61.2	4.6	34.2
Drudge Report	148	70.1	8.2	78.3	10.7	11.0
Mark Levin	101	87.7	3.9	91.6	2.7	5.7
Laura Ingraham	88	76.7	7.2	83.9	2.5	13.7
Michael Savage	85	77.9	10.5	88.4	4.2	7.3
Average		70.7	13.1	83.8	4.0	12.1
Liberal Sources						
CNN	528	17.5	15.3	32.8	6.4	60.9
Anderson Cooper	482	14.4	13.1	27.5	5.4	67.1
NPR	458	10.7	13.2	23.9	7.5	68.5
Jon Stewart	457	7.0	7.4	14.4	5.0	80.5
MSNBC	449	20.7	14.3	35.0	6.2	58.8
New York Times	374	8.1	17.9	26.0	4.2	69.8
Stephen Colbert	370	8.0	11.1	19.1	4.3	76.6
Huffington Post	334	16.2	9.5	25.7	6.3	68.0
Frontline	250	15.9	9.2	25.1	5.5	69.3
Chris Matthews	247	9.0	6.3	15.3	3.0	81.7
Washington Post	201	24.8	7.9	32.7	6.8	60.6
Average		13.8	11.4	25.2	5.5	69.3
Mainstream Sources						
60 Minutes	1,198	16.3	18.2	34.5	6.9	58.6
NBC Nightly News	1,121	18.3	19.7	38.0	6.6	55.4
CBS Evening News	1,019	19.0	18.1	37.1	7.8	55.2
20/20	976	16.3	20.3	36.6	8.8	54.6
Dateline	949	15.3	20.2	35.5	6.7	57.3
ABC World News	855	16.5	18.9	35.4	7.6	57.2
Nightline	722	18.4	18.6	37.0	6.8	56.2
Meet the Press	492	21.7	16.6	38.3	6.6	55.1
USA Today	405	24.2	25.0	49.2	7.0	43.8
Face the Nation	403	23.0	13.8	36.8	9.7	53.5
Average		18.9	18.9	37.8	7.5	54.7

this survey), express modal opinions quite distinct from those expressed by other Republicans on a wide variety of political opinions and beliefs, especially those involving Barack Obama. Not only are they more likely to take conservative positions, but on most questions their mean responses differ more from those of other Republicans than the other Republicans differ from independents (Bradberry and Jacobson 2013). Thus they are treated as a separate category in some analyses here.

The data on the distribution of partisans reported in Table 1 confirm the prevalence of selective attention by partisans. Republicans in general and Tea Party Republicans in particular are highly overrepresented among users of conservative media. On average, 84 percent of the audiences for conservative sources are Republicans, and 71 percent of them are Tea Party supporters. Only 12 percent are Democrats, and pure independents are also typically underrepresented. Liberal media, in contrast, attract audiences that are skewed Democratic (average, 69 percent), although they attract twice the proportion of Republicans (25 percent) as conservative media do Democrats. Audiences for mainstream media are about six percentage points more Democratic and five points less Republican than the national average for these categories – presumably reflecting Republican distrust of mainstream media (Morales 2012) – and mainstream outlets attract a relatively larger share of independents as well, although independents are still underrepresented, a sign of their comparative political indifference.

Within the conservative and liberal categories, a few sources have less highly skewed audiences. The national newspapers fall into this category; more Democrats read the *Wall Street Journal* than attend to any other conservative source, and more Republicans read the *Washington Post* than attend to any other liberal source except CNN and MSNBC. Cable news networks such as CNN, MSNBC, and Fox News also tend to more balanced audiences. The most lopsided audiences belong to most enthusiastic ideologues, who apparently preach mainly to the choir.

Overall, about 54 percent of all Republicans, and 69 percent of Tea Party Republicans, reported using at least one of the conservative sources, compared to only 23 percent of independents and 18 percent of Democrats. About 54 percent of Democrats reported using at least one liberal source, compared to 39 percent of independents and 33 percent of Republicans (same percentage for both factions). Majorities in all categories used mainstream sources, although Tea Party Republicans were less likely (56 percent) than other Republicans (68 percent), independents (61 percent), or Democrats (70 percent) to say they did so.

Most voters attend to more than one type of outlet (Table 2). Few use one type of partisan media exclusively (17 percent of the total); more common is the use of partisan sources plus mainstream sources (28 percent); 16 percent expose themselves to both liberal and conservative sources; 19 percent use only mainstream media, and 20 percent report using none of these sources at all.

TABLE 2. *Media Source Combinations*

Sources	Percent
None	19.8
Mainstream only	18.9
Conservative only	8.0
Conservative and mainstream	9.3
Liberal only	9.4
Liberal and mainstream	18.3
Liberal and conservative	3.8
All three	12.5

Arceneaux and Johnson (2013: 151) argue that, even though "partisan news shows have a substantial effect on political attitudes in the expected direction," the audiences for the cable news shows whose effects they investigate are so small that their contribution to national polarization can only be very modest. The 2012 ANES data indicate that when a broader range of partisan media are considered, a clear majority of voters – more than 60 percent – were exposed to their messages, so their potential impact should not be underestimated.

To analyze the relationship between partisan media and the polarized electorate in 2012, I created five-point additive scales based on the number of sources in each category the respondent reported using; the scales range from 0 to 4 or more for each type. Table 3 reports the distribution of partisan voters on this scale for each media category. Tea Party Republicans are the most distinctive group by this measure; they are much heavier users of conservative media than any other group and pay less attention to mainstream media as well. The relatively heavy use of conservative media by the Tea Partiers is only partially a consequence of the large contingent of Fox News personalities on the list; if we count them together as only one source, 18 percent of Tea Party Republicans still report using four or more conservative sources. Again, the tendency toward selective exposure by partisans is unmistakable. But did it make any difference?

MEDIA USE AND OPINION POLARIZATION

Barack Obama was without question the primary focal object of electoral polarization in 2012. His immediate predecessor, George W. Bush, had received the most divergent partisan evaluations since surveys began asking about presidential approval in the 1930s (Jacobson 2011a: 4–6). In 2012, Obama not only matched but by a small margin exceeded Bush in this regard.[6] Obama also received the coldest average feeling thermometer ratings

---

[6] During the final quarter of 2004, the partisan difference in approval of Bush's performance in Gallup Polls averaged 79 percentage points (Republicans at 92 percent, Democrats at 13 percent);

TABLE 3. *Use of Media Sources, by Party*

		Republicans		Independents	Democrats
		Tea Party	Other		
Conservative sources	None	31.1	64.7	76.9	81.7
	1	14.2	16.6	12.3	12.8
	2	10.0	7.6	3.5	3.3
	3	8.4	5.3	2.8	1.3
	4 or more	36.4	5.8	4.4	0.9
Liberal sources	None	66.4	66.8	61.5	46.1
	1	19.5	18.0	21.2	21.9
	2	8.6	8.2	7.3	12.2
	3	2.8	3.6	3.1	8.0
	4 or more	2.7	3.3	6.9	11.9
Mainstream sources	None	44.5	32.7	38.7	30.0
	1	17.3	16.4	17.0	17.3
	2	11.5	14.4	9.7	13.3
	3	10.3	8.7	12.1	12.6
	4 or more	16.4	27.8	22.5	26.8

from the other party's voters of any president running for reelection, and the partisan difference in mean temperature was wider in 2012 than in any previous year.[7] Thus, I begin my examination of the relationship between partisan media consumption and polarized opinions and beliefs by examining responses to questions about the president. For this exercise, I computed a net index of partisan media use by subtracting the number of liberal sources mentioned from the number of conservative source mentioned (up to 4 each) that ranges from −4 (4 or more exclusively liberal sources) to 4 (4 or more exclusively conservative sources).[8] About 10 percent of voters were at the extremes on this scale; about 32 percent had net scores in the −2 to −4 or 2 to 4 ranges and so were distinctly partisan in their choice of media.[9]

during the comparable quarter of 2012, the gap was 81 points (Democrats at 91 percent, Republicans at 10 percent.)

[7] Obama's average thermometer rating from Republicans in 2012 was 29.2 degrees; G.W. Bush's average rating from Democrats in 2004 was 29.8 degrees; the partisan gap in 2012 was 53.0 degrees, in 2004, 52.7 degrees. The largest previous gap was 42.9 degrees for Bill Clinton in 1996.

[8] With minor exceptions, responses to the questions analyzed here did not vary according to respondents' use of mainstream media and I, therefore, ignore this variable here, although it will be included in later multivariate analyses of these relationships.

[9] The distribution of voting respondents on this scale was:

−4	4.7%	−1	16.0%	2	4.5%
−3	5.4%	0	43.6%	3	3.7%
−2	7.7%	1	9.0%	4	5.5%

Figure 2A and 2B displays the distribution of voters' opinions and beliefs about Obama across locations on the partisan media use scale. The relationships between attention to partisan media and views of Obama are all very strong, and the greater the difference in net partisan media used, the more polarized are responses to Obama. Approval of Obama's job performance ranges from 90 percent at the liberal source maximum to less than 1 percent at the conservative source maximum. Very few below the midpoint on the index think Obama is an extreme liberal, while large majorities of those at the right end of the scale do so. In 2012, partisan differences in the ideological location attributed to the Democratic presidential candidate, and the proportion of voters rating him as an extreme liberal, were the widest ever observed in the ANES time series going back to 1972, when the question was first asked. The charge that Obama is an extreme leftist was a central theme of the McCain-Palin campaign in 2008 and has been a common motif of conservative attacks ever since (Jacobson 2011b). Republican voters located Obama further to the left in 2012 than any previous Democratic candidate, including George McGovern (Jacobson 2013a) – this for a president whose first-term DW-NOMINATE score, based on his positions on legislation considered in Congress, identified him as "the most ideologically moderate Democratic president in the post-war period" (Hare, Poole, and Rosenthal 2013).

Consumers of conservative media were also inclined to accept the even more dubious claims about the president's birthplace and religion. The notion that Obama is foreign born and thus ineligible to be president, circulating among some of his detractors since he first sought the presidency, has proven impervious to disconfirming information. The same is true of the claim that he is Muslim rather than a Christian (Bradberry and Jacobson 2013). More than half of the heaviest users of conservative media accept these bogus claims, which are rejected by a huge majority of respondents favoring liberal media.

Net partisan media use is also strongly related to other beliefs about reality (Figure 3A and 3B). Climate change denial, a rejection of the overwhelming scientific consensus that human activity is heating up the planet, increases as net partisan media use becomes more conservative, as does the unfounded belief that the Affordable Care Act establishes government panels to make end-of-life decisions for people on Medicare (the so-called death panels). Media use also influenced perceptions of how the economy had progressed over the year leading up to the election, with consumers of conservative media believing it had gotten worse (by the usual objective indicators it had improved, albeit modestly[10]) and whether the administration's policies were biased in favor of blacks over whites.[11]

[10] The nation's GDP, real per capita income, and median family income grew, though slowly, over the election year, and unemployment declined by about one percentage point.

[11] The ANES also asked about two dubious claims thought to be more common on the left: that the George W. Bush administration had foreknowledge of the terrorists attacks of September 11, 2001, and that the Army Corps of Engineers let Hurricane Katrina flood African-American

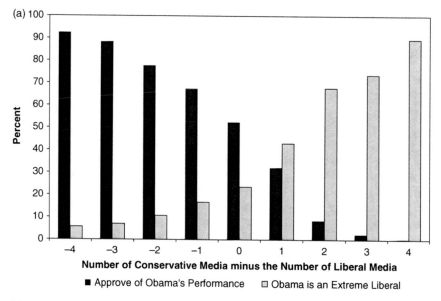

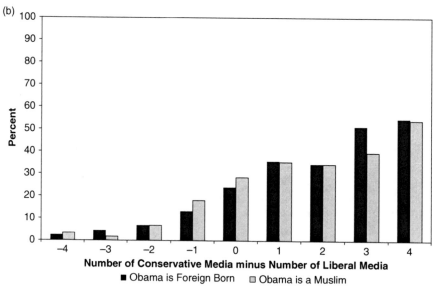

FIGURE 2. Opinions and Beliefs about Barack Obama

section of New Orleans to protect white sections. Media use had little effect on responses; respondents at the liberal end of the scale (−2 or less) were only about six points more likely to believe the claim than respondents at the conservative end of the scale (2 or higher). Belief in these claims decreased with the increasing use of media of all three types.

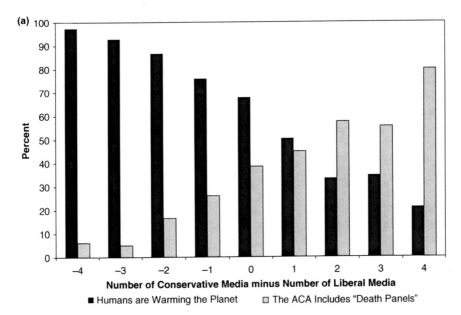

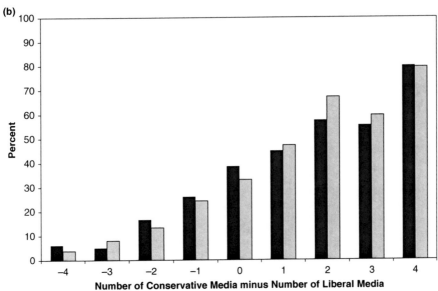

FIGURE 3. Beliefs about Reality

I have focused here largely on beliefs rather than opinions. Similar, sometimes even sharper illustrations of polarization across the net partisan media use scale appear in opinions on policy questions, such as the Affordable Care Act or whether to tighten gun regulation (Figure 4A and 4B). Such examples could be multiplied almost endlessly, but these figures are sufficient to demonstrate how strongly polarized opinions and beliefs reflect voters' use of partisan media and how widely voters at the opposite ends of the scale diverge – by more than 90 percentage points in some cases, approaching the mathematical limit.

IS IT ONLY SELECTIVE EXPOSURE?

In principle, these relationships could be entirely the consequence of the strong tendency toward selective exposure documented in Tables 1 and 3. If so, however, they should vanish if we control for the characteristics of voters that determine their choice of partisan media. To test for this possibility, I estimated two logit models with responses to the questions analyzed for Figures 2 and 3 as the dependent variables. For the first, the independent variables are simply the three media use scales (each ranging from 0 to 4). Selective exposure guarantees that these estimates are subject to omitted variables bias, and thus for the second equation, I include a set of variables that should influence the selective choice of media sources: party identification, self-location on the seven-point liberal-conservative scale, the seven-point Tea Party support scale, and the three standard ANES scales measuring racial resentment, egalitarianism, and moral traditionalism.[12] Table 4 displays estimates derived from these equations of the difference in probability of a positive response to each question moving from the lowest to highest use of each type of media when the other variables are set at their mean values. Estimates based on coefficients failing to meet the $p < .05$ level of statistical significance are in parentheses.

---

[12] All of these variables are in fact significant predictors of partisan media consumption. The racial resentment scale is based on respondents' agreement or disagreement with four statements: (1) "Irish, Italians, Jewish, and many other minorities overcame prejudice and worked their way up. Blacks should do the same without any special favors." (2) "Over the past few years blacks have gotten less than they deserve." (3) "It's really a matter of some people not trying hard enough; if blacks would only try harder they could be just as well off as whites." (4) "Generations of slavery and discrimination have created conditions that make it difficult for blacks to work their way out of the lower class." The four items generated a single factor (eigenvalue = 2.60, absolute factor loadings ranged from .79 to .82); Cronbach's Alpha for the four items is .81. The factor scores are recoded to range from 0.0 to 1.0. The moral traditionalism scale is based on respondents' agreement or disagreement with four statements about social morality and tolerance. The four items generated a single factor (eigenvalue = 2.3, absolute factor loadings ranged from .69 to .78); Cronbach's Alpha for the four items is .72. The egalitarianism scale is from a six-item battery of agree-disagree statements regarding equality; the six items generated a single factor (eigenvalue = 3.01, absolute factor loadings ranged from .66 to .75); Cronbach's Alpha for the six items is .80.

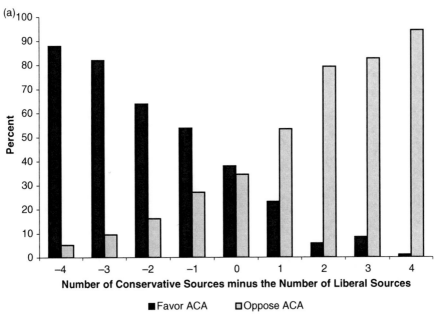

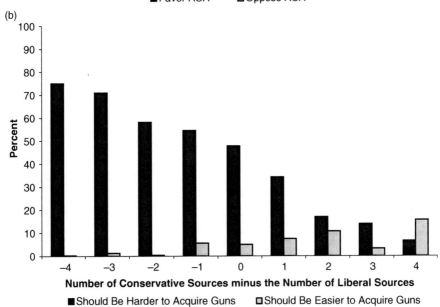

FIGURE 4. Opinions on Issues

TABLE 4. *Difference in Probability of Holding Selected Opinions and Beliefs*

	Media Type					
	Conservative		Liberal		Mainstream	
	No Controls	Controls	No Controls	Controls	No Controls	Controls
Approve of Obama's job performance	-.65	-.34	.52	(.12)	.17	(.01)
Obama is an extreme liberal	.67	.34	-.27	-.10	-.10	(-.02)
Obama is foreign born	.33	(-.02)	-.28	-.09	(.03)	(.03)
Obama is Muslim	.25	(-.06)	-.25	-.12	(.01)	.06
Human-induced climate change	-.54	-.30	.31	.21	.11	.08
ACA has "death panels"	.44	.16	-.33	-.22	-.13	-.10
Economy worse over past year	.49	.11	-.34	-.17	(.05)	(.02)
Administration favors blacks	.50	.11	-.24	-.13	-.06	(.04)
Support the ACA	-.65	-.16	.44	.12	.23	.10
Favor stricter gun control	-.46	-17	.26	(.03)	.15	.06

Notes: Entries are based on logit equations estimating the probability of holding each opinion or belief and indicate the difference in probability of holding an opinion or belief between the least (0) and most (maximum of 4) use of each type of media with the other variables set at their mean values. Estimates based on coefficients below the .05 level of statistical significance are in parentheses.

The first column in each set reiterates the strong relationship between partisan media use and responses to these questions, with the level of attention to conservative media having the largest effect on predicted responses in all but one question (Obama's religion is the exception – a tie here). The estimated effects of the use of mainstream media are all considerably smaller and in three cases are based on insignificant coefficients; the significant coefficients do, however, all have the same signs as the estimates based on liberal media use.

The second column in each set displays estimates of the remaining effects of media use once the six variables contributing to selective exposure are taken into account. They are in every case notably smaller than the initial estimates. For partisan media, however, most effects remain substantively meaningful and statistically significant. The residual estimated effects of conservative media use remain particularly large for approval of Obama's performance, perceptions of him as an extreme liberal, and acceptance of human-induced climate change. Conservative media use is unrelated to beliefs about Obama's alleged foreign birth and Muslim religion when these additional variables are taken into account, but greater liberal media use continues to predict a lower probability

TABLE 5. *Polarizing Effects of Partisan Media Use, Controlling for Selective Exposure*

	Difference between Respondents at −4 and +4 on the Net Partisan Media Scale	
	No Controls	Controls
Approve of Obama's job performance	−.97	−.47
Human-induced climate change	−.76	−.44
Support the ACA	−.87	−.42
Obama is an extreme liberal	.84	.39
ACA has "death panels"	.74	.34
Economy worse over past year	.74	.27
Favor stricter gun control	.68	.26
Administration favors blacks	.76	.16
Obama is Muslim	.51	.05
Obama is foreign born	.52	(.03)

of accepting these canards. Liberal media use also continues to have a substantial effect on answers to other factual questions (climate change, death panels, the economy's performance over the past year), but not on approval of Obama or opinion on gun control. The estimated effects of mainstream media use also shrink and are not significant for half of the ten questions when the controls are introduced; no remaining probability difference is greater than .10.[13]

These same control variables can be used to gauge the effects of net partisan media use on the polarization of opinions and beliefs. The entry in the first column in Table 5 is the difference between the mean responses of voters at the extreme ends of the net partisan media scale as displayed in Figures 2 and 3 (shown here as proportions rather than percentages). The second column lists, in order of their absolute magnitudes, the estimated differences when the six variables that determine selective exposure to partisan media are taken into account.[14] If the control variables eliminate most or all of the omitted variables bias arising from selective exposure, then the results suggest that partisan media did indeed contribute to a polarized electorate in 2012. The largest effects are for evaluations of Obama's job performance, views of his ideology, and opinions on his signature legislative achievement, the Affordable Care Act, along with factual questions about climate change and the existence of death panels. By this evidence, partisan media helped make Obama the focal object

---

[13] The one curiosity is the belief that Obama is Muslim actually increases significantly (albeit quite modestly) with the use of mainstream media; perhaps the idea would never occur to people who had little or no exposure to sources that at least mentioned the claim, if only to dismiss it.

[14] Estimated from logit equations in which the net partisan media scale replaces the three individual media use scales used to produce the estimates listed in Table 4.

around which partisan voters polarized in 2012 while also contributing to
divergent perceptions of reality regarding global warming and death panels.
The residual effects of media use on polarized views of the economy, gun
control, and administration favoritism toward blacks are smaller but still
appreciable. But respondents' polarized beliefs about Obama's birthplace and
religion were not, by this analysis, influenced by media use but rather reflect
prior beliefs held by the self-selected partisan media users.

THE EFFECTS OF INDIVIDUAL MEDIA SOURCES

The data examined so far indicate some asymmetry between conservative and
liberal media, with the former attracting the more ideologically homogeneous
audience (Table 1) but nonetheless having a relatively larger residual effect on
opinions and beliefs when the variables predicting selective exposure are taken
into account (on average about 35 percent larger according to the estimates in
Table 4). To examine this asymmetry and partisan media source effects more
generally, I chose the two exemplary measures of polarization in 2012 for
further analysis: the difference in voters' thermometer ratings of Obama and
Romney and of the Democratic and Republican parties. Recall from Figure 1
that partisan differences in these ratings were the highest in the entire ANES
time series. As with the other opinions analyzed here, the degree of polarization
of thermometer ratings on the candidates and parties in 2012 varies strongly
with the use of partisan media (Figure 5). To assess the relationship between

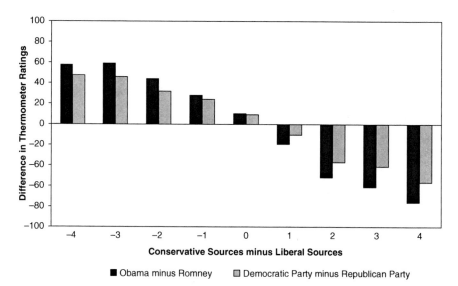

FIGURE 5. Net Partisan Media Use and Differences in Thermometer Ratings of the
Presidential Candidates and the Parties in 2012

individual media sources and the degree of polarization, I regressed these variable on the use of each of the 34 media sources by itself (as a categorical variable) and again with the 6 selective exposure control variables; the results are reported in Table 6.

The estimated coefficients for each source without the selective exposure variables reflect with great precision the partisan composition of each source's audience as displayed in Table 1; the correlations between the proportion of Republicans and Democrats in the audience and the net differences in candidate and party thermometer scores for each source are in all four cases greater than. 99. Thus, users of conservative sources rate Romney much higher than Obama and the Republican Party much higher than the Democratic Party, whereas users of liberal media clearly favor Obama and the Democratic Party over their rivals, but to a smaller extent. The audiences for mainstream sources also mostly tilt toward Obama and the Democrats but by much smaller margins. The six control variables by themselves explain a very large proportion of the variance (75 percent for the candidate thermometer differences, 76 percent for the in party thermometer differences), and their inclusion reduces the estimated source effects sharply. The effects of using all but a few liberal sources cease to be significantly different from zero, and of the five of the 26 coefficients that do meet the conventional $p < .05$ standard, three have the "wrong" (negative) sign. With these controls, mainstream sources have almost no evident effect on voters' affective reactions to the candidates and parties. Thus relationships observed in the first column of each set for liberal and mainstream sources arise from selective exposure rather than from any messages to which the voters have exposed themselves.

Attention to many of the conservative outlets, in contrast, continues to have a significant effect on thermometer differences, particularly with regard to the presidential candidates. Ten of the 13 coefficients for the Obama-Romney differences remain significant at $p < .05$, averaging about −8.6 degrees. Notably, the coefficients for all of the Fox News commentators and Fox News itself remain substantial and statistically significant, averaging −10 degrees. Estimated conservative source effects on relative party thermometers are smaller, with only six of them remaining significantly different from zero when the control variables are added. Again, however, five of these six belong to the Fox News stable. This is clear if circumstantial evidence that the Fox audience absorbed messages from the network's personalities that magnified their affective reactions to the presidential candidates and, to a lesser extent, the national parties. These source effects registered on thermometer ratings of both Romney and Obama when they are examined separately (results not shown); if anything, the media source coefficients for Romney's ratings tended to be larger. Thus insofar as Fox News commentators influenced their audience's affective reactions to the candidates, it was to boost Romney at least as much as to hurt Obama. Perhaps this is one reason why, although Romney won the Republican nomination by defeating several rivals with greater intrinsic appeal to the

TABLE 6. *Media Bias and Polarized Net Thermometer Ratings of Obama and Romney and the Political Parties*

	Obama minus Romney (Average = 5.4°)		Democratic Party minus Republican Party (Average = 6.3°)	
	No Controls	Controls	No Controls	Controls
Conservative Sources				
Mark Levin	−78.9	−10.9	−53.8	(0.2)
Sean Hannity	−78.2	−14.2	−57.3	−4.8
Mike Huckabee	−77.5	−8.3	−62.3	−6.5
Glenn Beck	−71.2	−6.3	−55.4	(−3.1)
Bret Baier	−70.8	−8.3	−53.5	(−3.3)
Bill O'Reilly	−70.3	−10.9	−53.8	−6.0
Greta Van Susteren	−68.5	−12.4	−53.2	−8.1
Rush Limbaugh	−68.5	−7.4	−50.0	(−0.4)
Michael Savage	−63.3	(−5.9)	−47.8	(−2.5)
Laura Ingraham	−61.2	−8.1	−47.8	−6.6
Fox News	−55.7	−8.2	−42.3	−3.6
Drudge Report	−51.9	(−1.3)	−38.2	(2.6)
Wall Street Journal	−15.6	(−1.4)	−13.8	(−1.2)
Any	−55.5	−8.5	−42.0	−3.5
Liberal Sources				
Chris Matthews	52.9	(−1.6)	42.1	(1.8)
Jon Stewart	46.0	(−2.4)	36.0	(−1.1)
Stephen Colbert	39.8	−3.8	30.5	(−2.5)
New York Times	37.2	(−.0.0)	27.6	(0.1)
NPR	34.3	(−1.6)	25.7	(−1.5)
Huffington Post	29.7	−4.0	20.8	−4.5
Frontline	28.4	(−0.2)	24.2	(1.9)
Anderson Cooper	24.2	(−2.3)	19.6	(−1.9)
CNN	22.4	4.1	13.0	(−1.0)
Washington Post	18.7	(−0.2)	12.6	(−0.1)
MSNBC	15.0	3.6	8.2	(0.1)
Any	30.4	(−1.4)	22.2	−2.4
Mainstream Sources				
60 Minutes	13.6	(−2.2)	13.4	(0.6)
NBC Nightly News	12.1	(0.5)	10.0	(0.5)
ABC World News Tonight	11.7	(0.9)	9.7	(1.1)
Dateline	11.5	(0.0)	9.3	(−0.7)

	Obama minus Romney (Average = 5.4°)		Democratic Party minus Republican Party (Average = 6.3°)	
	No Controls	Controls	No Controls	Controls
Meet the Press	11.2	(−2.7)	11.3	(1.0)
20/20	9.2	(−0.1)	8.8	(0.7)
Nightline	7.4	(0.0)	6.0	(−1.0)
CBS Evening News	6.6	(−1.8)	6.1	(−1.3)
Face the Nation	(5.0)	−4.0	8.4	(0.9)
USA Today	(−1.7)	(0.5)	(−1.7)	(1.0)
Any	14.6	(0.0)	12.0	(0.1)

Note: Coefficients not meeting the $p < .05$ level of statistical significance are in parentheses.

party's dominant conservative faction, the Republicans most sympathetic to the Tea Party eventually became the largest, most loyal, and most active component of his electoral coalition (Bradberry and Jacobson 2013).

MEDIA USE AND EXPECTATIONS ABOUT THE ELECTION OUTCOME

One of the oddities of the 2012 presidential election was the apparently sincere confidence expressed by the Romney camp and much of the conservative commentariat that most published polls were wrong and that Romney would emerge the winner on election day, according to some by a wide margin. Prominent conservatives who predicted a Romney victory included Newt Gingrich, Karl Rove, Michael Barone, George Will, Dick Morris, William Kristol, Glen Beck, Ann Coulter, Peggy Noonan, and Charles Krauthammer; Gingrich, Morris, Barone, Will, and Beck predicted Romney would get more than 300 electoral votes (Greenfield 2012). They were thus stunned when Obama outpolled Romney by nearly 5 million votes while winning a 332–206 electoral-college majority.

Ordinary Republicans had shared the partisan optimism permeating the conservative media; 70 percent of Republican voters in the ANES survey's pre-election wave predicted a Romney victory, 25 percent an Obama victory. In contrast, 90 percent of Democrats thought Obama would be reelected, with only 7 percent predicting a Romney victory.[15] It is normal for a far larger share of supporters than opponents to predict a candidate's victory, but expectations this divergent are unusual (Granberg and Brent 1983). Because predictions of a

[15] Five percent of Democrats and 7 percent of Republicans were unsure or thought someone else would win. A Gallup poll taken in late October 2012 got similar results; 71 percent of Republicans predicted a Romney victory (19 percent, Obama), and 86 percent of Democrats predicted an Obama victory (8 percent, Romney).

Romney victory were so prevalent in the conservative media – Krauthammer, Rove, Coulter, Noonan, Morris, and Gingrich had made or repeated their forecasts on various Fox News programs, among other venues – it is not surprising that their Republican audiences were persuaded by what they heard, insofar as they needed any persuading. Obama supporters could and did rely on liberal or mainstream sources that interpreted the polls as pointing to an Obama victory, most prominently in Nate Silver's widely cited FiveThirtyEight blog on the *New York Times* website, where his poll aggregation model, updated daily, had Obama ahead throughout the campaign. Not by much, however, and published surveys taken during the last month of the campaign gave Obama an average margin of less than one percentage point, with virtually all of the results indicating that the election was, statistically speaking, too close to call.[16] Considering the high level of uncertainty left by these polls, it is not surprising that voters resolved it in a manner consistent with their hopes. More to the point here, if partisan media messages are ever going to influence partisan beliefs about who will win, it should be when ambiguity is high and the desire for the preferred outcome is intense, as in 2012.

Figure 6 displays the incidence of predictions of a Romney victory according to the voter's pre-election presidential preference and net use of partisan media. Virtually everyone intending to vote for Obama thought he would win regardless of their attention to partisan media. Most of these voters

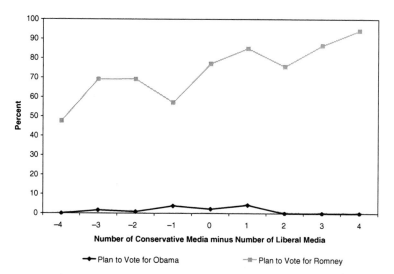

FIGURE 6. Media Use and Prediction that Romney Will Defeat Obama

---

[16] That is, either outcome fell within the 95 percent confidence interval; the average from 49 surveys taken by 20 polling firms between October 1 and the election gave Obama 50.4 percent of the two-party vote (based on data gathered from PollingReport.com and Pollster.com).

were of course Democrats (90 percent), but 90 percent of the small contingent of Republicans intending to vote for Obama, comprising 6 percent of the total, also thought he would win. Most voters planning to vote for Romney expected him to be elected, and the more so the more conservative the mix of media they used. These voters were mainly Republicans (87 percent); among Democrats planning to vote for Romney (5 percent of Romney's total), 67 percent thought he would win. In light of the Fox channel's role in spreading the news that prominent conservative pundits forecast a Romney victory, it is worth noting that Romney supporters' expectations of his victory rose monotonically with their level of attention to the five Fox News commentators on the list, from 72 percent if they tuned into none of them up to 92 percent if they tuned in to all five.[17]

Presidential preferences dominated expectations about who would win, but partisan media use remains a significant predictor of expectations when preferences and party identification are controlled. It also remains a significant predictor when a variable almost as potent as (and of course strongly related to) presidential preference is added: relative affect as measured by the difference in the candidate feeling thermometers (Table 7). Earlier research produced evidence that greater intensity of preferences strengthened the links between presidential preferences and predicted outcomes (Granberg and Brent 1983). This was certainly the case in 2012; the stronger the motive (as measured by relative candidate affect), the greater the inclination to motivated reasoning about the election outcome. The coefficient on media use shrinks when the thermometer difference variable is included, not

TABLE 7. *Logit Models of Prediction of a Romney Victory*

	Coefficient	Robust S.E.	Coefficient	Robust S.E.
Media use index (−4 to 4)	.26***	.05	.12*	.05
Party ID (7-point scale)	.23***	.05	.06	.06
Plan to vote for Romney	3.79***	.28	1.75***	.36
Obama-Romney thermometer difference			−2.78***	.36
Constant	4.11***	.20	2.45***	.29
Pseudo R^2	.54		.57	
Percent correctly predicted (Null = 64.3)	87.0		87.3	
Number of cases	3,568		3,568	

Note: The dependent variable is 1 if the respondent predicted a Romney victory, 0 otherwise; the thermometer difference has been divided by 100 to make the coefficient easier to read.
* $p < .05$;
*** $p < .001$.

[17] The percentages were 0: 72.0%; 1: 72.9%; 2: 81.0%; 3: 83.5%; 4: 88.3%; and 5: 91.5%.

surprisingly given the strong relationship between partisan media use and relative affect displayed in Figure 5. But partisan media use continues to contribute significantly to the popular divergence of opinion on who was going to win in 2012 even when powerful sources of motivated reasoning are taken into account.

PARTISAN MEDIA AND THE VOTE

One prominent manifestation of electoral polarization in 2012 was the record-high levels of partisan loyalty reported by voters in the presidential election. Neither candidate had any significant crossover appeal, and Obama's electoral coalition was more lopsidedly partisan than that of any previous winner in the entire ANES time series.[18] Still, party loyalty varied with the use of partisan media, as Figure 7 illustrates. In this chart, the sign on the media use scale is reversed for Democratic voters, so that the higher the number, the greater the voter's exposure to congenially biased media. The horizontal axis labels also display the proportion of partisan voters within each category, mainly to document how few are found at the lowest three points on this scale. Party loyalty clearly grows as the partisan media mix becomes more asymmetrically favorable to the respondent's party. The handful of voters below −1 on the scale

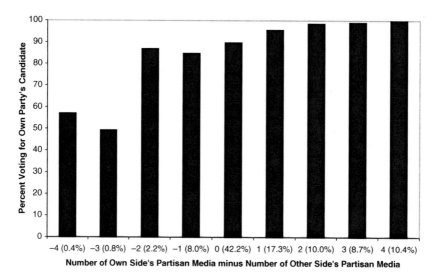

FIGURE 7. Partisan Media Use and Party Loyalty in the Presidential Election

[18] In the ANES face-to-face component, 89.9 percent reported voting for their party's nominee; both the National Exit Poll and the Cooperative Congressional Election Survey reported loyalty levels in excess of 93 percent (Jacobson 2013a); in the ANES data, 87.5 percent of Obama's electoral coalition consisted of Democratic identifiers; only 8 percent were Republicans.

are the least loyal (68 percent on average); above that level, party loyalty increases monotonically to reach 99.9 percent at 4 or more.

To consider once again whether this was merely a product of selective exposure, I estimated several logit models of the presidential vote that included the original net partisan media use index as an independent variable along with fourteen attitudinal and demographic variables that might be expected to influence the vote.[19] The first model omitted the Obama approval and candidate thermometer difference variables, which are so strongly predictive of the vote that they come close to measuring the same thing (presidential approval by itself accurately predicts 93.6 percent of reported votes, relative thermometer rating, 95.8 percent). The estimated coefficient on the partisan media use variable in the initial equation is −.35 (standard deviation, .08, $p < .001$); simulations suggest that, for example, among weak Democrats, the difference in probability of voting for Obama falls by −.40 across the full range of the scale, while the probability of a weak Republican voting for Romney rises by .41. When Obama approval is added to the equation, the coefficient shrinks to −.29 but is still statistically significant (standard deviation, .08, $p < .001$). However, when relative thermometer ratings are added the coefficient on partisan media use becomes notably smaller (−.17) and no more than marginally insignificant (standard deviation, .10, $p = .07$).[20]

These results suggest that, insofar as partisan media contributed independently to party-line voting in 2012, they did so mainly through their effect on how voters assessed the two candidates. As we saw from the analyses reported in Table 6, attention to conservative media evidently had the greater independent impact on candidate affect than attention to liberal or mainstream media. This is also true for the vote; if we replace the net partisan media use index with the two separate 0–4 scales for conservative and liberal media use, coefficients for conservative media are large and significant in the first two equations (−.55, standard deviation .12, $p < .001$ in the first, −.48, standard deviation, .12, $p < .001$ in the second). The coefficients for liberal media use are less than half as large but remain at or close to the standard level of significance (.20, standard deviation .10, $p = .047$ in the first equation, .18, standard deviation, .10, $p = .065$ in the second). Neither of the coefficients meet the $p < .05$ level of statistical significance when relative affect is taken into account in the third equation, although that for conservative media use remains the

---

[19] These variables included party identification, ideology, opinion of the Tea Party, the racial resentment scale, the egalitarianism scale, the traditional values scale, beliefs about Obama's birthplace and religion, race (black, Hispanic), age and age squared, gender, and religiosity. Coefficients for age, gender, and religiosity were not statistically significant in any of the models; for a complete description of these variables, see Bradberry and Jacobson (2013).

[20] The predictive accuracy of the equations rises from 93.2 percent to 95.5 percent and then to 96.6 percent with each additional independent variable.

larger of the two and comes close (–.28, standard deviation, .15, p = .063, compared to .09, standard deviation .12, p = .433, for liberal media use).

DISCUSSION

The evidence presented here suggests that partisan media did contribute independently to the record levels of partisan polarization in the electorate that ultimately gave Barack Obama his second term. Selective exposure was widespread, with partisans showing a clear preference for sources of news and opinion that reliably fit their biases, so it is no surprise that modal opinions, beliefs, and behaviors varied strongly with variations in the use of partisan media. Nonetheless, taking factors that determine the choice of media into account, exposure to partisan media continued to have a substantively and statistically significant effect on voters' responses to a variety of the survey questions examined.

The estimated effects of media source use varied across questions, and these variations also point to genuine media influence. For example, opinions of Obama, his ideological leanings, and the Affordable Care Act (and beliefs in the accompanying "death panel" myth) were all affected by attention to conservative media. Attacks on Obama, charges that he is a radical leftist or worse, and scathing attacks on his proposals for health care reform have been staples of conservative commentary almost since the day he took office (Jacobson 2011b). In contrast, specious notions about Obama's birthplace and religion, although popular among conservative media audiences, were not promoted by major conservative pundits. Some Fox News shows gave platforms to people questioning the authenticity of Obama's birth certificate, but none of the Fox hosts expressed doubts that Obama was a citizen; Bill O'Reilly even argued that birtherism helped Democrats aiming to marginalize Republicans "by painting them as nuts."[21] Fox News commentators also sometimes accused Obama of being overly sympathetic to Muslims, but none claimed he was one himself. Thus, when determinants of selective attention are controlled, attention to conservative sources had no discernable effect on beliefs that Obama is foreign born or a Muslim. On the other hand, liberal sources – including Matthews, Stewart, Colbert, Cooper, and the Huffington Post – gleefully ridiculed these notions and their proponents, and greater attention to liberal media significantly diminished the likelihood of accepting them.

The climate change question is also instructive here. Back in the 1990s, beliefs about global warming did not differ by party, but a partisan divide opened up after Al Gore raised the alarm, most prominently in his Academy

---

[21] *The O'Reilly Factor*, February 16, 2011, at http://www.youtube.com/watch?v=8rAqhdL1BUs. Accessed March 21, 2014.

Award–winning documentary, *An Inconvenient Truth*.[22] By 2012, skepticism or outright denial of human-induced climate change was modal if not universal on the right (Levin, Beck, Hannity, Limbaugh, Savage, O'Reilly, Ingraham, the *Wall Street Journal*'s op-ed pages, and Fox News are examples; Huckabee is something of an exception). Liberal and mainstream outlets, in contrast, treated global warming as established fact, and liberal pundits and programs (including Matthews, Stewart, Colbert, and Cooper, the Huffington Post, CNN, and PBS's *Frontline*) regularly skewered its deniers.[23] Thus, it is not surprising to find large residual effects of partisan media attention on beliefs about climate change (see Table 4) and that polarization on this issue was unusually high (see Table 5). In sum, the effects of partisan media use varied in ways that echoed variations in the emphasis of partisan messages and were most pronounced on issues where conservative and liberal media took clear and emphatic contrary positions.

As I cautioned at the outset, causality is difficult to demonstrate unambiguously in a cross-sectional study like the 2012 ANES. And of course a single study cannot show that the spread of partisan media has contributed to the growing partisan polarization of the American electorate over the last several decades. But results reported here do, I think, stand as strong circumstantial evidence that partisan media did contribute measurably to making 2012 the most partisan and polarizing election in at least sixty years.

Under current electoral configurations, party-line voting by a polarized electorate delivers a polarized, gridlocked national government. The high level of party-line voting was a net plus for Obama because the Democrats had a clear advantage among party identifiers in 2012,[24] and the distribution of partisans across the states also favored Democrats in the Electoral College.[25] In House elections, however, a comparable level of party-line voting produced a Republican majority because, mainly as a consequence of coalition demography, Republican voters are distributed more efficiently than Democratic voters across congressional districts, enabling Republicans to win a majority of seats (53.8 percent) with a minority of the major-party vote (49.3 percent; see Jacobson 2013b, for details).

The intense partisanship expressed in the 2012 election amplified intense partisan conflict in Washington because Obama and the House Republican

---

[22] In at 1997 Gallup Poll, 46 percent of Democrats and 47 percent of Republicans agreed that human beings were already warming up the planet; by the 2008 poll, the comparable division was Democrats, 76 percent Republicans, 41 percent.

[23] For these and all of the other assessments of outlets' positions in this section, I used numerous sources on the web that provided such information.

[24] Of 4.4 to 9.4 percentage points; see footnote 1.

[25] According to Gallup's calculation of party affiliation by state from their tracking poll, January–June 2012, Democrats outnumbered Republicans in 26 states (and the District of Columbia) with 334 electoral votes, Republicans outnumbered Democrats in 24 states with 204 electoral votes; data at http://www.gallup.com/poll/156437/Heavily-Democratic-States-Concentrated-East.aspx#2, accessed August 20, 2013.

majority owed their elections to thoroughly disjunctive coalitions with starkly opposed opinions and beliefs. After 2012, only 15 percent of House Republicans' electoral constituents (those who voted for the winning Republicans) also reported voting for Obama; this is the smallest proportion of voters shared by the president and members of the rival party in any Congress on record (the record going back to 1952).[26] The House Republicans' electoral constituents gave Obama the lowest thermometer ratings from the opposing congressional party's coalition ever recorded for a president. More than 86 percent disapproved of his performance, 74 percent strongly. More than 40 percent said he was foreign born or a Muslim, and a majority (54 percent) viewed him as an extreme liberal. They were overwhelmingly opposed to the Affordable Care Act and stricter gun control. The ideological distance between the president's and the opposing congressional party's electoral coalitions has also reached a peak during Obama's administration.[27] No wonder, then, that Obama's reelection only intensified Republican intransigence and tightened legislative gridlock.

REFERENCES

Abramowitz, Alan I. 2010. *The Disappearing Center: Engaged Citizens, Polarization, and American Democracy.* New Haven, CT: Yale University Press.

American National Election Study. 2013. User's Guide and Codebook for the Preliminary Release of the ANES 2012 Time Series Study. Ann Arbor, MI, and Palo Alto, CA: the University of Michigan and Stanford University.

Arceneaux, Kevin, and Martin Johnson. 2013. *Changing Minds or Changing Channels? Partisan News in an Age of Choice.* Chicago: University of Chicago Press.

Baumer, Donald C., and Howard J. Gold. 2010. *Parties, Polarization, and Democracy in the United States.* Boulder, CO: Paradigm Publishers.

Bishop, Bill. 2008. *The Big Sort: Why the Clustering of Like-Minded Americans Is Tearing Us Apart.* Boston: Houghton Mifflin.

Bradberry, Leigh, and Gary C. Jacobson. 2013. "Does the Tea Party Still Matter? Tea Party Influence in the 2012 Elections." Presented at the Annual Meeting of the American Political Science Association, Chicago, August 29–September 1.

Fiorina, Morris P., with Samuel Adams. 2009. *Disconnect: The Breakdown of Representation in American Politics.* Norman: University of Oklahoma Press.

Fiorina, Morris P., Samuel J. Adams, and Jeremy C. Pope. 2006. *Culture War? The Myth of a Polarized America.* New York: Longman.

Gaines, Brian J., James H. Kuklinski, Paul J. Quirk, Buddy Peyton, and Jan Verkuilen. 2007. "Same Facts, Different Interpretation: Partisan Motivation and Opinion on Iraq," *Journal of Politics* 69 (4): 957–974.

Granberg, Donald, and Edward Brent. 1983. "When Prophecy Bends: The Preference-Expectation Link in U.S. Presidential Elections, 1952–1980," *Journal of Personality and Social Psychology* 45 (3): 477–491.

---

[26] Among Republican Senate electoral constituents, the overlap was even lower: 10 percent, the lowest on record.

[27] Measured by mean locations on the seven-point liberal-conservative scale.

Greenfield, Rebecca. 2012. "How Pundits Are Explaining Their Totally Wrong Election Predictions," *The Atlantic Wire*, November 7. Retrieved from http://www.theatlanticwire.com/politics/2012/11/how-pundits-are-explaining-their-totally-wrong-election-predictions/58796/. Accessed August 19, 2013.

Hare, Christopher, Keith T. Poole, and Howard Rosenthal. 2013. "An Update on the Presidential Square Wave," *Voteview Blog*, January 18. Retrieved from http://voteview.com/blog/?p=735. Accessed July 8, 2013.

Hetherington, Marc J., and Jonathan D. Weiler. 2009. *Authoritarianism and Polarization in American Politics*. New York: Cambridge University Press.

Iyengar, Shanto, and Kju S. Hahn. 2009. "Red Media, Blue Media: Evidence of Ideological Selectivity in Media Use," *Journal of Communication* 59 (1): 19–39.

Jacobson, Gary C. 2013a. "Barack Obama and the Nationalization of Electoral Politics in 2012." Presented at the Conference on the Confirming U.S. Presidential Election of 2012, Mershon Center, the Ohio State University, October 10–11.

Jacobson, Gary C. 2013b. "Partisan Polarization in American Politics: A Background Paper," *Presidential Studies Quarterly* 43 (December): 688–708.

Jacobson, Gary C. 2011a. *A Divider, Not a Uniter: George W. Bush and the American People*, 2nd edition. New York: Pearson Longman.

Jacobson, Gary C. 2011b. "Polarization, Public Opinion, and the Presidency: The Obama and Anti-Obama Coalitions." In Bert A. Rockman and Andrew Rudalevige, eds., *The Obama Presidency: Appraisals and Prospects*. Washington, DC: CQ Press, 94–122.

Jacobson, Gary C. 2010. "Perception, Memory, and Partisan Polarization on the Iraq War," *Political Science Quarterly* 125 (Spring): 1–26.

Jamieson, Kathleen Hall, and Joseph N. Cappella. 2008. *Echo Chamber: Rush Limbaugh and the Conservative Media Establishment*. New York: Oxford University Press.

Jones. David. 2002. "The Polarizing Effects of New Media Messages," *International Journal of Public Opinion Research* 14 (2): 158–174.

Kull, Steven, Clam Ramsay, and Evan Lewis. 2003. "Misperceptions, the Media, and the Iraq War." *Political Science Quarterly* 118 (Winter): 563–598.

Kunda, Ziva. 1990. "The Case for Motivated Reasoning," *Psychological Bulletin* 108 (3): 636–647.

Levendusky, Matthew. 2013. *How Partisan Media Polarize America*. Chicago: University of Chicago Press.

Levendusky, Matthew. 2009. *The Partisan Sort: How Liberals Became Democrats and Conservatives Became Republicans*. Chicago: University of Chicago Press.

Lodge, Milton, and Charles S. Taber. 2001. "Three Steps Toward a Theory of Motivated Political Reasoning." In Arthur Lupia, Mathew D. McCubbins, and Samuel L. Popkin, eds., *Elements of Reason: Cognition, Choice, and the Bounds of Rationality*. New York: Cambridge University Press.

Morales, Lymani. 2012. "U.S. Distrust in Media Hits New High." Retrieved from http://www.gallup.com/poll/157589/distrust-media-hits-new-high.aspx, September 12.

Mutz, Diana C. 2006. *Hearing the Other Side: Deliberative Versus Participatory Democracy*. New York: Cambridge University Press.

Prior, Markus. 2007. *Post-Broadcast Democracy: How Media Choice Increases Inequality in Political Involvement and Polarizes Elections*. New York: Cambridge University Press.

Stroud, Natalie Jomini. 2011. _Niche News: The Politics of News Choice._ New York: Oxford University press.

Tabor, Charles S., and Milton Lodge. 2006. "Motivated Skepticism in Evaluation of Political Beliefs," _American Journal of Political Science_ 50 (3): 755–769.

13

News as a Casualty

District Polarization and Media Coverage of U.S. House Campaigns

Danny Hayes and Jennifer L. Lawless

Although scholars have noted a variety of consequences of polarization – from legislative gridlock to a decline in political comity to increasingly negative views of government – virtually no work has considered district polarization's effects on local political news coverage. Using an original, detailed content analysis of local newspaper coverage from every congressional district during the 2010 midterms, we examine how district polarization shapes media coverage of U.S. House races. The data reveal that:

- District polarization affects the competitive context of House campaigns. Lopsided districts – those safe for one party – are less likely than more evenly split districts to see competitive contests.
- Competitiveness then influences the attention congressional races receive from the news media. Districts that are lopsided see less coverage than more evenly split districts do.
- Competitiveness also affects the substance of local news coverage in U.S. House campaigns. The more competitive the race is, the more substantive coverage there is. This is true whether we examine the number of stories that mention both candidates, the number of issue mentions across the campaign's coverage, or the number times the candidates' personal traits are discussed in the coverage.

By linking polarization to competitiveness, and competitiveness to news coverage, we show that polarization impoverishes the news environment. These findings are consequential because a growing body of research suggests that a diminished news environment can depress citizens' political knowledge and engagement.

INTRODUCTION

When Carol Shea-Porter and Frank Guinta took the debate stage at Saint Anselm College on a mid-October day in 2010, most voters in New Hampshire's 1st

Congressional District already knew where the two candidates stood. Shea-Porter, the two-term Democratic incumbent vying to keep her seat, surprised no one in the audience when she blamed the Bush administration for the struggling national economy and persistent federal budget deficits. She was just repeating a central theme in her months-long campaign. "The reality is that when the Republicans came into power," she said, "we were running a surplus." And when Guinta lambasted Shea-Porter's support for the 2009 stimulus package that had promoted only anemic job growth in New Hampshire as "not effective management of money," debate watchers could have guessed his next line. The Republican former mayor of Manchester had been making the same argument since he entered the race. "When," he asked Shea-Porter, "are you going to start taking responsibility for the four years you've been in Congress?"[1]

By the time of the debate – just three weeks before the November election that would see Guinta defeat Shea-Porter and take her seat – 1st District voters had been exposed to a deluge of coverage of the race. In just the last month of the campaign, the *New Hampshire Union-Leader* published 43 stories discussing the contest, an average of more than one per day. And this wasn't merely the kind of vacuous horse race coverage that scholars and political observers often deride. An attentive reader would have seen 122 mentions of the candidates' positions on issues from health care to the economy to national security. Those articles also included 58 references to Guinta and Shea-Porter's personal attributes, such as their integrity and leadership abilities. In short, voters would have gone to the polls with a wealth of knowledge about their choices on election day.

Three thousand miles away, in California's 31st District, the story could hardly have been more different. Had residents of Democratic Representative Xavier Becerra's district been curious about their congressman's contest against Republican Stephen C. Smith, they would have been hard-pressed to find anything about it in the local media. The race – which Becerra went on to win – received virtually no coverage. One story in the *Los Angeles Times* mentioned Becerra briefly, but provided no serious discussion of his campaign or Smith's arguments about why Becerra shouldn't be returned to Capitol Hill. Especially diligent citizens might have visited the candidates' websites, where they could have read up on Becerra's record in Congress and where Smith, an electronics salesperson, discussed his qualifications: "I have listened to and filled the electronic needs of every type of person who lives in The City of the Angels."[2] But otherwise, little information was available.

---

[1] Jake Berry, "1st Congressional District Debate Has Candidates Disagreeing from Start to End," *The Telegraph*, October 13, 2010. Retrieved from http://www.nashuatelegraph.com/news /879225-227/1st-congressional-debate-has-candidates-disagreeing-from.html. Accessed on July 21, 2014.

[2] An archive of Smith's 2010 website is available at http://digital.library.ucla.edu/websites /2010_995_089/index.php%5Ep=1_7_Biography-and-History.htm. Accessed on July 24, 2014.

Considering the competitive landscape of the two districts, this is hardly a surprise. New Hampshire's 1st District was closely split along partisan lines, a district where in 2008 Barack Obama eked out a narrow victory over John McCain with 54 .percent of the vote. The contest between Shea-Porter and Guinta was rated a "toss-up" by the *Cook Political Report*, reflecting the presence of two experienced candidates who collectively spent more than $3 million on the race.[3] Meanwhile, California's 31st District was a Democratic bastion, giving 82 percent of the 2008 vote to Obama and leaving it essentially abandoned by Republicans during the 2010 midterms. Smith was a sacrificial lamb who spent only $14,000 in his quixotic campaign to defeat Becerra, a prominent incumbent seeking his tenth term in office. In New Hampshire, reporters had plenty to cover. In California, not so much.

This pattern would be of little concern if most congressional districts in the country looked like the New Hampshire 1st. But since the end of World War II, more and more U.S. House seats look like California's 31st. The vast majority of congressional districts have become safe for one party; incumbent reelection rates have increased, and district polarization has rendered the outcomes of most contests predictable before the campaign even begins. This change is evident in the number of close House elections. In the congressional elections of the 1950s, 39 percent of seats each cycle on average were decided by 20 points or less. By the 1970s, that figure was down to 24 percent. And after a slight uptick in the 1990s, it had fallen even further by the 2000s.[4] The number of Americans living in competitive House districts has shrunk to a small minority.

While scholars have noted a variety of consequences of polarization – from legislative gridlock (Binder 2003; Theriault 2008) to a decline in political comity (Jamieson and Falk 2000; Iyengar, Sood, and Lelkes 2012) to increasingly negative views of government (Nye, Zelikow, and King 1997; Keele 2005; Bafumi and Herron 2010) – virtually no work has considered district polarization's effects on local political news coverage. But to the extent that the media's propensity to cover House elections depends on the presence of competitive contests, then the proliferation of polarization and the decline of truly marginal districts should affect the information environment in which citizens operate. And an erosion of media coverage of congressional elections could have important consequences. After all, when citizens are exposed to news coverage about politics, they are not only more likely to know about their representatives, communities, and issues facing the nation (e.g., Chaffee, Zhao, and Leshner 1994; Delli Carpini and Keeter 1996; deVreese and Boomgaarden 2006; Jerit, Barabas, and Bolsen 2006), but they

---

[3] The two just couldn't quit each other. In a 2012 rematch, Shea-Porter would defeat Guinta to regain the seat. In 2014, Guinta would again claim victory.

[4] We calculated these figures from Gary Jacobson's widely used data on congressional elections. Other measures (e.g., Abramowitz, Alexander, and Gunning 2006: 76) show a similar trend (see also Mayhew 1974; Cox and Katz 1996).

are also more likely to participate (e.g., Eveland and Scheufele 2000; Tolbert and McNeal 2003; Hayes and Lawless 2015). If polarization diminishes the news environment by making more and more congressional districts uncompetitive, then the foundation of democracy – citizen engagement – may be imperiled.

In this chapter, we examine how district polarization shapes media coverage of U.S. House races. Using an original, detailed content analysis of local newspaper coverage from every congressional district during the 2010 midterms, we demonstrate that district polarization affects the competitive context of House campaigns. We then show that levels of competitiveness influence the attention congressional races receive from the news media. Ultimately, by linking polarization to competitiveness, and competitiveness to news coverage, we make a strong – and until now, overlooked – case that polarization impoverishes the news environment. It is not just legislative productivity or a spirit of political cooperation that is threatened by polarization. Local news is a casualty too.

POLARIZATION AND THE MEDIA: WHAT WE KNOW AND WHAT WE DON'T KNOW

With the rise of cable television and the Internet, Americans' options for political news have expanded dramatically – and that adverb may well be an understatement. One of the most important consequences of the proliferation of outlets has been the emergence of news organizations devoted to advocating ideological positions and repeating partisan talking points, a development that has reshaped the kind of information to which citizens have ready access. Whereas Walter Cronkite, David Brinkley, and their broadcast news counterparts were once the face of the American media, they have been replaced by a new generation of partisan and sharp-elbowed media personalities: Bill O'Reilly, Sean Hannity, Rachel Maddow, Lawrence O'Donnell.

This change has spawned a large body of work that explores the consequences of a more partisan and polarized news environment for political attitudes and behavior (see Prior 2013 for a review). One line of research focuses on the extent to which citizens engage in selective exposure, consuming news from outlets that confirm their political beliefs and eschewing sources that challenge them. Both experimental and observational data suggest that people do indeed have a preference for ideologically friendly news (Iyengar et al. 2008; Iyengar and Hahn 2009; Stroud 2011), although the magnitude of these selection effects is open to debate (Gentzkow and Shapiro 2011; Prior 2013). A second line of work examines whether exposure to partisan news polarizes the public – that is, whether it moves the attitudes of Democrats and Republicans, for instance, farther apart. While there is little doubt that exposure to "like-minded" programming can reinforce political beliefs and, in some cases, promote attitude extremity (e.g., Jamieson and

Cappella 2008; Levendusky 2013), it remains unclear how widespread such effects are. Because relatively few people actually tune in to cable news programs, there is limited potential for polarization (Arceneaux and Johnson 2013). Changes to the media environment may be contributing to mass polarization, but so far the size of that contribution is modest at best.

As this brief review makes clear, the research that examines media and polarization tends to focus on how polarized media affect the public's attitudes, not whether polarization itself may be reshaping the media environment. Moreover, the focus of the existing literature has been almost entirely on national news; political communication scholars have largely ignored the relationship between polarization and the volume and content of local political news. Yet, as a practical matter, polarization is most evident at the district level, and it is on local news that voters still rely most for information about local political campaigns. Theoretically, there are good reasons to expect that the rise in district polarization – an increasing number of seats becoming safe for one party – should affect the availability of information about U.S. House races in local media outlets.

HOW POLARIZATION SHOULD AFFECT MEDIA
COVERAGE OF HOUSE ELECTIONS

Districts that are closely split in terms of partisanship, such as New Hampshire's 1st District, are considered winnable by both the Democrats and the Republicans. In such locales, the parties can recruit well-qualified candidates to run against incumbents. Ambitious, strategic politicians, after all, are most likely to run in districts where they believe they have a good chance of winning (Black 1972; Jacobson and Kernell 1983; Stone and Maisel 2003; Maestas et al. 2006; Lawless 2012). In lopsided districts where one party is dominant, such as California's 31st District, it is far less likely that experienced out-party candidates will emerge. (Those are the kinds of districts where you get electronics salespeople.) This dynamic is critical because the emergence of quality candidates can have a profound effect on the competitiveness of House races (Jacobson 1989). Quality candidates are more likely to be able to raise large amounts of money, hire professional campaign staff, and build a campaign infrastructure. In short, closely split districts with two well-heeled candidates breed competitive, active campaigns.

The relationship between polarization and electoral competitiveness is important because competitiveness strongly affects the calculus for journalists and, therefore, carries profound consequences for the quality of local news coverage. Because close elections have uncertain outcomes, they generate more drama and are inherently more newsworthy (e.g., Graber 2010; Bennett 2011). In addition, competitive races produce more campaign activity (and more conflict between candidates), so they offer more campaign-trail developments for reporters to cover (e.g., Bruni 2002; Dunaway and Stein

2013). Indeed, numerous studies have found a strong relationship between competitiveness and news attention (Clark and Evans 1983; Goldenberg and Traugott 1984; Kahn and Kenney 1999; Vinson 2003; Arnold 2004; Gershon 2012). And because competition leads to more coverage, competitive contests also produce reporting about candidates' issue positions (Westlye 1991; Kahn and Kenney 1999; though see Hayes 2010). Competitiveness, then, tends to breed a news environment that more closely approximates democratic ideals. The corollary, of course, is that when races are not competitive, the news media tend to ignore them. Less electoral competition produces an information environment with less volume and substance. Thus, we expect district polarization to have an indirect effect on news coverage of House races by shaping the competitive context in which those contests take place.

As straightforward as these propositions might sound, they are based on very little empirical evidence. Over the course of the last 40 years, only a dozen studies have investigated news coverage in U.S. House elections (Manheim 1974; Clarke and Evans 1983; Tidmarch and Karp 1983; Goldenberg and Traugott 1984; Orman 1985; Vermeer 1987; Larson 1992; Vinson 2003; Arnold 2004; Gershon 2012, 2013; Fogarty 2013). And most of this research is quite limited in scope. None of the studies analyzes coverage in more than 100 districts, and some focus on just one (Orman 1985; Larson 1992). Many can say little about House coverage specifically because the analyses combine House and Senate races. Still others restrict their inquiries to specific types of candidates and contests by focusing only on incumbents, contested races, or members implicated in scandals (e.g., Fogarty 2013). This has left us with an incomplete understanding of the conditions under which journalists will be more or less likely to cover House races, which is central to developing a fuller understanding of the consequences of district polarization.

RESEARCH DESIGN AND DATA SET

To study the relationship between polarization and local news coverage of U.S. House campaigns, we rely on three sets of data. First, we conducted an unusually detailed content analysis of the general election coverage in all House districts during the 2010 midterm elections. In each of the 435 congressional districts across the country, we identified the largest circulation local newspaper that we could access through one of several electronic databases or the newspaper's online archives. We focus on local newspapers because most of the information available to voters during congressional election campaigns comes from local print media (Vinson 2003; Graber and Dunaway 2014). In addition, local print coverage has been found to affect voter attitudes toward members of Congress, but local television has not (Schaffner 2006).[5] After identifying the

[5] We do not analyze national newspapers, cable television, blogs, or social media because there is very little coverage of individual congressional campaigns in outlets such as the *New York Times* and Fox News, and the audiences for political information in many newer venues remain very

appropriate newspaper in each district, we collected every article that mentioned at least one of the two major-party candidates for the House seat and analyzed the content of the coverage in the month leading up to election day (October 2–November 2, 2010).

We focus on four measures that allow us to assess the volume and substance of political coverage: (1) the number of articles published about each House race, (2) the share of stories that mentioned both candidates (in contested races), (3) the number of mentions of issues in news coverage, and (4) the number of mentions of candidates' traits. We assume that more coverage, coverage that provides information about both candidates, and coverage that includes attention to issues and the candidates' personal attributes (as opposed to topics such as fundraising, campaign strategy, or the horse race) are likely to give voters more useful information about their electoral choices, and promote knowledge and participation. In all, we coded 6,003 news stories, editorials, and op-ed columns. (See the Appendix for details about the newspapers included in the content analysis, as well as the issues and traits we coded.)

Second, we collected data that allow us to gauge both the level of polarization in a district and the competitiveness of its House race. To measure district polarization, we rely on the percentage of the vote in each congressional district that Barack Obama and John McCain received during the 2008 presidential election. Because the presidential vote closely reflects district partisanship, districts in which Obama or McCain won by a small margin are far more likely to generate competitive House contests than are districts where one candidate won in a landslide. Thus, our measure of polarization is the presidential election margin of victory in percentage points. In other words, by how many points did the winner take the district? A district where Obama beat McCain by six points has the same "polarization score" as a district where McCain defeated Obama by the same margin. To gauge the competitive context of the race in each district, we rely on three measures. The *Cook Political Report* classifies House races on a four-category scale: safe for one party, likely to be won by one party, leaning toward one party, or toss-up. We collected the Cook Report rating for each district as of October 5, 2010. We also collected data on whether the race featured a "quality challenger" (someone with previous office-holding experience), as well as the total amount of money the candidates (combined) spent on the race.[6]

small. For instance, blog readers constitute just a fraction of the public (Lawrence, Sides, and Farrell 2010), fewer than one in five Americans are on Twitter (Smith and Brenner 2012), and just 9 percent of consumers in 2010 said they regularly got news from a social networking site (Rainie and Smith 2012). Although Facebook and Twitter are growing in importance for both candidates and news consumers, they do not yet constitute a significant source of political information for most Americans. Despite changes to the media environment, local newspaper coverage remains the most thorough and influential political news source during House campaigns, which is why we train our focus there.

[6] For simplicity, our use of the term "quality challenger" encompasses open-seat candidates who have held previous electoral office, even though these individuals are not challenging incumbents.

Third, we collected contextual information about each congressional district and the newspaper that serves it. We tracked the district's median income, percentage of college graduates, racial composition, and "market convergence," which is the level of overlap between a district and a media market.[7] Previous work has identified these as potential influences on news content (Schaffner and Sellers 2003; Arnold 2004; Cohen, Noel, and Zaller 2004; Napoli and Yan 2007; Dunaway 2008). By accounting for these attributes, we can be confident that any polarization or competitiveness effects we uncover are not an artifact of other district or newspaper characteristics.

RESULTS: DISTRICT POLARIZATION, ELECTORAL COMPETITIVENESS, AND LOCAL NEWS COVERAGE

Perhaps the best place to begin the analysis is with a summary of the landscape of local newspaper coverage in the 2010 midterm elections. In terms of the volume of coverage, the average number of stories per race was 14.4, which is about one article every other day in the month leading up to the election. In districts with contested races, an average of 44.5 percent of stories mentioned both candidates. The average number of issue mentions over a month's worth of campaign coverage was 48.6, and the average number of trait mentions was 6.4.

If district polarization is related to the volume and content of local news, then we should see a lower volume of coverage and less attention to candidates' issue positions and personal traits in lopsided districts than in more evenly split ones. That is exactly what we find. Figure 1 presents the bivariate relationships between district polarization and the number of stories written about the race, the percentage of articles mentioning both candidates, and the total number of times issues and traits were mentioned in the coverage. The upper left panel of the figure, for example, shows that the districts where Obama or McCain saw the largest margins of victory in 2008 were the districts that were least likely to garner House race coverage in 2010. Whereas more evenly split districts (those that delivered no more than a five-point victory to Obama or McCain) saw an average of 17.2 stories written about the 2010 House race, lopsided districts (where the presidential race was decided by at least a 20-point margin) saw on average only about 7.8 stories.

The same pattern emerges when we turn to the number of stories that mentioned both candidates, and the total number of times issues and traits were mentioned in relation to the candidates. In the most closely split districts, 55.8 percent of stories mentioned both candidates. As for the substance of the coverage, these evenly split districts saw on average 64.2 mentions of issues and

We thank Gary Jacobson for providing the candidate quality and campaign spending data. We also coded whether the race in each district was contested and whether there was an open seat, since both of these measures reflect the extent to which the electoral context is competitive.

[7] We thank Hans Noel for the media market data.

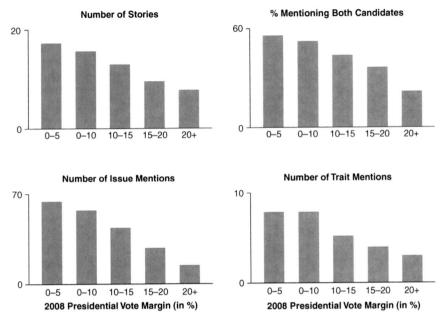

FIGURE 1. District Polarization and Campaign News Coverage
Note: News data come from a content analysis of local newspaper campaign coverage (6,003 stories overall) in all 435 House districts from October 2–November 2, 2010. Data for percentage of stories mentioning both candidates include only contested districts.

7.9 references to the candidates' traits. On the other hand, in the most lopsided districts, just 21.9 percent of stories referenced both candidates, and throughout a month's worth of coverage, there were on average only 14.3 issue mentions and a meager three references to candidate traits. Regardless of the measure we use, a district where Obama or McCain won narrowly saw more than twice as much – and far more substantive – coverage of the 2010 House race than a district where the presidential contest was a landslide. This leaves little doubt that polarization is closely connected to House campaign coverage.

By moving into a multivariate context, we can provide a more refined assessment of the relationship between district polarization and the information environment in House races. Here, we account for some basic features of the race, such as whether it is for an open seat and whether it is contested, as well as the demographics of the district and overlap between the district and its media market. Table 1 presents four OLS regression models, each of which predicts a measure of coverage in the House race. In each equation, the coefficient on the 2008 presidential vote margin is negative and significant. This means that as the margin of victory increases – indicating that the district is more lopsided – the volume and substance of House race coverage

TABLE 1. *The Relationship between District Polarization and the Volume and Substance of Newspaper Coverage in House Elections, 2010*

	Number of Stories	Both Candidates Mentioned	Number of Issue Mentions	Number of Trait Mentions
District Polarization				
2008 presidential vote margin	−0.25 *	−0.83 *	−1.19 *	−.014 *
	(0.06)	(0.15)	(0.27)	(0.04)
District and Newspaper Features				
Open seat	0.81	16.62 *	8.87	1.83
	(2.33)	(4.14)	(13.01)	(1.79)
Uncontested	−5.63 *	−	−28.66 *	−4.73 *
	(1.45)		(4.69)	(0.94)
Percent white	0.07	0.25 *	0.45 *	0.02
	(0.39)	(0.09)	(0.14)	(0.03)
Median income	−0.81	−1.61	−3.05	−0.46
	(0.67)	(1.51)	(3.04)	(0.45)
College educated(%)	0.17	−0.14	0.79	0.18 *
	(0.11)	(0.29)	(0.46)	(0.08)
Market convergence	8.19	33.52 *	39.23	6.93
	(7.45)	(13.45)	(27.83)	(5.13)
Constant	10.71 *	41.67 *	39.23	3.56
	(4.39)	(8.95)	(27.83)	(2.59)
R^2	0.09	0.23	0.13	0.06
N	435	380	435	435

Notes: Cell entries are OLS regression coefficients. Robust standard errors clustered on newspaper are in parentheses. For the "Both Candidates Mentioned" equation, we restrict the analysis to contested races. Levels of significance: * $p < .05$.

decreases. For instance, controlling for other factors, an eight-point increase in the presidential vote margin reduces by two the number of stories published about the congressional race. Given that the average number of stories in a district is 14, a decline of about 14 percent is not insubstantial. The multivariate results, in other words, confirm the bivariate relationships presented in Figure 1. Voters in more evenly split districts have access to more local newspaper coverage of their House races, and to coverage that is more likely to inform them about both candidates and the candidates' issue positions and personal traits.

As we discussed earlier, though, we do not expect polarization, in and of itself, to affect journalists' assessments of what is newsworthy in a congressional race. That is, the margin by which Obama or McCain won a district in 2008 should not directly influence the volume or substance of newspaper coverage about the 2010 midterms. Rather, because lopsided districts tilt heavily in favor of one of the two parties, the congressional races in those districts should be less competitive and, accordingly, less newsworthy to the journalists covering them. The competitive context of the race – a function of district polarization – is the mechanism that should drive down coverage.

In order to determine whether this is the case, we turn once again to a series of bivariate relationships – this time, between district polarization and the features of a congressional race that reflect its competitiveness: the Cook Report rating, the total amount of campaign spending, and whether the race includes a quality challenger. The data displayed in Figure 2 support our expectations, and the inverse relationships between polarization and competitiveness are striking. The leftmost panel of the figure plots the percentage of races that the Cook Report classified as toss-up or leaning against the 2008 presidential election vote margin in the district. Nearly 40 percent of the districts that Obama or McCain won by no more than five points saw competitive House races in 2010. Compare that to the only 2.5 percent of competitive House races in districts that McCain or Obama swept by at least 20 points. The relationship is similarly robust and monotonic when we consider average campaign spending in a district and the presence of a quality candidate. The most competitive districts saw nearly $3 million in spending, whereas the least competitive saw less than half that. And although 42.7 percent of the most closely split districts had a race with a candidate who previously held elective office, that was true in just 5 percent of landslide districts.

Although these cross-tabulations are suggestive, we can use regression analysis to gain a better handle on whether the competitive context of the House race, as opposed to district polarization itself, affects news coverage. We supplemented the four regression equations we presented in Table 1 with our three measures of competitiveness. Table 2 presents the four fully specified models. In three of the four models, the 2008 presidential vote margin is no longer statistically significant. Once we account for the Cook Report rating, campaign spending, and the presence of a quality challenger, district polarization does not exert a direct effect on the volume or substance of local news coverage. But the gauges of competitiveness do.

Consider the effects of the Cook Report rating. Congressional races rated toss-up saw an average of 26 stories, districts rated leaning saw 23, and districts rated likely to go for one party received on average 20 stories. But in the 72 percent of districts rated as safe for one party – districts that are very lopsided – the average number of news stories was just 10. Indeed, in every model, the more competitive the race is, the more coverage (or substantive coverage) there is. This is true whether we examine the total number of stories published about a race, the number of stories that mention both candidates, the number of issue mentions across the campaign's coverage, or the number of times the

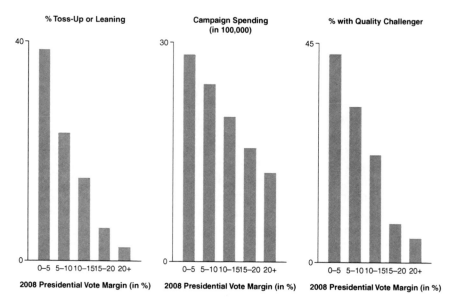

FIGURE 2. District Polarization and the Campaign Context of the 2010 Midterms
Note: Competitiveness data are from the *Cook Political Report*, as of October 5, 2010.

candidates' personal traits are discussed in the coverage. All are indicators of an information environment that could help inform citizens' choices, and all are strongly related to the competitiveness of the House race, controlling for a host of other factors that might also plausibly be related to media attention. Campaign spending has slightly weaker effects than competitiveness, but it is significant in every model as well. The presence of a quality challenger does not exert as strong or consistent an effect, but that variable still affects the overall volume of coverage.

Only in the model for the percentage of stories mentioning both candidates does the 2008 presidential vote margin remain significant. It is not entirely clear why polarization would exert an independent effect here, and not for the other measures of coverage. But even here, two results underscore the importance of campaign context as a mediator of polarization's effect on news coverage. First, the size of the coefficient on presidential vote margin (−0.42) is far smaller than it was in Table 1 (−0.83). The inclusion of the campaign measures reduced its effect by half. Second, the fact that the indicators of campaign activity behave similarly as they do in the models predicting volume of coverage and issue and trait mentions show that journalists appear to be responding primarily to the competitive context of the race.

In sum, the results – which emerge from more than 6,000 articles and hundreds of local newspapers, House races, and candidates – are clear: the

TABLE 2. *The Relationship between Campaign Context and the Volume and Substance of Newspaper Coverage in House Elections, 2010*

	Number of Stories	Both Candidates Mentioned	Number of Issue Mentions	Number of Trait Mentions
District Polarization				
2008 presidential vote margin	−0.03 (0.06)	−0.42 * (0.16)	−0.23 (0.25)	−0.01 (0.04)
Competitive Context				
Cook Report rating	3.20 * (1.03)	7.96 * (1.48)	17.63 * (4.75)	2.27 * (1.02)
Campaign spending	0.15 * (0.05)	0.17 ^ (0.10)	0.52 * (0.23)	0.09 ^ (0.05)
Quality candidate	4.27 * (1.97)	−0.42 (3.48)	10.29 (8.56)	2.58 (1.67)
District and Newspaper Features				
Open seat	−2.13 (2.12)	14.67 (4.14)	−1.02 (11.23)	−0.04 (1.89)
Uncontested	−2.10 (1.49)	−	14.09 * (4.51)	2.41 * (0.85)
Percent white	0.46 (0.03)	0.23 * (0.09)	0.35 * (0.12)	0.01 (0.03)
Median income	−0.38 (0.60)	−0.73 (1.44)	−0.89 (2.78)	−0.16 (0.41)
College educated(%)	0.14 (0.11)	−0.17 (0.29)	0.66 (0.44)	0.16 * (0.08)
Market convergence	8.09 (6.92)	34.02 * (11.80)	40.14 (25.71)	6.90 (4.55)
Constant	2.09 (4.06)	25.43 * (9.09)	18.60 (12.77)	−2.17 (2.32)
R^2	0.29	0.34	0.30	0.20
N	435	380	435	435

Notes: Cell entries are OLS regression coefficients. Robust standard errors clustered on newspaper are in parentheses. For the "Both Candidates Mentioned" equation, we restrict the analysis to contested races. Levels of significance: $*p < .05$; $^ p < .10$.

competitive context of a district is a central driver of election coverage. This is the case across a variety of measures of news content. Because lopsided districts are less likely than more evenly split districts to see competitive contests, district polarization contributes indirectly to the richness – or, more to the point, the poverty – of the information environment of U.S. House races.

CONCLUSION

Given the large body of research devoted to the effects of district polarization, it is surprising that the relationship between polarization and news coverage in congressional elections has been largely overlooked. But as the results presented in this chapter now make clear, polarization does more than hinder Congress's ability to pass legislation or generate ill will between partisans in the public. By shaping the competitive context of congressional districts, polarization influences the information environment during House campaigns. Lopsided districts receive less, and less substantive, coverage than more evenly split ones.

These findings are consequential because a growing body of research suggests that a diminished news environment can depress political knowledge and engagement. Consider, for example, the effects of recent newspaper closures on political participation. Although the *Cincinnati Post* had a daily circulation of less than 30,000 when it folded in 2007, in subsequent elections relatively fewer people went to the polls in the places where the *Post* served as the main newspaper (Schulhofer-Wohl and Garrido 2011). When newspapers closed in Seattle and Denver between 2008 and 2009, citizens' political engagement dropped more in those two cities than in other major cities that did not lose a newspaper (Shaker 2014). Of course, the effects of a reduction in local political news can emerge even when a newspaper does not close. Citizens in districts with less campaign coverage are less able to evaluate their incumbent and not as capable of making ideological judgments about the candidates vying for office (Hayes and Lawless 2015). By making it more difficult for citizens to gain the information that would help them hold their local officials accountable, district polarization chips away at the foundation of electoral democracy.

Given the trends in contemporary American politics, there is no reason to expect that a renaissance of local political coverage is anywhere on the horizon. District polarization has increased over time, and because the decline in competitiveness is principally a product of polarization, uncompetitive elections – which generate few incentives for journalists to cover them – are likely here to stay. Moreover, at the local level, mainstream news organizations constitute the main – and sometimes only – source of information about House races and other lower-level contests. In an analysis of more than a thousand local news and information sources in the top 100 U.S. television markets, Hindman (2010) reports that less than 2 percent of local news websites are unaffiliated with traditional print or broadcast media. When local news outlets like daily newspapers devote less coverage, and less substantive coverage, to politics, there are few alternative sources to which citizens can turn. For all the recent efforts to save local news (Abernathy 2014), the vast majority of U.S. communities are beholden to local newspapers for information about local politics.

This, of course, doesn't mean that citizen knowledge and participation in congressional elections are doomed. Indeed, there is evidence in a recent report that some Americans are becoming increasingly politically engaged (Pew Research Center 2014). And as the media environment continues to evolve, new outlets may emerge to provide coverage of House elections where mainstream news has fallen away. But both of these developments are likely to contribute to a more ideologically extreme electorate. The individuals who polarization has spurred to action tend to be "the most ideologically oriented and politically rancorous Americans" (Pew Research Center 2014: 7). And the fastest-growing online political news sites are those that are more likely to inflame than inform. If polarization continues to contribute to the diminishment of the mainstream news environment, this may pose yet another barrier to broad-based participation in congressional elections. To the extent that the electorate is made up primarily of impassioned partisans, political leaders will have even fewer incentives to pursue the compromises that are the antidote to political gridlock.

REFERENCES

Abernathy, Penelope Muse. 2014. *Saving Community Journalism: The Path to Profitability*. Chapel Hill: University of North Carolina Press.

Abramowitz, Alan, Brad Alexander, and Matthew Gunning. 2006. "Incumbency, Redistricting, and the Decline of Competition in U.S. House Elections." *Journal of Politics* 68 (1): 75–88.

Arceneaux, Kevin, and Martin Johnson. 2013. *Changing Minds or Changing Channels? Partisan News in an Age of Choice*. Chicago: University of Chicago Press.

Arnold, R. Douglas. 2004. *Congress, the Press, and Political Accountability*. New York: Russell Sage Foundation, and Princeton, NJ: Princeton University Press.

Bafumi, Joseph, and Michael C. Herron. 2010. "Leapfrog Representation and Extremism: A Study of American Voters and Their Members in Congress." *American Political Science Review* 104 (3): 519–42.

Bennett, W. Lance. 2011. *News: The Politics of Illusion*, 9th edition. New York: Longman.

Binder, Sarah A. 2003. *Stalemate: Causes and Consequences of Legislative Gridlock*. Washington, DC: Brookings Institution Press.

Black, Gordon S. 1972. "A Theory of Political Ambition: Career Choices and the Role of Structural Incentives." *American Political Science Review* 66 (1): 144–159.

Bruni, Frank. 2002. *Ambling into History: The Unlikely Odyssey of George W. Bush*. New York: Harper Collins.

Chaffee, Steven H., Xinshu Zhao, and Glen Leshner. 1994. "Political Knowledge and the Election Campaign of 1992." *Communication Research* 21 (3): 305–324.

Clarke, Peter, and Susan H. Evans. 1983. *Covering Campaigns: Journalism in Congressional Elections*. Stanford, CA: Stanford University Press.

Cohen, Marty, Hans Noel, and John Zaller. 2004. "Local News and Political Accountability in U.S. Legislative Elections." Paper presented at the annual meeting of the American Political Science Association. Chicago: September 2–5.

Cox, Gary W., and Jonathan N. Katz. 1996. "Why Did the Incumbency Advantage in U.S. House Elections Grow?" *American Journal of Political Science* 40 (2): 478–497.

Delli Carpini, Michael X., and Scott Keeter. 1996. *What Americans Know about Politics and Why It Matters*. New Haven, CT: Yale University Press.

de Vreese, Claes H., and Hajo Boomgaarden. 2006. "How Content Moderates the Effects of Television News on Political Knowledge and Engagement." *Acta Politica* 41: 317–341.

Dunaway, Johanna. 2008. "Markets, Ownership, and the Quality of Campaign News Coverage." *Journal of Politics* 70 (4): 1193–1202.

Dunaway, Johanna, and Robert Stein. 2013. "Campaign News Coverage and Early Voting." *Political Communication* 30 (2): 278–296.

Eveland, William P., and Dietram A. Scheufele. 2000. "Connecting News Media Use with Gaps in Knowledge and Participation." *Political Communication* 17(3): 215–37.

Fogarty, Brian J. 2013. "Scandals, News Coverage, and the 2006 Congressional Elections." *Political Communication* 30 (3): 419–33.

Gentzkow, Matthew, and Jesse M. Shapiro. 2011. "Ideological Segregation Online and Offline." *Quarterly Journal of Economics* 126 (4): 1799–1839.

Gershon, Sarah. 2013. "Voter Reaction to Media Coverage of Anglo, Latino and African American Congresswomen: An Experimental Study." *Political Research Quarterly* 66 (3): 702–714.

Gershon, Sarah. 2012. "Press Secretaries, Journalists, and Editors: Shaping Local Congressional News Coverage." *Political Communication* 29 (2): 160–183.

Goldenberg, Edie, and Michael Traugott. 1984. *Campaigning for Congress*. Washington, DC: CQ Press.

Graber, Doris A. ed. 2010. *Media Power in Politics*, 6th edition. Washington, DC: CQ Press.

Graber, Doris A., and Johanna Dunaway. 2014. *Mass Media and American Politics*, 9th edition. Washington, DC: CQ Press.

Hayes, Danny. 2010. "The Dynamics of Agenda Convergence and the Paradox of Competitiveness in Presidential Campaigns." *Political Research Quarterly* 63 (3): 594–611.

Hayes, Danny, and Jennifer L. Lawless. 2015. "As Local News Goes, So Goes Citizen Engagement: Media, Knowledge, and Participation in U.S. House Elections." *Journal of Politics* 77 (2): 447–462.

Hindman, Matthew. 2010. "Less of the Same: The Lack of Local News on the Internet." Washington, DC: Federal Communications Commission. Retrieved from http://www.fcc.gov/encyclopedia/2010-media-ownership-studies. Accessed December 3, 2013.

Iyengar, Shanto, and Kyu S. Hahn. 2009. "Red Media, Blue Media: Evidence of Ideological Selectivity in Media Use." *Journal of Communication* 59: 19–39.

Iyengar, Shanto, Kyu S. Hahn, Jon A. Krosnick, and John Walker. 2008. "Selective Exposure to Campaign Communication: The Role of Anticipated Agreement and Issue Public Membership." *Journal of Politics* 70 (1): 186–200.

Iyengar, Shanto, Guarav Sood, and Yphtach Lelkes. 2012. "Affect, Not Ideology: A Social Identity Perspective on Polarization." *Public Opinion Quarterly* 76 (3): 405–431.

Jacobson, Gary C. 1989. "Strategic Politicians and the Dynamics of House Elections, 1946–1986." *American Political Science Review* 83 (3): 773–793.

Jacobson, Gary C., and Samuel Kernell. 1983. *Strategy and Choice in Congressional Elections*. New Haven, CT: Yale University Press.

Jamieson, Kathleen Hall, and Joseph N. Capella. 2008. *Echo Chamber: Rush Limbaugh and the Conservative Media Establishment.* New York: Oxford University Books.

Jamieson, Kathleen Hall, and Erika Falk. 2000. "Continuity and Change in Civility in the House." In J. Bond and R. Fleisher, eds., *Polarized Politics: Congress and the President in a Partisan Era.* Washington, DC: CQ Press, 96–108.

Jerit, Jennifer, Jason Barabas, and Toby Bolsen. 2006. "Citizens, Knowledge, and the Information Environment." *American Journal of Political Science* 50 (2): 266–282.

Kahn, Kim Fridkin, and Patrick J. Kenney. 1999. *The Spectacle of U.S. Senate Campaigns.* Princeton, NJ: Princeton University Press.

Keele, Luke. 2005. "The Authorities Really Do Matter: Party Control and Trust in Government." *Journal of Politics* 67 (3): 873–886.

Larson, Stephanie Greco. 1992. *Creating Consent of the Governed: A Member of Congress and the Local Media.* Carbondale: Southern Illinois University Press.

Lawless, Jennifer L. 2012. *Becoming a Candidate: Political Ambition and the Decision to Run for Office.* New York: Cambridge University Press.

Lawrence, Eric, John Sides, and Henry Farrell. 2010. "Self-Segregation or Deliberation? Blog Readership, Participation, and Polarization in American Politics." *Perspectives on Politics* 8 (1): 141–157.

Levendusky, Matthew. 2013. *How Partisan Media Polarize America.* Chicago: University of Chicago Press.

Maestas, Cherie D., Sarah Fulton, L. Sandy Maisel, and Walter J. Stone. 2006. "When to Risk It? Institutions, Ambitions, and the Decision to Run for the U.S. House." *American Political Science Review* 100 (2): 195–208.

Manheim, Jarol B. 1974. "Urbanization and Differential Press Coverage of the Congressional Campaign." *Journalism Quarterly* 51 (4): 649–653.

Mayhew, David. 1974. "Congressional Elections: The Case of the Vanishing Marginals." *Polity* 6: 295–317.

Napoli, P. M., and M. Z. Yan 2007. "Media ownership regulations and local news programming on broadcast television: An empirical analysis." *Journal of Broadcasting and Electronic Media* 51 (1): 39–57.

Nye, Joseph S., Philip Zelikow, and David C. King, eds. 1997. *Why People Don't Trust Government.* Cambridge, MA: Harvard University Press.

Orman, John. 1985. "Media Coverage of the Congressional Underdog." *PS: Political Science and Politics* 18 (4): 754–759.

Pew Research Center. 2014. "Political Polarization in the American Public." Retrieved from http://www.people-press.org/2014/06/12/political-polarization-in-the-american-public/. Accessed July 31, 2014.

Prior, Markus. 2013. "Media and Political Polarization." *Annual Review of Political Science* 16: 101–27.

Rainie, Lee, and Aaron Smith. 2012. "Politics on Social Networking Sites." Washington, DC: Pew Research Center. Retrieved from http://pewinternet.org/Reports/2012/Politics-on-SNS.aspx. Accessed August 18, 2013.

Schaffner, Brian F. 2006. "Local News Coverage and the Incumbency Advantage in the U.S. House." *Legislative Studies Quarterly* 31 (4): 491–511.

Schaffner, Brian F., and Patrick J. Sellers. 2003. "The Structural Determinants of Local Congressional News Coverage." *Political Communication* 20 (1): 41–57.

Schulhofer-Wohl, Sam, and Miguel Garrido. 2011. "Do Newspapers Matter? Short-Run and Long-Run Evidence from the Closure of the *Cincinnati Post*." Working Paper 686. Minneapolis: Federal Reserve Bank of Minneapolis.

Shaker, Lee. 2014. "Dead Newspapers and Citizens' Civic Engagement." *Political Communication* 31 (1): 131–148.

Smith, Aaron, and Joanna Brenner. 2012. "Twitter Use 2012." Washington, DC: Pew Research Center. Retrieved from http://pewinternet.org/Reports/2012/Twitter-Use-2012/Findings.aspx. Accessed August 18, 2013.

Stone, Walter J., and L. Sandy Maisel. 2003. "The Not-So-Simple Calculus of Winning: Potential U.S. House Candidates' Nominations and General Election Prospects." *Journal of Politics* 65 (4): 951–977.

Stroud, Natalie Jomini. 2011. *Niche News: The Politics of News Choice*. New York: Oxford University Press.

Theriault, Sean M. 2008. *Party Polarization in Congress*. New York: Cambridge University Press.

Tidmarch, Charles M., and Brad S. Karp. 1983. "The Missing Beat: Press Coverage of Congressional Elections in Eight Metropolitan Areas." *Congress and the Presidency* 10 (1): 47–61.

Tolbert, Caroline J., and Ramona S. McNeal. 2003. "Unraveling the Effects of the Internet on Political Participation?" *Political Research Quarterly* 56 (2): 175–185.

Vermeer, Jan Pons. ed. 1987. *Campaigns in the News: Mass Media and Congressional Elections*. Westport, CT: Greenwood Press.

Vinson, Danielle C. 2003. *Local Media Coverage of Congress and Its Members: Through Local Eyes*. Cresskill, NJ: Hampton Press.

Westlye, Mark C. 1991. *Senate Elections and Campaign Intensity*. Baltimore: Johns Hopkins University Press.

APPENDIX

NEWSPAPER SELECTION

Very little political science research has sought to analyze media coverage of House elections from more than a handful of districts. Thus, there is no accepted method for identifying the local news outlets that serve a particular House contest. To identify the appropriate newspaper for each House race, we first consulted maps of each congressional district and identified the largest city in each district. We then determined whether the city had a daily newspaper that we could access through one of several electronic databases or the newspaper's online archives. In the vast majority of cases, this was a straightforward, though time-consuming, task. In the few cases for which we could not gain access to newspaper coverage from the district's largest-circulation daily paper, we relied on coverage from the next largest paper.

We identified every news story in each congressional district from October 2 through November 2, 2010 (election day) that mentioned at least one of the two major party candidates. We included in the sample straight news reports, news analyses, editorials, and op-ed columns. We did not code letters to the editor. We

TABLE A1. *Summary Statistics on Newspaper Sample and News Stories*

	Mean	Standard Deviation	Minimum	Maximum
Daily circulation of newspaper	195,149	202,379	6,772	876,638
Number of stories	14	13	1	81
Average number of words in a story	696	274	34	3,275

Notes: Circulation and number of stories reflect data from all 435 congressional districts. Average number of words reflect data from the 405 districts with at least one story mentioning a major-party candidate. The total number of stories is 6,003.

did not restrict the analysis strictly to "campaign" stories because we assume that any information about the House candidates is potentially relevant for voters. As a result, our coding includes a comprehensive analysis of the media coverage to which voters could have been exposed in the lead-up to the election. Our analyses do not include independent and minor-party candidates.

Table A1 provides an overview of our media data. The figures in the table represent summary statistics on the circulation size of the newspapers in our sample, the number of stories about the congressional race, and the length of those stories. The circulation of the newspapers and the amount of attention to the House race varies quite a bit, as one would expect, given differences in district composition and competitiveness.

NEWS CONTENT ANALYSIS

We tracked every time an issue was mentioned, beginning with a list of issues commonly included in previous studies and then recording references to additional issues as they emerged in the coverage. We then classified each issue into eight broad categories following previous scholars' coding schemes: (1) Defense, Security, and Military, (2) Taxes and Spending, (3) Race and Social Groups, (4) Civil and Social Order, (5) Social Welfare, (6) Economy, (7) Foreign Affairs, and (8) Government Functioning. Table A2 presents a list of the 173 issues we identified.

Coders also recorded the number of explicit references to candidate traits, both positive and negative (e.g., "honest" and "dishonest"). These references could come from candidates themselves ("I have shown the leadership abilities to represent this district effectively"), their opponents ("My opponent does not care about the people of this district"), or reporters ("Questions about Thompson's trustworthiness have been a problem for her campaign"). We coded for traits that fell into one of the four dimensions that previous research has identified as salient for voters: competence, leadership, integrity, and empathy. In total, we coded for 131 separate specific trait references that fell into the four trait dimensions. Table A3 displays the full list.

Defense, Security, and Military
Afghanistan, defense, defense
spending, GI bill, Guantanamo
Bay, intelligence, Iran, Iraq,
military issues (bases, benefits,
health care, pay), NASA/space,
national security, nuclear
weapons, Pakistan, Patriot Act,
security, veterans' affairs, war

Taxes and Spending
arts programs, balanced budget,
budget/spending, Bush tax cuts,
business, debt ceiling, debt or
deficit, earmarks/pork, funding for
local projects, government size/
power, oil subsidies, other
program funding, research and
development, spending, taxes/tax
breaks

Civil and Social Order
abortion, alcohol, assisted suicide,
bullying, civil liberties, crime,
criminal justice system, death
penalty, domestic violence, English
as the national language, gambling
and casinos, guns, hate crimes,
hunting rights, illegal drugs,
immigration, police or fire
funding, pornography, privacy,
public safety, religion/religious
issues/creationism taught in
schools, school prayer, securing
the border, separation of church
and state, social issues, stem cell
research

Race and Social Groups
advocacy for women, affirmative
action, civil rights, Don't Ask
Don't Tell, ERA/pay equity, gay
rights, marriage equality, Native
American issues, race advocacy,
racial equality, seniors, workplace
discrimination, workplace
diversity

Government Functioning
campaign finance reform,
constitutional amendments,
decreasing partisanship in
Congress, disaster relief/FEMA,
ethics, FDA, government reform/
transparency, insurance reform
(not health care), lobbying, PACs,
personal scandal, reforms to

Social Welfare
9/11 workers health plan, birth
control/contraception, BP oil spill,
cap and trade, children's issues/
child care, climate change,
education, energy/electricity/coal/
nuclear power, entitlements,
environment, family planning,
health care/health insurance/

Economy
agriculture, auto industry, bailout,
banks, business, Cash for
Clunkers, consumer protection,
credit card reform, economy,
ethanol subsidies, farms, federal
employee wages, Freddie Mac/
Fannie Mae, free enterprise, gas
prices, global currency, housing/

Foreign Affairs
Africa, China, diplomacy, foreign
policy, human rights, international
issues in health, Israel, Mexico,
Middle East, other specific
country, spending on foreign aid,
trade

Obamacare, homelessness, Medicaid, medical research, Medicare, mining, natural gas, oil drilling, oil pipelines, prescription drugs, school vouchers, social security, social services, student loans, teacher salaries, utilities, water, welfare, wildlife/forests, women's health, women's issues (not abortion, contraception), work safety, workers' compensation

foreclosures, inequality (economic), infrastructure, jobs, labor, manufacturing, minimum wage, mortgage rates, net neutrality, outsourcing, personal finances, poverty, redistribution of wealth, regulations, retirement, stimulus, TARP, technology, tourism, transportation, unemployment, unions, Wall Street reform

congressional campaigns, term limits, tort reform, wages for members of Congress and other elected officials

TABLE A3. *Specific Trait References Coded from News Coverage*

	Competence	Leadership	Integrity	Empathy
Positive	accomplished, articulate, assertive, careful, cautious, competent, consistent, contemplative, creative, dedicated, determined, diligent, effective, experienced, focused, good speaker/orator, hardworking, has common sense, intelligent, knowledgeable, open-minded, pragmatic, proactive, rational, reasonable, reliable, responsible, savvy, thoughtful, understated, wonky	active, ambitious, brave, committed, confident, consistent, courageous, decisive, direct, effective, energetic, enthusiastic, entrepreneurial, feisty, fighter, independent, independent thinker, maverick, optimistic, passionate, persistent, straight shooter, strong, strong leader, team player, tough	decent, earnest, ethical, has integrity, honest, honorable, principled, reliable, sincere, trustworthy	accessible, affable, caring, compassionate, concerned with needs of district, courteous, empathetic, engaging, friendly, good listener, in touch, kind, likeable, listens to constituents, nice, personable
Negative	careless, clueless, incompetent, ineffective, inexperienced, irrational, irresponsible, not pragmatic, reactive, superficial, unfit, uninformed, unintelligent, unprofessional	adversarial, afraid, argumentative, combative, fearful, flip-flopper, inconsistent, lack of confidence, lackadaisical, lacks vision, not independent, party puppet/lapdog, rigid, scared, unsure, weak, weak leader	dirty fighter, dishonest, disingenuous, greedy, hypocritical, immoral, lacks integrity, liar, malicious, manipulative, not trustworthy, unethical	aloof, not caring, not engaged, out of touch

14

More a Symptom Than a Cause

Polarization and Partisan News Media in America

Kevin Arceneaux and Martin Johnson

Many observers blame partisan news media for the high level of partisan polarization in U.S. government and the American electorate. In this chapter, we discuss the emergence of partisan news media in the United States and review disparate sources of evidence to assess its effect on political polarization. Taken together, we contend that the emergence of partisan news media is more a symptom of a polarized political system than a source.

- Political parties in the U.S. Congress polarized before the advent of partisan news media.
- The expansion of entertainment options on television and the Internet has limited the reach of both mainstream and partisan news.
- Although exposure to partisan news programs can polarize political attitudes, exposure to mainstream news can *also* polarize.
- News programs are polarizing, in part, because they communicate to the public the degree to which politicians are polarized along party lines. Consequently, if political elites were to become less partisan, the electorate would likely follow.

The debate over the Affordable Care Act in 2009 and 2010 offers a prime example of the polarized polity in the United States. It was cast in ideological terms, with supporters advancing access to medical care as a universal human right to be afforded by government and opponents decrying any government intrusion into the provision of medical care as creeping socialism. President Obama, attempting to craft the image of a "post-partisan" politician, met publicly with congressional Republicans multiple times and made a show of including some of their proposals. Whether these attempts were genuine is a matter of perspective, but their ineffectiveness is not. Not one Republican in either the House of Representatives or the Senate voted in support of the health care bill (Herszenhorn and Pear 2010).

Things were somewhat different in 1965, when 13 Republican senators and 70 Republican representatives joined their Democratic colleagues to support the creation of Medicare, providing health care for the elderly. Nearly half of the Republican caucus supported the bill (Social Security History 2014). What changed? The passage of Medicare was not a fait accompli ordained by overwhelming popularity or a lack of a credible opposition. The public was just as ambivalent about the proposed legislation in 1965 as it was in 2009, with opponents denouncing the plan as "socialized medicine" (Klein 2010). Moreover, the American Medical Association, which endorsed the Affordable Care Act, firmly opposed and openly lobbied against Medicare. The difference between then and now is that the 1965 Congress was filled with moderates in both the Democratic and Republican Parties who were willing to negotiate and hash out compromises on major pieces of legislation, such as Medicare (Jacobs and Shapiro 2000). Today, there are few moderates in the halls of Congress.

In accounting for where the moderates went, some political observers and scholars point fingers at the emergence of the partisan news media in the 1990s. The availability of ideologically driven news on the radio and then cable television as well as the Internet allows people to fashion an information environment in which they only receive like-minded news, if they wish. In doing so, the argument goes, people's political attitudes become more extreme and ossified, polarizing the mass electorate in the process (e.g., Slater 2007; Jamieson and Cappella 2008; Sunstein 2009). With an increasingly polarized electorate, partisan media outlets mobilize the extremists in the Democratic and Republican Parties, giving extreme candidates a boost in congressional primaries and, ultimately, pushing moderate candidates out of the way (Brock, Rabin-Havt, and for America 2012; Levendusky, 2013). Partisan news media also provide a platform for legitimating and promoting outlandish and incendiary claims to spread fear and anger. It is one thing for a moderate in Congress to vote for "socialized medicine," and quite another to support a bill that creates "death panels" that deny insurance to those whose care costs too much, an erroneous claim widely featured on partisan news outlets during the 2009 health care debate.

In this chapter, we draw upon an array of available evidence – from public opinion surveys, randomized experiments, and congressional voting patterns – to evaluate the claim that partisan news media are to blame for partisan polarization. Our assembly of evidence makes a circumstantial case that partisan news media are more likely a symptom of a polarized party system than a cause. Political elites appear to have polarized before rank-and-file partisans in the mass public and the emergence of partisan news media. Moreover, because right-slanted media got a head start on left-slanted outlets, the initial emergence of partisan news outlets did more to move *both* Democrats and Republicans in Congress to the right. Among the mass public, exposure to partisan news media can be polarizing, but they are not unique in this respect. Exposure to mainstream news can also polarize. Partisan elites are central to explaining why (see also Davis and Dunaway n.d.). As long as Democratic and Republican legislators line up on opposite sides of the issues, they signal party adherents to adopt polarized positions. In contrast to the notion that the mass public is deeply and irrevocably polarized, we find that people are willing to moderate their positions if party elites move toward the center.

PARTISAN POLARIZATION THEN AND NOW

Since the 1970s, American politics has become more partisan. It was not always this way. By the middle of the twentieth century, the American Political Science Association Committee on Political Parties bemoaned the lack of "responsible parties" in the United States – parties that adopt clear ideologically rooted positions and vote in coherent blocks in the legislature (American Political Science Association Committee on Political Parties 1950). Rather than resembling coherent teams in opposition, as is commonplace in parliamentary systems, the Democratic and Republican Parties were a loose coalition of career-minded politicians more interested in advancing the parochial interests of their districts than an overarching ideological vision (Mayhew 1974). A Republican legislator from Connecticut might well be to the left of a Democratic colleague from Mississippi. However, since the 1970s, the ranks of liberal Republicans and conservative Democrats have shrunk considerably. The civil rights movement ultimately drove a wedge between racially liberal Northern Democrats and racially conservative Southern Democrats in Congress, while giving the Republican Party inroads into the solid Democratic south (Schickler, Pearson, and Feinstein 2010). As Figure 1 illustrates, beginning in the 1980s, the Democratic and Republican delegations in the U.S. House of Representatives have become more ideologically polarized (Poole 2014). These data show that Republicans in the U.S. House have become more conservative, while Democrats have become more liberal. Gone are the days of liberal Republicans and conservative Democrats; even moderates are rare in both parties. Republicans and Democrats now resemble the ideologically coherent teams envisioned by the APSA Committee on Political Parties.

What about the mass public? The advent of scientific polling in the 1940s allowed researchers to undertake large-scale systematic studies of public opinion. Like their representatives in Congress, Americans in the late 1940s and 1950s did not seem like an ideological bunch. Voting choices tended to reflect group identities and social pressures more than they did sober reflection on political debates (Berelson 1954). People formed psychological attachments to political parties for sure, but save for a sliver of the electorate, most people did not possess well-formed attitudes rooted in an overarching belief system, and rank-and-file Democrats and Republicans were not separated all that much on political issues (Campbell et al. 1960; Converse 1964). Times have changed. Nowadays, knowing someone's party identification tells you more about their

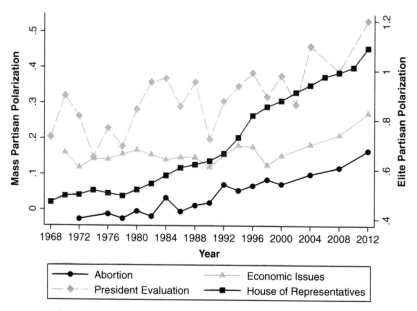

FIGURE 1. Elite and Mass Partisan Polarization, 1968–2012
Source: Elite polarization based on DW-Nominate scores (Poole 2014). Mass polarization based on survey data drawn from the American National Election Studies (see text for details).

political opinions than it did in the 1950s (Lewis-Beck et al. 2009). Not only do Democrats and Republicans tend to hold more distinct opinions on political issues today, they are also more likely to hold members of the other party in contempt. In the abstract, Democrats are less likely to say they feel warm toward Republicans and Republicans are less likely to say they feel warm toward Democrats. Partisans today are also more likely than they were in 1960 to say they would be upset if their child married someone from the other party (Iyengar, Sood, and Lelkes 2012).

To help illustrate trends in the attitudes of Democrats and Republicans in the mass public over the past 40 years, we recruit survey data collected by the American National Election Study (ANES) during presidential elections and most midterm elections from 1968 to 2012.[1] Because moral and economic issues occupy different conceptual dimensions, we separate the two. For moral issues, we focus on attitudes toward abortion, since the ANES has consistently included an item on abortion policy since 1972 and it is one of the primary moral fissures in American politics (Adams 1997). For economic issues, we recruit three items that have been consistently included on the ANES

---

[1] The ANES conducted a brief survey following the 2002 midterm election and did not conduct surveys in the 2006 and 2010 elections.

since 1970: one that asks respondents whether the federal government should provide health care or leave it to individuals; one that asks whether the federal government should guarantee jobs or leave it to individuals; and one that asks people whether they think there should be fewer (or more) government services. We combined all three of these items into one economic issues index. Finally, we gauge the affective charge of political evaluations with the help of the "feeling thermometer" question that asks respondents to say how cool or warm they feel toward the president of the United States. See the Appendix for question wording.

We rescaled all of these items so that 0 represented the most liberal response and 1 represented the most conservative response. To measure the degree of partisan polarization on political issues and affective evaluations of the present, we averaged the survey responses for self-identified Democrats and Republicans and took the difference.[2] A negative number indicates that, on average, Republicans were to the left of Democrats on the issue, while a positive score indicates that Democrats were to the left of Republicans. Large values indicate that Democrats and Republicans are further apart from one another on the issue. Because partisans always evaluate the president of their party more warmly than the president of the opposing party, we take the absolute difference between Democrats and Republicans on this item, so that a positive value simply indicates how far apart Democrats and Republicans are in how much they like presidents from their party and dislike presidents from the other party.

The trends in mass polarization are also shown in Figure 1. Echoing Adams' (1997) analysis of similar data, Republicans were actually to the left of Democrats on abortion until the mid-1980s. Since then, Republicans have become increasingly pro-life, whereas Democrats have become increasingly pro-choice. On economic issues, Democrats have always been to the left of Republicans, but partisans have become increasingly polarized on these issues since 2000 (see also Fiorina, Abrams, and Pope 2005; Abramowitz 2010). We observe a similar pattern with respect to affective evaluations of the president. On balance, Democrats tend to like Democratic presidents better than Republican ones and vice versa for Republicans. Yet the 2004, 2008, and 2012 data show a marked uptick in the degree to which partisans like their party's guy and dislike the other party's guy. Like Iyengar, Sood, and Lelkes (2012), we also find that affective polarization dwarfs the magnitude of partisan polarization on political issues.

---

[2] More precisely stated, we performed the following calculation:

$$Polarization = \frac{1}{n_{Dem}}\sum_{i=1}^{n_{Dem}} A_i - \frac{1}{n_{Rep}}\sum_{j=1}^{n_{Rep}} A_j$$

where A = survey measure of a political attitude, i = index for self-identified Democrats in the survey, and j = index for self-identified Republican.

While many scholars agree that partisans in the U.S. Congress and the public have become more polarized over the past few decades, there remains a great deal of disagreement over why it is happening. With respect to mass polarization, some scholars contend that these trends reflect an increasingly ideological public (Abramowitz 2010). Others argue that Americans have not become more ideological, but that as partisan elites have become more polarized, ideologues are better able to sort into the party that suits them ideologically (conservatives become Republicans and liberals become Democrats) while non-ideological partisans receive clearer cues and align their preferences to be consistent with party messages (Fiorina, Abrams, and Pope 2005; Levendusky 2009). Our analysis does not help resolve this debate, but merely confirms that polarization at both the elite and mass levels is real. In the remainder of this chapter, we speak to this debate by considering an oft-cited source of polarization in American politics – partisan news.

ARE PARTISAN MEDIA TO BLAME?

As with most social phenomena, when it comes to describing the effects of mass media, simple questions rarely receive simple answers. For the task of pondering whether partisan news media are responsible of partisan polarization, we find it useful to compartmentalize the effects of partisan media along two dimensions: (1) the level at which the polarization occurs (among political elites or the mass public) and (2) the causal route by which polarization occurs (direct or indirect). See Table 1 for our simplified typology.

In order for polarization to occur via the direct route, partisan news must influence individuals – at the elite or mass level – through direct exposure. It is this causal route that many scholars have in mind when theorizing about or gauging the effects of partisan news, and it is a potentially potent one. At the mass level, exposure to like-minded news shows reinforce preexisting beliefs and

TABLE 1. *Typology of Partisan News Media Effects*

Causal Pathway	Level of Polarization	
	Elite	Mass
Direct effect	Politicians view news content as indication of public opinion	Exposure to partisan news polarizes
Indirect effect	Partisan news activates partisans in electorate to contact politicians	Partisan news content spreads through social networks

induce people to adopt more extreme attitudes (Jamieson and Cappella 2008; Sunstein 2009; Stroud 2011; Arceneaux and Johnson 2013). The polarizing power of like-minded news shows lies in the fact that they send powerful signals about what in-group members believe (or should believe), while denigrating and mocking the other side (Sobieraj and Berry 2011). The same heavy-handed tactics that bolster the attitudes of like-minded viewers also antagonize viewers who hail from the other side of the political spectrum and, as a result, exposure to oppositional news programs can *also* polarize audience members (Arceneaux and Johnson 2013). Consequently, it may not matter if people selectively seek out like-minded news, as some scholars contend (e.g., Jamieson and Cappella 2008), or if they do not as others contend (e.g., Garrett, Carnahan, and Lynch 2013). Exposure to partisan media – no matter what its orientation – has the power to polarize.

At the elite level, politicians are not immune to the influence of news media. Like their constituents, politicians interpret news stories as a signal for what is important (Yanovitzky 2002). Beyond simply using news media as a source of information, many elected officials also view it as an indication of public opinion (Herbst 1998). As such, news coverage can enter into politicians' strategic calculus and influence their public position on issues (Edwards and Wood 1999). Because career-minded politicians prioritize their reelection, they are motivated to respond to what they think their constituents want (Miller and Stokes 1963). Consequently, political elites should be pulled in the direction of the loudest partisan network – irrespective of whether its content is ideologically congenial. For instance, if conservative news outlets hold sway, we should expect to see all politicians move to the right.

Direct exposure is only one way in which partisan news outlets can shape mass and elite behavior. At the mass level, in fact, it is quite possibly not even the primary route. On a daily basis, only a small fraction of the electorate consumes partisan news, limiting its reach and impact (Arceneaux and Johnson 2013). Political elites are voracious consumers of news. Consequently, one can make a more plausible case that partisan news media have a large direct effect on politicians. Nonetheless, partisan news media may influence political outcomes even if it does not have massive direct effects. At the mass level, partisan news may influence political discussion, allowing polarization to spread through social networks (Siegel 2013). In this way, partisan news may indirectly influence mass polarization via a two-step flow of information in which small audiences communicate partisan messages to political discussants who are not members of partisan news audiences (Katz and Lazarsfeld 1955; Huckfeldt and Sprague 1995). Partisan news shows may also inspire a subset of audience members to contact their elected officials (Levendusky 2013). Because legislators are typically responsive to constituent appeals (Bergan 2009), partisan news may indirectly influence elite behavior, as well.

It's All in the Timing

Cable television began in the 1940s as a mechanism for transmitting local broadcast network content to consumers who had difficulty receiving signals over the airwaves (e.g., people who lived in mountainous or highly dense urban areas). For a long while, the number of channels available on cable television was constrained by the meager capacity of analog converter boxes and the dearth of networks willing to provide programming, limiting the appeal of expensive cable packages over free broadcast television (Parsons 2008). The 1990s ushered in two innovations that led to the rapid expansion of cable television offerings. The first was technological, as digital converter boxes replaced analog ones, simply making it possible for cable companies to offer more channels. The second innovation was an agreement between broadcast networks and cable providers that paved the way for those channels to be filed with content. The 1992 Cable Act required cable companies to compensate local broadcast stations for retransmitting their highly valued content. The major broadcasting companies, led by Fox Broadcast Corporation, proposed that rather than demanding money for the rights to local affiliate feeds, the broadcast networks wanted channels on which to feature content that they developed (Lubinsky 1996). Everyone stood to profit from this proposal. Cable companies had the capacity to offer consumers lots of options, but they lacked the content. Broadcast networks, meanwhile, had access to plenty of content – it was their business to develop shows – but they were hemmed in by the availability of a handful of broadcast signals.

From the late 1990s through the early 2000s, there was an exponential explosion of channels on cable and satellite television. In 1985, the average American household had access to roughly 19 channels, by the end of the first decade of the 2000s, the average home had access to over 130 channels. The first partisan news channel to hit the cable television dial was Fox News, rolled out at the end of 1996. Fox News featured debate shows and talk shows that took a conservative take on issues of the day (see Groseclose and Milyo 2005). Other cable news networks, such as CNN and MSNBC, mimicked the approach of broadcast news networks by attempting to provide even-handed balance in reporting and the line-up of opinion programming. By 2005, MSNBC perhaps seeing an opportunity to play the liberal alternative to Fox News began shifting its opinion line-up to the left.

The timing of partisan news media's emergence does not line up well with the pattern of polarization reported in Figure 1. Partisan polarization at the elite level began well in advance of Fox News' debut (Davis and Dunaway n.d.). Indeed, one could just as easily make the case that the emergence of partisan news was a symptom of elite polarization, rather than a cause (Ladd 2012). Moreover, in research conducted with our colleagues René Lindstädt and Ryan Vander Wielen, we find that initial rollout of Fox News may have actually attenuated the rate of polarization in the U.S. House of Representatives (Arceneaux et al. 2015). Taking advantage of natural variation in the presence of Fox News in congressional districts created by its haphazard rollout (DellaVigna and Kaplan 2007), we were able to compare the voting behavior of Congress members in districts with Fox News to members whose districts did not yet have Fox News. In line with the notion that elected officials strategically respond to partisan news media content (direct route) or to constituents activated by exposure to partisan news (indirect route), it appears that Fox News caused both Republicans and Democrats legislators to cast more Republican votes as the general election approached (see Arceneaux et al. 2015, figure 2). If anything, it appears that the initial rollout of Fox News may have done more to pull elites of all stripes to the right than to polarize them (Hacker and Pierson 2005; see also Clinton and Enamorado 2014).

With respect to mass-level polarization, Republicans and Democrats in the electorate began to polarize on abortion well in advance of partisan news media's emergence. In contrast, polarization on economic issues and presidential evaluations appear to increase more sharply after the emergence of partisan news media. It is possible that partisan news played some role in polarizing the mass public on these issues, yet we cannot be sure on the basis of these data alone. Partisan news media did not emerge in a vacuum. There were many other changes in the media landscape in the late 1990s and early 2000s – namely, the explosion of entertainment options.

Tuning In and Tuning Out

As of 2012, over 90 percent of American households subscribed to cable or satellite television, and the average household had access to over 130 channels. Only a handful of those channels are devoted to partisan news or any kind of political news for that matter. Forty years ago, there were times of day where the only choice on the dial was the news. Although people could have chosen to do something other than watch television at that time – read a book or play with their kids – millions of people who were not particularly interested in the news chose to watch television news nonetheless, creating a large "inadvertent" news audience. The expansion of entertainment options on the cable spectrum enabled people to change the channel and indulge their hedonic desires to be entertained (Prior 2007).

As Figure 2 shows, during the mid-1990s, there was a sharp drop of in the percentage of the country that reported tuning into the news more than four days a week.[3] When there was little choice, it appears that many people watched television news simply because there was nothing else on. Now that people can choose from a plethora of game shows, reality shows, documentaries, and movies on other television channels, not to mention the options for entertainment that exist on the Internet and services such as Netflix, it is

---

[3] See the Appendix for question wording. We define news seekers as those who reported watching the news five days or more a week. We find a similar pattern if we use a less stringent cut-off for entertainment seekers.

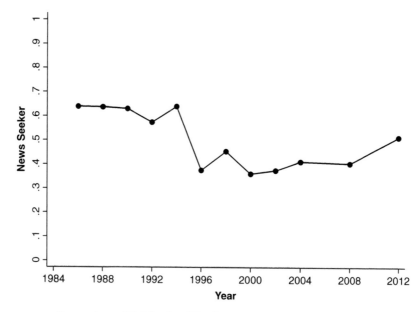

FIGURE 2. Proportion of Public that Watches News Five Times or More Last Week, 1986–2012

apparent that there were fewer news seekers in the 1980s than behavior suggested. More entertainment options freed entertainment seekers to be themselves.

If we break out the patterns in mass-level polarization by news seekers and entertainment seekers, we can observe whether trends in polarization differ after the introduction of partisan news. The results shown in Figure 3 suggest that they do. With the exception of abortion, news seekers appear to have become more polarized than entertainment seekers on economic issues and presidential evaluations since the emergence of partisan news media.[4] One interpretation of these results is that partisan news media are responsible for the gap in polarization between news seekers and entertainment seekers. After all, partisan news was not readily available on television dials prior to the late 1990s, and it just so happens that news seekers are primarily the ones expressing greater polarization since then. While this is a plausible interpretation of these trends, it is certainly not the only one.

As we saw in Figure 2, the emergence of partisan news was not the only change that occurred over the past 15 years. Fewer people are also tuning into the news. With entertainment seekers selecting out of the news audience, it is

---

[4] News seekers have polarized so recently on economic issues that we cannot rule out sampling variation as an explanation for this time trend ($p = 0.524$). The data offer unambiguous evidence of increasing partisan polarization on presidential evaluations ($p = 0.008$, two-tailed).

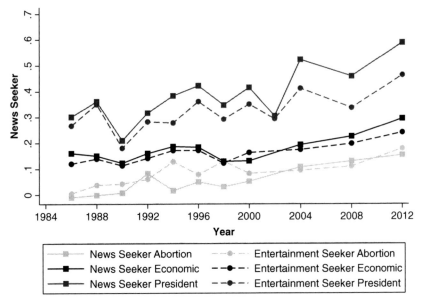

FIGURE 3. Mass Partisan Polarization by News and Entertainment Seekers, 1986–2012

possible that those left are simply more interested in politics, more partisan, and therefore, more polarized (Prior 2007). Moreover, in our previous research, we find that partisan news shows have *less* impact on people who seek them out than it does on those who do not (Arceneaux and Johnson 2013).[5] At first blush, this may seem counterintuitive. Why wouldn't partisan news seekers get caught in a "reinforcing spiral" of polarization (Slater 2007: 281)? Our answer is twofold. First, across a variety of domains, people tend to habituate to repeated exposure to stimuli, such that each exposure has a diminishing marginal effect (Thompson 2009). Second, people who chronically expose themselves to news tend to have stronger, more stable opinions and are less likely to exhibit large shifts of opinion in response to persuasive messages (Zaller 1992). Partisan news may play a role in polarizing partisan news seekers on novel issues (Levendusky 2013), but it is unlikely to escalate polarization on attitudes central to their political belief system, such as party evaluations.

[5] Levendusky (2013) offers countervailing evidence using similar methods. He finds that exposure to partisan news polarizes partisan news seekers to a larger degree than it does those who do not wish to watch partisan news shows. It is possible that his results are different from ours because he uses different stimuli. Another possibility is that because he does not offer entertainment options, some of his subjects may have selected partisan news even though they preferred an entertainment show. If entertainment seekers really are more susceptible to media effects, as our theoretical model asserts, then Levendusky's results are consistent with our model's prediction, and the only inconsistency would be in the interpretation.

Another issue is that the ANES measure of news media exposure does not separate mainstream and partisan news. We cannot tell on the basis of this measure the degree to which people are exposing themselves to partisan news media. When measurement error and selection bias are present, it is difficult to infer causal relationships from correlations. More disconcerting, if researchers attempt to account for selection bias by including covariates that explain media choices, for instance, they may end up exacerbating the problem (Achen 1986). So, constructing a more complicated statistical model would do little to help explain why we observe what we observe in Figure 3. In instances like these, randomized experiments offer a more promising approach (Arceneaux 2010). In an experiment, researchers test hypotheses by manipulating the variable (or variables) believed to influence human behavior. The standard practice is to first construct stimuli that isolate the theoretical variable (e.g., creating a news program) and then assign participants at random to a "treatment group" (or groups) exposed to the stimuli or a "control group" that is exposed to something else (or nothing at all). Random assignment insures that the treatment and control groups are comparable. Had the researcher not administered the treatment, we would expect both groups to have the same attitudes on average, for instance. If we observe a difference in attitudes or behavior between the treatment and control group *after* administering the treatment, we can more confidently conclude that something about the treatment caused some people to change their attitudes or behavior. Given the strength of the approach, randomized experiments have enjoyed a long and fruitful history in the study of media effects (Hovland, Janis, and Kelley 1953; Iyengar and Kinder 2010).

Unfortunately, a standard experimental design does not fully serve our purposes here. We are interested in understanding the effects of news media *given* people's media preferences. A conventional media effects experiment assumes away differences in media effects across individuals by simply averaging over them. If we are interested in the average overall effect of exposure to some media content, then this is a fine approach. In the days of the large inadvertent news audience, the standard experimental design may have even provided a useful estimate of the overall effect of news media (cf. Iyengar and Kinder 2010). Yet as Figure 2 demonstrates, we are no longer living in a time where we can assume large-scale exposure to news media, and we certainly cannot assume large-scale exposure to partisan news media. Fortunately, it is possible to tweak the standard experimental design in a way that serves our purposes. The participant preference experiment records study participants' preferences over the experimental stimuli (e.g., what they would watch if given a choice) before administering the treatment. As a result, it is possible to gauge whether media content affects people who seek it out differently from those who do not (Arceneaux and Johnson 2013, ch. 3; see also Gaines and Kuklinski 2011).

In a recent paper, we employ the participant preference experiment to estimate the effects of news programming delivered by mainstream, like-minded partisan, and oppositional partisan outlets (Arceneaux and Johnson 2014). The stimuli for the news programs covered allegations that the IRS unfairly scrutinized applications for nonprofit status from conservative groups. The mainstream news program (*CBS Evening News*) covered the story in line with the norms of journalistic balance by giving both sides in the controversy equal time. In contrast, the partisan news shows offered tendentious analysis of the controversy, with Fox News' *The O'Reilly Factor* characterizing the IRS's actions as clearly a plot against conservatives and MSNBC's *The Last Word with Lawrence O'Donnell* treating it as a non-story trumped up by rightwing groups. In order to get a baseline on participants' views on the matter, we randomly assigned some individuals to a control group in which they watched entertainment programming.[6] Before administering the treatment, we gave subjects a list of the shows to which they could be assigned (unbeknownst to them) and asked them to rank order their desire to watch these shows. We also asked subjects to tell us whether they identified as liberal or conservative using a six-point scale (very liberal, liberal, somewhat liberal, somewhat conservative, conservative, very conservative). We excluded "moderate" from the scale so that we could have a sense of all subjects' political predispositions.[7] After administering the treatment, we asked subjects thirteen questions to measure their opinion on the IRS story. We coded the items such that larger values indicate an ideologically consistent position (i.e., liberals dismissing the story and conservatives seeing it as a politically motivated scandal). We reduced these items to a single polarization scale using factor analysis.[8]

Ignoring subjects' viewing preferences, we found that mainstream news – and not partisan news – reliably increased the level of polarization on the IRS issue. How could that be? Parsing the effects of news shows by viewing preferences offered some insight. Partisan news shows did little to polarize either mainstream or partisan news seekers, while they did polarize entertainment seekers. Mainstream news shows, in contrast, appeared to polarize everyone. One explanation for these findings is that mainstream news seekers see mainstream news as credible (and thus worth taking seriously) and simply dismiss partisan news shows. Meanwhile, for the reasons we articulated earlier, partisan news seekers are inured to the content on partisan news shows, but at least find comfort in the fact that they are getting the facts right (yes,

---

[6] Consistent with our approach in other experiments, we chose entertainment programming that attracted audiences of similar sizes to partisan news shows. In this particular study, we selected segments from the basic cable shows *For Rent* and *Pet Stars*.

[7] Removing the "moderate" option from the response set inhibits people who lean in a particular ideological direction from masking their ideological orientation. At the same time, it forces true moderates to pick a side, but if anything this should introduce more noise into our results, creating a more conservative test for media effects. It does not appear that the response set caused many people to opt out of answering the question. Of the 843 subjects who participated in the experiment, only five failed to provide a response to the ideology question.

[8] See Arceneaux and Johnson (2014) for details about the sample and measurement.

everyone knows the other guys are wrong). In contrast, when partisans watch mainstream news coverage, they see bias in balanced coverage (how dare they report what the other side says as if it could be true!). Previous research demonstrates that balanced descriptions of controversies are capable of polarizing attitudes (Lord, Ross, and Lepper 1979; Taber and Lodge 2006). Consequently, it would not be surprising to find that mainstream news could be just as polarizing as partisan news.

NEWS CONTENT VERSUS PARTISAN CUES

If mainstream news can polarize, then why did we not observe higher levels of mass-level polarization before the advent of partisan news? Part of the answer may lie in the level of polarized discourse among elites. Employing a clever experiment, Druckman, Peterson, and Slothuus (2013) expose participants to arguments that either support or oppose legislation before Congress.[9] Some subjects received a strong argument and some received a weak argument.[10] Before exposing subjects to the policy argument, they provided a party cue that described the position taken by most Democrats and Republicans in Congress as well as an indication of whether the parties were polarized on the issue (most members of each party are on the same side as the rest of their party) or not (members of each party can be found on both sides of the issue). Partisans who were told that parties were not polarized on the issue found strong arguments more persuasive than weak arguments – irrespective of whether the argument was consistent with the party cue. In contrast, those who were told that the parties were polarized ignored the strength of the arguments. They always found the argument that was consistent with the party cue more persuasive, be it weak or be it strong. These results demonstrate that the distribution of elite polarization affects how much people weight their partisan identities when forming issue attitudes (see also Levendusky 2010).

Much of the extant research on the polarizing influence of partisan news, including our own, implicitly assumes that these media are polarizing because their content is polarizing. However, an implication of Druckman, Peterson, and Slothuus's findings is that news content may not be the only (or even primary) mechanism through which media exposure polarizes viewers. News stories also disseminate cues about where one's party stands on the issues. If people are responding to the opposing stands that party elites are taking on issues – and not just the arguments that they encounter in the debates that surround issues – then even balanced coverage on mainstream news channels can cause partisans to take opposite sides on issues. Under this scenario, party elites may bear more of the responsibility for the polarized state of the country. News media, including mainstream and partisan outlets, are megaphones more

---

[9] The authors included two issue conditions: one on a relatively recondite issue (oil drilling) and one on a hot button issue (immigration reform).

[10] Argument strength was determined empirically with the aid of a pilot study.

than motivators of partisan polarization. It is a plausible one, too, since political parties play an extremely important role in organizing political conflict in American politics (Aldrich 1995), and party elites, not rank-in-file voters, are in the driver's seat when it comes to many aspects of the electoral process (Cohen et al. 2009).

We evaluate the relative role of partisan news content and party cues with a participant preference experiment in which we hold the content constant while manipulating whether the source is a partisan news outlet or a party elite. In January 2013, we recruited 1,205 subjects through the *Amazon Mechanical Turk* online labor market (see Berinsky, Huber, and Lenz 2012). After completing a pretest instrument in which participants registered their media view preferences (using the same item reported in Arceneaux and Johnson 2014), they were asked to read an excerpt from an opinion column on one of four possible issues written by a fictional person, Fred Barnes, or assigned to a control group in which they were asked to answer one of the issue questions.[11] Subjects were either told that Fred Barnes was a co-partisan ("a chairman of the Republican Party" for conservatives and "a chairman of the Democratic Party" for liberals) or a "frequent contributor" to a like-minded news outlet (Fox News for conservatives and MSNBC for liberals).

Following a similar protocol employed by one of us (Arceneaux 2008), we account for the possibility that the ease with which people can understand issues may influence attitude strength (Carmines and Stimson 1980) by varying the four issues so that there would be two hot button social issues (gun rights and death penalty) and two regulatory issues (banking regulations and the appropriate role of the federal government in regulating environmental policy). We also held the content constant. No matter what issue or source condition subjects were assigned, all subjects (save for those in the control group) read an excerpt in which the source took a counter-stereotypical position (see Table 2). The conservative source made a case for gun regulations and called for a moratorium on the death penalty, more banking regulations, and federal control of environmental protection. The liberal source argued that gun regulations were futile, was against ending the death penalty, was for fewer banking regulations, and sought the devolution of environmental policy. If people are responding to source cues, then they should adjust their attitude in the direction of the opinion taken. If they are responding to content, then they should reject the counter-attitudinal information (Bergan 2012). After reading the opinion excerpt, participants were asked their opinion on the issue. See the Appendix for details regarding the sample and measures.

The results, shown in Figure 4, are consistent with the notion that partisan cues may be doing more of the work than the content of the arguments that people encounter on partisan news outlets. Except for the death penalty issue,

---

[11] In order to maintain parallelism between the treatment groups and the control group, control group subjects were randomly assigned to only one set of issue questions.

TABLE 2. *Issue Prompts for Liberals and Conservatives.*

Issue	Liberals Read	Conservatives Read
Gun control	It's time to talk some sense about guns. I believe in placing some curbs on individuals' access to guns. That's just commonsense. But, we have to face the fact that gun registries and waiting periods are not going to end gun-related violence. There are simply too many guns floating around on the black market for waiting periods and registries to stop the flow of guns to criminals who can get them illegally. These policies will just make it harder for law-abiding citizens to protect themselves.	It's time to talk some sense about guns. I'm all for the right to bear arms. It's right there in the constitution. But, no right is absolute. There is room for sensible laws that protect the rights of law-abiding citizens and stop criminals from getting their hands on guns. I'd start with reasonable waiting periods and a gun registry. These policies still allow upstanding citizens to buy guns, while giving law enforcement the tools to stop and track down the bad guys who want to use guns to hurt the innocent.
Death penalty	I am not a fan of the death penalty. It is often applied unfairly. Disadvantaged members of society are more likely to receive the ultimate punishment. At the same time, I don't agree with throwing the baby out with the bath water. Some crimes are so heinous, so despicable, that they deserve death. Criminals who intentionally rape and murder their victims, especially when those victims are children, do not deserve our sympathy. We need to fix how the death penalty is applied in this country, not end it.	The ultimate crime deserves the ultimate punishment. If someone takes an innocent person's life, they don't deserve to continue living. At the same time, it would be equally wrong to put to death someone who was wrongly convicted of a crime. As the saying goes, it is better for a thousand guilty people to go free than to put a single innocent person to death. Given the recent instances of DNA evidence exonerating people on death row, we should put a halt to the death penalty until we can create a less error-prone system.
Bank regulation	The federal government should play an active role in safe-guarding the interests of consumers. In the abstract it may seem like a good idea to restrict banks from using customer deposits to make speculative investments. In practice, however, such a move would only hamstring community banks, which rely on investments to maintain competitive	When it comes to economic growth, usually the best thing the federal government can do is to stand out of the way. When it comes to the financial industry, though, some regulations are needed. The financial meltdown of 2008 shows what can happen if banks are allowed to become "too big to fail." We need to

	rates on loans. Loans that go to average Americans, helping them be the engines of economic growth.	reinstate rules that limit banks from using customer deposits to make risky investments.
Federalism	State and local governments should have more responsibility developing and implementing environmental policy. The health of the environment is so important, so necessary for our communities' vitality, that states and cities – not the federal government – should play the most prominent role ensuring its protection. It's about empowering the people. State and local governments are closer to the people and can do a better job deciding what is best for the environment.	It is time to stop leaving state and local governments with unfunded mandates. The federal government should have more responsibility developing and implementing environmental policy. The health of the environment affects everyone in the country, not just people in a particular state. So, the federal government should take the lead ensuring its protection. It's in our national interest to have clean air and clean water.

Note: Subjects in the treatment conditions were randomly assigned to one issue prompt. Before reading the issue prompt, they were instructed, "Please read an excerpt from an opinion column recently written by Fred Barnes, [a chairman of the Democratic Party/a frequent contributor to MSNBC]." The text in the square brackets was randomized.

subjects' issue attitudes moved in the direction of either the party or media cue ($p < 0.05$). Conservatives (liberals) registered less (more) conservative opinions on gun control, banking regulations, and federal control of environmental policy. In short, we document an instance in which partisan cues *lessened* polarization. More important, we do not observe significant differences in the type of partisan source. On average, people were equally responsive to the cue whether it was attributed to a like-minded media outlet or a partisan elite ($M_{Media\ Source} - M_{Party\ Source} = -0.03$, $p = 0.761$). Also, the story does not appear to be different across media preferences. As Figure 5 illustrates, everyone moves in the direction of the partisan cue. Partisan news seekers are more polarized to begin with, but once they are given clear signals from a partisan source, their attitudes end up in roughly the same spot as others. Once again, we also do not observe large or statistically significant differences in the type of partisan source ($p > 0.2$).

CONCLUSION

Political parties in the United States have undoubtedly become more polarized over the past thirty years. Democrats and Republicans in Congress have moved further from each other, and rank-and-file partisans have followed suit. Although it is more likely than not that the reasons for the surge in party polarization as well as the forces that maintain it are complex, simple explanations are seductive. The emergence of partisan news media makes an

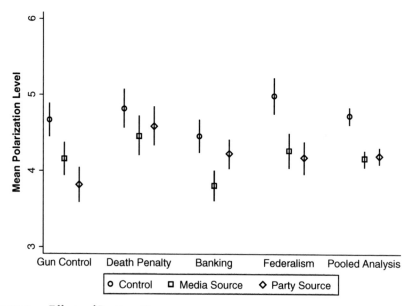

FIGURE 4. Effects of Partisan Cues

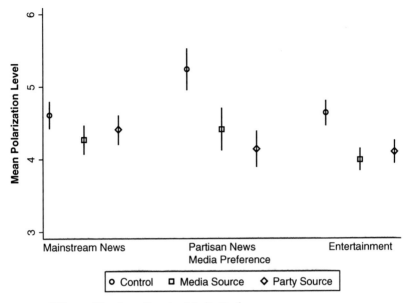

FIGURE 5. Effects of Partisan Cues by Media Preferences

easy target for a simple explanation. Talk show hosts on partisan news outlets deal in the worst form of agitprop. They are not interested in illuminating political debates. They are combatants on a partisan battlefield and offer support for the truism that anything is fair in warfare. If peddling misinformation, ad hominem attacks, and cherry-picked facts are what it takes to win, then so be it. How could these shows not be the cause of what ails the polity?

The problem with the partisan-media-did-it narrative is that it does not quite line up with the timing of polarization in Congress, and if anything, the asymmetry between conservative and liberal outlets in the early days appears to have moved Congress members to the right (at least when they were up for reelection). It also seems too pat of an explanation when we consider that a relatively small group of Americans tune into partisan news shows on a consistent basis. Moreover, given the rapid expansion of entertainment options, the news audience is smaller than it once was, and those who do seek out partisan news tend to be partisan to begin with. All things considered, it seems unlikely that partisan news media would be an all-encompassing force in American politics. Instead, a more plausible characterization is that partisan news media are a symptom of polarization, not its cause.

Exposure to partisan news media *can* polarize viewers – be it exposure to a like-minded or oppositional news source. Yet, exposure to mainstream news can also polarize. We believe that mainstream news' commitment to reporting both sides of a controversy helps explain why. Not only does it give partisans reasons to cling to their preferred worldview, it also communicates where party elites stand on the issues, and as our experiment demonstrates, partisan cues can indeed play an outsized role in how people form political attitudes on a range of issues. Fifty years ago, news coverage over the Medicare debate portrayed Democrats and Republicans in Congress on both sides of the issue. In today's polarized environment, mainstream news stories end up communicating that most party elites fall on opposite sides of the issue. As party elites grew increasingly polarized over the 1990s, news viewers learned about it from mainstream outlets just as well as they did from partisan outlets. In fact, it may have even caused them to seek out news on partisan outlets (Ladd 2012).

To be clear, we are not arguing that partisan news media are blameless when it comes to partisan polarization. They are normatively problematic. But we do not think it makes sense to single them out as the cause of polarization. If we are going to blame news media, we should include *all* news media, not just partisan outlets. More crucially, if we are going to point fingers, we believe the better place to start is with party elites, not TV shows. We are certainly not the first to observe that political parties shape the contours of public opinion (e.g., Key 1961; Zaller 1992). Yet it is interesting to note that fifty years ago, scholars fretted that Americans lacked coherent ideological belief systems to have a sophisticated understanding of politics (Converse 1964). In essence, scholars lamented that Americans were not polarized enough. Pushing against the caricature of the American voter as an ignorant fool, Key (1966: 2) wrote in his reckoning of voting patterns from 1940 to 1960, "The voice of the people is but an echo. The output of an echo chamber bears an inevitable and invariable relation to the input." If party elites fail to take consistently ideological positions on issues, then how could voters be expected to do the same? Today, the two major political parties behave ideologically, and many in the electorate follow suit. In contrast to the notion that the process of polarization is largely demand driven, our evidence suggests that elite-led depolarization is possible across a range of issues. If elites lowered the tone, the mass public would likely follow.

At the same time, we realize elite-led depolarization is not an easy solution. Now that the dance has already begun, party elites cannot simply go back to the way things were. The decentralized structure of political parties in the United States constrains the hands of legislative party leaders, and the extremes of both parties have more credibility and clout than they once did. They now play a major role in fundraising, motivating activists, and primaries. Even if party leaders wanted to move toward the center, it is unlikely that rank-and-file legislators would be willing or able to do so. Some members, such as Republicans who align with the Tea Party, are true believers who place their policy goals above career goals, and are willing to buck the party leadership. Career-minded legislators who typically want to go along to get along may resist centrist moves to avoid attracting a strong challenger in the primaries. The last two years of Obama's presidency will provide some insight into how much the two parties can work together. Now that the Republican Party has taken complete control of Congress, Republican congressional leaders may ultimately feel some pressure to demonstrate that the party can effectively govern and, in doing so, work with President Obama. However, Mr. Obama confronts challenges from the left as well as the right on issues such as trade, privacy, and energy policy, among others.

In the meantime, mainstream news media could help matters if journalists did not rely so much on reducing political stories to two sides. In his recent book, Patterson (2013: 7) advocates for "knowledge-based journalism" in which reporters possess expertise on the stories they cover, rather than acting as a simple pass-through. The current system encourages journalists to faithfully record and report what both sides of a political debate say, letting the public sort it out. In Patterson's alternative scenario, journalists would also act as arbitrators of facts by drawing deep knowledge of the topics that they cover and it would be more difficult for political elites to simply provide their "spin" on political issues. The hope is that this new journalistic model would force political elites to craft evidence-based arguments and, in the process, enrich the foundations of public opinion.

In addition to improving the quality of journalism, we should also figure out how to attract more people to watch the news. Fewer people watch the news today than they did 25 years ago because many do not find the news to be all that entertaining, and there are literally hundreds of entertainment alternatives from which to choose. Unless one has an abiding interest in public affairs, it is easy to see why. The structure of news shows, with the anchor behind a desk, is an efficient model for delivering news stories, but not an engaging one. Yet we can think of no reason why the news needs to be boring. Humans are drawn to narrative, and what is a news story if not a narrative? But, there are good storytellers and bad storytellers, and the way journalists are trained to structure news stories makes them bad storytellers, on average. The news is not inherently boring. Politics is filled with drama and conflict, for instance. Moreover, the content that draws viewers is not, on its face, more interesting than the stories that make up the news. After all, cable content producers figured out how to get 12 million people to watch a show about a family who manufacture duck calls and other sporting goods. So, we think it is possible to re-engineer the provision of the news and attract a larger audience in the process. Partnerships between news and entertainment channels could get more news to the people who are avoiding it.

REFERENCES

Abramowitz, Alan I. 2010. *The Disappearing Center: Engaged Citizens, Polarization, and American Democracy.* New Haven, CT: Yale University Press.

Achen, Christopher H. 1986. *The Statistical Analysis of Quasi-Experiments.* Berkeley: University of California Press.

Adams, Greg D. 1997. "Abortion: Evidence of an Issue Evolution." *American Journal of Political Science* 41 (3): 718–737.

Aldrich, John H. 1995. *Why Parties? The Origin and Transformation of Party Politics in America.* Cambridge: Cambridge University Press.

American Political Science Association Committee on Political Parties. 1950. "Toward a More Responsible Two-Party System." *American Political Science Review* 44 (3) Part 2, Supplement: 1–100.

Arceneaux, Kevin. 2010. "The Benefits of Experimental Methods for the Study of Campaign Effects." *Political Communication* 27 (2): 199–215.

Arceneaux, Kevin. 2008. "Can Partisan Cues Diminish Democratic Accountability?" *Political Behavior* 30 (2): 139–160.

Arceneaux, Kevin, and Martin Johnson. 2014. "Understanding How Individual Differences and Political Context Shape Media Effects." Presented at the Annual Meeting of the American Political Science Association, Washington DC.

Arceneaux, Kevin, and Martin Johnson. 2013. *Changing Minds or Changing Channels? Partisan News in an Age of Choice.* Chicago: University of Chicago Press.

Arceneaux, Kevin, Martin Johnson, René Lindstädt, and Ryan J. Vander Wielen. 2015. "Democratic Representation and the Emergence of Partisan News Media: Investigating Dynamic Partisanship in Congress." *American Journal of Political Science.* Advance online publication. doi:10.1111/ajps.12171.

Berelson, Bernard R. 1954. *Voting: A Study of Opinion Formation in a Presidential Campaign.* Chicago: University of Chicago Press.

Bergan, Daniel E. 2012. "Partisan Stereotypes and Policy Attitudes." *Journal of Communication* 62 (6): 1102–1120.

Bergan, Daniel E. 2009. "Does Grassroots Lobbying Work? A Field Experiment Measuring the Effects of an E-mail Lobbying Campaign on Legislative Behavior." *American Politics Research* 37 (2): 327–352.

Berinsky, Adam J., Gregory A. Huber, and Gabriel S. Lenz. 2012. "Evaluating Online Labor Markets for Experimental Research: Amazon.com's Mechanical Turk." *Political Analysis* 20 (3): 351–368.

Brock, David, Ari Rabin-Havt, and Media Matters for America. 2012. *The Fox Effect: How Roger Ailes Turned a Network into a Propaganda Machine.* New York: Anchor Books.

Campbell, Angus, Philip E Converse, Warren E Miller, and Stokes Donald E. 1960. *The American Voter.* New York: John Wiley.

Carmines, Edward G., and James A. Stimson. 1980. "The Two Faces of Issue Voting." *American Political Science Review* 74 (1): 78–91.

Clinton, Joshua D., and Ted Enamorado. 2014. "The National News Media's Effect on Congress: How the Spread of Fox News Affected Elites in Congress." *Journal of Politics* 76 (4): 928–943.

Cohen, Marty, David Karol, Hans Noel, and John Zaller. 2009. *The Party Decides: Presidential Nominations before and after Reform.* Chicago: University of Chicago Press.

Converse, Philip E. 1964. The Nature of Belief Systems in Mass Publics. In David E. Apter, ed., *Ideology and Discontent*. New York: The Free Press of Glencoe, 206–261.

Davis, Nicholas T., and Johanna L. Dunaway. N.d. "Competing Explanations for Partisan-Ideological Sorting: Media Fragmentation or Elite Polarization?" Unpublished MS, Louisiana State University, Baton Rouge, LA.

DellaVigna, Stefano, and Ethan Kaplan. 2007. "The Fox News Effect: Media Bias and Voting." *The Quarterly Journal of Economics* 122 (3): 1187–1234.

Druckman, James N., Erik Peterson, and Rune Slothuus. 2013. "How Elite Partisan Polarization Affects Public Opinion Formation." *American Political Science Review* 107 (01): 57–79.

Edwards III, George C., and B. Dan Wood. 1999. "Who Influences Whom? The President, Congress, and the Media." *American Political Science Review* 93 (2): 327–344.

Fiorina, Morris P., Samuel J. Abrams, and Jeremy C. Pope. 2005. *Culture War? The Myth of a Polarized America*. New York: Pearson Longman.

Gaines, Brian J., and James H. Kuklinski. 2011. "Experimental Estimation of Heterogeneous Treatment Effects Related to Self-Selection." *American Journal of Political Science* 55 (3): 724–736.

Garrett, R Kelly, Dustin Carnahan, and Emily K Lynch. 2013. "A Turn Toward Avoidance? Selective Exposure to Online Political Information, 2004-2008." *Political Behavior* 35 (1): 113–134.

Groseclose, Tim, and Jeffrey Milyo. 2005. "A Measure of Media Bias." *The Quarterly Journal of Economics* 120 (4): 1191–1237.

Hacker, Jacob S., and Paul Pierson. 2005. *Off Center: The Republican Revolution and the Erosion of American Democracy*. New Haven, CT: Yale University Press.

Herbst, Susan. 1998. *Reading Public Opinion: How Political Actors View the Democratic Process*. Cambridge: Cambridge University Press.

Herszenhorn, David M., and Robert Pear. 2010. "Final Votes in Congress Cap Battle on Health Bill." *New York Times*, March 25, A1.

Hovland, Carl I., Irving L. Janis, and Harold H. Kelley. 1953. *Communication and Persuasion: Psychological Studies of Opinion Change*. New Haven, CT: Yale University Press.

Huckfeldt, Robert, and John Sprague. 1995. *Citizens, Politics and Social communication: Information and Influence in an Election Campaign*. Cambridge: Cambridge University Press.

Iyengar, Shanto, and Donald R. Kinder. 2010. *News That Matters: Television and American Opinion, Updated Edition*. Chicago: University of Chicago Press.

Iyengar, S, G. Sood, and Y. Lelkes. 2012. "Affect, Not Ideology: A Social Identity Perspective on Polarization." *Public Opinion Quarterly* 76 (3): 405–431.

Jacobs, Lawrence R., and Robert Y. Shapiro. 2000. *Politicians Don't Pander: Political Manipulation and the Loss of Democratic Responsiveness*. Chicago: University of Chicago Press.

Jamieson, Kathleen Hall, and Joseph N. Cappella. 2008. *Echo Chamber: Rush Limbaugh and the Conservative Media Establishment*. New York: Oxford University Press.

Katz, Elihu, and Paul Felix Lazarsfeld. 1955. *Personal Influence, The Part Played by People in the Flow of Mass Communications*. New York: Free Press.

Key, Valdimer Orlando. 1966. *The Responsible Electorate*. New York: Vintage Books.

Key, Valdimer Orlando. 1961. *Public Opinion and American Democracy*. New York: Knopf.

Klein, Ezra. 2010. "Was Medicare Popular When It Passed?" Retrieved from http://voices.washingtonpost.com/ezra-klein/2010/03/was_medicare_popular_when_it_p.html.

Ladd, Jonathan McDonald. 2012. *Why Americans Hate the Media and How It Matters*. Princeton, NJ: Princeton University Press.

Levendusky, Matthew. 2013. *How Partisan Media Polarize America*. Chicago: University of Chicago Press.

Levendusky, Matthew. 2009. *The Partisan Sort: How Liberals Became Democrats and Conservatives Became Republicans*. Chicago: University of Chicago Press.

Levendusky, Matthew S. 2010. "Clearer Cues, More Consistent Voters: A Benefit of Elite Polarization." *Political Behavior* 32 (1): 111–131.

Lewis-Beck, Michael S., William G Jacoby, Helmut Norpoth, and Herbert F. Weisberg. 2009. *The American Voter Revisited*. Ann Arbor, MI: University of Michigan Press.

Lord, C. G., L. Ross, and M. R. Lepper. 1979. "Biased Assimilation and Attitude Polarization: The Effects of Prior Theories on Subsequently Considered Evidence." *Journal of Personality and Social Psychology* 37 (11): 2098–2109.

Lubinsky, Charles. 1996. "Reconsidering Retransmission Consent: An Examination of the Retransmission Consent Provision (47 U.S.C. 325(b)) of the 1992 Cable Act." *Federal Communications Law Journal* 49 (1): 99–165.

Mayhew, David R. 1974. *Congress: The Electoral Connection*. New Haven, CT: Yale University Press.

Miller, Warren E., and Donald E. Stokes. 1963. "Constituency Influence in Congress." *American Political Science Review* 57 (1): 45–56.

Parsons, Patrick R. 2008. *Blue Skies: A History of Cable Television*. Philadelphia: Temple University Press.

Patterson, Thomas E. 2013. *Informing the News: The Need for Knowledge-Based Journalism*. New York: Vintage.

Poole, Keith. 2014. "The Polarization of Congressional Parties." Retrieved from http://voteview.com/political_polarization.asp.

Prior, Markus. 2007. *Post-Broadcast Democracy: How Media Choice Increases Inequality in Political Involvement and Polarizes Elections*. Cambridge: Cambridge University Press.

Schickler, Eric, Kathryn Pearson, and Brian D. Feinstein. 2010. "Congressional Parties and Civil Rights Politics from 1933 to 1972." *Journal of Politics* 72 (3): 672–689.

Siegel, David A. 2013. "Social Networks and the Mass Media." *American Political Science Review* 107 (4): 786–805.

Slater, Michael D. 2007. "Reinforcing Spirals: The Mutual Influence of Media Selectivity and Media Effects and Their Impact on Individual Behavior and Social Identity." *Communication Theory* 17 (3): 281–303.

Sobieraj, Sarah and Jeffrey M Berry. 2011. "From Incivility to Outrage: Political Discourse in Blogs, Talk Radio, and Cable News." *Political Communication* 28 (1): 19–41.

Social Security. 2014. "*Legislative History*." Retrieved from http://www.ssa.gov/history/tally65.html.

Stroud, Natalie Jomini. 2011. *Niche News: The Politics of News Choice*. Oxford: Oxford University Press.

Sunstein, Cass R. 2009. *Going to Extremes: How Like Minds Unite and Divide.* New York: Oxford University Press.
Taber, Charles S., and Milton Lodge. 2006. "Motivated Skepticism in the Evaluation of Political Beliefs." *American Journal of Political Science* 50 (3): 755–769.
Thompson, Richard F. 2009. "Habituation: A History." *Neurobiology of Learning and Memory* 92 (1): 127–134.
Yanovitzky, I. 2002. "Effects of News Coverage on Policy Attention and Actions: A Closer Look Into the Media-Policy Connection." *Communication Research* 29 (4): 422–451.
Zaller, John. 1992. *The Nature and Origins of Mass Opinion.* Cambridge: Cambridge University Press.

APPENDIX

AMERICAN NATIONAL ELECTION STUDY QUESTION WORDING

Abortion: There has been some discussion about abortion during recent years. Which one of the opinions on this page best agrees with your view?

1972–1978 Response Set:

Abortion should never be permitted.
Abortion should be permitted only if the life and health of the woman is in danger.
Abortion should be permitted if, due to personal reasons, the woman would have difficulty in caring for the child.
Abortion should never be forbidden, since one should not require a woman to have a child she doesn't want.

1980–2012 Response Set:

By law, abortion should never be permitted.
The law should permit abortion only in case of rape, incest, or when the woman's life is in danger.
The law should permit abortion for reasons other than rape, incest, or danger to the woman's life, but only after the need for the abortion has been clearly established.
By law, a woman should always be able to obtain an abortion as a matter of personal choice.

Economic Issues: We summed the following three items and then took the mean.

Health Care: There is much concern about the rapid rise in medical and hospital costs. Some (1988,1994-LATER: people) feel there should be a government insurance plan which would cover all medical and hospital expenses (1984 AND LATER: for everyone). (1996, 2004: Suppose these people are at one end of a scale, at point 1.) Others feel that (1988,

1994–1996: all) medical expenses should be paid by individuals, and through private insurance (1984 AND LATER: plans) like Blue Cross (1984–1994: or [1996: some] other company paid plans). (1996, 2004: Suppose these people are at the other end, at point 7. And of course, some people have opinions somewhere in between at points 2, 3, 4, 5, or 6.) Where would you place yourself on this scale, or haven't you thought much about this?

Guaranteed Jobs: Some people feel that the government in Washington should see to it that every person has a job and a good standard of living. (1972–1978,1996–LATER: Suppose these people are at one end of a scale, at point 1). Others think the government should just let each person get ahead on his/their own. (1972–1978, 1996: Suppose these people are at the other end, at point 7. And, of course, some other people have opinions somewhere in between, at points 2, 3, 4, 5, or 6.) Where would you place yourself on this scale, or haven't you thought much about this?

Government Services: Some people think the government should provide fewer services, even in areas such as health and education, in order to reduce spending. (2004: Suppose these people are at one end of a scale, at point 1.) Other people feel that it is important for the government to provide many more services even if it means an increase in spending. (2004: Suppose these people are at the other end, at point 7. And of course, some other people have opinions somewhere in between, at points 2, 3, 4, 5, or 6.) Where would you place yourself on this scale, or haven't you thought much about this? [We reverse coded this item.]

President Evaluation: 1968–1974: (1968, 1972: As you know, there were many people mentioned this past year as possible candidates for President [1972: or Vice-President] by the political parties.) (1970: Several political leaders have already been mentioned as possible candidates for President in 1972.) (1968–1972: We would like to get your feelings toward some of these people.) (1974: Now I'd like to get your feelings toward some of our political leaders and other people who are in the news these days.) I have here a card on which there is something that looks like a thermometer. We call it a "feeling thermometer" because it measures your feelings toward these people. (1968: You probably remember that we used something like this in our earlier interview with you.) Here's how it works. If you don't feel particularly warm or cold toward a person, then you should place him in the middle of the thermometer, at the 50 degree mark. If you have a warm feeling toward him or feel favorably toward him, you would give him a score somewhere between 50 degrees and 100 degrees. (1968–1970 only: depending on how warm your feeling is toward that person). On the other hand, if you don't feel very favorably toward a person – that is, if you don't care for him too much – then you would place him somewhere between 0 degrees and 50 degrees. Of course, if you don't know too much about a person, just tell me and we'll go on to the next name.

1976: As you know, many people were mentioned this year as possible candidates for president or vice-president by the political parties. We would like to get your feelings toward some of these people. I'll read the name of each person and I'd like you to rate that person with what we call a feeling thermometer. Ratings between 50 and 100 degrees mean that you feel favorably and warm toward the person; ratings between 0 and 50 degrees mean that you don't feel favorably toward the person and that you don't care too much for that person. If you don't feel particularly warm or cold toward a person you would rate them at 50 degrees. If we come to a person you don't know much about, just tell me and we'll move on to the next one.

1978–Later: I'd like to get your feelings toward some of our political leaders and other people who are in the news these days (1990: have been in the news). I'll read the name of a person and I'd like you to rate that person using (1986–LATER: something we call) the feeling thermometer. Ratings between 50 and 100 (1986–LATER: degrees) mean that you feel favorably and warm toward the person; ratings between 0 and 50 degrees mean that you don't feel favorably toward the person and that you don't care too much for that person. (1986–LATER: You would rate the person at the 50 degree mark if you don't feel particularly warm or cold toward the person.) If we come to a person whose name you don't recognize, you don't need to rate that person. Just tell me and we'll move on to the next one. (1978–1984: If you do recognize the name, but you don't feel particularly warm or cold toward the person, then you would rate the person at the 50 degree mark.)

News Watching: How many days in the past week did you watch national news on TV? 0–7

PARTISAN CUES EXPERIMENT

In January 2014, we recruited 1,212 individuals from the *Amazon.com Mechanical Turk* online labor market, of which 1,205 agreed to participate. Participants were compensated $0.50 for completing the study, which took approximately five minutes to complete. The sample was broader and more diverse than the college student population at our respective universities, but was certainly not representative of the population. The average age of the sample was 31.75 (ranging from 19 to 80). The median income was close to the national median, falling between $35,000 and $50,000, but the sample skewed white (72.85 percent) and male (61.22 percent). With respect to political identities, 68.77 percent identified as liberal, 42.6 percent identified as Democrat, and 14.95 percent identified as Republican.

The experiment employs a 4 × 3 design, consisting of four issues (gun control, the death penalty, banking regulations, and federalism), and three source cues (party elite cue, partisan news cue, or none [control group]). Subjects were randomly assigned to one of these twelve cells: Gun Control × Party Cue (*n* = 100), × Media Cue (*n* = 107), × Control (*n* = 106); Death Penalty × Party Cue (*n* = 96), × Media Cue (*n* = 96), × Control (*n* = 97);

Banking Regulations × Party Cue ($n = 114$), × Media Cue ($n = 111$), × Control ($n = 92$); Federalism × Party Cue ($n = 108$), × Media Cue ($n = 93$), × Control ($n = 85$).

On the pre-test instrument, we measured subjects' demographic characteristics and media viewing preferences. Our media viewing preference question mirrored the one used in a previous experiment.* Subjects were asked, "Imagine you had a choice among the five television shows below. Please rank these shows based on how much you would like to watch them with your most preferred show at top and your least preferred show at bottom." The choices were: *The O'Reilly Factor with Bill O'Reilly* on the Fox News Channel, *The Last Word with Lawrence O'Donnell* on the MSNBC News Channel, *CBS Evening News with Scott Pelley, Pet Star* on the Animal Planet network, and *For Rent* on the HGTV network. Subjects who ranked either of the partisan talk shows as first were coded as partisan news seekers; those who ranked CBS news as first were coded as mainstream news seekers, and those who ranked either of the entertainment shows first were coded as entertainment seekers.

On the post-test instrument, subjects assigned to the Gun Control conditions were asked, "Gun control policies, such as registries and waiting periods, are effective at reducing gun violence." For all issue questions, subjects placed their answers on a seven-point scale that ranged from Strongly Disagree to Strongly Agree. Responses were coded such that larger values were consistent with their predispositions: higher values indicated agreement for liberals, while for conservatives, higher values indicated disagreement. Subjects assigned to the Death Penalty conditions were asked, "Although some crimes deserve punishment by death, the use of the death penalty should be halted until safeguards are put in place to ensure that it is fairly applied." Those assigned to the Banking Regulations conditions were asked, "The federal government should enact more regulations that restrict all banks from making investments with deposits." Finally, subjects assigned to the Federalism conditions were asked, "When it comes to protecting the environment, the federal government should be more involved than state governments."

---

* Kevin Arceneaux and Martin Johnson, "Understanding How Individual Differences and Political Context Shape Media Effects." Presented at the Annual Meeting of the American Political Science Association, Washington, DC, 2014.

15

The Polarizing Effects of Partisan and Mainstream News

Natalie Jomini Stroud and Alexander Curry

- Strong partisans gravitate toward like-minded partisan media.
- Like-minded media use can polarize attitudes and, in some instances, so can the use of counter-attitudinal media.
- An experiment using NBC, MSNBC, and Fox News coverage of the Keystone XL Pipeline's environmental impact shows that media coverage affects attitudes and beliefs.
- Drawing from inoculation theory, like-minded news polarized attitudes, and watching a combination of like-minded and mainstream news coverage did little to reduce polarization.

On January 31, 2014, the U.S. Department of State released its "Final Supplemental Environmental Impact Statement for the Keystone XL Project." The report garnered substantial attention. Would the pipeline have a devastating environmental impact as some groups had alleged?[1] Or was the effect minimal and offset by the prospect of a reliable source of oil and an influx of new jobs?[2] If you learned about this report from television, your answer to these questions would depend on which outlet you watched. According to Fox News, the report concluded that the environmental impact would be minimal. MSNBC, however, highlighted the environmentally damaging effects of not only the tar sands that would travel through the pipeline, but also the nation's continuing dependence on oil. NBC News noted that there would be some environmental impact, but it would be minimal and that although jobs would be created, there wouldn't be many and they would be short term. All three outlets covered exactly the same report, but each was unique in its coverage.

The Keystone Pipeline report is an illuminating case study of how information is presented in today's fragmented media environment. Partisan

---

[1] J. Eilperin. "Environmentalists Take Hard Line with Obama on Keystone XL," *Washington Post*, September 24, 2013.
[2] Ibid.

outlets have decidedly different takes on the day's news and events. Based on these divergent portrayals, audiences may rely on unique sets of facts to support polarized attitudes and opinions about important political matters. It is precisely this topic that we tackle in this chapter. To begin, we briefly describe evidence regarding partisan selective exposure, the selection of politically like-minded media. Our review lays the groundwork for why partisan media are relevant for understanding polarization. Next, we present an overview of research on how the media affect partisans' political beliefs, opinions, and attitudes. Equipped with this background, we turn to the Keystone Pipeline report and present original data on how people react to the coverage. Our case study illustrates the media's ability to polarize beliefs and attitudes. We conclude by discussing the broader role of the media in affecting political polarization.

PARTISAN AND MAINSTREAM NEWS MEDIA USE

Partisan selective exposure occurs when partisans display a preference for like-minded over counter-attitudinal information. The notion has captivated scholars for over half a century. In *Voting: A Study of Opinion Formation in a Presidential Campaign*, Berelson, Lazarsfeld, and McPhee (1954) noted that voters were attracted to information favoring their preferred candidate in the 1948 presidential election. Festinger (1962) formalized the concept of selective exposure as a prediction emerging from his theory of cognitive dissonance. To reduce the uncomfortable experience of having conflicting cognitions, Festinger proposed, people could select congenial information to bolster their views. Early research findings were mixed on selective exposure (Sears and Freedman 1967), but more recent scholarship has uncovered clearer evidence, particularly when focusing narrowly on politics (Hart et al. 2009).

The renaissance in selective exposure research has been spurred at least in part by the increased availability of partisan news options. Recent studies provide evidence that partisans are drawn to like-minded news. In *Niche News: The Politics of News Choice*, Stroud (2011) categorized the self-reported media diets of over 30,000 National Annenberg Election Survey respondents. A series of open-ended questions asked respondents to name the newspapers, talk radio programs, cable news outlets, and news websites that they used. Media outlets were coded as left-leaning, right-leaning, or neither and then compared to respondents' partisanship and political ideology. Newspapers named by the respondents were categorized on the basis of their presidential endorsements. Talk radio programs were grouped on the basis of previous content analyses, whether trade publications labeled the programs as partisan, and whether the programs described themselves as partisan. For cable news, Fox News was treated as right-leaning; CNN and MSNBC as left-leaning.[3] Finally, the few websites named by respondents as sources of political information were subjected to a content analysis to identify whether the sites aligned with the political left of right. Using both cross-sectional and panel survey data, the results were consistent: people's political leanings predicted the media outlets that they named. Democrats used more left-leaning outlets than Republicans, and Republicans used more right-leaning outlets than Democrats (see also Stroud 2008).

Numerous other studies also conclude that people are drawn to media matching their partisan beliefs. Iyengar and Hahn (2009) found that by randomly assigning articles to different partisan news labels, Republicans preferred articles labeled as coming from Fox News and Democrats preferred articles from CNN and National Public Radio (NPR). Knobloch-Westerwick and Meng (2009) created a news website containing articles with distinct viewpoints on important political issues. They unobtrusively logged people's browsing behavior and found that study participants selected more articles consistent with their beliefs than articles containing a different point of view. Stroud (2011) observed magazine browsing behavior in a library waiting room. Unsuspecting study participants could browse any magazine of interest from a set of political magazines strategically placed on a side table. The magazines selected were recorded by a confederate. Participants also were given a free subscription to a political magazine of their choosing. Partisanship again emerged as a predictor of people's browsing behavior and subscription decisions.

Although evidence of partisan selective exposure is widespread, one persistent question is whether partisan news audiences are large enough to warrant our attention. The question is notoriously difficult to answer because it isn't possible to definitively arrive at a single estimate of how often people use like-minded news. Rates will vary based on context – a presidential election, for instance, likely inspires more news use and selectivity than a year without a high profile election. Nonetheless, the first response is to look at the numbers (see a similar strategy in Prior 2013). We focus on Nielsen ratings for television news because these metrics are widely available and cable news outlets are acknowledged as having partisan leanings. This emphasis also reflects our focus on television news coverage in our Keystone Pipeline case study. Before turning to the numbers, it is important to note that Nielsen ratings aren't ideal for understanding the prevalence of partisan selective exposure. They cover only television viewership, neglecting use of the many other partisan media sources. Further, the data aren't broken down by partisanship. All we know from Nielsen data is the audience size for various programs, not whether the audience was like-minded or opposed to the partisan message. Nielsen data also can be tricky because rarely are the numbers presented in a comparable way. The Pew Research Center, for instance, reports *median* prime time viewership

---

[3] There is some question about whether CNN should be considered as left-leaning or as more middle of the road; see Stroud (2011) for more details on coding it as liberal in 2004.

for cable news and *average* viewing for the network evening news broadcasts in their 2014 State of the News Media report.[4] Median viewership was 1.75 million for Fox News, 619,000 for MSNBC, and 543,000 for CNN. On average, *ABC World News* attracted 7.7 million viewers, *CBS Evening World News* 6.5 million, and *NBC Nightly News* 8.4 million. Whether these numbers are comparable depends on how skewed the viewership distributions are.

Comparable data can be obtained more easily for important political events, such as the national conventions and presidential debates. These data are shown in Figure 1. For the conventions, cable and network news outlets are comparable in terms of the audience size. For the debates, however, the broadcast networks attracted larger audiences than cable. That partisan selective exposure explains some of these numbers seems to be a reasonable assumption given that the left-leaning MSNBC attracted more viewers during the Democratic National Convention (DNC) and right-leaning Fox News ratings outpaced both its cable and network news rivals during the Republican National Convention (RNC).

Whether any of these numbers are large or small is a matter of opinion. For comparison, the top two programs during the 2012–13 season were *NCIS*, which garnered a season average of 21.6 million viewers, and *Sunday Night*

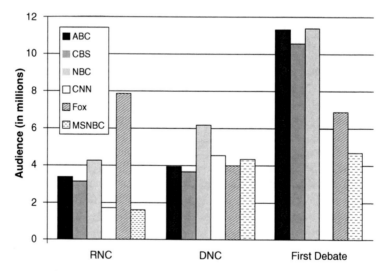

FIGURE 1. Nielsen Ratings for 2012 Presidential Campaign Events
Source: Data from the University of Virginia's Center for Politics (http://www.centerforpolitics.org/crystalball/articles/reviewing-the-convention-ratings/) and the *New York Times* (http://mediadecoder.blogs.nytimes.com/2012/10/04/presidential-debate-drew-more-than-70-million-viewers/).

[4] Available at http://www.journalism.org/2014/03/26/state-of-the-news-media-2014-key-indicators-in-media-and-news/.

Football, with an average of 21 million viewers.[5] Compared to these sports and entertainment programs, news and political events attracted smaller audiences on any one channel. *The Daily Show*, a political comedy program attracting extensive academic attention, had an audience of 1.4 million viewers during the week of June 23–27, 2014.[6] Compared to *The Daily Show*, network programming and, at least in some instances, cable news programming have greater reach. Although we find the rates of cable news viewing – particularly when considered as one of many different mediums containing partisan news – substantively important, others are less persuaded (Prior 2013).

A second argument is that even if few people use partisan media, the audiences attracted to these outlets are disproportionately influential. Partisan news viewers are more politically engaged. Research demonstrates that those using like-minded news media are more likely to vote and to participate in politics (Dilliplane 2011; Stroud 2011). This group thus has greater influence on elections and public affairs relative to other citizens. Partisan news viewers may include a high percentage of opinion leaders, spreading the information that they obtain from partisan programming to others. Although little systematic research evaluates opinion leadership and partisan news viewing, several have suggested its plausibility (Arceneaux and Johnson 2013; Levendusky 2013). Supportive of the idea, Tsfati, Stroud, and Chotiner (2013) found that like-minded news use predicted attempts to convince others to vote, an expected behavior for opinion leaders. This effect was mediated in part by polarized attitudes.

Taking a broad view, we contend that the research demonstrates that partisans display preferences for like-minded news. As the ratings data illustrate, not all partisans use partisan media. But some do. And these audiences – whether one regards the ratings as small or large – arguably play a disproportionate political role due to their high rates of political involvement.

THE POLARIZING EFFECTS OF THE MEDIA

Numerous studies confirm that the media can affect political polarization. In addition to the documented effect of congenial media on polarization, research has found that even counter-attitudinal media can increase political polarization. Less research has analyzed the polarizing effect of mainstream news media, but it is possible that even network news could polarize attitudes.

Turning first to partisan media, data support its polarizing effect. Again from *Niche News*, survey data supported the polarizing effects of partisan media. In the book, Stroud analyzed feeling thermometer measures of how favorably or unfavorably members of the American public felt toward then-presidential

[5] Data from *TV Guide* (http://www.tvguide.com/news/most-watched-tv-shows-top-25-2012-2013-1066503.aspx).
[6] Data from http://tvbythenumbers.zap2it.com/2014/07/03/late-night-tv-ratings-for-june-23-27-2014/279365/.

candidates John Kerry and George W. Bush. Cross-sectional survey analyses demonstrated that conservatives and Republicans using right-leaning sources and liberals and Democrats using left-leaning sources held more affectively polarized political attitudes than partisans not using like-minded media sources.

Although the relationships were consistent in the presence of numerous demographic and political controls, cross-sectional survey analyses are subject to well-known limitations. Most obviously, it is not clear which variable is the cause and which is the effect. In general, surveys are ill-suited to providing definitive evidence of causal relationships, but survey data gathered over time comes closer to identifying the temporal dynamics. Stroud (2010) analyzed four different panel surveys and rolling cross-sectional survey data to understand the relationships between partisan media use and polarization. The results consistently demonstrated that partisan selective exposure led to affective polarization. In the panel survey analyses, there also was some evidence of the reverse, that polarization can motivate greater like-minded partisan media use.

Experimental research also supports the proposed relationship between polarization and like-minded media use. For two controversial political issues, Taber and Lodge (2006) found that those accessing confirmatory information held more polarized political attitudes. Similarly, Levendusky (2013) discovered that experimental subjects viewing like-minded partisan media (Fox News for conservatives and MSNBC for liberals) held more polarized political attitudes than those viewing mainstream media (*PBS Newshour*). Arceneaux and Johnson (2013) argue that experimental effects may be overestimated because participants who wouldn't typically use partisan news are more affected by exposure. Although this conclusion suggests a more modest role for partisan media, it nonetheless demonstrates the potential for polarization particularly when broader audiences tune in.

Just as pro-attitudinal news coverage can increase polarization, so too can counter-attitudinal news. Research on the polarizing effect of counter-attitudinal news, however, suggests that the effect is more mixed. In some instances, viewing messages with a different political perspective can *increase* polarization, particularly among those with strong political attitudes (Taber and Lodge 2006). Presumably, encountering different views can increase one's political resolve and inspire counter-argument, thus increasing polarization. In other instances, however, counter-attitudinal media use is related to more modest attitudes and views closer to the political opposition's perspective (Stroud, 2010; Feldman 2011; Garrett et al. 2014).

Even less is known about the polarizing effects of mainstream news coverage (see also Prior 2013). Several possibilities exist. First, we know that partisans tend to see putatively neutral news coverage as hostile to their political viewpoint (Vallone, Ross, and Lepper 1985). Thus mainstream news exposure may produce mixed effects in much the same way that counter-attitudinal news exposure sometimes polarizes audiences and sometimes does not. Second, efforts to cover multiple viewpoints even-handedly may produce relatively little change in an audience's political outlook. If the mainstream news provides an equal number of confirmatory and contradictory claims, they may cancel each other out and leave audiences with essentially the same view. In our Keystone Pipeline case study, we compare the effects of mainstream and like-minded news exposure. We leave the task of exploring the effects of counter-attitudinal exposure to future research for the simple reason that research on partisan selective exposure suggests that counter-attitudinal news exposure is less prevalent than pro-attitudinal exposure.

EXPOSURE COMBINATIONS AND INOCULATION

The story that partisans use like-minded news media and then become more politically polarized is an obvious oversimplification. Although partisans gravitate toward like-minded news, some venture beyond the comfort of the echo chamber. Some, driven by any number of motivations from curiosity to a desire to counter-argue, use oppositional media (Garrett 2009; Knobloch-Westerwick and Meng 2009; Gentzkow and Shapiro 2011; Stroud 2011; Garrett and Stroud 2014). Others keep tabs on mainstream news coverage in addition to monitoring like-minded content (Garrett, Carnahan, and Lynch 2011).[7]

How people integrate multiple media portrayals has received little systematic attention. In one study, those watching Fox News *and* either CNN or MSNBC seemed to split the difference, forming opinions about the war in Iraq that fell in between the views of those watching only Fox News and the views of those watching only CNN/MSNBC (Muddiman, Stroud, and McCombs 2014). In our Keystone Pipeline case study, we focus not on the combination of left- and right-leaning exposure, but instead on the effects of mainstream and like-minded exposure in isolation and in combination.

Theoretically, like-minded media may have an inoculation effect – providing arguments that shield audiences from the contradictory information that they may obtain from other sources. In the book *Echo Chamber*, Jamieson and Cappella (2008) suggest that the partisan media may have this consequence. Writing about conservative talk radio host Rush Limbaugh, they noted that, "Limbaugh's use of inoculation – the presenting of the opposing frame in order to rebut it – can be expected to increase adherence to the conservatively framed argument because inoculation minimizes the likelihood of counterpersuasion" (142). Work on inoculation is a productive place to start when analyzing how people navigate multiple related messages from different sources.

---

[7] Note that ABC, CBS, and NBC sometimes are accused of having a liberal bias (Watts et al. 1999), the public at large – particularly conservatives – perceive a liberal bias (Stroud, Muddiman, and Lee 2014; Watts et al. 1999), and content analyses suggest that for at least some of these outlets, the coverage has a liberal tilt (Groeling 2008). Despite this, we argue that the evening news programs on these outlets are *less* partisan relative to the programming on Fox News and on MSNBC.

Inoculation theory takes its cue from the medical use of the term; following exposure to weakened versions of germs, people become immune to diseases such as smallpox and polio. In persuasion research, inoculation is the idea that "people can be stimulated to build up resistance to attacks on attitudes by being exposed to weakened attitude-threatening messages" (Szabo and Pfau 2002: 234). While Lumsdaine and Janis (1953) were the first to draw an analogy between medical inoculation and the potential to confer resistance to attitude change, it was McGuire (1964) who elaborated on the idea and brought inoculation theory to life. In the intervening fifty years, many scholars have validated the theory, particularly in the political realm. We know, for example, that inoculation can protect voters from persuasive attempts in political debates (An and Pfau 2004). Lin and Pfau (2007) showed that inoculation can guard against the effects of what Noelle-Neumann (1974) termed the spiral of silence, or a reticence of people to speak their minds when they believe their opinion is in the minority. Furthermore, we know that political campaigns can use inoculation strategies to guard a candidate's image and help lock in votes (Pfau et al. 1990). Applied to our current focus, like-minded news exposure may inoculate viewers from any possible depolarization resulting from exposure to counter-attitudinal information in mainstream news.

The time interval between an inoculation treatment and an attack has been the focus of much research (e.g., Compton and Pfau 2004). Drawing again from the medical use of the term, inoculation requires time to produce resistance to a disease. Although scholars proposed that a moderate delay between inoculation treatment and attack is ideal for conferring resistance, study results have been inconclusive (Banas and Rains 2010). Indeed, Pfau et al. (1990) found no significant difference in resistance to persuasion when a treatment was given before or after a counter-attitudinal attack. In essence, unlike medical inoculation, which requires that the vaccination precede a body's gaining resistance, Pfau et al. found that inoculation against persuasive messages does not necessarily require a similar chronological flow. This point is particularly significant in light of the case study presented later in this chapter, as like-minded news may inoculate viewers regardless of whether it is seen before or after mainstream news.

According to inoculation theory, threat and counter-argument are prerequisites for creating resistance to persuasion. Threat refers to a real or perceived challenge to a prevailing attitude, belief, or position (Compton 2013). Research suggests that mainstream news may be seen as threatening to partisan audiences. Although ideologically middle-of-the-road citizens may view a mainstream news report as unthreatening, partisans may perceive the same mainstream report as a threat to their closely held beliefs (Vallone, Ross, and Lepper 1985). Counter-arguing refers to the internal process that happens when people are faced with a threat and then, on their own, refute the threat using novel arguments (Compton 2013). Again, we know that partisans generate new counter-arguments when confronted with counter-attitudinal messages (Taber and Lodge 2006). Mainstream news can generate threat and provoke counter-argument by mentioning different political viewpoints, thus triggering an inoculation effect from exposure to like-minded news.

Although it was long thought that threats and counter-arguments were key to the process of inoculation-related resistance, scholars found a path between pretreatment and inoculation that is independent of threat and counter-arguing (Pfau et al. 1997a). A study by Pfau et al. (2003) suggested that attitude accessibility may provide an alternate path for conferring resistance, where inoculation treatments lead to stronger and more accessible attitudes, which then leads to a greater ability to resist counter-attitudinal attacks. Research demonstrates that choosing like-minded news articles increases the accessibility of partisanship (Knobloch-Westerwick 2012), thus providing another possible explanation for the inoculation effect of like-minded media.

We mentioned earlier the key role of inoculation treatments in conferring resistance to persuasion. Some researchers have suggested, and subsequently confirmed, that some threats may be significant enough that they do not require an inoculation pretreatment in order to confer resistance (Pfau et al. 1997b). In the context of our study, it could be that the presence of counter-attitudinal information in mainstream news constitutes enough of a threat to illicit resistance regardless of whether audiences also view like-minded news. Wyer (1974) suggested and Pfau et al. (1997b) confirmed that the presence of a threat eclipses the importance of a refutational preemption when conferring resistance. In this vein, Compton (2013) encouraged researchers to look at whether more subtle methods of inoculation exist than the traditional refutational pretreatment. Our case study seeks to answer this call as we look at whether mainstream news yields polarization even in the absence of like-minded news.

Closely related to our focus on particular media outlets is the notion that source derogation may be associated with inoculation. Instead of counter-arguing a message, source derogation means that individuals deem the information source untrustworthy. Several researchers have noted that source derogation may better explain resistance to persuasion (Tannenbaum and Norris 1965), while others have suggested that source derogation may be a consequence of inoculation (Ivanov and Miller 2011). It could be that political partisans who encounter news from mainstream sources counter-argue this news based on the source, not on what is being reported. This could result in either no attitude change or polarization as a result of viewing mainstream news.

By evoking alternative views, increasing the accessibility of partisanship, and providing refutations, like-minded news may inoculate viewers from counter-attitudinal messages. By appearing as a threat to partisans, mainstream news may elicit counter-argument or source derogation. This process may inoculate against potential persuasion from non-like-minded messages, "protecting" people from views unlike their own and exacerbating polarization.

THE KEYSTONE PIPELINE CASE STUDY

To illustrate how partisan media affect the public's thoughts and reactions, we conducted an experiment using the Keystone Pipeline coverage. We gathered clips of roughly comparable length from Fox News, MSNBC, and NBC News. We randomly assigned 274 respondents gathered through Amazon.com's Mechanical Turk to one of five different conditions: (1) a *control* condition where respondents did not watch any news coverage, (2) a *mainstream news* condition where respondents watched NBC News' coverage of the Keystone Pipeline report, (3) a *like-minded news* condition where Republicans watched the clip from Fox News and Democrats watched the MSNBC coverage, (4) a *mainstream–like-minded news* condition where respondents first watched the NBC News coverage and then like-minded coverage, and (5) a *like-minded– mainstream news* condition where respondents first saw a like-minded news clip followed by the NBC News segment. Although identifying a like-minded clip is easy for those identifying as Democrats or Republicans, it is not clear which clip would be like-minded for those without a partisan leaning. For this reason, and in keeping with prior literature, we focus only on the subset of respondents with a partisan leaning ($n = 225$).[8]

The broadcast segments selected for this study were all approximately two minutes in length and aired on January 31 on Fox News' *Special Report with Bret Baier*, MSNBC's *All in with Chris Hayes*, and NBC's *Nightly News with Brian Williams*. As described briefly in the introduction to this chapter, each clip varied in how it covered the State Department's report on the Keystone Pipeline. As will be seen shortly, the information conveyed reflected the partisan reputation of each source.

After viewing each clip, we asked respondents to tell us, based on the clip that they watched, whether the report found that: (a) the Keystone Pipeline will create more jobs, (b) the Keystone Pipeline won't affect demand for crude oil, (c) oil sands crude produces more carbon pollution than average crude, and (d) the Keystone Pipeline would have little environmental impact. They could check as many of these options as applied. For this analysis, we looked at reactions among all respondents, regardless of whether they saw other clips or the order in which they viewed the other clips.[9] As shown in Figure 2a, both Democrats and Republicans reached similar conclusions about the substance of the State Department report if they watched the mainstream, NBC News

---

[8] Following Petrocik (2009) and the 2014 Pew Research Center report on polarization (http:// www.people-press.org/2014/06/12/appendix-b-why-we-include-leaners-with-partisans/pp- 2014-06-12-polarization-a2-01/), we treat those leaning toward a party as partisans.

[9] In most instances, reports of what the clip said about the Keystone Pipeline report did not vary between those who saw a clip first (or who only saw one clip) and those who saw a clip after viewing another clip (*like-minded–mainstream news* and *mainstream–like-minded news* conditions). The one exception was perceptions of crude oil demand, where study participants were more likely to recognize this in the like-minded clip when they saw it second.

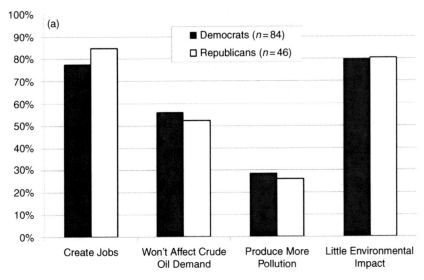

FIGURE 2A. Perceptions of How NBC News Covered the Keystone Report

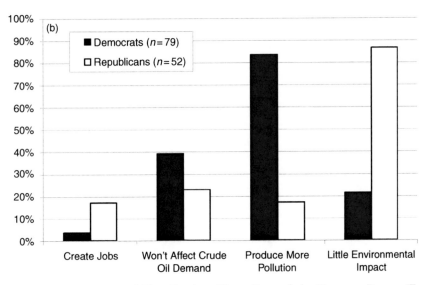

FIGURE 2B. Perceptions of How Partisan News Covered the Keystone Report (Fox News for Republicans, MSNBC for Democrats)

coverage. Partisans from both sides of the aisle learned from NBC News that the Keystone Pipeline would create jobs and would have little environmental impact. Just over 50 percent of partisans also remembered that the clip said that the pipeline would have little effect on demand for crude oil.

Those viewing like-minded partisan news (Democrats viewing MSNBC and Republicans viewing Fox News), however, came away with starkly different impressions of what the report found (see Figure 2b). Nearly 90 percent of Republicans viewing Fox News concluded that the report demonstrated that the pipeline would have little environmental impact. Reaching quite the opposite conclusion, over 80 percent of Democrats watching MSNBC determined that the report concluded that the pipeline would produce more pollution – precisely the opposite environmental impact. As these figures show, audiences recognized differences in how NBC, Fox News, and MSNBC covered the Keystone report.[10]

Answering factual questions about what the media reported is different from believing the information, however. We next asked respondents what they believed about the pipeline. After study participants viewed the clip(s) to which they were assigned, we elicited their opinions on whether the pipeline would affect the environment and whether the pipeline would create a significant number of jobs. As shown in Figure 3a, Democrats were more likely than Republicans to believe that the pipeline would pose a significant risk to the environment, regardless of the condition to which they were assigned. In addition to these persistent partisan differences, however, media exposure mattered. For the *mainstream* and *control* conditions, Democrats and Republicans had similar views on the environmental impact of the pipeline. For the *like-minded, like-minded–mainstream*, and *mainstream–like-minded* conditions, however, Democrats and Republicans had significantly different beliefs about the Keystone Pipeline's effects on the environment.[11]

A similar, albeit less pronounced, pattern appears when looking at beliefs about whether the pipeline would create a significant number of jobs. Here, more Republicans than Democrats thought that the pipeline would create jobs, regardless of the condition to which they were assigned (see Figure 3b). Again, there are no partisan differences when looking at the *mainstream* and *control* conditions. In the mixed conditions (*like-minded–mainstream* and *mainstream–like-minded*), differences between Democrats and Republicans are marginally significant. In the *like-minded* condition, Democrats and Republicans

---

[10] There were no significant differences in Democrats' and Republicans' reports about the NBC News coverage based on chi-square tests (Figure 2a). Democrats watching MSNBC and Republicans watching Fox News differed significantly in their reports about the coverage, although the difference was only marginally significant for perceptions of crude oil demand (Figure 2b).

[11] In ANOVA analyses conducted for Figures 3a and 3b, the interaction between party and condition was not significant for beliefs about the environmental impact of the pipeline ($F(4,213) = 1.73$, $p = .14$), or for the pipeline's ability to produce jobs ($F(4,213) = 0.95$, $p = .44$). If condition is treated as a continuous, as opposed to categorical, variable, it is significant in predicting the environmental impact of the pipeline ($F(1,219) = 6.76$, $p = .01$). Given our substantive interest in differences between Democrats and Republicans, we nonetheless look at the within condition differences between Democrats and Republicans using post-hoc tests and Sidak corrections; the significance of these comparisons are noted in text.

(a)

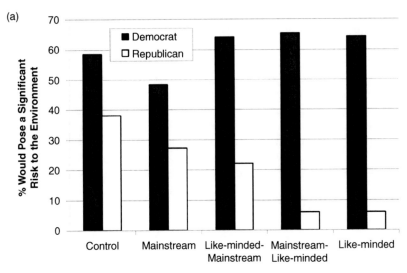

FIGURE 3A. Belief that the Keystone Pipeline Would Pose a Significant Risk to the Environment

(b)

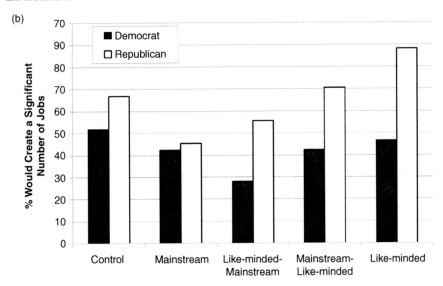

FIGURE 3B. Belief that the Keystone Pipeline Would Create a Significant Number of Jobs

significantly diverge from one another in their views about whether the Keystone pipeline would create jobs. These results suggest that not only did audiences pick up on differences in how the media organizations covered the Keystone Pipeline report, they also modified their views on the basis of the information. Like-minded news, whether by itself or paired with mainstream news, resulted in greater differences between Democrats and Republicans than mainstream news coverage by itself or no news coverage at all.

Thus far, we've shown that the three news segments transmitted different facts about the pipeline report (Figure 2a, 2b) and that like-minded news produced more polarized beliefs about the effects of the pipeline (Figure 3a, 3b). Our final analysis examined support for the pipeline as a function of partisanship and experimental condition. Using a Likert scale, we asked study participants whether they favored or opposed building the Keystone XL Pipeline. We analyzed whether these views varied based on respondents' partisanship and the media clips they viewed. The results, shown in Figure 4, follow a now-familiar pattern.[12] As is clear from the chart, partisanship is related to what people think of the Keystone Pipeline. Republicans are consistently more supportive of the pipeline than Democrats. The effect of partisanship on pipeline support, however, is moderated by the experimental conditions. Partisanship affects attitudes toward the pipeline similarly for participants in the *control* and *mainstream news* conditions. For the three remaining conditions (*like-minded—mainstream, mainstream–like-minded,* and *like-minded*), however, partisanship is a significantly stronger predictor of attitudes toward the pipeline relative to the control condition. Like-minded news, whether seen in isolation or in combination with mainstream news, increases partisan polarization.

Several lessons emerge from this case study. First, viewing mainstream news coverage did not increase the gap between Democrats and Republicans (Figures 3a, 3b, 4). In no instance did pipeline attitudes and beliefs vary between the *mainstream* and *control* conditions. On the one hand, this may be an artifact of the particular topic and clip used in this study. There may be something unique about the Keystone Pipeline report and the NBC coverage of it that produced little change in partisans' beliefs and attitudes. On the other hand, perhaps mainstream news coverage, in its effort to present both sides, has the effect of returning people to their previously held beliefs and attitudes. Mainstream news also could be dismissed outright. After all, we know that partisans tend to see hostile biases in neutral media coverage (Vallone, Ross, and Lepper 1985). This could lead partisans to discount information from the source.

Second, like-minded news exposure polarizes beliefs and opinions. This is true even if the like-minded news is paired with mainstream news coverage. It also holds regardless of whether respondents view mainstream news coverage before or after the partisan content. The result showcases the potency of like-minded news and coheres nicely with previous research on inoculation, where resistance to counter-persuasion was apparent regardless of whether the inoculating information was provided before or after the counter-attitudinal information (Pfau et al. 1990).

---

[12] In a regression analysis predicting attitudes about the pipeline, the interaction between condition and partisanship was significant (R-square change $F_{(4, 215)} = 3.20$, $p = .01$).

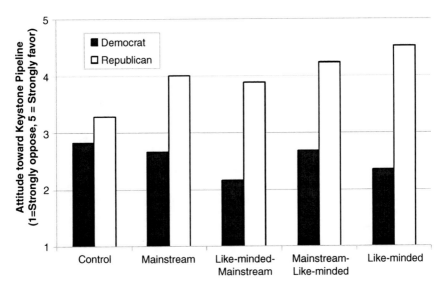

FIGURE 4. Support for the Keystone Pipeline by Partisanship and Condition

Of course, this is just one case study demanding replication and extension before generalizing the findings. With this important caveat, the differences in the coverage and opinions after viewing the coverage are noteworthy. It appears that, at least in this study, like-minded news polarized partisan viewpoints and a dose of mainstream news did little to counteract these effects.

CONCLUSION

The media both reflect and intensify partisan divides among members of the public. Outlets with sharply partisan bents attract like-minded audiences and intensify their political attitudes. Although not everyone uses partisan media, the audience that does may be particularly politically influential, making findings of increased polarization worrisome. Given that some like-minded news viewers also watch mainstream news, an optimistic outcome could be that doses of mainstream news counteract the polarizing effects of like-minded media. Our case study of the State Department's report on the Keystone XL Pipeline suggests otherwise. Like-minded news seems to override information presented within mainstream news reports. Like-minded media exposure, occurring in isolation or prior to or after mainstream news exposure, polarizes beliefs about the pipeline and strengthens the relationship between partisanship and attitudes about the pipeline. Our case study offers only a glimpse at the effects of partisan media. Future work is needed to better specify the direct and indirect reach of partisan media. Based both on this case study and the results of prior work, however, we conclude that partisan media contribute to polarization.

REFERENCES

An, C., and M. Pfau. 2004. "The Efficacy of Inoculation in Televised Political Debates." *Journal of Communication* 54 (3): 421–436.

Arceneaux, K., and M. Johnson. 2013. *Changing Minds or Changing Channels? Partisan News in an Age of Choice*. Chicago: University of Chicago Press.

Banas, J. A., and S. A. Rains. 2010. "A Meta-analysis of Research on Inoculation Theory." *Communication Monographs* 77 (3): 281–311.

Berelson, B. R., P. F. Lazarsfeld, and W. N. McPhee. 1954. *Voting: A Study of Opinion Formation in a Presidential Campaign*. Chicago: University of Chicago Press.

Compton, J. 2013. "Inoculation Theory." In J. P. Dillard and L. Shen, eds., *The SAGE Handbook of Persuasion*, 2nd edition. Thousand Oaks, CA: SAGE Publications, 220–236.

Compton, J., and M. Pfau. 2004. "Use of Inoculation to Foster Resistance to Credit Card Marketing Targeting College Students." *Journal of Applied Communication Research* 32 (4): 343–364.

Dilliplane, S. 2011. "All the News You Want to Hear: The Impact of Partisan News Exposure on Political Participation." *Public Opinion Quarterly* 75 (2): 287–316.

Feldman, L. 2011. "The opinion factor: The effects of opinionated news on information processing and attitude change." *Political Communication* 28 (2): 163–181.

Festinger, L. 1962. *A Theory of Cognitive Dissonance*. Stanford, CA: Stanford University Press.

Garrett, R. K. 2009. "Politically Motivated Reinforcement Seeking: Reframing the Selective Exposure Debate." *Journal of Communication* 59 (4): 676–699.

Garrett, R. K., D. Carnahan, and E. K. Lynch. 2011. "A Turn toward Avoidance? Selective Exposure to Online Political Information, 2004–2008." *Political Behavior* 35 (1), 113–134.

Garrett, R. K., S. D. Gvirsman, B. K. Johnson, Y. Tsfati, R. Neo, and A. Dal. 2014. "Implications of Pro- and Counterattitudinal Information Exposure for Affective Polarization." *Human Communication Research* 40 (3), 309–332.

Garrett, R. K., and N. J. Stroud. 2014. "Partisan Paths to Exposure Diversity: Differences in Pro- and Counterattitudinal News Consumption." *Journal of Communication* 64 (4): 680–701.

Gentzkow, M., and J. M. Shapiro. 2011. "Ideological Segregation Online and Offline." *The Quarterly Journal of Economics* 126 (4): 1799–1839.

Groeling, T. 2008. "Who's the Fairest of Them All? An Empirical Test for Partisan Bias on ABC, CBS, NBC, and Fox News." *Presidential Studies Quarterly* 38 (4): 631–657.

Hart, W., D. Albarracín, A. H. Eagly, I. Brechan, M. J. Lindberg, and L. Merrill. 2009. "Feeling Validated Versus Being Correct: A Meta-analysis of Selective Exposure to Information." *Psychological Bulletin* 135 (4): 555–588.

Ivanov, B., and C.H. Miller. 2011. "Boosting the Potency of Resistance: Combining the Motivational Forces of Inoculation and Psychological Reactance." Paper presented at the annual convention of the National Communication Association, New Orleans, LA, November.

Iyengar, S., and K. S. Hahn. 2009. "Red Media, Blue Media: Evidence of Ideological Selectivity in Media Use." *Journal of Communication* 59 (1): 19–39.

Jamieson, K. H., and J. N. Cappella. 2008. *Echo Chamber: Rush Limbaugh and the Conservative Media Establishment*. New York: Oxford University Press.

Knobloch-Westerwick, S. 2012. "Selective Exposure and Reinforcement of Attitudes and Partisanship before a Presidential Election." *Journal of Communication* 62 (4): 628–642.

Knobloch-Westerwick, S., and J. Meng. 2009. "Looking the Other Way: Selective Exposure to Attitude-Consistent and Counterattitudinal Political Information." *Communication Research* 36 (3): 426–448.

Levendusky, M. 2013. *How Partisan Media Polarize America*. Chicago: University of Chicago Press.

Lin, W-K., and M. Pfau. 2007. "Can Inoculation Work against the Spiral of Silence? A Study of Public Opinion on the Future of Taiwan." *International Journal of Public Opinion Research* 19 (2): 155–172.

Lumsdaine, A. A., and I. L. Janis. 1953. "Resistance to "Counterpropaganda" Produced by One-sided and Two-sided "Propaganda" Presentations." *Public Opinion Quarterly* 17: 311–318.

McGuire, W. J. 1964. "Inducing Resistance to Persuasion: Some Contemporary Approaches." In L. Berkowitz, ed., *Advances in Experimental Social Psychology*, vol. 1. New York: Academic Press, 191–229.

Muddiman, A., N. J. Stroud, and M. McCombs. 2014. "Media Fragmentation, Attribute Agenda Setting, and Political Opinions about Iraq." *Journal of Broadcasting and Electronic Media* 58 (2): 215–233.

Noelle-Neumann, E. 1974. "The Spiral of Silence. *Journal of Communication* 24: 43–51.

Petrocik, J. R. 2009. "Measuring Party Support: Leaners Are Not Independents." *Electoral Studies* 28 (4): 562–572.

Pfau, M., H. C. Kenski, M. Nitz, and J. Sorenson. 1990. "Efficacy of Inoculation Strategies in Promoting Resistance to Political Attack Messages: Application to Direct Mail." *Communication Monographs* 57 (1): 25–43.

Pfau, M., D. Roskos-Ewoldsen, M. Wood, S. Yin, J. Cho, K-H. Lu, and L. Shen. 2003. "Attitude Accessibility as an Alternative Explanation for How Inoculation Confers Resistance." *Communication Monographs* 70 (1): 39–51.

Pfau, M., K. J. Tusing, As. F. Koerner, W. Lee, L. C. Godbold, L. Penaloza et al. 1997a. "Enriching the Inoculation Construct: The Role of Critical Components in the Process of Resistance." *Human Communication Research* 24 (2): 187–215.

Pfau, M., K. J. Tusing, W. Lee, L. C. Godbold, A. Koerner, L. Penaloza et al. 1997b. "Nuances in Inoculation: The Role of Inoculation Approach, Ego-Involvement, and Message Processing Disposition in Resistance." *Communication Quarterly* 45 (4): 461–481.

Prior, M. 2013. "Media and Political Polarization." *Annual Review of Political Science* 16 (1): 101–127.

Sears, D. O., and J. L. Freedman. 1967. "Selective Exposure to Information: A Critical Review." *Public Opinion Quarterly* 31 (2): 194–213.

Stroud, N. J. 2011. *Niche News: The Politics of News Choice*. New York: Oxford University Press.

Stroud, N. J. 2010. "Polarization and Partisan Selective Exposure." *Journal of Communication* 60 (3): 556–576.

Stroud, N. J. 2008. "Media Use and Political Predispositions: Revisiting the Concept of Selective Exposure." *Political Behavior* 30 (3): 341–366.

Stroud, N. J., A. Muddiman, and J. K. Lee. 2014. "Seeing Media as Group Members: An Evaluation of Partisan Bias Perceptions." *Journal of Communication* 64 (5): 874–894.

Szabo, E. A., and M. Pfau. 2002. "Nuances in Inoculation: Theory and Applications." In J. P. Dillard and M. Pfau, eds., *The Persuasion Handbook: Developments in Theory and Practice*. Thousand Oaks, CA: SAGE Publications, 233–258.

Taber, C. S., and M. Lodge. 2006. "Motivated Skepticism in the Evaluation of Political Beliefs." *American Journal of Political Science* 50 (3): 755–769.

Tannenbaum, P. H., and E. L. Norris. 1965) "Effects of Combining Congruity Principle Strategies for the Reduction of Persuasion." *Sociometry* 28 (2): 145–157.

Tsfati, Y., N. J. Stroud, and A. Chotiner. 2013. "Exposure to Ideological News and Perceived Opinion Climate: Testing the Media Effects Component of Spiral-of-Silence in a Fragmented Media Landscape." *The International Journal of Press/Politics* 19 (1): 3–23.

Vallone, R. P., L. Ross, and M. R. Lepper. 1985. "The Hostile Media Phenomenon: Biased Perception and Perceptions of Media Bias in Coverage of the Beirut Massacre." *Journal of Personality and Social Psychology* 49 (3): 577–585.

Watts, M. D., D. Domke, D. V. Shah, and D. P. Fan. 1999. "Elite Cues and Media Bias in Presidential Campaigns: Explaining Public Perceptions of a Liberal Press." *Communication Research* 26 (2): 144–175.

Wyer, R. S., Jr. 1974. *Cognitive Organization and Change: An Information Processing Approach*. New York: John Wiley and Sons.

PART V

IMPLICATIONS AND CONCLUSIONS

16

Congressional Polarization and Its Connection to Income Inequality

An Update

Adam Bonica, Nolan McCarty, Keith T. Poole, and Howard Rosenthal

- Polarization in Congress is the highest since Reconstruction.
- Polarization is not an artifact of roll call voting. It also occurs in campaign contributions.
- Polarization in Congress is largely due to the Republican Party becoming more conservative.
- Polarization and income inequality appear to be mutually causal.

INTRODUCTION

This essay updates our findings on political polarization in Congress and elite political actors who work through Congress to affect public policy. We also link various threads of our research with the other essays in this volume. We begin with a discussion of the methodologies that enabled us to identify the emergence of political polarization in Congress, and then turn to substantive results.

A BRIEF HISTORY OF D-NOMINATE AND DW-NOMINATE

In 1984, we (Poole and Rosenthal) published a paper in the *Journal of Politics* titled "The Polarization of American Politics."[1] We found that beginning in the mid-1970s, American politics became much more divisive at the congressional level. More Democratic legislators staked out consistently liberal positions, and more Republicans supported wholly conservative ones. The primary evidence in that study, which focused exclusively on the Senate, were ratings issued by interest groups such as the Americans for Democratic Action and the United States Chamber of Commerce.[2]

---

[1] See Poole and Rosenthal (1984).
[2] A larger set of interest group data were analyzed in Poole (1990). The results confirm our 1984 analysis.

These early findings motivated us to develop better measures of legislative ideology. Because interest group ratings are in fact aggregations of legislator roll call voting decisions, we believed that much better information would be available by scaling the individual roll call votes directly. Consequently, we adapted the standard dichotomous logit (or probit) model to develop the NOMINATE (*Nominal* Three-step *Estimation*) procedure.

NOMINATE is based on a simple spatial model of voting behavior. Each legislator is represented by a single point, and each roll call is represented by two points – one for the "yea" position and one for "nay." These points form a *spatial map* that summarizes the roll calls. This spatial map is much like a road map. Tables in road atlases that tabulate the distances between every pair of sizable cities in the United States contain much the same information as the corresponding map of the United States, but a table gives you no idea what the U.S. looks like.[3] Indeed, atlases contain maps as well as a table. Much like a road map, a spatial map formed from roll calls gives us a way of visualizing the political world of a legislature. The closeness of two legislators on the map shows how similar their voting records are, and the distribution of legislators shows what the dimensions are.

The number of dimensions needed to represent the points is usually small because legislators typically cast votes on the basis of their positions on a small number of underlying evaluative or *basic* dimensions. For example, in recent congresses, we can easily predict how a "liberal" or a "conservative" will vote on most issues.

NOMINATE is based on a spatial model proposed by Melvin Hinich and Peter Ordeshook to account for the low dimensional spatial maps that they observed in scaling analyses of feeling thermometers (Cahoon 1975; Cahoon, Hinich, and Ordeshook 1976, 1978; Ordeshook 1976). Their theory was that there were two preference spaces. One was a low dimensional space and one a high dimensional space with the two linked by a projection shaped by some form of *constraint* (Converse 1964) or ideology. They dubbed the low-dimensional space recovered by the scaling programs a *basic space* and the high-dimensional space they dubbed an *action space* containing all "contemporary political issues [and] government policies" (Ordeshook 1976: 308).[4] Hinich and colleagues went on to develop the theory in great depth (Hinich and Pollard 1981; Enelow and Hinich 1984; Hinich and Munger 1994, 1997). Hinich and Enelow (1984) labeled the dimensions of the low dimensional space the *predictive dimensions*. More generally, these are latent or evaluative dimensions, commonly referred to as *ideological dimensions*

---

[3] We borrowed this analogy from Jordan Ellenberg, who used it in an article about our political polarization research. See Jordan Ellenberg, "Growing Apart: The Mathematical Evidence for Congress' Growing Polarization." *Slate*, December 26, 2001.

[4] Ordeshook (1976) proposed a model with *three* spaces – a common underlying preference space, an action space, and a third space identical to the action space but recording the positions of the candidates.

(Hinich and Munger 1994, 1997). We have consistently used Ordeshook's term *basic dimensions* or *basic space*.

The Hinich-Ordeshook spatial voting model embodies the fundamental insight of Philip Converse (1964) about ideology – or stated in his terms, a *belief system* – where issues are interrelated or bundled and that ideology is fundamentally *the knowledge of what-goes-with-what*. In contemporary American politics the knowledge that a politician opposes raising the minimum wage makes it virtually certain that the politician favors tax cuts, opposes the Affordable Care Act, opposes affirmative action, and so on. In short, a *conservative* and almost certainly a Republican. Converse called this bundling of issues *constraint* – the ability, based on one or two issue positions, to predict other (seemingly unrelated) issue positions.

These basic dimensions structure the roll call votes and are captured by the spatial maps.

A dynamic version of NOMINATE – D-NOMINATE – enabled the analysis of all the roll call votes in the first 99 congresses. In *Congress: A Political-Economic History of Roll Call Voting* (1997), Poole and Rosenthal found that the polarization surge had continued unabated through the 100th Congress (1987–88). Later, with McCarty (McCarty, Poole, and Rosenthal, 1997; Poole and Rosenthal, 2007), DW-NOMINATE, a more flexible version of D-NOMINATE, was developed.

POLARIZATION INTO THE TWENTY-FIRST CENTURY

The results of DW-NOMINATE show that polarization has continued to increase through 2013. Figure 1 shows the means of the Democratic and Republican Parties on the liberal-conservative dimension in the House of Representatives since the end of Reconstruction (a Senate figure is very similar).

We measure polarization as the distance between the two major party means. Changes in polarization over time are identified using overlapping cohorts of members of Congress. The Pennsylvania Senate seat once held by the moderate John Heinz was recently held by the conservative Rick Santorum, who in turn was replaced by the liberal Bob Casey. How can we claim that Santorum was more conservative than Heinz? Heinz served with Arlen Specter. Specter also served with Santorum. Heinz and Specter had very similar voting records. In contrast, Specter voted with the liberals (or Democrats) much more frequently than Santorum. Observations like this one form the basis for measuring increases in polarization. Replacements such as that of Heinz by Santorum[5] and Santorum by Casey in Pennsylvania or Sam Ervin by John Edwards in North Carolina are the symptoms of polarization. To nail down the polarization, we need to further assume that Heinz, Santorum, and all the other members of Congress have relatively stable ideological positions

---

[5] Heinz's direct replacement was the Democrat Harris Wofford. Wofford then lost to Santorum.

House 1879–2013
Party Means on Liberal-Conservative Dimension

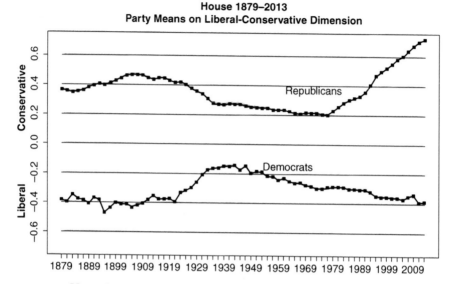

FIGURE 1. House Party Means on the Liberal-Conservative Dimension, 1879–2013

throughout their career. Considerable evidence suggests that this is the case, that by and large members of Congress die with their ideological boots (and polarized glasses) on (Poole 2007). We have found that any movement can be captured by simple linear shifts.

Specifically, a two-dimensional spatial model where each legislator is allowed to move linearly through time best fit the roll call data for Congresses 1–99 (Poole and Rosenthal 1991a, table 1). For example, if a member served in three or more Congresses, then four parameters were estimated using all the roll call votes cast by the member in all of the Congresses. Two were the mean two-dimensional coordinates for the member and two were the coefficients on the time trends. (Roll calls with less than 2.5 percent in the minority were excluded.) For the House, 9,759 members and 32,953 roll calls were included for a total of 8,110,702 choices. For the Senate, the numbers were 1,714 senators, 37,281 roll calls, and 2,317,915 choices. The overall fit was 85.2 percent (83.8 percent for "close" roll calls, those with at least 40 percent in the minority) for the House and 84.5 percent (83.6 percent for close roll calls) for the Senate. Poole and Rosenthal (1997) used another statistic, Aggregate Proportional Reduction in Error (APRE) that controls for the margins of the roll calls. The APRE for the House was 0.553 and for the Senate 0.543.

We found that the first dimension typically divided the two major parties on the fundamental issue of the role of government in the economy. The second dimension differentiated the members by region mainly over race and civil rights although in the latter part of the nineteenth century it reflected regional differences on bimetallism and the free coinage of silver. In the modern era, the primary dimension is liberal-moderate-conservative as it is commonly understood, and the second dimension captured the conflict over race and civil rights. We dubbed this a "1.5" dimensional result because "while a second dimension adds significantly in some Congresses, the second dimension is clearly less important than the first" (1991a: 232).

The two brief periods where the spatial model fails is for a few congresses during the Era of Good Feelings, when there was a one party system, and the 32nd Congress (1851–53), when the Compromise of 1850 unraveled. In these periods, there is a poor fit, even when 10 or more dimensions are used. Congressional voting was chaotic.

The original NOMINATE data set is frequently updated to include roll call voting in recent congresses. For Congresses 1–113 (through December 2013), the totals for the House are 10,723 members and 37,511 roll calls for a total of 13,677,311 choices. For the Senate, the numbers are 1,894 senators, 45,020 roll calls, and 3,072,058 choices. The overall fit for the two-dimensional dynamic model is 87.7 percent for the House and 86.0 percent for the Senate. The APRE for the House is 0.634 and for the Senate 0.588. The model now shows a better fit to the data than the results presented above for the first 99 congresses. The better fit clearly suggests that Congress has become more ideological in the past 14 congresses. As shown in Figure 1, the more ideological Congress is also more polarized.

The claim that voting in Congress was at most two dimensional over most of the history of Congress was contrary to the prevailing opinion of political scientists from the 1950s and 1960s. Scholars claimed that multiple policy dimensions were present in congressional roll call voting (MacRae 1958, 1970; Clausen 1973; Clausen and Van Horn, 1977).

Weisberg (1968) questioned the prevailing opinion and showed that if voting along the underlying dimensions is in accord with a standard spatial model, then a principal components analysis of the roll call by roll call Yule's Q matrix will reveal the dimensionality underlying the voting. Poole (1988) tests this for all congresses through the 99th and finds that at most three dimensions account for most of the variance in almost every House and Senate.

This did not settle the controversy about our claim of low dimensionality. Koford (1989, 1991, 1994) argued that a one-dimensional model would provide a good fit even when spaces have higher dimensionality. In a truly two-dimensional space, one dimension will have some success at classifying any vote that is not strictly orthogonal to the dimension. As a result, the marginal increases in fit, on the order of 2 or 3 percent may understate the importance of the second dimension. Poole and Rosenthal (1991b, 1994, 1997, ch. 3) showed that Koford's conjecture was not correct.

A lot of the confusion about dimensionality is likely due to our use of the two-space theory. We have never claimed that the basic space captures all of the issue dimensions underlying congressional voting. What we do claim is that our overlapping cohorts model captures the *systematic, basic dimensions over time.*

No one has succeeded in constructing a formal test of the dimensionality of a roll call matrix.[6] In our opinion, the closest is Poole, Sowell, and Spear (1992). They state a formal model of high dimensionality and then derive the exact probability distribution of the projection of roll call votes from a high dimensional space onto one dimension. This allows a formal test of the dimensionality of voting and the best fitting model is two dimensions for Congresses 1–99.

Recently there has been a spate of papers addressing dimensionality in congressional voting using simulation (Dougherty, Lynch, and Madonna 2012; Krehbiel and Peskowitz 2012; Aldrich, Montgomery, and Sparks 2014). Krehbiel and Peskowitz claim that the quadratic utility function is superior to the Gaussian utility function in modeling the deterministic portion of legislative utility. Results from Carroll et al. (2013) strongly support the exact opposite conclusion. Carroll et al. (2013) develop a mixture model in an MCMC framework that distinguishes between quadratic and Gaussian utility in one dimension with no imposition of constraints. The method – alpha-NOMINATE – has been implemented in R (Hare, Lo, and Poole 2014), and examples can be found in Armstrong et al. (2014, ch. 6).[7]

In addition, Krehbiel and Peskowitz (2012) echo Aldrich, Montgomery, and Sparks (2014) in that they use W-NOMINATE to make claims about artificial extremism and polarization. We have never used W-NOMINATE, a static model typically applied to a single congress, to study the dynamics of polarization.

Finally, Aldrich, Montgomery, and Sparks (2014) argue that there should be more focus on *intra*-party scaling to uncover the true dimensionality of roll call voting. In other words, one should recover the action space by looking at within-party divisions. This is essentially the view of MacRae (Poole 1988: 120): "Throughout my research in this area I tried to emphasize the contrast between ideological dimensions ... and strictly partisan dimensions, reflecting loyalty to the legislative party, which may not be so visible but which can be relevant to a legislator's career" (personal communication to Keith Poole, 1985).

These critiques of our finding of low dimensionality are subject to several technical criticisms. For example, the simulations of Aldrich, Montgomery, and Sparks (2014) fail to reproduce the roll call margins found in Congress. The

---

[6] Heckman and Snyder (1997) use the method of Cragg and Donald (1997) to claim that the covariance matrix computed from the roll call matrices they analyzed were anywhere from six to eight dimensional. The Cragg and Donald method has some very serious drawbacks, however. For a detailed discussion, see Poole (2005, ch. 5).

[7] See Carroll et al. (2009) for a discussion of W-NOMINATE versus the IRT-based IDEAL (Clinton, Jackman, and Rivers 2004), and Carroll et al. (2011) for the R implementation of W-NOMINATE.

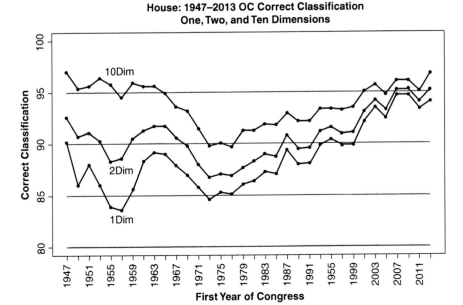

FIGURE 2. Optimal Classification: Correct Classification for the House (1947–2013) in One, Two, and Ten Dimensions

critiques are better laid to rest, however, by validating NOMINATE with independent methods. One is Optimal Classification. The other is scaling of campaign contributions.[8]

Optimal Classification (OC) (Poole 2000, 2005) is ideally suited to test the dimensionality of a binary choice matrix because it is non-parametric. It thus does not depend on assumptions about the shape of the spatial utility function or the process that generates errors and it does not face W-NOMINATE issues related to the constraining of ideal points. Figure 2 shows OC correct classification results for one, two, and ten dimensions since the end of World War II.

A case can be made that the action space was high dimensional in the mid-1950s, but since the mid-1970s the gain in classification from two dimensions to ten dimensions is only about 1 percent and about 2 percent or less over a one-dimensional rank ordering.

Finally the scaling of a totally independent data set, campaign contributions, yields results that correlate highly with the ideological positions found by DW-NOMINATE. The history of campaign contribution scaling reveals

---

[8] Barbera (2014) using Twitter data and Messing and Bond (n.d.) using Facebook data have uncovered similar ideological structure and recover candidate estimates that correlate strongly with roll call measures.

substantial technical improvement. In 1998, McCarty and Poole developed PAC-NOMINATE. This procedure models a contribution to one major party candidate in a race as a binary vote for that candidate over the candidate of the other major party. They thus scaled jointly both contributors and winners and losers of congressional races. Consequently, McCarty, Poole, and Rosenthal (2006) simply scaled a contributor as the money-weighted average and standard deviation of DW-NOMINATE positions of the incumbents that were supported by the contributor.

Combining ideas from PAC-NOMINATE and money-weighted averaging, Bonica (2013, 2014) showed that iterative procedures could mimic the alternating algorithms in NOMINATE and OC to obtain a scaling of contributors and candidates. The scaling procedures are, in the spirit of PAC-NOMINATE, totally independent of roll call votes. He developed two related models. The first is an item response theory (IRT) count model that controls for nonspatial candidate characteristics such as incumbency status and committee assignments (Bonica 2013). The second is an augmented version of correspondence analysis capable of handling large data sets with millions of contributors and tens of thousands of recipients (Bonica 2014). Both models incorporate information on the magnitude of contributions.

Bonica's work shows that the evidence for partisan polarization does not rest entirely on roll call voting in Congress.[9] In particular, his CF scores (Bonica 2013, 2014) also show that Congress has ideologically polarized over recent decades, closely tracking with common-space DW-NOMINATE scores since 1980 as shown in Figure 3.[10] The correlation between the two polarization trends is 0.97.

ASYMMETRIC POLARIZATION

Although both DW-NOMINATE and CF scores show the parties polarizing over the postwar period, the CF scores show the Democrats moving almost as much to the left as the Republicans move to the right. In DW-NOMINATE, the polarization is *asymmetric* – the Republicans move dramatically to the right beginning in the mid-1970s.

We can double-check our results by analyzing the roll call votes with OC in two dimensions (cf. Poole, 2007). Figure 4 shows the party means on the first dimension corresponding to the time period in Figure 3.

---

[9] Shor and McCarty (2011) show that many state legislatures have polarized and have become more polarized over the past 15 years.

[10] As the two measures are not on the same scale, a transformation is needed in order to display the two measures on a comparable metric. We regressed the common-space DW-NOMINATE scores on the common-space CF scores for all members of Congress who served during the 96th–113th Congresses using a bivariate linear errors-in-variables model to adjust for attenuation bias. The model was fit using the *leiv* R package. The linear transformation applied to the CF scores had an intercept estimate of –0.013 and a slope estimate of –0.503.

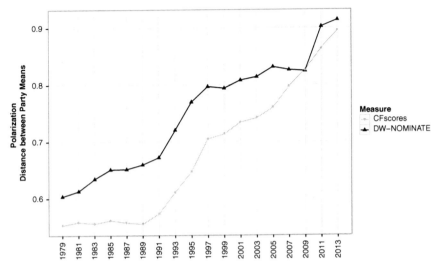

FIGURE 3. House Polarization, 1979–2013

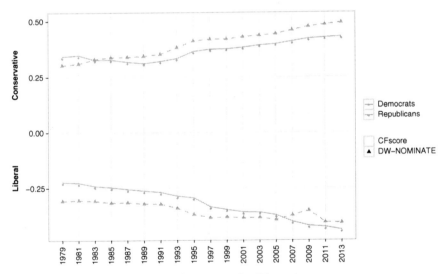

FIGURE 4. Party Means on Liberal-Conservative Dimension

Both trends are generated by *constant* or *static* scalings in that a single ideal point was estimated for each of the unique representatives who served in the House. That is, there was no linear shift term, as in DW-NOMINATE. Consequently, the changes in the party means in Figure 4 are entirely due to *replacement*.

We are just beginning to explore the differences between DW-NOMINATE scores and CF scores in Figure 4. In particular, the CF scores position many conservative southern Democrats much further to the right as compared to their DW-NOMINATE scores. This causes the mean Democrat to locate much nearer to the center during the 1980s and early 1990s. Second, the CF scores show Democrats moving to the left subsequent to their electoral gains in 2006 and 2008 whereas the DW-NOMINATE scores move in the opposite direction. In campaigns, very liberal Democrat contributors, primed by the campaign strategies of Rahm Emanuel, Chuck Schumer, and other congressional leaders, may have mobilized the partisan base to shower money on candidates in conservative-leaning districts who became relatively moderate in their roll call behavior. This would cause Democrats to move left in contribution scaling but right in roll call voting.

More generally, we conjecture that Democratic Party activists are moving to the left faster than the Democratic members of Congress who, in our opinion, are close to the left edge of the range of acceptable public policy on economic issues in the United States. Many policy options such as nationalization, steeply progressive taxation, and extensive regulation are off the table. The Northern Democrats moved to the left into the mid-1960s such that when they achieved absolute majorities in both chambers in the 1964 elections they were able to enact Medicare. After their reforms in the 89th Congress – the Voting Rights Act of 1965, Immigration Reform, Medicare – the Northern Democrats did not move further to the left and remained constant until the last two elections.

In this regard, the "liberal tradition in America" (Hofstadter 1948; Hartz 1955) has, so far, limited the reach of government. No real European-style socialist party has ever gained a lasting foothold in the United States.

Although the Republican Party has continued to move to the right, the GOP may not have reached the right edge of what, historically, has been the "liberal tradition." The Tea Party movement, absent the social and lifestyle issues of abortion, gay marriage, and so on, can claim to draw on the views of Thomas Jefferson and Andrew Jackson. The early Democratic Party opposed the concentration of power in the federal government and believed that the best government was the one closest to the people so that the people could be in control (Gerring 1998). However, voters have not completely reconciled these nineteenth-century views with their support for big government programs – Social Security, Medicare, and big chunks of the Affordable Care Act. So at some point the Republicans will not continue to win national elections if they keep moving to the right.

On the social issues of gay rights, abortion, immigration, and gun control, the Democrats have moved to the left relative to their positions 20 years ago. This has almost certainly had an effect on their donor base. In terms of voting in Congress, what has changed is how these issues have mapped from the action space to the basic liberal-conservative dimension. From "Don't Ask Don't Tell" in 1993 to open support of gay marriage in 2012, the mapping changed so that most Democrats support LGBTQ rights. In effect the cutting lines for roll calls on the social issues have moved from the left edge of the basic space into the left edge of the Republican Party (Hare and Poole 2014).

Figure 5 shows the movement of the Republicans in Congress to the right over the past forty years. The smoothed histograms are from the combined House and Senate Common Space DW-NOMINATE scores (Carroll et al. 2013).

For reference, we indicate the position of Senators John McCain, Barack Obama, and Hillary Clinton. Figure 5 not only shows the movement of the Republican mode to the right, it also shows the disappearance of the centrists in both parties. This, in a nutshell, shows why "Politics Is More Broken Than Ever" (Mann and Ornstein 2012; Mann 2014).

This movement to the right by Republicans has been politically costly for a number of legislators. A good example is Senator Richard Lugar (R-IN), who served in the Senate between 1977 and 2013. He was defeated in the 2012 primary. As Karol (2012) points out, Lugar himself did not change very much over time: he was a reliable conservative who moved only somewhat toward the center during a 30-plus year career (from a DW-NOMINATE first dimension score of 0.348 to 0.241). DW-NOMINATE scores range (with slight simplification) from −1 to +1 or a band of two units. So in 30 years, Senator Lugar moved just 5 percent on the liberal-conservative dimension, yet he was defeated by a Tea Party candidate who then lost in the general election.

Figure 6 shows the 113th Congress. The dark line shows the distribution of the House and the grey line shows the distribution of the Senate.

Quite naturally the Senate delegations are more moderate than the House delegations. What stands out is how extreme Ted Cruz and Rand Paul are relative to the rest of the Republicans in the Senate. In contrast, Hillary Clinton, Joe Biden, and Barack Obama were right at the mean of the Democratic Party in the Senate.

POLARIZATION AND INCOME INEQUALITY

Political polarization has had serious public policy effects. McCarty, Poole, and Rosenthal (2006) discuss at length the relationship between polarization and income inequality. Political polarization, income inequality, and immigration have all increased dramatically in the United States over the past three decades. The increases have followed an equally dramatic decline in these three social indicators over the first seven decades of the twentieth century. The pattern in the social indicators has been matched by a pattern in public policies with regard to taxation of high incomes and estates and with regard to minimum wage policy.

For example, Figure 7 shows the relationship between House polarization and the Gini index of household income since the end of World War II.

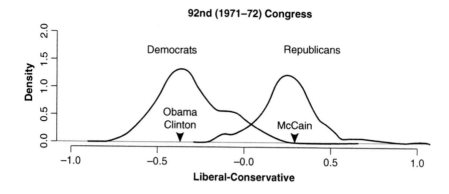

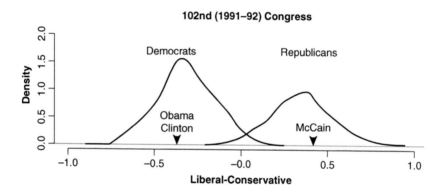

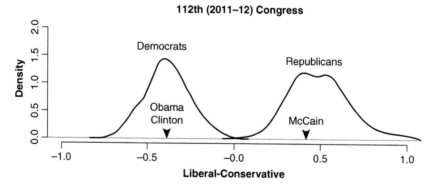

FIGURE 5. Common Space DW-NOMINATE Score Distributions by Party for the 92nd, 102nd, and 112th Congresses.

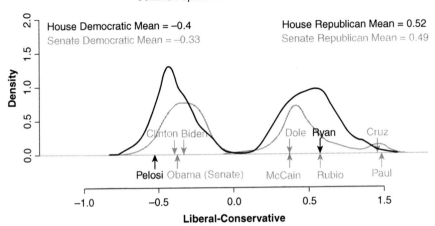

FIGURE 6. Common Space DW-NOMINATE Score Distributions by Party and Chamber for the 113th Congress

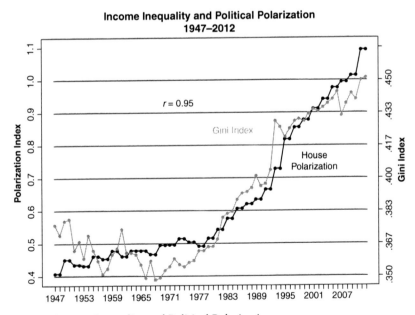

FIGURE 7. Income Inequality and Political Polarization

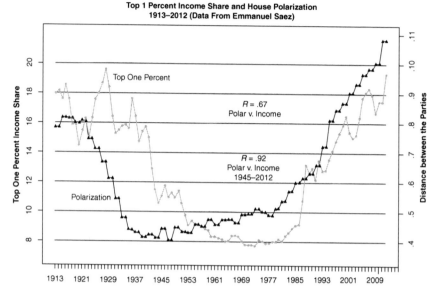

FIGURE 8. Top 1 Percent Income Share and House Polarization, 1913–2012

Similarly, Figure 8 shows the top 1 percent income share (Piketty and Saez 2003; Saez 2013) versus House polarization since 1913.

We argue that the separation of powers makes it difficult to generate coalitions large enough to produce policy change even when opinion shifts. We exploit this observation to get some leverage in disentangling the effects of political, economic, and social policies. For much of the period when polarization fell, immigration policy was restrictive and unchanged while income and estate taxes, defined in nominal terms, became more onerous. Ending low-wage immigration would have contributed to reducing pre-tax income inequality and resulted in the median voter being less concerned about sharing government expenditure with noncitizens. Increasing taxes would have allowed for a reduction in post-tax income inequality. These processes were reversed once immigration policy changed in 1965 and, starting with President Kennedy, marginal tax rates were reduced.

Clearly, since the onset of renewed polarization, the rich have received a disproportionate share of national income. In addition, the effects of social and tax policy have been especially dramatic as real minimum wages have fallen, welfare devolved to the states, and tax rates have diminished. Furthermore, polarization appears to be a leading indicator (Bonica et al. 2013). Lagging polarization by ten years increases the correlation with income share to 0.91.

McCarty, Poole, and Rosenthal (2013) discuss how political polarization affected the deregulation of the financial services industry and the subsequent

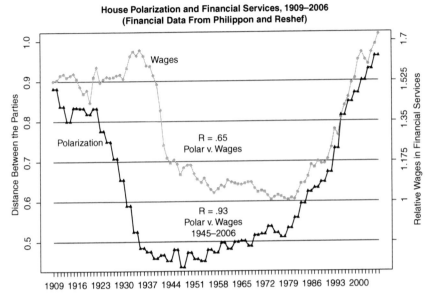

FIGURE 9. House Polarization and Financial Services, 1909–2006
Source: Financial data from Philippon and Reshef (2012).

housing price bubble. For example, Figure 9 shows the relationship between political polarization and the wages in the financial sector relative to other sectors of the economy (Philippon and Reshef 2012).

Figures 8 and 9 tell a similar story. Wages in the financial industry and the income of the rich lagged behind the depolarizing trend into the middle of the Great Depression, and then after World War II polarization and the income of the rich became tightly correlated. Again, lagging polarization by 10 years produces a correlation of 0.91 in Figure 9 (the same as in Figure 8).

We found strong evidence that gridlock resulted in a less activist federal government since the 1980s (McCarty, Poole and Rosenthal 2006, 2013). The passage of new laws has been curtailed due to the increasing difficulty of generating the requisite bipartisan coalitions (at the state level, see Chapter 11, this volume). The passage of the Affordable Care Act and the Dodd-Frank Act in 2010 took place after months of negotiation despite the 2008 elections having produced unified government, albeit one that was frequently subject to filibuster. After the Republicans took the House in the 2010 elections, gridlock reappeared in full force.

Meanwhile, the campaign contribution data suggests that, as income inequality increases, American democracy is tending to plutocracy. Figure 10 shows the percentage of the total campaign contributions accounted for by the top 0.01 percent of the contributors since 1980 (cf. Bonica et al. 2013, figure 5).

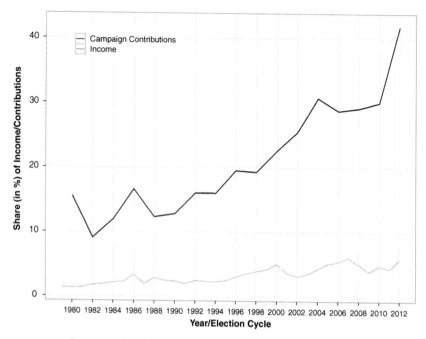

FIGURE 10. Concentration of Income and Campaign Contributions in the Top 0.01 Percent of Households and Voting Age Population

The figure speaks for itself. Some 40 percent of the total monies contributed to campaigns were given by a small slice of contributors. Among the very rich identified by the *Forbes* 400, the Adelsons, Sheldon and Miriam, stand out with over $100 million in contributions.

Figure 11 shows the distribution of Bonica's CF scores (Bonica 2013, 2014) for 2004–12 broken down by the mega-rich, big donors, and small donors (cf. Bonica et al., 2013, figure 7). The overall distribution of all three groups is strongly bimodal. Interestingly, it is the small donors who are the furthest left/ right. The important takeaway from Figure 11 is that neither party has the advantage when it comes to money (see also Chapter 10, this volume). The rich are active in both parties. The fact that the top income tax rate was "compromised" to be $450,000 for married couples is not surprising given this figure.

CONCLUSION

There is no question about the increasing polarization of Congress, but at least until the late 1990s, the American public did not appear to be polarizing (Fiorina 2010). However, more recent surveys have shown that activists and

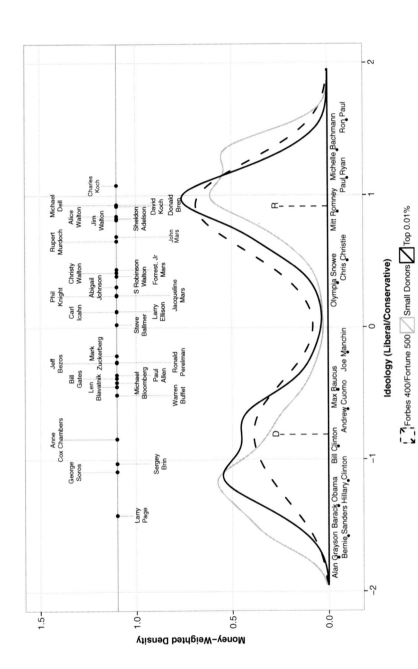

FIGURE 11. The Ideological Distribution of Dollars from Small Donors and the Top 0.01 Percent

voters who are strong party identifiers have polarized as well (Abramowitz 2010; Jacobson 2010; Chapter 3, this volume). Bonica's research on campaign contributors, a specific class of activists, also shows polarization. The disappearance of moderates means that it is increasingly difficult for the parties to govern effectively. It is difficult to fashion compromises when each side believes the other side is morally and ethically deficient. Moreover, both sides may be correct.

As of 2015, there is no sign that polarization has peaked. The last period of such intense polarization was just before World War I. Then the war and the dramatic increase in taxes to pay for it, and the success of Progressive Era reforms, lessened tensions and polarization declined for forty years. No resolution of this sort appears likely for this modern period of polarization.

REFERENCES

Abramowitz, Alan I. 2010. *The Disappearing Center.* New Haven, CT: Yale University Press.

Aldrich, John H., Jacob M. Montgomery, and David B. Sparks. 2014. "Polarization and Ideology: Partisan Sources of Low Dimensionality in Scaled Roll Call Analyses." *Political Analysis* 22: 1–22.

Armstrong, David, Ryan Bakker, Royce Carroll, Christopher Hare, Keith T. Poole, and Howard Rosenthal. 2014. *Analyzing Spatial Models of Choice and Judgment with R.* Boca Raton, FL: CRC Press.

Barbera, Pablo. 2014. "Birds of the Same Feather Tweet Together: Bayesian Ideal Point Estimation Using Twitter Data." Working paper, New York University.

Bonica, Adam. 2014. "Mapping the Ideological Marketplace," *American Journal of Political Science* 58: 367–387.

Bonica, Adam. 2013. "Ideology and Interests in the Political Marketplace," *American Journal of Political Science* 57: 245–260.

Bonica, Adam, Nolan McCarty, Keith T. Poole, and Howard Rosenthal. 2013. "Why Hasn't Democracy Slowed Rising Inequality?" *Journal of Economic Perspectives* 27 (Summer): 103–124.

Bonica, Adam, Howard Rosenthal, and David Rothman. 2014. "The Political Polarization of Physicians in the United States: An Analysis of Campaign Contributions to Federal Elections, 1991–2012." *Journal of the American Medical Association—Internal Medicine* 174 (8): 1308–1317.

Cahoon, Lawrence S. 1975. "Locating a Set of Points Using Range Information Only." Ph.D. diss., Department of Statistics, Carnegie-Mellon University.

Cahoon, Lawrence S., Melvin J. Hinich, and Peter C. Ordeshook. 1978. "A Statistical Multidimensional Scaling Method Based on the Spatial Theory of Voting." In P. C. Wang, ed., *Graphical Representation of Multivariate Data.* New York: Academic Press.

Cahoon, Lawrence S., Melvin J. Hinich, and Peter C. Ordeshook. 1976. "A Multidimensional Statistical Procedure for Spatial Analysis." Unpublished ms. Carnegie-Mellon University.

Carroll, Royce, Jeffrey B. Lewis, James Lo, Nolan McCarty, Keith T. Poole, and Howard Rosenthal. 2013. "Common Space DW-NOMINATE Scores with Bootstrapped Standard Errors." Retrieved from http://voteview.com/dwnomin_joint_house_and_senate.htm.

Carroll, Royce, Jeffrey B. Lewis, James Lo, and Keith T. Poole. 2011. "Scaling Roll Call Votes with wnominate in R." *Journal of Statistical Software* 42: 1–21.

Carroll, Royce, Jeffrey B. Lewis, James Lo, Keith T. Poole, and Howard Rosenthal. 2013. "The Structure of Utility in Spatial Models of Voting." *American Journal of Political Science* 57 (4): 1008–1028.

Carroll, Royce, Jeffrey B. Lewis, James Lo, Keith T. Poole, and Howard Rosenthal. 2009. "Comparing NOMINATE and IDEAL: Points of Difference and Monte Carlo Tests." *Legislative Studies Quarterly* 34: 555–592.

Clausen, Aage. 1973. *How Congressmen Decide: A Policy Focus.* New York: St. Martin's.

Clausen, Aage, and C. Van Horn. 1977. "The Congressional Response to a Decade of Change: 1963–1972." *Journal of Politics* 39: 624–666.

Clinton, Joshua D., Simon D. Jackman, and Douglas Rivers. 2004. "The Statistical Analysis of Roll Call Data: A Unified Approach." *American Political Science Review* 98: 355–370.

Converse, Philip E. 1964. "The Nature of Belief Systems in Mass Publics." In David E. Apter, ed., *Ideology and Discontent.* New York: Free Press, 206–261.

Cragg, John G. and Stephen G. Donald. 1997. "Inferring the Rank of a Matrix." *Journal of Econometrics* 76: 223–250.

Dougherty, Keith L., Michael S. Lynch, and Anthony Madonna. 2012. "Partisan Agenda Control and the Dimensionality of Congress." Unpublished manuscript.

Ellenberg, Jordan. 2001. "Growing Apart: The Mathematical Evidence for Congress' Growing Polarization." *Slate*, December 26.

Enelow, James M. and Melvin Hinich. 1984. *The Spatial Theory of Voting.* New York: Cambridge University Press.

Fiorina, Morris. 2010. *Culture War? The Myth of a Polarized America.* New York: Pearson Longman.

Gerring, John. 1998. *Party Ideologies in America, 1828–1996.* Cambridge: Cambridge University Press.

Hare, Christopher, James Lo, and Keith T. Poole. 2014. "anominate: alpha-NOMINATE Ideal Point Estimator." Retrieved from http://cran.r-project.org/web/packages/anominate/index.html.

Hare, Christopher, and Keith T. Poole. 2014. "The Polarization of Contemporary American Politics." *Polity* 46: 411–429.

Hartz, Louis. 1955. *The Liberal Tradition in America.* New York: Harcourt, Brace & World.

Heckman, James J., and James M. Snyder. 1997. "Linear Probability Models of the Demand for Attributes with an Empirical Application to Estimating the Preferences of Legislators." *Rand Journal of Economics* 28: 142–189.

Hofstadter, Richard. 1948 [1973]. *The American Political Tradition and the Men Who Made It,* 25th anniversary edition. New York: Knopf.

Hinich, Melvin J., and Michael Munger. 1997. *Analytical Politics.* New York: Cambridge University Press.

Hinich, Melvin J., and Michael Munger. 1994. *Ideology and the Theory of Political Choice*. Ann Arbor: University of Michigan Press.

Hinich, Melvin J., and Walker Pollard. 1981. "A New Approach to the Spatial Theory of Electoral Competition." *American Journal of Political Science* 25: 323–341.

Jacobson, Gary. 2010. *A Divider, Not a Uniter: George W. Bush and the American People*. New York: Pearson Longman.

Karol, David. 2012. "Defining Dissidence Down." *The Monkey Cage*, May 9, 2012.

Koford, Kenneth. 1994. "What Can We Learn about Congressional Politics from Dimensional Studies of Roll Call Voting?" *Economics and Politics* 6: 173–186.

Koford, Kenneth. 1991. "On Dimensionalizing Roll Call Votes in the U.S. Congress (Controversy with Keith T. Poole and Howard Rosenthal)." *American Political Science Review* 85: 955–975.

Koford, Kenneth. 1989. "Dimensions in Congressional Voting." *American Political Science Review* 83: 949–962.

Krehbiel, Keith, and Zachary Peskowitz. 2012. "Legislative Organization and Ideal-Point Bias." Research Paper No. 2124, Stanford University.

MacRae, Duncan, Jr. 1970. *Issues and Parties in Legislative Voting*. New York: Harper and Row.

MacRae, Duncan, Jr. 1958. *Dimensions of Congressional Voting*. Berkeley: University of California Press.

Mann, Thomas E. 2014. "Politics Is More Broken Than Ever – Political Scientists Need to Admit." *The Atlantic*. Retrieved from http://m.theatlantic.com/politics/archive/2014/05/dysfunction/371544/.

Mann, Thomas E., and Norman J. Ornstein. 2012. *It's Even Worse Than It Looks: How the American Constitutional System Collided with the New Politics of Extremism*. New York: Basic Books.

McCarty, Nolan, and Keith T. Poole. 1998. "An Empirical Spatial Model of Congressional Campaigns." *Political Analysis* 7: 1–30.

McCarty, Nolan, Keith T. Poole, and Howard Rosenthal. 1997. *Income Redistribution and the Realignment of American Politics*. Washington, DC: AEI Press.

McCarty, Nolan, Keith T. Poole, and Howard Rosenthal. 2013. *Political Bubbles: Financial Crises and the Failure of American Democracy*. Princeton, NJ: Princeton University Press.

McCarty, Nolan, Keith T. Poole, and Howard Rosenthal. 2006. *Polarized America: The Dance of Ideology and Unequal Riches*. Cambridge, MA: MIT Press.

Messing, Solomon, and Robert Bond. 2014. "Quantifying Social Media's Political Space: Estimating Ideology from Publicly Revealed Preferences on Facebook." Working paper, Stanford University.

Ordeshook, Peter C. 1976. "The Spatial Theory of Elections: A Review and a Critique." In Ian Budge, Ivor Crewe, and Dennis Farlie, eds., *Party Identification and Beyond*. New York: Wiley.

Philippon, Thomas, and Ariell Reshef. 2012. "Wages and Human Capital in the U.S. Financial Industry: 1909–2006." *Quarterly Journal of Economics* 127 (4): 1551–1609.

Piketty, Thomas, and Emmanuel Saez. 2003. "Income Inequality in the United States, 1913–1998." *Quarterly Journal of Economics*, 118 (1): 1–39.

Poole, Keith T. 2007. "Changing Minds? Not in Congress!" *Public Choice* 131: 435–451.

Poole, Keith T. 2005. *Spatial Models of Parliamentary Voting*. New York: Cambridge University Press.

Poole, Keith T. 2000. "Non-Parametric Unfolding of Binary Choice Data." *Political Analysis*, 8 (3): 211–237.

Poole, Keith T. 1990. "Least Squares Metric, Unidimensional Scaling of Multivariate Linear Models." *Psychometrika* 55: 123–149.

Poole, Keith T. 1988. "Recent Developments in Analytical Models of Voting in the U.S. Congress." *Legislative Studies Quarterly* 13: 117–133.

Poole, Keith T., and Howard Rosenthal. 2007. *Ideology and Congress*. Piscataway, NJ: Transaction Press.

Poole, Keith T., and Howard Rosenthal. 1997. *Congress: A Political-Economic History of Roll Call Voting*. New York: Oxford University Press.

Poole, Keith T., and Howard Rosenthal. 1994. "Dimensional Simplification and Economic Theories of Legislative Behavior." *Economics and Politics* 6: 163–172.

Poole, Keith T. and Howard Rosenthal. 1991a. "Patterns of Congressional Voting." *American Journal of Political Science* 35: 228–278.

Poole, Keith T. and Howard Rosenthal. 1991b. "On Dimensionalizing Roll Call Votes in the U.S. Congress (Controversy with Kenneth Koford)." *American Political Science Review* 85: 955–975.

Poole, Keith T. and Howard Rosenthal. 1984. "The Polarization of American Politics," *Journal of Politics* 46: 1061–1079.

Poole, Keith T., Fallaw B. Sowell, and Stephen Spear. 1992. "Evaluating Dimensionality in Spatial Voting Models." *Mathematical and Computer Modeling* 16: 85–101.

Saez, Emmanuel. 2013. "Tables and Figures Updated to September 2013." Retrieved from http://eml.berkeley.edu/~saez/TabFig2012prel.xls.

Shor, Boris, and Nolan McCarty. 2011 "The Ideological Mapping of American Legislatures." *American Political Science Review* 105 (August): 530–551.

Weisberg, Herbert F. 1968. "Dimensional Analysis of Legislative Roll Calls." Ph.D. diss., University of Michigan.

17

The Sources and Impact of Political Polarization

James A. Thurber and Antoine Yoshinaka

Partisan polarization has now been on the rise for several decades, and it has become a fact of life in twenty-first-century U.S. politics. At the elite level, the overwhelming evidence presented in this volume (and elsewhere) demonstrates clearly that our two major parties are ideologically as far apart as at any point in our nation's recent history. And at the mass level, while there are strong disagreements regarding the extent to which citizens are ideologically polarized along partisan lines and on a host of issues, it seems abundantly clear that the choices offered to them and the institutions (electoral, legislative, and others) in which social choices are made help to sustain – or at least fail to curb – partisan polarization.

That much seems fairly clear. When we commissioned the papers that form the basis for this volume's chapters, we asked contributors to examine polarization among voters and activists, among the states, in various federal institutions, and in the media. Our goal was to bring together all these disparate strands into a single volume that would provide the most up-to-date political science scholarship on this very important question. We now have in a single volume the state-of-the-art in the literature on polarization.

What can we conclude on the basis of this extensive research? While the bulk of the literature agrees that polarization is an illness that plagues our current political system (though there are exceptions – as will be shown shortly), some of the chapters in our volume raise serious questions about whether polarization is always deleterious and whether some of the cures may be worse than the disease. To be sure, the vast majority of contributors are of the opinion that polarization hurts the operation of our democracy.

But as scholarship on this topic moves forward, we believe that the debate would benefit from more theoretical and normative discussions about the costs and benefits of partisan polarization as well as a more thorough examination of the conditions under which polarization hurts various constituencies and, conversely, the conditions under which some groups may actually benefit from polarization and, its offshoot, gridlock. If polarization is here to stay – and most contributors to this volume seem to think it is – then we must think of possible solutions. But perhaps more importantly, scholars and practitioners must tackle the concept of polarization, its layers and its dimensions, in order to understand how and when it may be desirable (or at least tolerable) as opposed to unconditionally bad for our democracy. This is not to say that we must offer a wholesale "defense" of partisan polarization (although, as it has been done in the case of parties [see Rosenblum 2008] perhaps a serious defense of polarization is in order), but at the very least, the concept deserves to be unpacked and theorized about in a more sustained and nuanced fashion, if only because then we will be able to tackle its perniciousness without falling into the trap of eliminating all of its potential upsides, if any.

The challenge, then, is to take all this information and move forward, not just as a discipline, but also as a nation facing real pressing public policy issues in need of serious, careful, and long-term solutions. The strength of the chapters in this volume is not only that they identified and addressed one (or more) aspect of partisan polarization, but they also raised questions that we hope other scholars will wish to pursue further. We expand on three such questions here. First, if polarization has nefarious consequences, how do we reverse its march toward more ideological warfare (to borrow Sean Theriault's phrase) or, at the very least, mitigate its effects? Second, are there reforms that can help reduce or even eliminate partisan polarization and its offshoot of legislative gridlock (see Persily 2015)? And lastly, can polarization be "saved" by arguing that it has real benefits and that its "cures" may in fact be worse? In other words, perhaps a polarized polity may not be such a bad state of affairs after all; at the very least, the argument against polarization needs to be fleshed out in a more theoretically, normatively, and empirically compelling way than it has to date.

MITIGATING POLARIZATION

We are, in the words of Shea and Fiorina (2013), in an era of "rude, nasty, stubborn" politics. In Congress, for instance, the rise of incivility has been shown to be a product of our time (Uslaner 1993). If politicians are being uncivil toward each other (or toward the president by shouting "You lie!" when disagreeing with his remarks), and if they are merely mirroring trends in society whereby mistrust of the other side seems to dictate a loss of respect and comity, then what are we to do about that?

Perhaps the answer lies not so much in reducing the occurrences of incivility (though we wouldn't be opposed to that), but rather in finding ways to keep the government functioning well *in spite* of such behavior. More generally, assuming that polarization is here for a long period of time, what we might wish to highlight are the ways for government to respond to the needs of the citizenry even when Democrats and Republicans are at opposite ends of the ideological spectrum. Moving away from hyper-partisanship may be an outcome that is desired by most people in the aggregate, but as Harbridge and Malhotra (2011) show, many voters are quite comfortable with their *own* representative displaying partisan behavior – so long as they are in agreement with their representative's stances. To paraphrase Fenno, voters seem to like their polarized member even as they dislike their polarized legislature.

Must partisan differences necessarily dissolve into "partisan warfare" (see Chapter 7, this volume) or into breaches of decorum (Dodd and Schraufnagel 2013)? Can we count on our political leaders to negotiate agreement (Mansbridge and Martin 2013)? Can politicians disagree without being disagreeable? Surely the answer must be yes, though we think more work needs to be done in order to find the ways to achieve such outcomes. Norms, habits, and mores are amorphous concepts that may be difficult to measure, and even more difficult to change, but that doesn't mean we shouldn't keep trying. As Abramowitz concludes in Chapter 1 in this volume, "political scientists and others concerned about the future of American democracy should focus on finding ways to help the political system to function in an age of polarization."

REFORMING OUR INSTITUTIONS

Another avenue, which has spawned quite a bit of scholarship, pertains to potential reforms that could help alleviate the level of partisan polarization we see in our government institutions. Although many have written about these possible changes (e.g., Mann and Ornstein 2006, 2013; Nivola and Galston 2008; Fiorina 2011), as Seth Masket (Chapter 10, this volume) reminds us, we must be very careful about enacting reforms that may bring about unintended consequences. With this very important caveat in mind, we identify reforms that some suggest may help alleviate the harm caused by partisan polarization. We hope that scholars and practitioners will provide a more systematic assessment of their usefulness in mitigating, reducing, or even eliminating partisan polarization.

Possibilities for Reform in the Way Congress Works

Most of the problems in the way Congress works are linked to increased polarization and a lack of true bipartisanship. As Harbridge (2015) demonstrates, there may be an underlying desire for bipartisan lawmaking among members of Congress of both parties, but party leaders are structuring debates in ways that promote, rather than deter, partisanship on the floor. As a result, the chambers are more partisan and deadlocked than at any time since the 1860s (just prior to the Civil War). There is little consensus about major policy problems and solutions. It is harder than ever for a majority to get its way, especially in the U.S. Senate (although the Democratic majority has ushered a slightly more majoritarian era in 2013 by finally invoking the "nuclear option" and eliminating filibusters on many presidential appointments). However, important reforms could improve lawmaking and lead to more consistent and careful oversight, encourage deliberation, and fulfill Congress's constitutional mandate to represent the people. Here are some suggestions:

- Improve lawmaking through legislative procedural reforms. Return to the regular order, limit restrictive rules, and improve protection of the minority in the House. The Senate needs immediate filibuster reform in the vein of the nuclear option invoked in 2013. Senate filibuster rules must be changed to force members to actually perform, rather than simply threaten, a filibuster (see Wawro and Schickler 2007). A face-saving route to reduce frivolous filibusters and the resulting deadlock in the Senate must be found. Secretive and lengthy holds on bills and nominations must also be limited.
- Of particularly critical importance is requiring members of both chambers to spend more time on their jobs in Washington. The Tuesday to Thursday Club needs to be stopped with an enforceable required schedule of work in Washington. Members should be in Washington doing the work of committees, oversight, and lawmaking, as well as educating themselves. It is time for the party leadership in both chambers to set rules of attendance that have consequences. There needs to be a new schedule for Congress in session, which includes not only the show time on the floor, but the work time in committees and their offices. Congress also needs to return to real post-enactment conference committees that are transparent to the public and fair to both parties.
- Reforms should be made to the congressional budget process. Enforce the calendar and stop the growth of continuing resolutions and omnibus spending bills. Establish a biennial appropriations process with one year for appropriations and the next year for oversight of government programs. A two-year process is reasonable, as now the budget is often passed right on the heels of the next year's budget talks. Establish a true pay-as-you-go (PAYGO) rule covering expenditures, taxes, and authorizations. Abolish or reform significantly the debt limit requirements. Abolish earmarks in both the House and Senate by requiring open access to and discussion of all narrowly cast appropriations. Stop all new "backdoor spending" by authorization committees and require all permanently authorized legislation to be reviewed on a regular basis.
- A key part of representation in America is pluralism, the expression of interests, and lobbying through organized groups. The 2007 lobbying and ethics reforms were a weak down payment on improving the regulation of lobbying. There needs to be better definition of lobbying and better enforcement of the congressional rules and statutes. Codes of ethics in both the House and Senate are rarely enforced, but coupled with greater enforcement, the Senate should create an office of public integrity like the House Office of Congressional Ethics, and the House

should step up its investigations and public reporting of ethical violations. There should be an absolute ban on lobbyists raising money for those they lobby. Leadership political action committees have no role in good government and should be abolished. Fundraising quotas set for committee chairs and ranking members are an invitation to practice undue influence; the quotas benefit no one.

The inability of Congress – in the absence of a vigorous, bipartisan center – to address effectively known and crucial issues such as job creation programs, tax reform, the rising accumulation of public debt, a looming Medicare and Medicaid shortfall, immigration reform, gun control, a failing education system, and serious energy and environmental problems is a legitimate cause of public dissatisfaction. A Congress that cannot confront these critical public policy challenges will surely lack the reserves of comity and trust to face any unknown and sudden – and perhaps even more dangerous – crises.

Possibilities for Reform in the Way Elections Are Conducted

Another set of reforms pertains to the rules and regulations that govern the conduct of elections in the United States. Much of these proposals are not ours; many others, including some in this volume, have suggested them. The full extent of their effectiveness, however, is still unknown as very few seem able to find systematic evidence of their ability to curb partisan polarization. As such they deserve even more serious inquiry from scholars and practitioners.

- Increase the use of open, nonpartisan, and blanket primaries at the expense of closed or semi-closed primaries. Many states have been experimenting with various forms of nonpartisan or blanket primaries. Their effects are quite varied, with little systematic evidence of their effectiveness. What is needed, then, is a much better understanding of the conditions that lead to the effectiveness of more open systems in curbing polarization.
- Take the redistricting process out of the hands of politicians in order to create balanced districts where both parties can field competitive candidates. As with the case of primaries, the effectiveness of redistricting reform is not unambiguous. What we need once more is to understand why and when these reforms work as intended and under what conditions they fail to meet reformers' goals.
- Curb the influence of outside "dark" money in elections and increase parties' and individuals' ability to influence elections by raising contribution limits. While the *Citizens United* decision may have helped to usher in a new era of outside spending by corporations and unions in our elections, one response would be to increase contribution limits so that the flow of money would be more transparent and regulated via hard money contributions. The federal government could also tinker with the definition of "primary activity" of social welfare groups, also known as 501(c)(4) organizations, such that the

threshold of acceptable political activity would be lowered from the current 50 percent (or so) to a much lower percentage.

- Break the deadlock at the FEC by restructuring its membership and start enforcing campaign finance regulations much more systematically. Make it a more potent actor that does not shy away from enforcing both the spirit and the letter of the law. Allow it to be the watchdog and enforcer that keeps candidates and parties in check.

- The emergence of a third party, while unlikely in the current state-level legal frameworks, could also depolarize the political system, especially if that third party were to represent a more moderate, middle-of-the-road option relative to the two major parties. Of course, we are well aware of the difficulties inherent in the emergence of third parties in a political system such as that of the United States, but the fact remains that the current standoff could benefit from the appearance of another viable alternative vying for popular support of the electorate.

The way elections are administered in the United States is unique. Unlike most democracies, there isn't a single set of rules enforced by a national entity that applies across the entire country (see Massicotte, Blais, and Yoshinaka 2003). Although campaign finance for elections to federal offices is regulated at the federal level, much of the institutional setting varies from state to state (e.g., primaries, redistricting, ballot access laws).

This variation affords scholars the opportunity to assess empirically the effect of various institutions on electoral and legislative outcomes, but that assessment is made more difficult by the fact that these institutions aren't adopted in a vacuum. Reform efforts, where successful, do not occur by happenstance. Parties are also not completely at the mercy of reform efforts. When faced with reforms aimed at curbing their influence, parties may nonetheless find ways to strengthen their hold on politics (e.g., Masket and Shor 2015). It is therefore difficult – though of course not impossible – to assess systematically the effects of institutional reforms, but it is a task that we hope many will continue to undertake (e.g., Hirano et al. 2010; Masket, Winburn, and Wright 2012; Kousser, Phillips, and Shor 2014; McGhee et al. 2014; Masket and Miller 2015).

IN DEFENSE OF POLARIZATION?

In 1950, a committee of the American Political Science Association published a very thorough report on the state of two-party politics in the United States (Committee on Political Parties 1950). Its conclusions could not have been clearer: an effective two-party democratic system necessitates a strong opposition that proposes a clear set of alternative policies to those espoused by the governing party. In short, and perhaps at the risk of simplifying the APSA report, prominent political scientists declared that what the United States needed was somewhat *more* polarization (though not *too* much of it – the report was somewhat vague about how much delineation between the parties was desirable). The Association seems to have gotten just that (Rae 2007).

Did the APSA report get it wrong? Would it arrive at different conclusions had its members been able to see into the future and what would become of our politics? While we cannot answer this question other than speculatively, what we can do is to recall what prompted our discipline's leading professional organization to commission such a study in the first place.

On the heels of the bloodiest conflict the world had ever seen as well as the Great Depression, it was assumed that the policies needed to navigate this new world would be national in scope and nature. According to the committee, the structure of American political parties was not conducive to meet these new challenges. Despite large successive majorities and broad support for his policies, Franklin Delano Roosevelt was unable to overcome the very significant divisions between northern and southern Democrats in order to fulfill his New Deal agenda.

Thus, the impetus behind the study was the perceived lack of party responsibility that marked the U.S. political system in the mid-twentieth century. Due to their decentralized nature, American political parties were simply unable, according to the APSA report, to offer coherent policy proposals for which voters would hold them collectively accountable.

Yet the APSA report did not embrace unmitigated polarization. To the contrary, the report asserted:

Needed clarification of party policy will not cause the parties to differ more fundamentally or more sharply... Nor is it to be assumed that increasing concern with their programs will cause the parties to erect between themselves an ideological wall. (Committee on Political Parties 1950: 2)

In fact, the committee warned that failure to take action on this issue could

set in motion more extreme tendencies to the political left and the political right. Once a deep political cleavage develops between opposing groups, each group naturally works to keep it deep ... [Our proposal] is a significant step toward avoiding the development of such a cleavage. (Committee on Political Parties 1950: 14)

Thus, we think it safe to say that the authors of the APSA report would not look too kindly at the current polarized state of affairs. Nor would they embrace the role of various interest groups and outside money in influencing elections. Yet the report does set forth a series of proposals aimed squarely at strengthening national parties, allowing them to become the vehicles for clear alternatives to each other, with more homogeneity within parties and more delineation between them.

Can we have one (i.e., responsible parties) without the other (i.e., partisan polarization)? Can programmatic parties present clear alternatives to voters who have the means for choosing one team over the other and holding each team accountable at the next election? Assuming that the latter is desirable, don't we run the risk of throwing the baby out with the bathwater by attempting to decrease or eliminate polarization?

In order to answer this question, we call on political scientists to examine more carefully what it is about polarization that we dislike (and why) and what it is about polarization that perhaps might be desirable (and why). It is not clear, for instance, that a desirable outcome would be to "turn back the clock" to a time when the policy and ideological splits within the majority party ran so deep that they prevented action on important issues such as civil rights. Hopefully such research will allow us to provide an answer to William Galston when he asked, "Can a Polarized American Party System Be 'Healthy'?"[1] As of now, we do not think we can answer confidently either way.

Let's take, for instance, the relationship between polarization and gridlock. Surely it is more difficult to get 60 votes to pass legislation in the Senate when parties are polarized and the majority does not have enough votes to invoke cloture (see Chapter 6, this volume). Hence gridlock. But the U.S. political system was designed, at its founding, to have multiple veto points, preventing majorities from running roughshod over the minority. While it is certainly the case that the minority party has quite often used the filibuster as a tool to delay and ultimately block popular legislation, the fact remains that we must ask how much expediency and majority rule should be valued over enlarged coalitions and the search for common ground. That the current major parties (and voters and activists) often fail to find such common ground does not, by itself, negate the desirability of institutions that can foster its likelihood.

The issue, then, is for a better appreciation of the layers and dimensions of polarization and the tradeoffs involved in trying to curb its effects. What are the conditions under which polarization leads to positive outcomes for some (or many) constituencies? And what conditions lead to negative polarization effects? We hope that scholars will take up these and other questions that emanate from the research from this volume. No matter one's views on polarization among voters, activists, elites, and the media, and the role of various actors and institutions in fostering it, more research on its causes and consequences is needed in order to further our understanding of what is arguably today's most important political phenomenon with very serious and real policy implications for our representative democracy.

REFERENCES

Committee on Political Parties. 1950. "Toward a More Responsible Two-Party System: A Report of the Committee on Political Parties." *American Political Science Review* 44 (3, Part 2): v–96.

[1] William Galston, "Can a Polarized American Party System Be 'Healthy'?" *Issues in Governance* 34, April 2010.

Dodd, Lawrence C., and Scot Schraufnagel. 2013. "Taking Incivility Seriously: Analyzing Breaches of Decorum in the US Congress (1891–2012)." In Scott A. Frisch and Sean Q. Kelly, eds., *Politics to the Extreme: American Political Institutions in the Twenty-First Century*. New York: Palgrave Macmillan, 71–92.

Fiorina, Morris P. 2011. *Culture War? The Myth of a Polarized America*. Boston: Longman.

Harbridge, Laurel. 2015. *Is Bipartisanship Dead? Policy Agreement in the Face of Partisan Agenda-Setting in the House of Representatives*. New York: Cambridge University Press.

Harbridge, Laurel, and Neil Malhotra. 2011. "Electoral Incentives and Partisan Conflict in Congress: Evidence from Survey Experiments." *American Journal of Political Science* 55: 494–510.

Hirano, Shigeo, James M. Snyder, Jr., Stephen Ansolabehere, and John Mark Hansen. 2010. "Primary Elections and Partisan Polarization in the U.S. Congress." *Quarterly Journal of Political Science* 5 (2): 169–191.

Kousser, Thad, Justin Phillips, and Boris Shor. 2014. "Reform and Representation: A New Method Applied to Recent Electoral Changes." Retrieved from http://papers.ssrn.com/sol3/papers.cfm?abstract_id=2260083.

Mann, Thomas E., and Norman J. Ornstein. 2013. *It's Even Worse Than It Looks: How the American Constitutional System Collided with the New Politics of Extremism*. New York: Basic Books.

Mann, Thomas E., and Norman J. Ornstein. 2006. *The Broken Branch: How Congress Is Failing American and How to Get It Back on Track*. New York: Oxford University Press.

Mansbridge, Jane, and Cathie Jo Martin, eds. 2013. *Negotiating Agreement in Politics*. Washington, DC: American Political Science Association.

Masket, Seth E., and Michael G. Miller. 2015. "Does Public Election Funding Create More Extreme Legislators? Evidence from Arizona and Maine." *State Politics and Policy Quarterly* 15 (1): 24–40.

Masket, Seth, and Boris Shor. 2015. "Polarization without Parties: Term Limits and Legislative Partisanship in Nebraska's Unicameral Legislature." *State Politics and Policy Quarterly* 15 (1): 67–90.

Masket, Seth E., Jonathan Winburn, and Gerald C. Wright. 2012. "The Gerrymanderers Are Coming! Legislative Redistricting Won't Affect Competition or Polarization Much, No Matter Who Does It." *PS* 45 (1): 39–43.

Massicotte, Louis, André Blais, and Antoine Yoshinaka. 2003. *Establishing the Rules of the Game: Election Laws in Democracies*. Toronto: University of Toronto Press.

McGhee, Eric, Seth Masket, Boris Shor, Steven Rogers, and Nolan McCarty. 2014. "A Primary Cause of Partisanship? Nomination Systems and Legislator Ideology." *American Journal of Political Science* 58 (2): 337–351.

Nivola, Pietro S., and William A. Galston. 2008. "Toward Depolarization." In Pietro S. Nivola and David W. Brady, eds., *Red and Blue Nation? Volume Two: Consequences and Correction of American's Polarized Politics*. Washington, DC: Brookings Institution Press, 235–284.

Persily, Nathaniel (eds.). 2015. *Solutions to Political Polarization in America*. New York: Cambridge University Press.

Rae, Nicol C. 2007. "Be Careful What You Wish For: The Rise of Responsible Parties in American National Politics." *Annual Review of Political Science* 10: 169–191.

Rosenblum, Nancy L. 2008. *On the Side of the Angels: An Appreciation of Parties and Partisanship*. Princeton, NJ: Princeton University Press.

Shea, Daniel M., and Morris P. Fiorina. 2013. *Can We Talk? The Rise of Rude, Nasty, Stubborn Politics*. New York: Pearson.

Uslaner, Eric M. 1993. *The Decline of Comity in Congress*. Ann Arbor: University of Michigan Press.

Wawro, Gregory J., and Eric Schickler. 2007. *Filibuster: Obstruction and Lawmaking in the U.S. Senate*. Princeton, NJ: Princeton University Press.

Index